ADVANCED
PSYCHOLOGY

Child Development, Perspectives & Methods

ADVANCED
PSYCHOLOGY

Child Development, Perspectives & Methods

Donald Pennington • Julie McLoughlin • Richard Smithson
Dave Robinson • Karen Boswell

Hodder & Stoughton

A MEMBER OF THE HODDER HEADLINE GROUP

Orders: please contact Bookpoint Ltd, 130 Milton Park, Abingdon, Oxon OX14 4SB.
Telephone: (44) 01235 827720. Fax: (44) 01235 400454. Lines are open from 9.00 – 6.00,
Monday to Saturday, with a 24 hour message answering service. You can also order through our
website www.hodderheadline.co.uk.

British Library Cataloguing in Publication Data
A catalogue record for this title is available from the British Library

ISBN 0 340 85934 2

First Published 2003
Impression number 10 9 8 7 6 5 4 3 2
Year 2010 2009 2008 2007 2006 2005 2004 2003

Typeset by Dorchester Typesetting Group Limited, Dorset, England.
Printed in Great Britain for Hodder & Stoughton Educational, a division of Hodder Headline
338 Euston Road, London NW1 3BH by Martins The Printers Ltd, Berwick upon Tweed

Contents

How to use this book

This textbook has been designed to meet the needs of students and teachers following the GCE A2 level Psychology Specification B offered by the Assessment and Qualifications Alliance (AQA). Each of the 12 chapters covers all the topic areas in the compulsory Unit 5 Perspectives, Debates and Methods in Psychology, and the Child Development topics in Unit 4. The option topics of the Psychology of Atypical Behaviour, Health Psychology and Contemporary Topics are each covered in separate short texts, also published by Hodder & Stoughton.

Each chapter in this book covers all the syllabus content of Unit 5 Perspectives, Debates and methods in Psychology, and Child Development in Unit 4. Each chapter provides short descriptions of empirical studies and experiments directly relating to the topic areas. The chapters also provide two types of activities that individuals and small groups can engage in, both inside and outside the classroom. It is recommended that you carry out as many of these activities as possible since they will help you both with remembering the material and thinking more deeply and critically about psychology. The chapters offer numerous evaluative comments that will help you to analyse, discuss and make application of theory, concepts and research in psychology. The intellectual skills fostered by the evaluative comments will help you gain marks required to achieve high grades in the examinations.

Each chapter contains four different types of learning activities as follows:

Reflective Activity This invites you to engage in a reflective activity and gives you something to think about before continuing with your reading.

Practical Activity This invites you to conduct some kind of practical activity. Here a suggestion is made that may be either carried out on your own or with a small group of people. Some activities will take time outside of reading further in the chapter.

Study This indicates a description of a study or experiment in psychology. Studies have been selected that are important and/or highlight theory or key concepts in psychology. The study or experiment is presented in the way required when you are asked to describe a study in a examination question. When reading the study try to identify strengths and shortcomings, and think about ways in which the study could be improved.

Evaluative Comment This indicates an evaluative comment. These provide you with critical comment and analysis. Try to elaborate on the point being made, or use the comment as a basis for a small group discussion to explore other points of view. The skills of evaluation and analysis are essential to the study of psychology and are needed if you wish to gain high grades. Evaluative comments help with the second assessment objective (AO2) examined throughout the AS and A level in psychology. For more information about assessment objectives see Appendix 2 towards the end of the book.

Towards the end of each chapter you will find a number of questions. These have been set in the style that appears in the AQA Specification B A2 examinations. Each question shows the number of marks available for each sub-section and the marks for each of the three assessment objectives. Assessment Objective 1 (AO1) is concerned with knowledge and understanding of theory, concepts and research in psychology. Assessment Objective 2 (AO2) is concerned with the intellectual skills of critical evaluation, analysis and application of psychology. Assessment Objective 3 (AO3) is to do with the design, conduct and report of psychological investigations. This assessment objective applies to the Coursework required for Unit 6 and to the research methods section of Unit 5. Please read Appendix 2 for more details on assessment objectives. It is important that you understand what assessment objectives are and how they are examined since all examination questions are based on them.

Finally, at the end of each chapter you will find suggestions for further reading. This is given in two parts: first, introductory books and second, more specialist sources. The introductory texts should be easily accessible to all students. The specialist books are more demanding and may be of value to teachers and students who wish to try to achieve high grades or are just interested in finding out more about psychology.

Three Appendices have been provided towards the end of this book. Appendix 1 gives detailed guidance on the requirements for the Coursework in Unit 6 and advice on how to write it up. It is worth reading this before embarking on the Coursework and before attempting to write up the empirical investigation that you have conducted. Appendix 2 provides information about the principles used to guide how questions are set and structured for the AQA GCE Psychology Specification B at AS level. Also provided in Appendix 2 is information concerning Assessment Objectives – these are important to understand since they determine how marks are allocated to each question and how your answers are marked. Appendix 3 provides a range of statistical tables that you will need to use in conjunction with Chapter 12, Research Methods in Psychology.

We hope you enjoy reading this book both from the point of view of studying psychology and engaging in the suggested activities.

Acknowledgements

The authors of this book wish to acknowledge and thank the Assessment and Qualifications Alliance (AQA) for their support and help in producing teacher support material for the A2 Psychology, Specification B.

The authors would also like to thank Emma Woolf and Jasmine Brown, at Hodder & Stoughton, for guidance, advice and support in developing, designing and producing this book.

Finally, thanks to Kathleen Williams for typing many chapters of this book, and to Claire Thompson for putting the whole book together prior to sending to Hodder & Stoughton for publication.

Donald Pennington

The authors and publishers would like to thank the following for permission to reproduce photographs:

Bob Watkins/Photofusion for the photo on page 2 (left), Joanne O'Brien/Photofusion for the photo on page 13, PA Photos for the photo on page 16, Crispin Hughes/Photofusion for the photo on page 24, Farrell Grehan/CORBIS for the photo on page 34, Richard Alton/Photofusion for the photo on page 57, Richard Young/Rex for the photo on page 111, Associated Press for the photo on page 113, Underwood & Underwood/CORBIS for the photo on page 122, Brian Mitchell/Photofusion for the photo on page 137, Steve Eason/Photofusion for the photo on page 141, Archivo Iconografico, S.A./CORBIS for the photo on page 143, Dennis Marsico/CORBIS for the photo on page 146, Bettmann/CORBIS for the photo on page 162, Bettmann/CORBIS for the photo on page 165, Steve Eason/Photofusion for the photo on page 181, Roger Ressmeyer/CORBIS for the photo on page 182, Ann Kaplan/CORBIS for the photo on page 187, Ray Tang/Rex for the photo on page 198, Sam Tanner/Photofusion for the photo on page 199, David Trainer/Photofusion for the photo on page 202, Phanie Agency/Rex for the photo on page 205, PA Photos/EPA for the photo on page 211, Caroline Mardo/Photofusion for the photo on page 212, Archivo Iconagrafico, S.A./CORBIS for the photo on page 213, IPC Magazines: CHAT for the photo on page 220, Chris Lisle/CORBIS for the photo on page 222, Fotex Medien Agentur GMBH for the photo on page 229, Eric C Pendzich for the photo on page 230, Bettmann/CORBIS for the photo on page 234, Photofusion for the photo on page 243.

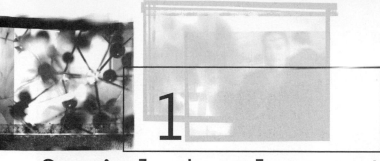

1

Social development

1.1 Introduction

The topic of social development includes some of the most compelling issues in developmental psychology. Research into the effects of early **attachment** relationships and the consequences of loss of an **attachment figure** have sometimes made for depressing reading, suggesting that children who do not receive continuous and loving care can grow up to be emotionally and cognitively damaged. This idea has been extremely powerful, leading to a tendency to think that many of our adult problems can be blamed on inadequate 'mothering'. Looking beyond the early relationship between infant and carer, psychologists have investigated how young children develop a sense of who they are – a sense of self. Looking further still we see how as children get older, wider social relationships become much more important, with friends acting as a source of social support, and relationships with friends serving as a bridge between complete dependence on parents/immediate family and the independence and self-sufficiency of adult life.

1.2 Attachment and separation

Attachment has been defined as 'a long-enduring, emotionally meaningful tie to a particular individual' (Schaffer 1996). This affectional bond or tie is usually characterised by a desire for closeness or proximity to a particular individual and by separation distress when the tie is broken or disrupted. The attachment object, usually the mother, offers comfort and acts as a source of security.

REFLECTIVE Activity

Think of someone or something you are attached to. It might be a person, an old toy, or even a place. How do you feel when you think about that person or thing now? On what is the attachment based? Is it simply a matter of familiarity, or is it for a feeling of security? How do you feel when separated from that person or thing for a while? And how do you feel when you are re-united after you have spent some time apart?

(a) Attachment,   (b) Separation

Caregiver-infant interactions

Research in the 1970s suggested that mother and baby should have immediate contact after birth because such skin-to-skin stimulation was important for the formation of a bond. Klaus and Kennell (1976) argued that mothers who cuddled their baby in a **critical period** after birth enjoyed better relationships with the child than those mothers who did not have that opportunity. Not all research has supported this suggestion. However, in the short term it seems that mothers who have immediate contact are more tender in their interactions with the child and spend more time looking at them than mothers who do not. Longer-term effects of early contact are less reliably demonstrated but, in some cases, early contact does appear to be related to general adequacy of parenting (Bee 1989).

Leaving aside the debate about the necessity for immediate contact we can see many behavioural interactions between baby and carer that function to develop and maintain an attachment. For example, parents will employ basic strategies such as focusing their communications to the child on objects of current interest (Messer 1978), thus ensuring that the child attends to the communication. In many more subtle ways adults interacting with babies seem to be especially tuned into the baby's needs, modifying their speech and actions accordingly. Even though a baby cannot speak, communication between carer–infant pairs is rich and complex. The following provides some examples of the ways in which babies and carers have been found to communicate:

INTERACTIONAL SYNCHRONY

Condon and Sander (1974) noted how babies would co-ordinate their actions in time with adult speech, taking turns to contribute to the 'conversation'. Frame-by-frame analysis of film recordings of babies' movements was matched to sound recordings of adult conversation. It was found that the babies would move in time with the rhythm of the conversation, engaging in a subtle form of turn-taking. In real interactions between baby and carer this results in reciprocal behaviour, with both parties able to elicit responses from the other even though only the adult can speak. Such synchronised interaction might be described as similar to a 'dance' between mother and baby.

More recently, Isabella *et al.* (1989) found that securely attached mother–infant pairs were those who had shown more instances of interactional synchrony in home observations during the first year.

Murray and Trevarthen (1985) deliberately interfered with the interactional turn-taking by asking mothers to adopt a 'frozen face' expression with their babies. In such circumstances infants become extremely upset as indicated by their turning away from the mother's face and crying. Furthermore, infants make deliberate attempts to draw the mother back into the interaction, suggesting that the infant is an active and intentional partner in the communication.

Babies can still have a 'conversation' even though they cannot speak

MODIFIED LANGUAGE OR MOTHERESE

Snow and Ferguson (1977) identified distinctive language patterns demonstrated by adults conversing with young children. Initially this was referred to as **motherese** although it is sometimes referred to as 'parentese' or 'care-giverese'. Motherese differs from normal linguistic style in a number of ways, all of which help communication between adult–baby pairs and draw the child into the communication, helping to establish and cement a relationship. Motherese is usually slow, high-pitched, repetitive, varied in intonation and comprises short, simple sentences. One of the most distinctive characteristics of motherese is the sing-songy nature of the communication, almost as if the speaker were singing rather than speaking.

PRACTICAL Activity

Find a mother–child or carer–child pair to listen to and observe. If you do not know anyone with a young baby then perhaps you could ask a friend if you could observe them with their baby brother or sister. Listen to the adult conversation and consider the elements of their speech style in relation to the features of motherese described above. Tick off the elements of motherese as you hear them.

IMITATION

The capacity of even very young infants to imitate adults' facial expressions has provided some of the most compelling evidence that children are innately social beings and take an active part in relationship formation in the first months of life.

Study 1.1

Aim Melzoff and Moore (1977) investigated imitation of facial expressions in two and three-week-old infants.

Method Infants were presented with a set of three facial expressions (tongue pull, lip protrusion and open mouth) and one hand movement involving sequential finger movement. A dummy was positioned in the infant's mouth to prevent any movement before and during presentation of the behaviour by the adult model. After presentation of the behaviour by the model, the dummy was removed from the infant's mouth and the child's immediate response/behaviour was recorded on a close-up video. Independent judges were then asked to rate the infant's response for likeness to any of the four target behaviours. Raters were not aware of which expression or movement the child had been exposed to.

Results The independent ratings showed there was a significant association between the model's behaviour and the behaviour produced by the child, with children able to imitate specific facial expressions or hand movements.

Conclusion Very young infants will spontaneously imitate facial and hand movements of adult models. The same effect was later demonstrated in infants of less than three days old.

EVALUATIVE COMMENT

Critics have suggested that babies will respond in a similar way to inanimate objects such as an approaching pen (Jacobsen 1979). However, Abravanel and DeYong (1991) found that 5- and 12-week-old babies would imitate tongue pulling and mouth opening in human models, but not when the expressions were simulated using objects. The question of whether the imitation shown in this type of study is intentional is arguable, and the exact role of imitation in the development of the child's social understanding is unclear. However, there is no doubt that the infant's capacity for imitation demonstrates how babies seem to be able to behave as if they were social beings almost from the day they are born. Although not initially intentional, behaviours such as imitation, crying, etc. might appear to the adult to be intentional, and thus lead the adult carer to feel closer to the child.

For any infant–caregiver interaction to be enjoyable and successful the more competent of the two partners, the adult, has to be highly sensitive to the child's behaviours and needs. Researchers have argued that **sensitive responsiveness** is the key to the development of successful attachments. Ainsworth *et al.* (1978) carried out a **longitudinal study** in which it was found that a mother's responses to her child's efforts at communications in different situations, such as feeding, distress, and face-to-face play could be linked to the quality and security of their attachment relationship at the end of the child's first year.

Human infants are not alone in their need for early social interaction. Animal studies, for example, Harlow's rhesus monkey research (see Study 1.4), indicate that, in certain species, early social interaction is extremely important for developing social relationships and for the infant's psychological adjustment. Research in other species has tended to focus on the more practical consequences of maternal responsiveness. For example, Schneirla *et al.* (1963) showed how the mother cat's cleaning of her kitten influenced the ability of the kitten to recognise the mother.

Functions of attachment

Initially it was thought that human infants attach to the person who provides nurture in the form of food. This **secondary drive theory** of attachment or 'cupboard love' theory, as it is sometimes known, can be criticised on several grounds, not least because babies do not necessarily attach to the person who feeds them.

Evolutionary theorists suggest that attachment behaviour has a critical survival value for an infant but not necessarily in the way that cupboard love theory would have predicted. Animals that are immediately mobile at birth, known as **precocial species**, need to remain close to the mother and have the protection of their group in order to avoid predators. Early views about attachment were often based on observations of other species, for example, Lorenz (1935) studied the innate following behaviour demonstrated by greylag geese. He reared young goslings away from other members of their species and found that they would follow and attach themselves to the first large moving object they saw. In normal circumstances this would usually be the mother, and so, this behaviour, known as **imprinting**, functions to keep the young gosling safe from harm. Thus, according to evolutionary theory, the innate following behaviour would confer survival value on members of the species that behave in this way.

EVALUATIVE COMMENT

How sensible is it to assume that behaviours shown in one species, in this case, the greylag goose, are relevant to human behaviour? There might be some similarities between newly hatched goslings and human babies, but many people would argue that such research tells us little, if anything, about human behaviour. According to Darwin's theory of evolution however, all species are genetically related in some way and it therefore makes sense to generalise findings from one species to another. The field of *comparative psychology* involves studying other species and then making extrapolations or comparisons from those findings to human behaviour.

Other explanations can also be linked to survival value. **Psychoanalytic** theorists explain attachment in terms of an innate, instinctual drive to maintain proximity to the caregiver, who would most usually be the mother. Drawing on animal research and his own psychoanalytic background, Bowlby (1969) proposed that attachment was rooted in the need to maintain proximity or closeness, the chief benefit of which would be survival. Survival value of a different sort was proposed by Bower (1979) in his **communication theory** of attachment. According to Bower, infants are selective in their choice of attachment figure, choosing as their preferred figure whoever is best able to communicate with them. This need not be the person who spends most time caring for the child, but instead would be the person who the child can use most effectively as a means to accessing the things he or she needs. For example, the child would prefer an attachment figure who can recognise from a cry exactly what is required, over someone who might often be present, but who is unable to interpret the child's attempts at communication. This theory about attachment can be linked to the earlier information about sensitive responsiveness.

Aside from offering survival value to the infant, attachment may serve a function in the longer term. In 1969, Bowlby proposed that attachment provides the child with an **internal working model** of relationships. This model acts as an internal representation or mental view of the relationship with the primary caregiver, for example, a child who has a secure and loving attachment would have an internal representation of the caregiver as responsive and sensitive. This mental model enables the child to have expectations of the caregiver and makes future interactions easier and more predictable. As the child comes into contact with more and more people, the internal working model can be used as a framework on which to build other similar relationships. If this notion is correct, then quite simply, the child's earliest relationship sets the scene for all relationships that are to follow, for example, with teenage and adult friends, and in intimate relationships.

EVALUATIVE COMMENT

Whilst the idea that early relationships act as a foundation for later relationships is an appealing one, critics have argued that the internal working model is too general to be useful

(Dunn 1993). The notion of continuity in relationships also leads to a fairly pessimistic, determinist view: if your first relationships are unhappy and insecure then this will be the pattern for all future relationships. In support of the internal working model, Barnes (1995) suggests that the model's appeal lies in its ability to combine several perspectives in psychology, for example the *cognitive perspective* (understanding of attachment) and the *behaviourist perspective* (behaviours that are rewarding are likely to be repeated).

Measuring attachment – secure and insecure attachments

It is easy enough to know when you are attached to someone because you know how you feel when you are apart from that person, and, being an adult, you can put your feelings into words and describe how it feels. However, most attachment research is carried out using infants and young children, so psychologists have had to devise subtle ways of researching attachment, usually involving the observational method.

PRACTICAL Activity

Think of a person to whom you are attached, perhaps a relative or a close friend. Now write down a series of statements explaining how you know you are attached to the person you have chosen. Here's one to start you off:

'I get upset if I am apart from X for very long.'

Some of the reasons you have given in the practical activity above are what psychologists consider when they try to observe and measure attachment in children. Now look at Figure 1.1 for the sorts of observable, attachment behaviours psychologists have used in their studies of attachment.

Watching – the child will keep his or her eyes on the attachment figure as they move about the room.
Crying – when the attachment figure moves out of sight.
Following – children who are able to crawl or walk will attempt to keep contact with the attachment figure by following and clinging to them.
Using as a safe base – a child will play in close proximity to the attachment figure, perhaps venturing away to get a toy but returning frequently and playing close by. This behaviour is especially obvious when the child is startled by, or suspicious of, something. For example, a child playing in the centre of the room might run back to the mother and hold on to her if a stranger enters or a sudden noise occurs.
Greeting – the child will show obvious pleasure at the return of an attachment figure, smiling and holding up his or her arms as a signal to be picked up.
Stranger fear – the child will show a dislike of strangers, demonstrated by turning away and crying if the stranger attempts contact.

Figure 1.1: Table of attachment behaviours

Study 1.2

Aim Ainsworth *et al.* (1978) studied the reactions of young children to brief separations from their mother in order to determine the nature of attachment behaviours and types of attachments. Ainsworth's procedure is known as the **strange situation.**

Method Over a period of approximately 25 minutes infants were exposed to a sequence of three-minute episodes. Initially the infant and mother were introduced to the observation room by the researcher, then the researcher left the room. After a while a stranger entered and had a brief conversation with the mother. The mother then left quietly, leaving the infant and stranger together for a maximum of three minutes. If the child became very distressed at this point the mother would return earlier than planned. This sequence of events was then repeated with a further 'stranger' episode. The child's behaviours were recorded throughout the sequence of events.

Results Using a combination of behavioural measures, mainly proximity seeking and maintenance of proximity, Ainsworth classified infants as securely attached, anxious avoidant or anxious resistant. In middle-class US samples approximately 65% of infants were found to fall into the secure category, with around 15 to 20% in the other two categories. These three types are described in Figure 1.2.

Conclusion There are different types of attachments and these types are differentiated in observed attachment behaviours. Furthermore, the type of attachment between a mother and child is dependent upon the mother's sensitivity and responsiveness to the child. Although the original work was carried out with Ugandan infants, the study has been replicated many times in different cultures.

Later research by Main and Solomon (1990) led to the identification of a fourth type of attachment, which they called 'disorganised'. This type is characteristic of high-risk families where children have perhaps been abused or neglected. A child showing disorganised attachment will appear confused and apprehensive, with no consistent response to the events of the Strange Situation.

Type of attachment	Demonstrated behaviours	Percentage of children
Anxious avoidant	Baby ignores mother and seems indifferent. Easily comforted by stranger. Treats mother and stranger the same.	21
Secure	Baby happy in mother's presence and distressed when mother leaves. Calms down at mother's return. Wary of stranger.	65
Anxious resistant	Fussy difficult child who cries a lot. Distressed when mother leaves but unable to be comforted on her return. Shows anger. Resists stranger.	14

Figure 1.2: Percentages of types of attachment (using data from 32 cross-cultural studies) (Barnes 1995)

EVALUATIVE COMMENT

Ainsworth's paradigm has been replicated many times to see whether (a) the classifications show good reliability over time with the same mother–child pairs, and (b) the category

percentages are similar across cultures. Although Ainsworth's own study (Ainsworth *et al.*1978) failed to show good test-retest reliability of classification, other studies have found fairly stable classification over time, for example, Antonucci and Levitt (1984) found strong consistency between classifications at seven and 13 months. However, although this indicates that the classification scheme may be relatively stable, Bremner (1994) questions the validity of the measures used in the Strange Situation. The assumption that proximity seeking and maintenance of proximity are key measures of security of attachment seems to neglect the frequent observation that securely attached infants are happier to explore their environment, and thus do not feel the need to maintain continual proximity to mother (Cassidy 1986). Indeed it could be argued that proximity seeking is a sign of insecurity rather than a sign of a secure attachment.

Cross-cultural replications of the Strange Situation indicate that the category percentages defined by Ainsworth using an American sample are not universal. Grossman *et al.* (1981) found that the majority of German infants demonstrated anxious-avoidant attachments, whilst Takahashi (1990) found a higher than average percentage of anxious-resistant types in Japan. Takahashi suggested that this could perhaps be attributed to the excessive stress Japanese infants might experience during the Strange Situation separation, as infant–mother separation is not the norm in the Japanese culture. Takahashi's explanation does suggest that it could be inappropriate to use the same measure of attachment in widely differing cultures.

According to Ainsworth, the type and quality of attachment between mother and child is largely dependent on the mother's behaviour towards the child. She suggested that mothers of securely attached infants tended to be more sensitive to the child's needs, more responsive, more co-operative and more accessible than mothers of either of the anxious types. Main *et al.* (1985) explored the relationship between the mother's behaviour and type of attachment and found that mothers who themselves had satisfactory attachment experiences would be more likely to foster secure attachments in their own children.

Using a procedure known as the **adult attachment interview**, Main *et al.* (1985) classified parents according to their recollections of their own attachment experiences. Autonomous (secure) adults, those who discussed their own childhood experiences openly, were more likely to have children identified as securely attached in a Strange Situation. Dismissing and pre-occupied adults however, tended to have children identified as insecure in the Strange Situation. According to Main *et al.* (1985), a mother's own childhood experiences affects how she interacts with her child, and the type of relationship established between the mother–child pair. Main's findings can be related to the internal working model function of attachment proposed by Bowlby (1969).

Belsky (1984) noted that explanations for attachment security proposed by

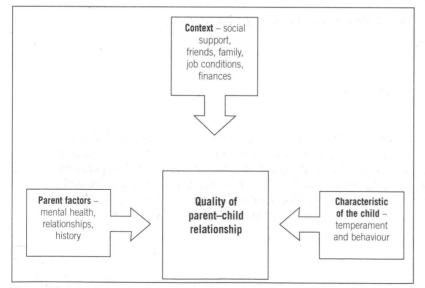

Figure 1.3: Wider determinants of attachment security (Belsky 1984)

Ainsworth emphasise the mother's sensitivity and neglect wider influences on attachment. Figure 1.3 shows how additional factors might interact to result in either secure or insecure attachments.

Consequences of privation and deprivation

Deprivation might be defined as losing something which a person once had, whereas **privation** might be defined as never having had something in the first place. Linking this idea to the concept of attachment, we can understand deprivation as having had a secure relationship or bond with a mother or attachment figure, which has since been lost, and privation as never having had any secure and loving relationship with any attachment figure at all.

DEPRIVATION

In the short term, deprivation results in distress of the type observed when a child has to be separated from the carer for a short while, perhaps because of hospitalisation or an extended holiday. A commonly observed sequence of behaviours can be seen in this sort of separation. Initially the child will protest, by crying and struggling to keep contact with the carer. This protest will then give way to despair where the child appears to be more calm, but perhaps cries quietly and appears very unhappy. Eventually, as the separation goes on, the child enters a period of detachment showing little emotion towards others and being apparently unconcerned. If the attachment figure returns, the child often rejects contact and appears almost to resent the attachment figure, who is treated just like a stranger by the child.

An excellent illustration of the **protest**, **despair**, **detachment** sequence is presented by Robertson and Robertson (1968), who filmed separations of young children going into care for a short time. The Robertson studies illustrated the short-term effects of separation and had a significant impact on the way health and child-care professionals viewed children's needs in separation situations.

Not surprisingly, young children between seven months and three years are most vulnerable to suffering from the distress of separation. However, Schaffer (1996) identified other characteristics that predispose children to suffer more in separation situations. Problems are more likely where the child

- is male (in early childhood, although females suffer more in adolescence)
- has a 'difficult' temperament
- has a history of family conflict
- has parents who are psychologically unavailable
- suffers repeated separations.

Long-term effects of deprivation are difficult to determine because other variables may influence the child's behaviour. However, studies of children who have experienced separations suggest that one long-term consequence may be a fear that separation will occur again. This **separation anxiety** may be seen in a variety of behaviours such as increased clinging, aggression towards the carer and physical stress-related reactions. In adulthood separation anxiety may result in a general fear of abandonment or insecurity in relationships making it difficult to trust other people.

Study 1.3

Aim Belsky (1988) investigated the effects of day-care on attachment relationships.

Method Using a **meta-analysis** Belsky collated the results of a number of previously published studies. Data gathered included the time per week young children spent in non-maternal care and information about their type of attachment.

Results In a review of 464 children, 26% of those in day-care for less than 20 hours per week showed insecure attachments, whereas 41% of those in day-care more than 20 hours per week were categorised as insecure.

Conclusion Belsky concluded there was some evidence that 20 hours or more per week in non-maternal care has a negative effect on attachment security. This effect was especially marked for children under one year. Barnes (1995) notes that these differences in attachment type may be due to other factors, such as the type of substitute care and the reasons for mothers needing to work longer hours.

One of the commonest separation situations occurs when parents divorce. Studies of children of divorced parents show some negative life outcomes such as lower academic attainment and a higher incidence of delinquency. However, such data is correlational and does not show that separation following divorce causes negative effects. Schaffer (1996) summarises the effects of divorce-related separations and suggests several factors that help reduce the effects of separation:

• Regular contact with absent parent

• Reduced parental conflict

• Behaviour of the parent who has custody and his or her ability to provide stability

• Lifestyle maintenance – many separated parents find themselves worse off financially, which affects continuity for the child

• Avoidance of further disruption, such as moving school

• Positive relationships with step-parent where there is re-marriage.

It is also important to realise that not all children are equally affected by such separations, with many finding ways of coping with their loss. Jenkins *et al.* (1989), for example, found that a common coping mechanism for 9/10-year-old children separated from a parent after divorce was to increase contact with siblings and friends.

PRIVATION

If children can be adversely affected by deprivation then it is likely that there would be negative consequences where infants and young children have no chance to form an attachment relationship at all. Since it is not possible, for ethical reasons, to carry out controlled studies of privation with children, any evidence showing cause and effect has tended to come from animal research.

Study 1.4

Aim Harlow (1959) studied the behaviour of infant monkeys separated from their mothers at birth to see what effects the separation had on their later behaviour.

Method Infant rhesus monkeys were taken from their mothers and kept in a cage with two substitute mothers; a 'cloth mother' covered with a soft blanket and a 'wire mother' incorporating a feeding bottle. The monkeys were kept in these conditions for a period of time, and then released into a cage with a group of normally reared monkeys.

Results The infant monkeys preferred to spend time close to the cloth mother even though they got their food from the wire mother. When returned to the company of other monkeys, Harlow's monkeys showed signs of inappropriate social behaviour and delinquency. They were aggressive towards other monkeys, unable to form normal relationships and attacked any monkey that tried to mate with them. If they did have offspring, the deprived monkeys were extremely poor, neglecting mothers.

Conclusion Two conclusions can be drawn from Harlow's work. First, it seems the privated monkeys suffered emotionally, resulting in delinquent and anti-social behaviour. Secondly the study showed that infant monkeys did not attach for food. Bremner (1994) describes this finding as inconsistent with what is known as the secondary drive theory of attachment, which sees the attachment to the mother simply as a consequence of the need for food (see Section 1.2.2).

EVALUATIVE COMMENT

The Harlow study was used to support Bowlby's hypothesis (see Section 1.2.5) that babies need a secure attachment by a certain age if they are to develop normally and be able to relate to others satisfactorily. Although it was initially thought these consequences of privation were irreversible, Suomi and Harlow (1972) found that it was possible to socialise six-month-old isolated monkeys by introducing female monkeys three months younger than themselves (monkey therapists). In this way delinquent and stereotyped behaviours were found to be much reduced. Harlow's research might also be criticised on ethical grounds. Certainly it seems unethical to deliberately deprive infant monkeys of the company of their own species, although it could be argued that the benefits in terms of knowledge outweigh the ethical problems.

Aside from the experimental work of Harlow, most evidence for effects of privation has come from case studies of children who have been raised in conditions of neglect. Some cases, for example the case of Genie (Curtiss 1977), suggest that severe privation has permanent effects. Genie had been severely neglected and maltreated by her parents. At the age of 13 years she was unable to speak, physically underdeveloped and showed inappropriate emotional responses. Despite fostering and intellectual stimulation Genie apparently never recovered from her years of privation, although there was a suggestion that other factors may have contributed to her problems. Certainly in other cases, severely privated children seem able to overcome the effects of their early suffering.

Study 1.5

Aim Rutter et al. (1998) investigated the progress of Romanian orphans brought to Britain for adoption in the 1990s. These children had been raised in very poor institutions with little chance to develop close attachments.

Method The Romanian children were assessed on a variety of measures of physical and intellectual ability on arrival in Britain, and had periodic assessments until the age of four years. A control group of British-adopted children was also tested to see whether it was separation from mother or the severe circumstances in Romania that was responsible for any negative effects.

Results Approximately half the Romanian group showed intellectual deficits at the start, and most were very underweight. The British children showed no such negative effects. Four years later the two groups of adopted children showed no significant differences in either intellectual or physical development, however, children from both groups who were older at the time of adoption tended to perform less well on both measures.

Conclusion Rutter et al. concluded that (a) the negative outcomes shown by the Romanian children could be overcome through adequate substitute care, and (b) separation from mother alone is not sufficient to cause negative outcomes as the British children had been separated but were not developmentally delayed.

EVALUATIVE COMMENT

The results in the above study should be contrasted with Kreppner *et al*. (1999). Kreppner reported that 104 Romanian children adopted into British families before the age of two years showed lower frequency of pretend play, role play and ability to appreciate other people's mental states than a UK control group. These differences did not appear to be related to general cognitive or verbal ability so the negative outcomes were assumed to be due to their early privation.

Bowlby's theory of attachment

Bowlby was a psychoanalyst and psychiatrist who thought that many mental health and behavioural problems could be directly attributed to early childhood experiences. In 1951, the World Health Organisation (WHO) published a document in which Bowlby stated that mother love in infancy is just as important for a child's mental health as are vitamins and minerals for physical health. In his 1953 book, *Child Care and the Growth of Love*, Bowlby stated the following:

> **What is believed to be essential for mental health is that an infant and young child should experience a warm, intimate and continuous relationship with his mother (or permanent mother-substitute – one person who steadily 'mothers' him) in which both find satisfaction and enjoyment.**

Remember how the **psychodynamic approach** emphasises the role of innate, instinctual drives in the motivation of our behaviour. This theoretical background led Bowlby to suggest that a child had an instinctual need to be close to the mother, which he called 'proximity seeking'.

The main points of Bowlby's (1951) theory are as follows:

- A child has an innate need to attach to one main attachment figure. This idea of the need for a single and exclusive bond became known as **monotropy** theory. Although Bowlby did not exclude the possibility of other attachments for a child, he did believe that there should be a primary bond which was much more important than any other

- A child should receive the continuous care of this single most important attachment figure for approximately the first two years of life. If the attachment is broken or disrupted during the critical two-year period the child will suffer irreversible long-term consequences of this **maternal deprivation**

- The consequences of maternal deprivation might include the following: delinquency, affectionless psychopathy and intellectual retardation. **Affectionless psychopathy** is an inability to empathise with other people, or, as Klein 1987 described it, 'permanent lack of feeling for others'.

EVALUATIVE COMMENT

When the maternal deprivation hypothesis was originally proposed some mothers questioned their own child-care arrangements. Mothers who were in work might have felt guilty for leaving their children in alternative care and stay-at-home mothers probably thought that they should continue to do so for the good of the child. As such, Bowlby's work affected the way in which at least a generation of children were raised. In other areas too there were consequences for social and welfare policy and practice: child-care workers reading Bowlby's work might have concluded that it was better for a child to be brought up by a 'bad' mother than to be sent to an

institution or children's home. However, Bowlby's work also had positive consequences. Hospitals changed their practices so that mothers of young children were encouraged to stay with the child in hospital and the importance of continuity of care was recognised for children in institutions.

PRACTICAL Activity

Interview a working parent about their child-care arrangements and how they feel about the issue of substitute care. Ask them to consider the benefits and the disadvantages of working and having a young child at the same time. Make a list of the issues mentioned and draw up a table to see whether there is a balance of pros and cons.

Support for the maternal deprivation hypothesis came from a variety of sources. Drawing initially on the evidence from animal studies such as that of Lorenz and Harlow, Bowlby then looked at research into the effects of institutional care. One such study was the work of Goldfarb (1943) who carried out a longitudinal study on 15 pairs of children up to the ages of 10 to 14. One group were fostered soon after birth, whilst the other group spent three years in an institution and were then fostered. Goldfarb found that the institution group performed significantly less well on a range of emotional and cognitive measures, concluding that their deficits could be attributed to their lack of an attachment figure during their institutionalised years.

REFLECTIVE Activity

Consider Goldfarb's conclusion that the institution group showed emotional and cognitive problems due to the lack of an attachment figure. Imagine what it was like for a young child in a children's home in the 1940s. Was it a stimulating environment? Did the children have many toys and books? Also consider why the 15 children were chosen for fostering and the other 15 were not. Perhaps the fostered group were brighter, more sociable children to start with and that is why they were chosen for fostering.

What are the effects of being a working parent, on both parent and child?

Study 1.6

Aim Bowlby (1946) set out to investigate causes of delinquency.

Method Bowlby interviewed 44 juvenile thieves at a clinic, asking them about themselves, their behaviour and their childhood experiences. Bowlby also interviewed members of their families about the boys' behaviour and aspects of family history, including whether the boys had been separated from their families in early childhood. A control group of non-delinquent young people was used as a baseline for comparison.

Results The clinic group included 14 individuals identified as affectionless psychopaths, and of these, 12 had been separated from their mothers for a long period during their first two years. Only five of the delinquents who were not suffering affectionless behaviour had been similarly separated from their mothers, and only two of the control group had been separated for any prolonged period.

Conclusion Bowlby concluded delinquency is linked to childhood maternal deprivation, since the group of delinquents were more likely than the average population to have had a deprivation experience in childhood. Critics have argued that the retrospective interviews he conducted might have yielded invalid data. Quite simply, the interviewees might not have been able to recall accurately events from many years ago.

	Control group	Juvenile Thieves
Evidence of maternal deprivation	2	17
No evidence of maternal deprivation	42	27

Figure 1.4: Table to show the association between cases of antisocial behaviour and maternal deprivation. (Bowlby 1946)

Alternative views on attachment

Whilst not denying the importance of attachment, many people have criticised aspects of Bowlby's maternal deprivation hypothesis. Five issues are discussed here.

MONOTROPY

Bowlby's notion of a monotropic attachment has been criticised by Schaffer and Emerson (1964) who showed that children develop more than one strong attachment, and that attachment need not be to the mother, but will be to those who are most responsive to the child's needs.

Study 1.7

Aim Schaffer and Emerson (1964) investigated the number of attachment relationships infants have, in the light of Bowlby's theory of monotropism.

Method In a longitudinal study of Scottish infants throughout their first 18 months, infants were observed and mothers were interviewed about the child's responses to separation.

Results By 18 months most children had formed more than one attachment figure and some children had as many as five. Although the mother was the most commonly selected attachment figure, 75% of infants also selected the father at 18 months.

Conclusion Babies do not normally demonstrate monotropy and it is usual for a child to have several attachment figures. This finding is supported by other research. For example, Lamb (1977) noted how infants establish several attachments simultaneously.

EVALUATIVE COMMENT

Schaffer and Emerson's research into multiple attachments is consistent with cross-cultural studies of childrearing. Schaffer (1996) also states that there is no evidence from societies where infant care is shared between members of the community that shared care is diluted care. Tronick *et al.* (1987) described the infant care arrangements of the Efe people from Zaire, where children are collectively cared for by members of the group, and where the average number of carers for a group of infants is 14.2. Such collective responsibility seems to have no damaging psychological effects on the children and brings many benefits, including the provision of various sources of security and wider social experience for the child.

DELINQUENCY

Rutter (1981) argued that there is no simple cause and effect relationship between delinquency and maternal deprivation since other important variables need to be taken into account, such as the reason for the separation from the mother and the way the separation is handled. Not all cases of maternal separation result in delinquent behaviour. Rutter suggested that Bowlby had confused deprivation and privation (discussed in Section 1.2.4). Deprivation happens when a child has had an emotionally satisfactory relationship which is then broken, whereas privation is never having had an emotionally satisfactory bond in the first place. Note the consistency between Rutter's suggestion that privation is the main cause of delinquency and Harlow's work (Study 1.4).

In 1970, Rutter *et al.* carried out a large-scale study of children on the Isle of Wight using a rating scale to measure disturbed behaviour. Parents and teachers were asked to assess a child's character and behaviour by indicating agreement or disagreement with a series of statements such as, 'Often destroys or damages own or others' property' and 'Not much liked by other children'. Rutter *et al.* concluded that approximately 6% of 10 and 11-year-olds showed substantial emotional and behavioural problems. Subsequent investigation showed that these children had suffered from an accumulation of stresses, including, but not exclusively, separation from mother. The types of stresses identified by Rutter included marital discord, overcrowding, psychiatric illness in one or both parents and death of a close relative. Rutter concluded that maternal deprivation on its own was not a sufficient explanation for delinquency and that the reason for the separation of mother and child was a more important determinant of problem behaviour. Separations that were well handled and included satisfactory alternative emotional support for the child were much less likely to lead to delinquency than separations involving family discord and argument.

CRITICAL PERIOD FOR ATTACHMENT

Despite Bowlby's assertion that 'good mothering is almost useless if delayed until after 2½ years of age', Hodges and Tizard (1989) showed how children adopted as late as 7 years of age could establish strong affectional relationships with adopted parents. Clarke and Clarke (1976) argued against the view that the effects of deprivation are permanently damaging and suggested that children have a **resilience**, which enables them to cope with and overcome even the most difficult circumstances.

THE EFFECTIVENESS OF SUBSTITUTE CARE

Freud and Dann (1951) showed that six war orphans who had been living in concentration camps before they were brought to Britain were relatively emotionally sound. They proposed that the children had survived emotionally because they had established bonds with peers who acted as an effective substitute for a primary attachment figure.

PRACTICAL Activity

Consider the following reasons why young children might have to be separated from their primary caregiver and make a list of people or organisations that might provide substitute care for the child. Then consider whether the substitute care would be similar to that provided by the primary caregiver? Would the substitute care compensate for the loss of the primary carer? The reasons are:

- Death of a parent
- Long-term hospitalisation either of the parent or of the child
- Going to nursery all day when parent returns to work
- Parent moving away from the family home.

THE ROLE OF THE FATHER

Fathers are sometimes the most preferred attachment figure

In the 1940s/1950s when Bowlby was studying attachment, fathers had very little to do with child-care and childrearing. According to Bowlby the child would have one attachment figure and, most usually, this would be the mother. However, with changes in social attitudes and employment patterns fathers nowadays take an increasingly active role in the care of their children. Studies have shown that some fathers are just as responsive to their infants as mothers are (Parke and Sawin 1980), and Schaffer and Emerson (1964) found that around half the infants in their Scottish study showed a stronger attachment to someone other than the mother, usually the father.

Lamb (1977) focused on the reasons why young children prefer to attach to the father and concluded that the time that fathers spend with their children is taken up with fun, playtime activity, whereas mothers spend their time with the child carrying out care-focused duties such as cleaning and dressing. Generally, evidence from fathering research indicates that that fathers have a valuable role to play in attachment.

PRACTICAL Activity

Interview a couple with a young child and ask how each of them spends time with the child. Questions you might like to ask could include:

Who looks after the child during the day?

How much time a week does each partner spend on their own with the child?

Who looks after the child when he or she is sick?

Who has responsibility for taking the child to and from school?

Who plays most with the child, you or your partner?

Do your findings support what researchers have discovered: that mothers have greater responsibility for caring and fathers spend more time playing?

1.3 Self and others

Aspects of the self

The self-concept is usually thought to consist of three components: **self-image** – how we think we look; **self-esteem** – how much we value ourselves, and the **ideal self** – the type of person we would like to be. As adults, most of us have a fair idea of what we look like and what our qualities and weaknesses are. We have some notion of how we appear to other people and whether we think we are 'nice' people or not. This ability to know and understand ourselves is so well developed by the time we reach adulthood, it is really quite difficult for us to imagine what it must have been like not to have any awareness of self.

REFLECTIVE Activity

Read the description of infant behaviour below and try to imagine what is going on in Caitlin's mind.

> **Nine-month old Caitlin had started constantly to hold her hand in front of her face. Watching Caitlin was intriguing. She would hold her hand close up to her face then slowly and deliberately make a fist with her little fingers. She would then unclench her tiny fist and spread out her fingers, before repeating the whole activity. As she performed this simple, repetitive activity she would continue to look intently and purposefully at her own hand, a part of her own body over which she had control.**

The reflective activity above seems to describe a child who is just learning about her own existence. Psychologists refer to the understanding that the self exists as a separate entity, with a past and a future, as the **existential self**. Another way to describe the existential self might be self-awareness, since it really refers to an awareness of oneself as separate to other people.

Study 1.8

Aim Lewis and Brooks-Gunn (1979) set out to find out the age at which self-recognition develops.

Method Children aged between 9- and 24-months-old were placed in front of a mirror in which they could see their own face. The researchers took a control measure of how often they touched their noses as they played. The researcher then wiped the children's faces with a cloth, deliberately putting a spot of rouge onto their noses. The researcher then watched to see whether the children reached for the spot on their own nose or tried to touch the spot on the mirror image.

Results As can be seen in Figure 1.5, the number of children touching the spot on their own face increased from 0% at 9 months to approximately 75% at 24 months. Using the mirror to explore the spot on the face rather than the mirror image could indicate that a child has developed self-recognition and knows what he or she looks like.

Conclusion The majority of children have developed some degree of self-awareness by the ages of 15 to 21 months.

EVALUATIVE COMMENT

Results from a similar study using photographs indicates that self-recognition from still, unmoving images is much more difficult. Self-awareness and the development of the existential self seems to develop gradually, meaning that a child may have some degree of self-awareness at a given age, but only in certain contexts. Perhaps because the image of self in the mirror is moving in time with the child's movements, this simultaneous movement provides another clue for the child that it is his or her own reflection in the mirror. With a photograph there is no simultaneous movement to use as an extra clue to self-recognition and this makes the rouge test more difficult.

The **categorical self** refers to an understanding of the characteristics that define the self, such as our age and sex. This ability to understand oneself in terms of categories develops as the child becomes aware of the existence of different categories of people in the world. In a typical study

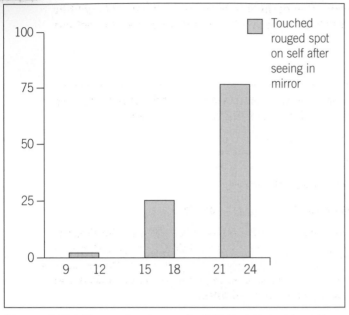

Figure 1.5: The percentage of children touching the rouge spot on their own nose

children are shown photographs of boys and girls and asked, 'Which of these children is like you?' Children who are able to point correctly to either the boy or the girl might be assumed to have developed a categorical self in relation to gender. Most research suggests that the ability to label the genders and identify one's own gender correctly develops at around two to three years of age. However, some studies show that even very young infants have some understanding of the categorical self.

Kujawski and Bower (1993) investigated **gender concept** in a novel way by showing 10- to 14-month-olds light point displays of male and female babies running and walking. A light point display shows up as a set of dots of light, each dot corresponding to joints on the model's body. Thus, the infants could see the way the bodies moved but not see the bodies themselves. In this study male infants spent more time looking at the male model display, with female infants preferring the female display. These results indicate the infants could discriminate between the male and female model and the preferential looking suggests they identified more with their own sex category.

Self esteem in children

Self-esteem is the evaluative dimension of self, or the extent to which we like and value ourselves. Argyle (1983) suggested that self-concept, which includes self-esteem, is dependent upon four factors: the reaction of others, identification with others, comparison with others and social roles. Although Argyle's theory was not particularly a developmental theory, all of these

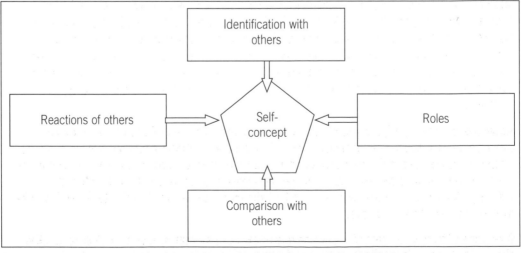

Figure 1.6: Factors affecting the self-concept (Argyle 1983)

factors can be related to child development quite easily. For example, children who get low marks in class tests might compare their results with the results other children get and feel less good about themselves.

REFLECTIVE Activity

Consider how Argyle's four factors might affect a child's developing self-esteem in each of the following scenarios. For each example identify the factor and think whether the child's self-esteem would go up or down.

Being the person that lots of people want to sit next to on the school bus.

Being given the job of register monitor or milk monitor.

Being the only person in your group of friends who has not got a Play-Station.

Being told that you look a bit like David Beckham (assuming you're a boy who wants to)!

The importance of the reaction of others for developing self-esteem is consistent with theories of self such as Cooley's Looking Glass Theory (1902). Cooley, a sociologist, proposed that in their behaviour towards us, other people act as a looking glass or mirror in which we see a reflection of our self. If people smile at us and choose to spend time with us, these actions and reactions give us a positive view of 'self' and enhance our self-esteem.

Although parental reactions are obviously very important for children's self-esteem, other sources of social support such as classmates, friends and even teachers become increasingly influential with age. Rosenberg (1979) asked children how much they cared about what parents, friends, siblings and others thought about them. Responses from the younger children referred to parents as the most significant influence, with peers becoming more important for older children and adolescents being most concerned about what their friends thought. According to the concept of the **significant other**, different people's reactions to us will matter to a greater or lesser extent depending on how much we value their opinion in respect of a particular area. Thus, our self-esteem would be much enhanced if a friend thought our clothes were great, but not if our parents did.

Study 1.9

Aim Coopersmith (1967) investigated the origins of self-esteem and the effects of self-esteem over time.

Method Using a questionnaire, teachers' evaluations and a projective personality test (**the Thematic Apperception Test – TAT**), the self-esteem of a large sample of 10/11 year-old-boys was assessed. The questionnaire comprised 58 statements, derived from adult self-esteem questionnaires, with which the boys were asked to agree or disagree. A typical statement was 'I'm popular with kids my own age'. Mothers of those children classified as high or low in self-esteem were interviewed about their relationships with their child and various aspects of childrearing.

Results Boys with high self-esteem were confident, more sociable and did better at school, whilst those with low self-esteem were isolated, lacking in confidence and did poorly at school. Furthermore, mothers of the high self-esteem group tended to be authoritative and accepting of their children whereas the mothers of the low self-esteem group tended to be harsh and unloving. Coopersmith's data also revealed that the boys' own levels of self-esteem tended to be similar to those of their parents.

Conclusion The development of self-esteem is related to parental behaviour. Follow-up studies showed that the positive effects of high self-esteem continued as the boys grew older.

EVALUATIVE COMMENT

Since Coopersmith's data was correlational it is impossible to say that a child's self-esteem is directly affected by parental treatment. It could even be that having such positive, high-achieving children caused the mothers of the high self-esteem boys to treat them more positively. The questionnaire measure used by Coopersmith may have been too insensitive and more recent studies have opted to assess aspects of self-esteem separately. Harter (1988) measured self-esteem in relation to five different domains: schoolwork, athletic ability, peer relationships, behaviour and physical appearance. Taken together these five measures provide a more sensitive measure of self-esteem than Coopersmith's global score.

Using a five-dimensional profile, Harter (1988) found that children could feel very positive about some aspects of themselves and at the same time quite unhappy about other aspects. For example, a boy might have a high level of self-esteem in the domain of sport because he is really good at sport, but feel very inadequate about his schoolwork because he is doing badly in exams at school. However, Harter found that levels of self-esteem were only lowered by inadequacy if a child thought that performance in that domain was important. Thus, failing tests at school would not have any effect on self-esteem for a student who thought that schoolwork was unimportant anyway.

PRACTICAL Activity

Consider the following five pairs of statements derived from Harter's Self-Perception Profile for children and see if you can identify which statement relates to which of Harter's proposed domains. Respondents have to choose one statement from each pair and say whether the statement they have chosen is 'like me' or 'a bit like me'. You could think what your own responses might be and what they would suggest about your own self-esteem for the five domains. The five domains are schoolwork, athletic ability, peer relationships, behaviour and physical appearance.

Pair 1
Some people are really good at all sorts of sports.
Some people don't think they're very good at sport at all.

Pair 2
Some people get into trouble a lot because of how they behave.
Some people usually behave well and stay out of trouble.

Pair 3
Some people wish they looked different.
Some people like the way they look.

Pair 4
Some people find schoolwork difficult.
Some people do really well at school.

Pair 5
Some people are really popular.
Some people are not really popular.

CONSEQUENCES OF HIGH AND LOW SELF-ESTEEM

In general, for children as for adults, high self-esteem is associated with positive outcomes whereas low self-esteem is associated with negative outcomes. Bee (1989) summarises the effects of high self-esteem on children and this is shown in Figure 1.7.

Higher academic ability
Feelings of control over own achievements and failures
More popular with peers
More positive relationships with parents
Know who they are and what they want to be
Psychologically more healthy – less likely to be depressed

Figure 1.7: Characteristics of children with high self-esteem (Bee 1989)

1.4 The development of friendship

Friendship is described by Flanagan (1996) as 'An emotional relationship which includes elements of mutual trust, assistance, respect, understanding and intimacy'. According to Erwin (1998), children's friendships have a number of important functions. They act as a means to develop interactional and cognitive skills, as a route to intimacy and as a way of exchanging and testing knowledge about people and the world. Friends can also be an important emotional buffer in times of stress, for example, when parents are arguing and the child is unhappy at home.

Age-related change in friendship

Observation studies often show that 2-year-old children have a sustained preference for a particular playmate and by the age of four, approximately 50% of children have a preferred friend, with whom they spend at least 30% of their time at nursery school (Hinde *et al.* 1985). The number of friendships increases up until adolescence, when depth of relationship rather than number of friends becomes important. Levitt *et al.* (1993) found that even 7-year-olds reported 'feeling close' to friends as well as members of their family, and Buhrmester (1996) found that, whereas 7/10-year-olds are most likely to **self-disclose** to parents, 15-year-olds are most likely to self-disclose to friends.

Just as children seem to value friends more as they get older and prefer the company of peers to the company of adults and family, so their understanding of friendship seems to change with age. This age-related change in understanding friendship might be explained through lessening **egocentrism** and an increase in the ability to take the perspective of another person.

To assess age-related differences in the understanding of friendship, Damon (1977) asked children questions like 'Tell me about your best friend' or 'Tell me a story about two children who are friends'. From analysis of the replies Damon proposed three levels of understanding. Under 7 years the child is still egocentric so has few feelings of like or dislike – friends are just people with whom the child spends time; friendships are quickly formed and quickly dissolved, for example, if a child takes away a toy from another. Between 8–11 years friendships are based on shared mutual interests with trust and responsiveness to others' needs; kindness is seen as an important criterion. From 12 years upwards friendships are seen as deep, enduring relationships with mutual understanding and sharing of intimacies.

Cognitive representations of friendship were similarly investigated by Selman (1980) who presented children with a social dilemma. A typical dilemma might involve a story about a girl who lied to her friend because she did not want to go out with her. The story was then followed by interview questions about the characters in the story and about friendship in general. Selman categorised the responses and proposed five stages in social understanding of friendship.

Selman's stages of social understanding (1980)

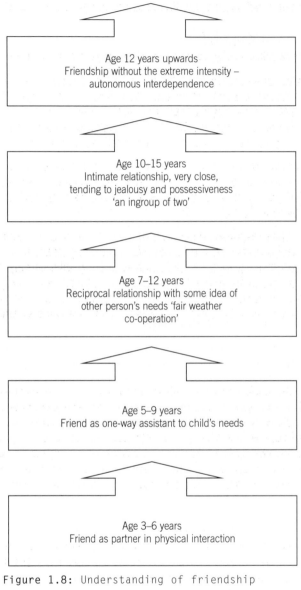

Age 12 years upwards
Friendship without the extreme intensity –
autonomous interdependence

Age 10–15 years
Intimate relationship, very close,
tending to jealousy and possessiveness
'an ingroup of two'

Age 7–12 years
Reciprocal relationship with some idea of
other person's needs 'fair weather
co-operation'

Age 5–9 years
Friend as one-way assistant to child's needs

Age 3–6 years
Friend as partner in physical interaction

Figure 1.8: Understanding of friendship becomes increasingly sophisticated with age

Study 1.10

Aim Bigelow and LaGaipa (1975) studied children's understanding of 'a friend'.

Method Essays about 'a best friend' written by children between the ages of 6 and 14 years were analysed and each was rated on 21 dimensions including reciprocity and sharing.

Results The dimensions referred to in the stories changed as children got older. For young children the emphasis was more on general play, and giving to a friend, whereas for older children the focus was more on similarity, acceptance, loyalty, etc. Bigelow confirmed the original age-related findings in a later study of 480 Scottish children.

Conclusion Children move from egocentric to empathic expectations of friendship, and understanding of the concept 'friend' becoming more sophisticated with age. With age there is increasing emphasis on psychological qualities rather than physical interaction.

EVALUATIVE COMMENT

There are three main criticisms of research into the understanding of friendship:

- The increasingly complex and abstract understanding of friendship shown in older children may be due to the increase in ability to express such ideas in language. Maybe younger children understand friendship in a very complex way, but cannot express their ideas. Just because a child does not talk about characteristics like trust and empathy in their answer, it does not mean that they do not appreciate and recognise such qualities in a friend

- Many studies involve the use of the clinical interview and lack formal structure and control. Usually the interview is followed by analysis and categorisation of responses, a procedure that can be subjective. This is especially likely where responses take a completely open-ended form like an essay (see Study 1.10)

- Hypothetical dilemma responses have been used in many contexts, including investigations of moral and pro-social reasoning and it has often been suggested that hypothetical reasoning tends to be more advanced than real-life understanding. Interestingly, Serafica (1982) found that responses to questions about hypothetical friends and real friends yielded descriptions which were quite different; not all studies are testing same thing – some ask about 'a friend', 'a best friend' and others ask about 'friendship' which is a complex and abstract notion for a young child.

Sex differences

Before two years, interaction between children tends to be in twosomes or pairs, with little evidence of same sex preference. However, even before the concepts of 'boy' and girl' are properly developed, children start to prefer the company of their own sex, and by 3/4 years play mostly in same sex groups (Erwin 1998). This 'cleavage of the sexes' might occur because boys and girls prefer different sorts of activities, for example, boys engage in much more rough and tumble play. By five years of age boys show greater same-sex preference than girls and by 11/12 years groups have become very important and sex segregation is almost complete.

PRACTICAL Activity

Carry out a mini-observation in a playground or at a nursery school. Remember to ask permission first, either from parents or from the head teacher at the school. Draw up a tally chart and observe selected children individually for a fixed time, say 10 minutes. Use a time sampling technique, recording every 30 seconds whether the child is playing alone, with a child of the same sex or with a child of the opposite sex. Time sampling allows you to see how much time the child spends in interaction, and with whom. When you have collected enough data calculate the percentages of time spent alone and with different social partners. How much cross-sex play did you observe?

Waldrop and Halverson (1975) have described boys' and girls' peer relationships as extensive (boys) and intensive (girls). For boys most time is spent in the larger group with the focus on shared activities or tasks. Boys view the friendship group as a collective entity and value its solidarity. Girls' relationships are described as intensive because they view the group as a network of intimate two-person friendships, with the focus on closeness and sharing of emotion rather than joint activities.

Boys spend more time in large friendship groups, whereas girls prefer to be in pairs

Study 1.11

Aim Serbin *et al.* (1977) set out to increase **cross-sex play** in 4-year-olds.

Method Teachers in two classes reinforced instances of cross-sex play with verbal positive comments. For example, if a boy and a girl were playing with building bricks the teacher would give verbal, positive reinforcement such as 'I like the tower Kathy and John are building with the blocks'. The amount of time the children spent playing with the opposite sex was recorded by observers. At the end of the two weeks the teacher ceased giving positive reinforcement for cross-sex play and again, the amount of time spent in cross-sex play was recorded.

Results Over the two-week experimental trial cross-sex play increased from 5% to over 20% of the children's time. However, once the reinforcement ceased, children reverted to their original low level of cross-sex play.

Conclusion It is possible to increase the amount of time children spend playing with a child of the opposite sex by selective reinforcement. Serbin's results seem to suggest that sex segregation in childhood may perhaps be attributed to subtle and unintentional reinforcement of same-sex play by parents, teachers or even peers.

Sex differences in friendship during adolescence tend to be similar to those observed in younger children. Although there is no apparent difference in the number of friends that boys and girls have, boys are much less concerned with forming close, intimate relationships. Whereas girls see individual friends as confidantes and a source of emotional support, boys are more likely to focus on the importance of the group and allegiance to the group. Considering reasons for differences in social behaviour between adolescent males and females, Douvan and Adelson (1966) suggested that boys need the group to support the quest for autonomy and defy authority, whilst girls are not as defiant and do not need to focus on the group as a source of strength.

Study 1.12

Aim Lever (1976) investigated sex differences in friendship attitudes and friendship behaviours.

Method 10-year-old boys and girls in American city and suburban schools were interviewed about their attitudes towards friends and their interactions with friends.

Results Several sex differences emerged:

- Girls were most comfortable with a single best friend, being less likely than boys to admit a third person into a friendship

- Girls openly showed affection, for example, by handholding and writing notes, whereas such behaviour was rarely seen in boys

- Girls were more sensitive to the fragility of the intimate relationship, worrying more about falling out with a friend

- Girls shared personal intimacies whereas boys shared group secrets and information about group strategy or rules

- Girls were more likely to be jealous of a third party than boys.

Conclusion Girls are more emotionally involved with friends and prefer more intimate two-person relationships, whereas boys' friendships are more open

PRACTICAL Activity

Interview a teenage boy and girl about their friendships. Devise a series of statements based on what you have read so far about sex differences and ask your interviewees how much they agree or disagree with the statements on a scale. The scale might look something like the example below.

	Agree				Disagree
I worry a lot when I fall out with a friend.	**1**	**2**	**3**	**4**	**5**

EVALUATIVE COMMENT

How do psychological perspectives relate to sex differences in children's friendships? The biological perspective would explain male preference for larger friendship groups as a means of fulfilling the need to compete within the dominance hierarchy of a group. Females on the other hand have a need to nurture and care and therefore prefer quieter activities using friends as a source of individual support. Traditional behaviourists would argue that males and females are reinforced for what is seen as sex-appropriate behaviour, so girls are encouraged to play quietly in twos and boys to play competitively in groups. These reinforced behaviours are thus acquired through the process of operant conditioning. *Social learning* theorists would suggest that boys and girls are simply copying the behaviour of adult models.

Popularity and rejection

Coie and Dodge (1983) carried out a **sociometric study** of primary-school-aged children in which each child was asked to identify who in the class they 'liked most' and who they 'liked least'. From the responses the researchers identified five types of children: popular children; average children; controversial children; neglected children and rejected children.

PRACTICAL Activity

What makes some children popular and much sought after, and why are other children neglected or actively rejected by their peers? Make a list of playground behaviours that might make a child (a) popular, (b) neglected and (c) rejected. Now check your list against those in Figure 1.9

Popular	Rejected	Neglected
Popular = smiley cartoon face	Rejected = angry cartoon face	Neglected = sad, lonely looking cartoon face
Physically attractive, positive, lots of two-some play, co-operative, low in aggression, able to share	Disruptive, argumentative, antisocial, highly active, talkative, unco-operative, unable to share, lots of solitary play	Shy, unaggressive, not antisocial, unassertive, solitary, avoids two-some play, prefers groups

Figure 1.9: Behaviours typical of popular, rejected and neglected children (Schaffer 1996)

Children prefer to be friends with those who are attractive and even young children have been found to prefer to look at attractive rather than unattractive peers. Higher status individuals and those who are perceived to be more competent, for example, those good at sport, tend to be more popular. Children also prefer familiar people and will choose friends who live near, or who are seen regularly. As we find similarity reinforcing, children will choose playmates from similar background, of the same sex, with similar interests, etc. Rubin (1980) refers to strong pressures to exclude the 'deviant' or different child.

Kandel (1978) carried out a longitudinal study of adolescent friendships from the start to the end of a school year, which suggests similarity is important in friendship. Three types of friendships were identified: maintained friendships – existed at the start and the end of the year; dissolved friendships – existed at the start, but not at the end of the year; newly formed friendships – started up at some time during the year. Kandel noted that maintained and newly formed friendship pairs were more similar in attitude, behaviour and interests than dissolved friendship pairs. He concluded that either similarity may be the key to friendship or, successful friendships may be those where partners come to adopt each other's interests and characteristics.

EXPLANATIONS FOR POPULARITY AND REJECTION

According to attachment theory and the **internal working model** the relationship between child and mother figure sets the pattern for future relationships, thus the rejected child is one who has not had the satisfactory care of a single loving adult, and who therefore has no model on which to base future relationships.

Hazan and Shaver (1987) proposed that the three types of attachment shown in Ainsworth's Strange Situation (Study 1.2) are carried through to later relationships with other people, so that an infant defined as 'Secure Type' according to Ainsworth's category system, would grow up to be a person who has similarly positive experiences in later relationships. Although Hazan and Shaver relate the three types to later romantic relationships, it follows that the 'anxious-resistant' and 'anxious-avoidant' types would probably be more likely to have difficulty in childhood and adolescent relationships too. For example, the anxious-resistant type would be afraid of getting too close to other people and tend to resist any attempts at intimacy from others, therefore finding it very difficult to sustain friendships.

REFLECTIVE Activity

Review the characteristics described in Hazan and Shaver's types of adult relationship. Consider them in relation to (a) yourself and how you manage your relationships and (b) a friend and how they cope in their relationships with others. It is likely that you will not be able to define either yourself or your friend as exclusively one type or another, but you may recognise some of the behaviour patterns outlined in Figure 1.10.

Type	Relationship Characteristics
Secure	No trouble getting close to others Happy depending on others Comfortable if others are dependent Not worried about being abandoned Not afraid someone will get too close
Anxious-avoidant	Somewhat uncomfortable being close to others Difficulty trusting others Difficulty depending on others Nervous when anyone gets too close Feels partners want to be too intimate
Anxious-ambivalent	Concerned partner will leave Disappointed other people will not get close enough Desire for intense closeness frightens others away Afraid others are not really committed

Figure 1.10: Adult relationship characteristics displayed by secure and anxious types (Hazan and Shaver 1987)

Whilst attachment theory may explain why some children have difficulty relating to peers, there are other possible explanations. A number of studies have shown that one reason for rejection by peers may be that a child has poor social skills and therefore experiences difficulty interacting with others.

Study 1.13

Aim Dodge *et al.* (1983) investigated playground behaviour to see whether there were behavioural differences between popular and unpopular children.

Method In a naturalistic observation, five-year-olds were observed in the playground. Researchers focused on pairs of children at play and watched to see how a third child would approach and try to join in with the game. Behaviours such as the time spent watching, the types of verbal comments made and the style of approach were recorded.

Results It was found that popular and unpopular children differed significantly in their approaches to the other children. Popular children watched and waited, made group-oriented statements and were gradually accepted. Neglected children watched but shied away from attempting interaction. Rejected children were highly active and aggressive, disrupting play of the others, being generally uncooperative and making critical comments.

Conclusion The unpopularity of rejected and neglected children relates to deficits in social skills.

EVALUATIVE COMMENT

There is no clear-cut cause and effect relationship here – perhaps initial peer group rejection leads to an expectation of social failure. Because a child expects to be rejected he/she may then avoid social opportunities to practise peer social skills. As a result the child becomes more and more deficient at social interaction. Ladd and Golter (1988) followed 3 to 4-year-old children for a year to see if they could detect a cause and effect relationship between social incompetence and unpopularity. Assessing each variable three times they found that early argumentative behaviour predicted later unpopular status.

If poor social skills are at the root of the problem for an isolated child then training in social skills ought to lead to an increase in popularity. Oden and Asher (1977) set up a programme of social skills training for 8–9 year-old isolates. The unpopular children were given coaching in the following skills:

• How to join in

• Turn taking

• Sharing

• Communication

• Giving attention to others

• Helping.

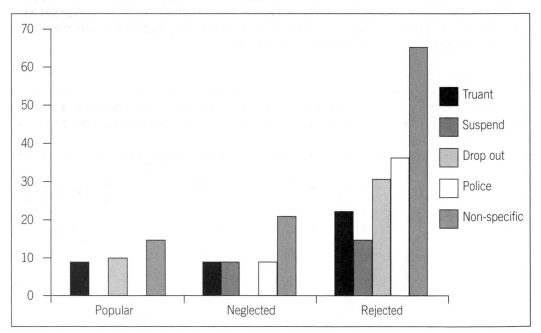

Figure 1.11: Graph to show the relationship between popularity status and negative outcome (Kupersmidt and Coie, 1990)

At the end of the programme they were no longer isolated from their peers, and were more outgoing, more positive towards other people and had improved social status.

Consequences of popularity and rejection

Cowen *et al.* (1973) carried out a longitudinal study with 800 children to investigate the long-term effects of peer relationships on psychological well-being. It was found that children rated negatively by peers at eight-years-old were more likely to suffer from a variety of psychiatric problems throughout childhood and adolescence and into their adult lives. Duck (1991) similarly found that rejected children were more likely to grow up to suffer from a range of behavioural and mental disorders including: alcoholism, depression, schizophrenia, delinquency and psychotic behaviour.

Kupersmidt and Coie (1990) identified a link between **sociometric status** and a number of negative life outcomes, including truancy and being in trouble with the police. In a seven-year longitudinal study they found that children identified as rejected at the age of 11 were much more likely to drop out of, or be suspended from, school and three times more likely than averagely popular children to have been in trouble with the police by late adolescence. Interestingly, neglected children did not show any increased evidence of negative outcomes.

EVALUATIVE COMMENT

Although these studies suggest that rejection has serious consequences, determining a cause and effect relationship is impossible. It might be that these individuals were rejected as children because they already showed disordered behaviours and that the behaviour was a cause and not a consequence of their rejection. Schaffer (1996) discusses the role of aggressiveness in negative outcomes and suggests that an aggressive temperament may be a more reliable indicator of negative life outcomes than peer rejection. Only some of the rejected children in the Kupersmidt and Coie study were identified as being aggressive and these were the children more likely to show social maladjustment.

PRACTICAL Activity

Draw up a table like the one in Figure 1.12 below with space for more causes and consequences. Read back over the section on popularity and rejection and see how many more causes and consequences you can add to the table.

Popularity		Rejection	
Causes	**Consequences**	**Causes**	**Consequences**
Good social skills	More social interactions	Poor social skills	Fewer social interactions – loneliness

Figure 1.12: Causes and consequences of popularity and rejection

1.5 Sample questions

SAMPLE QUESTION 1

(a)   Explain what is meant by *existential self*.
  (AO1 = 2, AO2 = 1)   *(3 marks)*

(b)   Outline and briefly discuss *one* aspect of age-related change in friendship.
  (AO1 = 2, AO2 = 3)   *(5 marks)*

(c)   Describe and discuss *either* causes *or* consequences of rejection in childhood.
  (AO1 = 6, AO2 = 6)   *(12 marks)*

(Total marks AO1 = 10, AO2 = 10)

QUESTIONS, ANSWERS AND COMMENTS
SAMPLE QUESTION 2

a)   Describe *one* way in which caregiver–infant interactions might contribute to the formation of attachment.
  (AO1 = 3, AO2 = 0)   *(3 marks)*

(b)   Outline and briefly discuss *one* method used by psychologists to measure attachment.
  (AO1 = 2, AO 2 = 3)   *(5 marks)*

(c)   Discuss *at least one* function of attachment.
  (AO1 = 5, AO2 = 7)   *(12 marks)*

(Total marks AO1 = 10, AO2 = 10)

Answer to 2(A)

One behaviour that helps in the formation of attachment is the way language is used to the child. Most adults use a special language when talking to young infants. This language, known as 'motherese', is specially designed to help the baby understand and to allow the mother and baby to become more close. Motherese is high pitched and repetitive so the baby understands more easily. Although a child may not understand the words, the special tone used in motherese allows the child to understand and they become closer.

Comment: 3 marks for identification of a way and elaborated description.

Answer to 2(B)

One method used is the strange situation, which is where a baby is exposed to a stranger with the mother either present or not. One problem with the strange situation is that children in different cultures behave differently. Also, it has been suggested that the kinds of behaviours observed are not always a good indication of attachment. Ainsworth believes that proximity seeking shows secure attachment, when, in fact, children who are happy to explore might be securely attached and therefore more confident to leave the mother.

Comment: 1 description mark is awarded for reference to the strange situation. Further description marks would have been awarded for reference to either the use of observation, or for emphasis on the sequence of events. 2 marks were given for evaluation: the candidate mentions two problems and clearly describes one of them, namely the validity of the measures. Altogether this part of the question is given three marks.

Answer to 2(C)

Attachment has many functions but one of the most important is the way that childhood attachments act as a model for later relationships. If we have a good relationship with our parents when we are young we can model later relationships, with friends, partners and even our own children on this. Bowlby referred to this as the internal working model of relationships. This view of attachment suggests that our understanding of the relationship is extremely important because this cognitive understanding affects later relationships. Main and Hazan and Shaver have shown that there may be some continuity between what happens in our childhood relationships and later relationships we form. Hazan and Shaver thought you could relate infant relationships to the kind of love relationships we have as adults. Main found that mothers who had had secure relationships themselves would carry forward the same pattern of attachment behaviours in interactions with their own children.

This view is not the same as the traditional view of attachment – that babies attach because of what they will gain out of the relationship (cupboard love theory – babies attach to people who feed them). This is consistent with the behaviourists' view of attachment, as behaviourists thought that behaviours that were rewarded would be more likely to be repeated. So, if a child is rewarded through positive and pleasant interactions with the carer, then they are more likely to perform the kinds of behaviours that would lead to more positive interactions, and therefore, more likely to become attached.

One very important function of attachment is to allow the child to stay close to the mother. Many researchers (Bowlby) have identified proximity seeking as the main attachment behaviour and staying close to the mother must have survival value. In the Ainsworth study children were observed as they tried to maintain proximity to the mother, following and crying when she left the room. This behaviour would be important for the child's survival and is seen in many species like the greylag geese (Lorenz). However, studies with geese may not tell us much about human behaviour.

So there may be many reasons for attachment. It is not likely we attach for food and Harlow's study with the cloth and wire monkeys showed this was not the case. However, we probably do attach for survival and we also use attachments as a foundation for later relationships.

Comment: Here the candidate gains all four AO1 marks for descriptive information about three possible functions – internal working model, cupboard love and evolutionary theory. There are several relevant evaluative comments and the candidate makes useful reference to studies, although some of these could have been elaborated further. The internal working model view is adequately presented with reference to studies. However, cupboard love theory is less well explained and it is a shame the Harlow reference was not made here rather than later. Proximity seeking as a function is explored with relevant reference and some discussion. In all, five AO2 marks were awarded, with a total of nine marks overall for this section. (AO1 = 4, AO2 = 5)

Overall mark: 15/20 (AO1 = 8, AO2 = 7) A competent answer that is wide-ranging, shows a good understanding of the specific area and attempts to link attachment to wider perspectives in psychology.

1.6 FURTHER READING

Introductory texts

Bee, H. 1999: **The developing child**. 9th Ed. Longman, New York.

Flanagan, C. 1996: **Applying psychology to early child development**. Hodder and Stoughton, London.

Harris, M. & Butterworth, G. 2002: **Developmental psychology: a student's handbook**. Psychology Press, Hove.

Jarvis, M. & Chandler, E. 2001: **Angles on child psychology**. Nelson Thornes, Cheltenham.

Smith, P. K., Cowie, H. & Blades, M. 1998: **Understanding children's development**. 3rd Ed. Blackwell, Oxford.

Specialist sources

Barnes, P. 1995: **Personal, social and emotional development of children**. Open University Press, Milton Keynes.

Bremner, J. G. 1994: **Infancy**. 2nd Ed. Blackwell, Oxford.

Erwin, P. 1998: **Friendships in childhood and adolescence**. Routledge, London.

Rutter, M. 1981: **Maternal deprivation reassessed**. 2nd Ed. Penguin, Harmondsworth.

Schaffer, H. R. 1996: **Social development**. Blackwell, Oxford.

2

Cognitive development

2.1 Introduction

What is cognitive development?

Most humans are able to make sense of the world around them. We can make plans, solve problems, recall events from the past, and understand the behaviour of other humans. We tend to take such abilities for granted, but they have to be acquired. They do not appear to be present in newborn humans (neonates). As far as we can tell, babies are not born with knowledge or understanding. Babies do not appear to think. Of course it is impossible to be certain about the cognitive abilities of human neonates – they do not have language, so we cannot ask them.

A child's cognitive development is not just about acquiring knowledge. The child has to develop or construct a mental model of the world. For example, a family of two parents and four children usually eat their evening meal together. One day the eldest boy is absent on a school trip. The youngest child notices that his elder brother is missing. To be able to do this, the child must have a stored representation of the family which includes all its members. This is just part of the mental model of his world that the child has constructed. During the meal, a parent asks the little boy what he would like for Christmas. To deal with this question, the boy has to have some idea of what Christmas is, and some ability to predict what will please him. His mental model of the world includes the idea of Christmas, but also an idea of himself.

Another way of understanding this cognitive ability is to imagine what it would be like if you did not have a mental model of your world. It would mean that you would not be able to make so much use of information from your past experience, or to plan future actions. You would simply respond to events and stimuli which affected you at the moment. As a result your behaviour would be much more like the behaviour of many non-human animals – you would spend most of your time seeking to meet your present needs and avoiding present threats.

2.2 Piaget's contribution to the study of cognitive development

Jean Piaget.

Jean Piaget (1896–1980) was born in Switzerland. He studied zoology, but soon became interested in child development. He was the first psychologist to make a systematic study of cognitive and moral development. His contributions include a theory of cognitive development, detailed observational studies of cognition in children, and a series of simple but ingenious tests to reveal different cognitive abilities.

Before Piaget's work, the common assumption was that children are merely less competent thinkers than adults. Piaget showed that young children think in strikingly different ways compared to adults.

Here is an example. A 5-year-old-boy's father was German, and his mother was English. When he found this out, he asked his mother whether he was German or English. His mother told him he was half German and half English. A few weeks later he had a fall and bruised his left arm. He ran to his mother, saying 'Mum, I've hurt my German arm!'

The boy had obviously assumed that one half of his body was English and the other half was German. He took his mother's statement literally and made sense of it in his own way – but in a way that few adults would ever do. We tend to laugh when children say things which reveal the difference between their way of understanding the world and ours. The child seems to be making a silly mistake. But a more careful consideration reveals that there is a kind of logic underlying the child's view of the world. In the example above, the little boy has made sense of his mother's statement. He understands how he can be half German and half English – even though adults would understand this in a different way.

Another example illustrates the same point. A 4-year-old-girl and her father are sitting on rustic wooden chairs in a garden. The father comments that his chair is wobbly. He asks his daughter why this is, not really expecting a reply. Immediately the girl responds, 'It's made of wobbly wood'. Notice that the girl does not have a problem in dealing with the question. She attributes the wobbliness to the material. Adults would be unlikely to do this, because they understand that it is the structure of the chair – perhaps the length of each leg – which makes it wobbly, and that a chair of the same structure would be wobbly whether it was made of wood, metal or plastic. Piaget noticed this qualitative difference in the way adults and children think.

Piaget also made careful, detailed observations of children. These were mainly his own children and the children of friends. Often the behaviour observed was stimulated by Piaget himself, intervening in the child's play, as in the following observation of his son, Laurent.

At . . . [4 months old] . . . I place a large rubber monkey in front of Laurent: the mobile limbs and tail as well as its expressive head constitute an absolutely new entity for him. Laurent reveals, in effect, lively astonishment and even a certain fright. But he at once calms down and applies to the monkey some of the schemata which he used to swing hanging objects; he shakes himself, strikes with his hands, etc., gradating his effort according to the result obtained. (Piaget 1952)

PRACTICAL Activity

List three ways in which Piaget's method of study illustrated by the extract above differs from the usual scientific method used in psychology.

Schemas

Piaget emphasised the importance of schemas in cognitive development, and described how they were developed or acquired. A **schema** can be defined as a set of linked mental representations of the world, which we use both to understand and to respond to situations. The assumption is that we store these mental representations and apply them when needed. For example, a person might have a schema about buying a meal in a restaurant. The schema is a stored form of the pattern of behaviour which includes looking at a menu, ordering food, eating it and paying the bill. (This is an example of a type of schema called a 'script'.) Whenever they are in a restaurant, they retrieve this schema from memory and apply it to the situation. The schemas Piaget described tend to be simpler than this – especially those used by infants. He described how – as a child gets older – his or her schemas become more numerous and elaborate.

Piaget believed that newborn babies have some schemas – even before they have had much opportunity to experience the world. These neonatal schemas are the cognitive structures underlying innate reflexes. These reflexes are genetically programmed into us. For example babies have a sucking reflex, which is triggered by something touching the baby's lips. A baby will suck a nipple, a comforter (dummy), or a person's finger. Piaget therefore assumed that the baby has a 'sucking schema'. Similarly the grasping reflex which is elicited when something touches the palm of a baby's hand, or the rooting reflex, in which a baby will turn its head towards something which touches its cheek, were assumed to result from primitive schemas.

Students often find the concept of a schema difficult to grasp. It is made easier if you get the idea that underlying any behaviour pattern or routine is a schema. So if a child is able to throw things (rattles, plastic hammers, food) s/he must have a 'throwing schema'.

These simple schemas can be applied to a range of situations. From an early age, infants will apply the sucking schema to their clothes, blankets, fingers and other objects within their reach.

REPETITION

If you have the opportunity to observe the behaviour of infants, you are likely to notice repeating patterns of behaviour. An example is simple 'turn-taking'. Infants sometimes play a game with an adult in which they give an object to an adult, then reach for it until the adult gives it back. Then the infant gives the object back to the adult and the cycle repeats itself. So you could say that the child has a 'turn-taking schema' – which it might apply to different forms of give and take, such as the alternate speaking and listening which occurs in conversations. As children grow older, their schemas become less linked with specific behaviours, and more like habits or patterns of thought which can be applied to a range of situations, such as the turn-taking schema.

Piaget noticed that children often repeat actions many times – especially in infancy. The implication is that frequent repetition of an action assists the acquisition of the new schema which underlies it. This is illustrated in Piaget's description his son Laurent aged 10 months.

. . . Laurent lets go of a series of objects while varying the conditions in order to study their fall. He is seated in an oval basket and lets the objects fall over the edge, sometimes to the right, sometimes to the left, in different positions. Each time he tries to recapture it, leaning over and twisting himself around . . . '

Piaget (1952), called these repetitions 'circular reactions'.

Adaptation, assimilation and accommodation: how schemas develop

For Piaget, an important aspect of cognitive development is **adaptation**. In this context adaptation means that the child constructs a set of schemas which fit his or her world. The better the child's schemas are adapted to their environment, the more able the child will be to make sense of events, and respond appropriately. Since different children grow up in a wide variety of different environments, they will acquire different schemas.

According to Piaget, adaptation takes place through two processes: assimilation and accommodation. **Assimilation** means applying a schema to a new situation – or choosing an appropriate one. For example a child might try to assimilate a piece of coloured modelling clay by picking it up and chewing it. A chewing schema is not the ideal response in this situation – the clay does not taste very nice. However the main point of having a schema is that it enables the child to respond – to deal with – the stimulus, rather than having no way of interacting with it. A second example is of a child who is used to drawing with thick crayons. The child uses a 'power grip' to hold the crayon. This means that the child clamps the crayon between the palm of the hand and the fingers. Then for the first time the child is given a much thinner coloured pencil. The child assimilates the pencil by grasping it with the power grip. This works up to a point, but it is hard to control the pencil.

According to Piaget, when a child assimilates an object or situation using a schema that does not quite fit that situation, the child experiences **disequilibrium**. In the examples above, disequilibrium might be caused by the fact that the clay tastes awful, or the pencil wobbles about. The child attempts to restore balance or equilibrium by a process called accommodation.

Accommodation means modifying a schema in order to deal more effectively with a new situation. In the modelling clay example, the child may modify the chewing schema by not putting the clay in his or her mouth, but by doing the 'chewing' with the hands. The clay will be squashed and shaped as a piece of food is squashed and shaped in the mouth – but using the hands only.

In the drawing example, the child may modify the power grip by holding the pencil more between the thumb and finger ends – in what is called the 'precision grip' – as most people hold pencils. These modifications enable the child to accommodate the new experiences. Notice that the result of these processes of assimilation and accommodation is that the child ends up with more schemas. For example the child has two ways of grasping objects instead of one.

Opportunities for adaptation frequently occur in a child's everyday life. Children spend many hours playing – and sometimes do so with such determination that to an onlooker they seem to be working hard at it. Piaget believed that play provided opportunities for developing new schemas – and was therefore important in aiding cognitive development. Construction toys such as sets of plastic bricks which clip together present a series of challenges which use and extend the abilities, or schemas, children have.

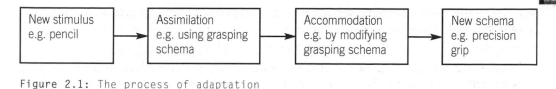

Figure 2.1: The process of adaptation

REFLECTIVE Activity

1. A 1-year-old child often uses a one-handed grasping schema. On her birthday she is given a large furry cube.

Using the words 'assimilate' and 'accommodate', suggest how the child is likely to deal with the cube, and what new schema may result.

2. Refer back to Piaget's observation of Laurent on page 35. What new situation is presented to Laurent, and how does he assimilate it?

Discovery learning

Piaget's view of cognitive development is sometimes described as **constructivist**. This means that the child builds up a mental model of the world and the processes which happen. For Piaget, it is the child's own actions in dealing with situations which are most important. The child's understanding of the world is acquired by discovery. Piaget's idea of **discovery learning** has been influential in early years education. Discovery learning means learning things by discovering them for yourself as a result of active exploration. Piaget's assumption that children learn through active self-discovery during play rather than by instruction is reflected in the emphasis on play in nursery schools and in the first year of primary education.

However, Piaget recognised that social interaction also contributes to cognitive development. He noticed that children begin to imitate the actions of other people from around 8- to 12-months-old. He also recognised that parents and others can provide the kind of stimulating experiences that increase the speed with which children's cognition develops.

Piaget's stages of intellectual development

Piaget's theory of intellectual (or cognitive) development is a **stage theory**. This means that it describes a universal and invariant sequence of stages through which an individual passes. Each child goes through the stages in the same order, and no stage can be missed out – although some individuals may never attain the later stages. There are individual differences in the rate at which children progress through stages – Piaget did not claim that a particular stage was reached at a certain age – although descriptions of the stages often include an indication of the age at which the average child would reach each stage.

Piaget believed that these stages are universal – i.e. that the same sequence of development occurs in children all over the world, whatever their culture. He claimed that a child's thinking was qualitatively different in each stage, but also that each stage built on, added to and reorganised the previous stage.

EVALUATIVE COMMENT

When child development follows a sequence, the obvious assumption to make is that it is strongly influenced by maturation. An example of this is motor development in the first year of life, which features a sequence of 'milestones' such as sitting up, crawling and finally walking. However Piaget did not regard the cognitive abilities he described as genetically determined.

According to Piaget, concepts are not inherited. However, biology contributes to cognitive development in two ways:

1. The biological structures necessary for cognition – including sense organs and the nervous system.

2. The innate tendency to interact with the environment in such a way as to acquire new ways of handling it – both physically and cognitively. Piaget referred to this tendency as adaptation.

Although this is partly a biological theory, it does not assume that maturation is involved. A maturational theory of cognitive development would claim that a series of growth events affecting the central nervous system would be triggered according to a maturational timetable – and that these would explain dramatic developments in cognitive ability.

Piaget's description of stages of cognitive development were based on his very detailed observations of his own children and the children of friends. These studies could be regarded as case studies, because of their in-depth nature, and the very small sample used. As well as observation he also asked children probing questions (the so-called 'clinical interview' method). Piaget devised a number of simple but ingenious tests of development, which provided the basis for a lot of subsequent research by other investigators.

THE SENSORIMOTOR STAGE: BIRTH TO 2 YEARS

Piaget divided this stage into six sub-stages.

At birth children are only able to interact with their world by means of reflex responses. The neonate has a repertoire of reflex behavioural schemas with which to explore the world. Sucking is the first to be used to explore objects.

In the first three sub-stages (from birth to 8 months) there is little evidence of what we would recognise as thinking. The child's way of dealing with the world is mainly through sensations and movements – hence the title 'sensorimotor' – and it is limited to the 'here and now'. The child responds to things which are present at the time, but shows little or no awareness of past, future, or objects which are not present.

The child shows no awareness of him- or herself as an individual in an environment. In other words the child does not have a self-concept. Equally the child shows no awareness that other objects or people exist independently of him- or herself. It is as though the child has experiences but cannot distinguish between self and the rest of the world.

During the last three sub-stages (from 8 to 24 months), the child's actions become more obviously intentional. For example the child might push a chair aside in order to get access to the space behind it. Trial-and-error behaviour becomes more apparent. For example a child who has a toy plastic duck which squeaks when it is squeezed, may try squeezing other objects to see whether they squeak. The child begins to show simple pretend play – for example, the child pretends to eat from a toy plate, or pretends to be sleeping. Language development also occurs at this stage. The child also acquires a self-concept and also object-concept.

Object-concept can be defined as the awareness that objects exist independently of us in the world, and continue to exist even if we are not observing them. Piaget devised a simple test of object-concept – which is often called a test of **object permanence**.

Piaget's test of object permanence
Object permanence means knowing that an object still exists, even if it is hidden.

It requires the ability to form a mental representation of the object. Alternatively it can be defined as the ability to react to the disappearance of a previously present object, for example by searching for it.

Aim Piaget (1963) wanted to find out at what age children acquire object permanence.

Method Piaget hid a toy under a blanket, while the child was watching, and observed whether or not the child searched for the hidden toy. Searching for the hidden toy was evidence of object permanence. Piaget assumed that the child could only search for a hidden toy if s/he had a mental representation of it.

Results Piaget found that infants searched for the hidden toy when they were around 8-months-old. However if the toy was removed from under the blanket and then hidden in another place, the infant continued to search for the toy in its first hiding place – under the blanket.

Piaget found that infants began to search for the toy in its most recent hiding place from around 12-months-old.

Conclusion Object permanence develops at around 8 months.

THE PREOPERATIONAL STAGE: 2 TO 7 YEARS

At this stage children show clear evidence of thinking, but thought is typically not logical. The name of this stage refers to the fact that during this stage a child is not yet able to perform mental operations (see page 42).

Piaget divided this stage into two periods: the preconceptual period (from 2–4 years); the intuitive period (from 4–7 years).

The preconceptual period

In the **preconceptual period** children begin to make more use of symbols, such as words and images. For example a child can pretend that a row of wooden blocks is a series of carriages in a train. Piaget pointed out that during this period children show several characteristic errors in thought. These include egocentrism, animism and centration.

Egocentrism: this refers to the child's inability to see a situation from another person's point of view. According to Piaget, the egocentric child assumes that other people see, hear and feel exactly the same as the child does. For example a little girl covers her eyes up and says 'You can't see me, can you Mummy.'

When he used the term egocentrism, Piaget was not suggesting that young children are selfish, but simply that they are unaware of a point of view that is not their own. They do not suspect that the world might look different to other people.

Aim Piaget and Inhelder (1956) wanted to find out at what age children decentre – i.e. become no longer egocentric.

Method They devised the 'three mountains test'. This was a board on which were placed three different mountain shapes. The mountains were different, with snow on top of one, a hut on another and a red cross on top of the other. The child was allowed to walk round the model, to look at it, then sit down at one side. A doll was seated at another side. The child was given 10 pictures representing the scene from different angles, and asked to pick out the card which showed the scene as the doll would see it. Piaget assumed that if the child correctly picked out the card showing the doll's view, s/he was not egocentric. Egocentrism would be shown by the child who picked out the card showing the view s/he saw.

Results Piaget and Inhelder found that 4-year-olds always chose the card which showed the view from their own position. Six-year-olds often chose a different perspective, but not always the correct one. Only 7- and 8-year-olds chose the right picture consistently.

Conclusion Children remain egocentric during most of the preoperational stage.

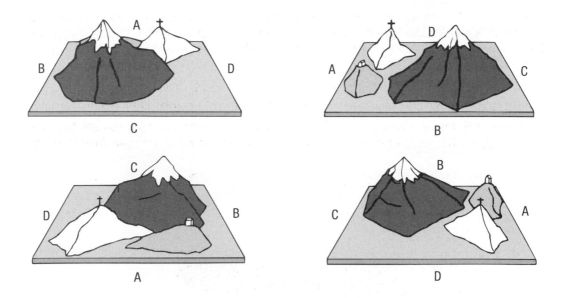

Egocentric children assume that other people will see the same view of the three mountains as they do

Animism is the child's belief that inanimate objects have feelings and intentions. There are many examples of children's statements which suggest that they think this way. For example, a child hearing some church bells start ringing said, 'The bells have woken up.' Another child, referring to the result of a recent collision said, 'It hurts where the wall hit me.' The children seem to assume that these inanimate objects (bells, walls, etc.) act in the same way as living things.

Statements such as 'The bicycle bit my leg', do seem to suggest that the inanimate object (bicycle) acted intentionally (biting is typically an intentional act). However it may be that the child, instead of actually attributing feelings and intentions to inanimate objects, is talking this way because it is an easy way of saying what they want to communicate. When an adult says of a broken-down car that 'The battery's dead', we do not assume they have an animistic view of the battery.

Centration refers to a child's tendency to only deal with one aspect of a situation at a time. The pre-operational child finds it difficult to take into account the effect of two factors. For example, if you give a child a box of plastic squares and triangles, some of which are red and some blue, and ask the child to pick out 'all the blue triangles', the child is likely to concentrate on only one of the two attributes (shape or colour). A typical response would be for the child to pick out all the triangles, regardless of colour, or alternatively to pick out all the blue objects, regardless of shape.

The ability to **de-centre**, i.e. to take into account more than one factor at a time is not achieved, according to Piaget until the stage of concrete operations.

The intuitive period

The **intuitive period** is the latter part of the preoperational stage. During this period a child's judgements are strongly influenced by the appearance of objects, rather than by logical reasoning. For example, if you take two identical tins of beans and bash one against a table so as to put a big dent in it, preoperational children will probably tell you that there are fewer beans in the dented tin.

The errors in thought typical of the preconceptual period, especially egocentrism, begin to decline. However, children are still unable to perform mental operations – such as conservation. **Conservation** is the ability to understand that redistributing material does not affect its mass, number or volume.

Conservation of mass is shown by giving a child two equal balls of modelling clay and asking whether one has more clay than the other or whether there is the same amount in both.

On getting the answer 'Same', you roll out one ball into a long sausage, and ask the same question again. The pre-operational child is likely to say that there is more clay in the sausage.

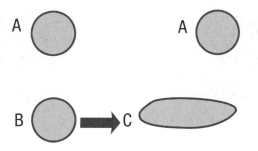

Conservation of mass. The two balls of clay are equal (A). When one ball is rolled into a sausage (C) the pre-operational child is likely to say that there is more clay in it than in B

Conservation of number is shown by counting out two sets of six beads, and putting them in two parallel lines of equal length. After asking whether one row has more beads than the other or whether they are the same, and getting the expected answer, spread one row out so that it is longer. The child is likely to respond that there are more in the longer row.

Conservation of number. Pre-operational children are likely to say that there are more beads in B than in C

Study 2.3

Aim Piaget and Szeminska (1941) wanted to find out at what age children could conserve volume (of liquid).

Method The researchers presented children with two identical beakers filled up to the same level with water. They asked each child whether there was the same amount of water in the two beakers or more in one than the other. Most children said there was the same. The researchers then poured the water from one of the beakers into a third, taller, thinner beaker. The previous question was repeated.

Results Piaget and Szeminska found that most children under 7-years-old said that there was more water in the taller, thinner beaker. In other words, they failed to conserve. In contrast, most children aged 7 years and over answered that there was the same amount in both beakers. The researchers asked each child for an explanation of their answer, to check that they had understood.

Conclusion The researchers concluded that a very significant change in cognitive ability occurs at around 7 years on average, when the ability to conserve is achieved and the child enters the stage of concrete operations.

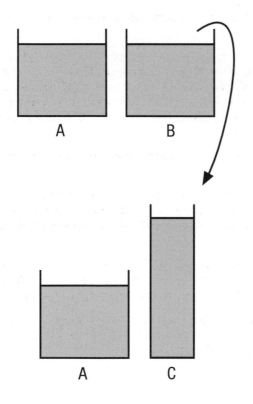

Conservation of volume. The 'three beakers test'. The pre-operational child is likely to say the amount of water in beaker C is different – even though they saw the researcher pour the water from B. From about 7 years old, children are no longer fooled by this test.

PRACTICAL Activity

1. Decide whether each of the following descriptions is an example of:

- animism
- egocentrism
- intuitive thought
- centration.

(a) A 5-year-old child is more impressed with a toy packaged in a large box than the same toy packaged in a small box.

(b) A boy is cutting out star shapes marked on cardboard to make a collage. After a while, his father joins in. After five minutes more, the boy pauses, looks at the pile of stars beside him, and the smaller pile his father has cut out. 'I've got more 'cos I'm quicker', he says.

(c) A boy who got into a fight with his sister understands when she is told off, but cannot understand why he should be told off.

(d) A child sees the sun setting and explains that it is hiding because it is afraid of the dark.

(e) A 6-year-old-boy has one sister and no brothers. Someone asks him 'Have you got a sister?' He answers 'Yes'. Then he is asked 'Has your sister got a brother?' His answer is 'No'.

2. Use the concepts of (a) *centration* and (b) *intuitive thought* to explain why a child in the preoperational stage thinks there is more liquid in a tall narrow beaker than a short, wide beaker.

REFLECTIVE Activity

Piaget assumed that if a child gave the wrong answer in a conservation of volume test, it was because the child lacked the understanding that the volume of a quantity of substance does not change if you change its shape or location. Think of two alternative reasons why a child might give the wrong answer.

The stage of concrete operations: 7 to 11 years

An **operation** is a rule-following transformation which we can make using our mental representations. In other words it is a type of logical thought process. Examples of operations include arithmetical operations such as adding, subtracting, multiplying and dividing. The ability to conserve requires mental operations including **reversibility** – the understanding that a transformation can be undone, and **compensation** – the recognition that one change – e.g. flattening a ball of clay will make it thinner but larger in area. Another example of an operation is converting a statement into its opposite, as illustrated by the child who said, 'When I grow *down* I will be *small*'.

During the stage of concrete operations, children can perform mental operations with real situations only. 'Concrete' means real and tangible.

An example is of a child at a family meal who looks at the other people round the table and asks, 'Are you the oldest one Dad?', and having this confirmed comments, 'That means you'll die first'. Here the child is applying a simple rule: first assuming that everybody lives for the same length of time, and then deducing that they will die in the same order as they were born. The assumption is faulty, but the logical operation is correct. The father, with the advantage of greater knowledge, merely replies, 'I hope so, son'.

This ability to perform operations means that children at this stage succeed in the conservation tests described above.

They can also manage **seriation** tasks. This means they can put concrete objects (or their representations) in order. For example if you told a child that Malcolm is taller than his brother Simon, who is taller than their sister Leonie, they could tell you which child was shortest.

Children in this stage can also perform **transitivity** operations – these involve making new deductions from information given. For example, given the information about the three children above, they could correctly answer the question 'Is Malcolm taller or shorter than Leonie?'

They can also demonstrate the ability of **class inclusion**. Piaget's 'class inclusion' test is an example of this. Piaget and Szeminska (1941) showed children 20 wooden beads. Eighteen were brown and two were white. Each child was asked several questions:

1. Are the beads all wooden?

2. Are there more brown beads or white beads?

3. Are there more brown beads or more wooden beads?

Pre-operational children usually answered the first two questions correctly. However they usually answered question 3 by saying that there were more brown beads. Children in the stage of concrete operations usually answered all three questions correctly. Notice that in question 2 the child has to think about two separate classes of beads – the brown ones and the white ones.

But in question 3 the two classes are not separate – they overlap. The class of brown beads is included in the class of wooden beads (this is class inclusion). The wrong answer is given, perhaps because the child assumes that if brown beads are one class, and they are the majority, they must have more members than any other possible class.

The stage of formal operations: 11 years and beyond

In this stage, adolescents can apply operations not only to concrete situations but also to abstract concepts. One example of a formal operation is *substitution* used in algebra. The individual is able to use a symbol – such as 'a' to stand for an unknown variable. This enables them to perform other arithmetical operations on 'a'. For example, if told that $3a = 21$, they can discover that $a = 7$. They can also perform transitivity tasks with unknown variables, such as this one. A number, 'x' is three times another number 'y', which itself is three times another number 'z'. How many times is x greater than z?

During the stage of formal operations adolescents can acquire and use abstract concepts. These are concepts which refer not to real objects or situations, but to invented or hypothetical ones. For example, many psychological concepts are abstract. One example is the concept of conservation. Conservation is an idea used to make sense of how children perform on tests like the three beakers test described above. You cannot see or touch conservation – you can only infer that it is occurring when a child gives the 'right' answer. Other abstract concepts you may have come across while studying psychology or other subjects include: repression, energy, bias, validity, health, inflation and justice.

Adolescents also begin to think *hypothetically*. This means they can suggest what might be the result if something were to happen. For example, being able to say what might happen if all the polar ice melted.

REFLECTIVE Activity

Dworetsky (1981) gave examples of likely responses to the question, 'What would it be like if people had tails?' Write down two possible answers to this question, before looking at Dworetsky's suggestions.

The responses he suggested include:

'People would leave lifts in a great hurry.' and 'Dogs would know when you were happy'.

The stage of formal operations also features greater flexibility in thinking. For example, adolescents are able to try one way of solving a problem, then if it is unsuccessful, they discard it and think of another way. They have a range of strategies instead of being limited to one approach. This is illustrated by mathematics problems in which students have first to decide on the most appropriate method for solving the problem and then to use it.

Piaget devised several tests of formal operational thought. One of the simplest was the 'third eye problem'. Children were asked where they would put an extra eye, if they were able to have a third one, and why. Schaffer (1988) reported that when asked this question, 9-year-olds all suggested that the third eye should be on the forehead. However, 11-year-olds were more inventive, for example suggesting that a third eye placed on the hand would be useful for seeing round corners.

The 'four beaker problem' (Inhelder and Piaget 1958) is a more demanding test which requires systematic hypothesis formulation and testing. Participants are given four beakers labelled 1 to 4, each containing colourless liquid, plus spare empty beakers and another chemical labelled 'g' which could be added with an eye-dropper. The researcher then shows the participant two more unlabelled beakers containing colourless liquid, and puts a few drops of 'g' in each. In one of these beakers, the liquid (which is a mixture of the chemicals in beaker 1 and 3) turns yellow. The liquid in the other beaker remains colourless. Participants are asked to use the liquid in the four beakers so as to get the same yellow colour as the researcher.

Participants usually start by adding 'g' to some of the liquid from beaker 1, then trying beaker 2 and so on. Younger participants (who are in the stage of concrete operations) typically decide that the task is impossible. Others may begin to try combinations of liquids – mixing liquids from three of the beakers for example. This haphazard approach is unlikely to be successful because participants forget which combinations they have tried, and so repeat some and miss others out.

The approach which is most likely to succeed is to work through all the possible combinations of liquids until the correct one is found. This systematic approach is likely to follow a sequence of trials like this:

1 + g, 2 + g, 3 + g, 4 + g

These will be followed by trials combining liquids in pairs like this:

1 + 2 + g, 1 + 3 + g, 1 + 4 + g, 2 + 3 + g, 2 + 4 + g, 3 + 4 + g, and so on to combinations of liquids from three beakers.

A participant using this systematic approach will get the right combination on the sixth trial.

Another task Piaget used was to give participants some string and some weights which could be attached to the string, and to use these to find out what factor or factors determine how fast the pendulum swings. Participants can vary the length of the pendulum string, and vary the weight. They can measure the pendulum speed by counting the number of swings per minute.

To find the correct answer the participant has to grasp the idea of the experimental method – that is to vary one variable at a time (e.g. trying different lengths with the same weight). A participant who tries different lengths with different weights is likely to end up with the wrong answer.

PRACTICAL Activity

Decide which of Piaget's four stages a child is likely to be in if they show the following behaviours (you should assume in each case, that the behaviour shown is at the upper limit of what they can achieve at that time).

The child can . . .

1. Design an effective experiment to test whether the growth of pea plants is influenced by noise.

2. Pretend to be sunbathing on a beach.

3. Guess that a small piece of wood will float in water, but assume that a much larger, heavier piece would sink.

4. Deal with a new toy by sucking it.

5. Give the correct answer to the question, 'Are there more vehicles or cars on the motorway today?'

Stage		Characteristics	Typical age
Sensorimotor stage	Substages 1–3	Ability to deal with situations is limited to: 1. having sensations and producing actions (including reflex responses) 2. the 'here and now'.	0–8 months
	Substages 4–6	Intentional actions emerge Trial and error behaviour Object concept develops Simple pretend play Language acquisition.	8–24 months
Preoperational stage	Preconceptual period	Symbolic thought develops Egocentrism Animism Centration	2–4 years
	Intuitive period	Judgements based on appearance not logical thought Less egocentric Unable to conserve	4–7 years
Stage of concrete operations		Can perform operations with real situations, including: conservation seriation transitivity class inclusion	7–11 years
Stage of formal operations		Can perform operations on unreal, abstract situations Abstract concepts acquired Hypothetical thinking Flexibility in thinking	12+ years

Figure 2.2: Summary table showing Piaget's stages of intellectual development

Was Piaget right?

1. WAS PIAGET RIGHT ABOUT THE TIMING OF OBJECT CONCEPT DEVELOPMENT?

One problem with Piaget's test of object permanence is this: if a child searches for the object, it is reasonable to conclude that they have achieved object permanence, but if they do not search, the opposite conclusion may not be justified. There could be several explanations for failing to search. For example, the child might lose interest in a toy which is not visible – especially if other toys are present and visible. It is quite possible that a child grasps object permanence earlier than at 8 months, but does not demonstrate it.

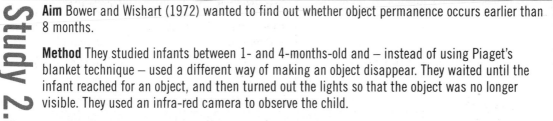

Study 2.4

Aim Bower and Wishart (1972) wanted to find out whether object permanence occurs earlier than 8 months.

Method They studied infants between 1- and 4-months-old and — instead of using Piaget's blanket technique — used a different way of making an object disappear. They waited until the infant reached for an object, and then turned out the lights so that the object was no longer visible. They used an infra-red camera to observe the child.

Results The researchers found that the infants continued to reach for the object for up to 90 seconds after it became invisible.

Conclusion Bower claimed that infants acquire object permanence much younger than Piaget stated. He explained their lack of success with Piaget's task as being due to an inability to understand the results of moving an object to a different location. In Piaget's test the object was moved when it was hidden, but in Bower and Wishart's procedure the object was not moved.

In an earlier study, Bower (1971) presented 4- to 8-month-old infants with a situation in which an object is moved from right to left, passes behind a screen and reappears. Bower observed the direction of the infant's gaze when the object disappeared behind the screen, and found that the older infants continued to track the invisible object with their eyes.

These studies demonstrate that it is possible to find evidence of object permanence earlier than Piaget claimed.

2. ARE YOUNG CHILDREN REALLY EGOCENTRIC?

Study 2.5

Aim Donaldson (1978) cites a study in which Hughes aimed to find out whether preoperational children really are egocentric. Hughes suspected that Piaget's mountains test was not a valid indicator of a child's ability to decentre. One problem with the test was that for many children, looking at an arrangement of mountains is an unfamiliar situation (although perhaps not in Piaget's native Switzerland).

Method Hughes redesigned the test using a situation likely to be more familiar to most children. The apparatus consisted of a model of four walls in a cross layout, a boy doll and a policeman doll. The child was asked to stand facing the model, in the position shown on the diagram below. The policeman doll was placed in different locations, and children were asked whether the policeman could see the boy doll.

First the policeman doll was placed so that he could see the areas B and D shown in the illustration above. He could not see areas A and C because of the wall.

The boy doll was placed in section A, and the child was asked if the policeman could see the boy. Then the boy doll was moved to section B, then C then D. If the child made a mistake (for example said that the policeman could not see the boy doll when it was placed in section D) the researcher pointed out the child's mistake.

Next the policeman was moved to the opposite side of the model — so that he could see sections A and C. The child was then asked to hide the boy doll where the policeman could not see him. Once again, any mistakes were pointed out — though Hughes reported that few mistakes were made.

The actual test of egocentrism came next. A second policeman doll was placed on the model, as shown on page 47. The child was told to hide the boy doll so that neither policeman could see him.

In the figure, section C was the correct answer. This was repeated with the policemen in different positions.

Results Hughes tested 30 children aged from three-and-a-half to five years. Ninety per cent of their responses were correct.

Conclusion This contradicts Piaget's own findings. Hughes's findings did not support Piaget's claim that children believe that the viewpoint of others is the same as their own. The study implies that in Piaget's mountains test, children did not understand what they had to do. Hughes made sure that children understood the task. He did this, first by choosing a situation which made sense to children (a policeman is looking for a boy who has been naughty), and second by his use of practice tests in which children were given the right answers.

The problem with the mountains test is that it does not really matter to the child what the doll can see. In Hughes' test, however, there is an implied story in which the child is likely to identify with the boy and be motivated to get the right answer.

EVALUATIVE COMMENT

You might be tempted to conclude that Piaget was wrong about egocentrism. However another way of interpreting the evidence of egocentrism studies is this: young children are able to decentre in situations that are easy for them to understand and which have personal relevance, but are egocentric in situations where it is more difficult to take another person's viewpoint, or where they are not motivated to do so. Young children are more likely to show egocentrism than older children or adults, but decentring is not absolutely impossible for them.

Flavell (1978) carried out a different study which questioned Piaget's belief in egocentrism. The experimenter sat opposite the child, with a Snoopy doll on a table between them. The child was asked to cover his/her eyes with their hands, and was then asked whether the experimenter could see them, or Snoopy, or both. The youngest children (aged 3) often replied that the experimenter could not see them, but all replied that the experimenter could see Snoopy. According to Piaget's concept of egocentrism, the children would deny that the experimenter could see anything which they themselves could not see.

3. ARE PREOPERATIONAL CHILDREN REALLY UNABLE TO UNDERSTAND CLASS INCLUSION?

Piaget's class inclusion test used wooden beads, some white and some brown. He found that children in the preoperational stage were unable to give the right answer to the question, 'Are there more brown beads or more wooden beads?'

Donaldson (1978) cites a study by McGarrigle which used a slightly different version of this test. He used four model cows, three of them black, and one white. He laid all the cows on their sides, as if they were sleeping. Six-year-old children were then asked:

1. Are there more black cows or more cows? (This is the question Piaget asked.)

2. Are there more black cows or more sleeping cows?

Twenty-five per cent of the children answered question 1 correctly, but 48% of the children answered question 2 correctly. This suggests that children are capable of understanding class inclusion rather earlier than Piaget believed. Once again, this is probably because the task was made easier.

Do children acquire object concept at around 8 months?	Studies have found object concept in much younger children.
Are children in the preconceptual period egocentric?	Under favourable conditions pre-school children can decentre.
Are children in the pre-operational stage unable to understand class inclusion?	Under favourable conditions they can.
Do children begin to conserve at around 7 years?	Under favourable conditions they do this a little earlier – but not much.

Figure 2.3: Was Piaget right?

4. WAS PIAGET RIGHT ABOUT THE AGE AT WHICH CHILDREN TYPICALLY BEGIN TO CONSERVE?

In the reflective activity on page 42 you were asked to think about why children might give wrong answers in conservation tests.

One possibility is that they misunderstand the language used in the task. For example, in the conservation of volume task, it could be that when children say there is 'more' in one beaker than the other, they are using 'more' in a different way from the adult. The adult means 'a greater volume'. The child's 'more' might mean 'higher' or 'fuller', in which case children may not be failing to conserve after all.

Another possibility is that children misunderstand the intentions of the researcher. Rose and Blank (1974) pointed out that if you asked the question 'Are these two different or the same?' twice, some children would think that the first answer they gave must be wrong, and so give a different answer.

Rose and Blank carried out a conservation of number test, but left out the first question. They only asked the 'same or different?' question after the transformation had been made (one row of counters or beads spread out). They found that 6-year-olds made fewer mistakes under this condition than the two-question condition.

McGarrigle and Donaldson (1974) thought that children might believe that the intentional transformation in a conservation test was supposed to lead to a different answer to the second question (an adult would not change something if it made no difference). They redesigned the conservation of number test by having 'naughty Teddy' appear out of a box, then mess up and spread out one of the rows of beads. The adult would seem annoyed with Teddy and ask the child to put him back in his box. The impression was given that the spreading out of the beads was not intentional. Then children were asked the conservation question.

Sixty per cent of 6-year-olds successfully conserved in this condition, compared with 16% in the normal version. Studies like these show that a child's understanding of language and intentions are factors which influence success on conservation tasks. However they do not disprove Piaget's view of the development of conservation, although they suggest that the ability to conserve is present rather earlier than he believed.

Evaluation of Piaget's work

CRITICISMS OF PIAGET'S THEORY

1. Are there distinct stages?

One problem for Piaget is the finding that children tend to be able to conserve number and mass earlier than they conserve volume. A child who can conserve number, but not volume, seems to show some features of the preoperational stage, and some features of the stage of concrete operations. This casts doubt on whether these stages are really distinct.

Piaget tried to get round this problem for his stage theory by introducing the term **horizontal decalage**. By this he meant that for some abilities a child could show characteristics of more than one stage. This seems rather confusing and contradictory. However it is reasonable to suppose that children (and adults) sometimes use ways of thinking characteristic of earlier stages of development. Adults may sometimes rely on intuitive judgements based on appearance rather than logical judgements. For example, some people refuse to fly in aeroplanes because they are sure that something that big and heavy could not get off the ground safely.

Piaget pointed out that the ways of thinking featured in the earlier stages are not lost but 'built on'. So it could be that some conservation situations are easier to apply operational thought to than others.

Piaget's account of several distinct stages is not really supported by evidence. However his underlying idea that there are qualitative differences in the way children think at different ages does seem to be true. The consistency and confidence with which children aged under 6 give wrong answers in conservation tests illustrates this.

2. Are Piaget's stages universal?

Piaget's stages were devised as a result of observing and testing a small number of Swiss children. His research did not allow him to generalise these findings to children growing up in other cultures. However, Goodnow (1969) reported the results of cross-cultural studies using large samples of children from the USA, Britain, Africa and China. These showed the same sequence of developing abilities described by Piaget.

Nyiti (1982) carried out a cross-cultural study of children aged 7–12 years. The sample included English-speaking Canadians and Canadian native Americans. The mean age of success with tests of conservation of mass and volume were very similar in the two groups and also similar to those in European children.

Dasen (1975) in a similar cross-cultural study found that all children studied eventually reached the stage of concrete operations, but those from non-industrial societies (which tend to have less education provided by the state) reached each stage later. King (1985) found that only a minority of adults show the formal operational abilities required for scientific reasoning – even in industrial societies.

This evidence supports Piaget's view that aspects of cognitive development are universal – even if the existence of stages is questionable.

3. Is discovery learning the key process in cognitive development?

Vygotsky and others (see p.52) have argued that cognitive development does not usually occur as a result of the child's individual interactions with play materials. Instead, they argue that support and teaching from adults is the main factor leading to development. Piaget's own descriptions of the cognitive development of his children show that he often prompted and supported their discovery learning.

However, Gelman (1969) attempted to teach the concept of conservation to 4- and 5-year-old children. If she had succeeded, this would support Vygoytsky's view of the importance of

Key questions	Comments
Are there distinct stages?	Stages are not distinct – they overlap. So perhaps development is continuous and not in stages at all.
Are Piaget's stages universal?	Cross-cultural studies show a similar pattern of development.
Is discovery learning the key process?	Vygotsky said that instruction was more important.
Does cognitive development consist of the development of schemas?	Acquisition of knowledge is important too.

Figure 2.4: Summary of criticisms of Piaget's theory

instruction. She found that it was extremely difficult to get the children to conserve. It took two days of repetition (192 trials in all) before these children were consistently successful with conservation tasks. This suggests that teaching and support are not sufficient for the achievement of new cognitive tasks, which supports Piaget's view.

4. Does cognitive development consist of the development of schemas?
Since Piaget's theory emphasises the development of cognitive structures (schemas), it tends to ignore the importance of acquiring knowledge. Some people would regard the acquisition of knowledge as the most important aspect of cognitive development.

CRITICISMS OF PIAGET'S METHODOLOGY

1. Sampling and reporting
The sample of children Piaget studied was small, and not representative. Although later studies using his procedures confirmed his findings, there is no doubt that Piaget's research lacked the methodological rigour with which A2 psychology students are familiar. For example, he often neglected to specify the number and ages of participants he used, and rarely provided any statistical analysis.

2. Use of tests
As several studies have shown (see p.52) Piaget underestimated the abilities of children because his tests were sometimes confusing or difficult to understand. He failed to consider the effects of the context, of the child's motivation, memory and understanding of language and intentions on test performance.

3. Use of the clinical method
Piaget's clinical method failed to control variables – he did not use standardised procedures, and he failed to control for experimenter effects. In the clinical method, a researcher does not stick to a prepared schedule of questions or use standardised instructions. The interaction between researcher and participant is quite informal, and the line of questioning is influenced by the participant's responses. This means that each participant is treated slightly differently. For example, using a test of conservation of liquid volume, using orange juice, the researcher might not be sure whether the child understood the question. So the researcher might try the test again with a different question – for example, 'Supposing you were really, really thirsty and could choose one of these beakers of orange to drink. Would you prefer one to the other – or wouldn't it make any difference?'

Although this criticism is valid, there are good reasons for using the clinical method in the way Piaget did, when working with children. First, it is important to get the child to relax and feel

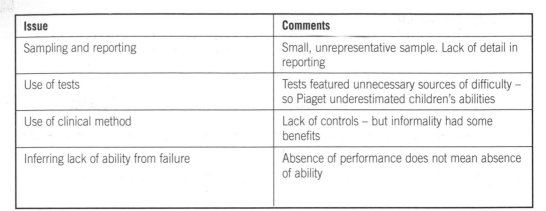

Issue	Comments
Sampling and reporting	Small, unrepresentative sample. Lack of detail in reporting
Use of tests	Tests featured unnecessary sources of difficulty – so Piaget underestimated children's abilities
Use of clinical method	Lack of controls – but informality had some benefits
Inferring lack of ability from failure	Absence of performance does not mean absence of ability

Figure 2.5: Summary of criticisms of Piaget's methodology

An awareness of Piaget's ideas can help parents with young children to enjoy, understand and support their cognitive progress

comfortable. An informal approach helps here. Second, if you want to find out what a child thinks, it will be necessary to explore their answers and get them to explain. Inevitably each interview will follow a slightly different course.

4. Inferring inability from failure

Piaget seemed to assume that a child's failure to perform correctly on a test was evidence of a lack of that particular competence. In fact absence of performance does not imply absence of ability. You can conclude that a child who succeeds reliably in a conservation test has the ability to conserve, but you cannot conclude that a child who does not succeed lacks the ability.

POSITIVE EVALUATIONS

1. Piaget's work laid the foundations of the study of cognitive development. A vast amount of research was stimulated by the need to replicate and extend his work.

2. Piaget's own observations were detailed and very extensive.

3. He created a number of simple but ingenious tests of cognitive ability.

4. His view that there are universal qualitative differences in thinking at different ages is broadly supported by cross-cultural research.

5. He influenced practice in early years education by presenting the view that play is an important tool for learning and development.

6. More generally, Piaget influenced the way people think about children. He listened carefully to them, and took them seriously.

2.3 Alternatives to Piaget

Vygotsky's approach to children's learning

Lev Vygotsky (1896–1934) was a Russian developmental psychologist who was a contemporary of Piaget. His work was not published in English until after his death. He believed that Piaget's theory ignored the influence of culture on cognitive development. Vygotsky suggested that an important part of cognitive development was a child's acquisition of *cognitive tools* developed by their culture. These tools include language, writing, number systems and scientific concepts.

Whereas Piaget emphasised the importance of discovery learning through a child's interactions with play materials, Vygotsky emphasised the importance of interactions with other children and adults – through social learning and direct support and instruction. Vygotsky pointed out that the skills acquired during cognitive development are those which are needed for the culture in which the child is growing up. Today that culture requires the ability to process numbers, to read and write, to plan and co-operate. However human cultures have not always required these skills. The development of these abilities in children must therefore be more influenced by social learning than by biological processes.

Richardson (1994) gives the following example. When children first attend nursery school, they come across some interesting new toys and want to play with them. This raises a problem the child might not experience at home – the toys are not for one child only. This leads to conflicts where two children want to play with the same toy. Through the responses of adults and peers children begin to understand the need to regulate or control behaviour, and accept systems like queuing, or rules about who can play with what and at what time. This understanding of regulation becomes internalised, so that the child becomes able to delay his or her own gratification – to acquire the ability to wait for things they want. This is important in modern cultures which use money. Adults in many developed nations save money so that they can spend it later, or delay having children in order to make progress in a career.

According to Vygotsky, children can acquire some concepts through their own unaided play, but most concepts are acquired with the help of others – often adults. For example, the child might enjoy playing with coloured beads, but might not sort them into colours unless an adult suggests it. This support is particularly important for the acquisition of abstract concepts. Vygotsky claimed that abstract thought occurred most in technologically advanced societies which have systems of formal education.

The zone of proximal development

According to Vygotsky, the **zone of proximal development** can be defined as the gap between what a child can achieve unaided, and what s/he can achieve with the help and support of other people. In this case 'proximal' means 'what comes next'. The idea is that a child is only able to take the next step in their cognitive development if another person – typically an adult – supports and prompts them to do so. This sort of assistance has been called **scaffolding** by Wood, Bruner and Ross (1976). In other words much cognitive development requires informal teaching. Discovery is not enough.

For example, a child begins to read because teachers prompt each step, structure the task, and give direct help. There follows a stage in which the inexperienced reader is seen to help themselves in a similar way – by pointing at parts of words, by saying strings of letters ('d', 'o', 'g') and then the word 'dog', and by reading out loud.

Vygotsky (1978) stated:

> **The zone of proximal development defines those functions that have not yet matured, but are in the process [of doing so] . . .**

> **. . . what is the zone of proximal development today will be the actual developmental level tomorrow – that is, what a child can do with assistance today she will be able to do by herself tomorrow.**

The following study provides some support for Vygotsky's view.

Study 2.6

Aim Wood and Middleton (1975) designed a study to find out whether parents do support children's development of concepts.

Method They designed a set of wooden blocks which could be fitted together, and observed the interactions between 4-year-old children and their parents as the child tried to assemble the blocks. The task was designed to be too difficult for most 4-year-olds to manage alone.

Results They found that at first parents tended to show the child how to put the blocks together. As the child became more skilled, the parent would simply give verbal instructions or prompts.

Wood and Middleton described the different levels of parental support as follows:

1. Parent demonstrates e.g. by fitting blocks together.

2. Parent prepares assembly e.g. by lining blocks up correctly.

3. Parent indicates materials e.g. points to the next block required.

4. Parent gives specific instructions e.g. 'You need a big block next'.

5. Parent gives verbal prompt e.g. 'See if you can make something'.

At the start, parents tend to give the kind of support shown at the beginning of the list. As the child becomes more skilled, the parents tends to give the kind of support shown lower down the list.

Conclusion Parents support the child's development of concepts by arranging the child's experience, rather than by formal instruction.

EVALUATIVE COMMENT

The study shows that as a child becomes more skilled, a parent gives less specific support. This is not surprising. Most people require less specific support as they become more familiar with a task. For example a driving instructor with a new learner driver will start off saying things like 'Slacken off the accelerator, depress the clutch and push the gear lever away from you'. A few lessons later, the instructor is more likely to say, 'Are you in the right gear?'

The study shows the acquisition of a particular skill, but this is not exactly what we mean by cognitive development. For example, conservation is not a particular skill, but a concept applicable to many different situations. It could be argued that Wood and Middleton's task was not a valid test of cognitive development. It illustrates Vygotsky's concept of a zone of proximal development, but does not demonstrate its correctness.

Hatano and Inagaki (1992) made a distinction between 'routine' knowledge which is restricted to specific situations and 'conceptual' knowledge which can be applied across a range of different situations.

An example of routine knowledge is knowing how to tie a reef knot. An example of conceptual knowledge is the understanding of conservation – which applies to number, mass, volume and so on. Cognitive development as described by Piaget and Vygotsky is really about acquiring conceptual rather than routine knowledge.

REFLECTIVE Activity

Use the distinction between routine and conceptual knowledge to decide whether or not Wood and Middleton's task was a valid test of cognitive development.

EVALUATIVE COMMENT

Vygotsky's account of the zone of proximal development can be interpreted as suggesting that a child's development can be artificially accelerated. This conflicts with Piaget's view that development will not occur until a child is ready for it – in which case attempts to accelerate development would be pointless.

Another criticism is that the emphasis on instruction is likely to reduce the child's ability to think independently – to think for themselves.

Vygotsky seems to assume that the role of parents in a child's cognitive development is entirely supportive. However this is unlikely to be so. Parents sometimes confound a child's attempts to understand the world by making mystifying statements. For example, when children ask direct questions about sex or death, some parents are too embarrassed to give accurate answers – or believe that children should not know the truth about such topics.

PRACTICAL Activity

Ask your friends for examples of mystifying statements they have heard adults make to young children. Try to decide why adults sometimes do this, and what the effects on children might be.

REFLECTIVE Activity

When Edward was 4-years-old, he enjoyed listening while his parents read him stories. One of his favourite story books was a simple illustrated version of well-known ancient Greek myths – such as Jason and the Argonauts. One day late in December, after hearing this story he asked, 'Dad, is Father Christmas mythical?'

Evidently Edward had been trying to make sense of what he knew about Father Christmas – a contradictory set of facts about an overweight person who enters millions of homes simultaneously, not by the door, but by the central heating flue – and his conclusion was that this had to be a myth. Edward had got it exactly right. (This may come as a shock to younger readers.) Decide how you would have answered Edward's question, and why.

Differences between Piaget's and Vygotsky's views of cognitive development

Vygotsky's view of cognitive development contrasts with Piaget's as follows.

THE SOURCE OF COGNITIVE DEVELOPMENT

Whereas Piaget emphasised the role of an inbuilt tendency to adapt to the environment, by a process of active self-discovery, Vygotsky emphasised the role of culture and experience. Vygotsky believed that what drives cognitive development is social interaction – a child's experience of other people. The child acquires skills and concepts such as language by interacting with others, particularly parents.

CONCEPT ACQUISITION

According to Piaget, children acquire concepts by applying existing schemas to new situations – typically in solitary play. According to Vygotsky, children acquire concepts by internalisation – learning from their social experiences.

An example is Vygotsky's explanation of the development of pointing. This starts with an infant trying to grasp something which is out of reach. The arm and fingers are extended towards the object. A parent sees this, and is likely to point at the object themselves with one finger extended. Then the parent might pick up the object and give it to the child. The infant learns to imitate the parent's pointing behaviour.

THE ROLE OF INSTRUCTION

Piaget felt that teaching or instruction for young children led to learning of procedures, but not cognitive development. He believed that 'discovery learning' though play was more effective in cognitive development.

Vygotsky believed that the ability to learn from a teacher (typically the child's parent) was what made human cognitive development so extensive.

VIEWS OF LANGUAGE AND THOUGHT

Vygotsky's view of the relationship between language and thought contrasted with Piaget's view.

Issue	Piaget's view	Vygotsky's view
Source of cognitive development	An inbuilt tendency for active self-discovery	Culture, transmitted by social interaction
Concept acquisition	A mainly solitary process of adaptation of schemas	Results from social experience
Role of instruction	Produces learning but not cognitive development	Increases scope of cognitive development, by enabling learning
Language and thought	Language is a product of cognitive development	Social speech leads to the development of verbal thought

Figure 2.6: Differences between Piaget and Vygotsky

For Piaget, language is a product of cognitive development. In other words, cognitive development determines language use.

Vygotsky believed that language develops from social interactions, for communication purposes. Later language ability becomes internalised as thought and 'inner speech'. Thought is the result of internalising language.

Bruner's approach to children's learning

Jerome Bruner was influenced by Piaget's theory. He agreed that biological organisation underlies cognitive development, and that children actively explore their environment in order to make sense of it. However, Bruner's (1966) theory differs from Piaget's in two ways.

1. BRUNER'S CONCEPT OF SCAFFOLDING

Wood, Bruner and Ross (1976) introduced the idea that adults (especially parents) scaffold children's behaviour. Taken literally, scaffolding is a temporary support arrangement used in building. Wood, Bruner and Ross use the term to refer to the support parents give to children in everyday play interactions. This support is temporary, in that parents who are sensitive to the needs and abilities of a child gradually give less support as a child gains a particular skill, up to the point that the child can perform the skill independently.

Scaffolding in action. This grandfather is helping his grandson to relate the words of the story to the picture

Examples of scaffolding in action

1. A grandfather is reading a story to his grandson. He pauses and directs the child's attention to a picture, saying 'Can you point to the sheep?' 'Is someone hiding there?'. This supports the child's growing ability to relate the words of the story to visible features of the pictures.

2. An older sister sits by her young brother who is playing with coloured blocks. The sister says 'I'm going to sort out all the red blocks and put them over here'. After demonstrating this she asks her brother, 'Now can you sort out all the blue ones?'

3. A child is playing with a construction toy and needs one particular block to complete a model. A parent holds out two blocks, one of which is the right one and asks, 'Which

one of these do you need now?' If the child had been left to pick the right block from many different-sized blocks, she would have been less likely to succeed.

Each example of scaffolding features actions which improve a child's chances of acquiring skills and achieving success. In the first case, a child's attention is directed to what is most relevant. In the second case a skill is demonstrated and an opportunity given to model that behaviour, and in the third example, the child's choices are limited to those which will result in success.

2. BRUNER'S THEORY IS NOT A STAGE THEORY

When we think about objects, situations or concepts, we must somehow have representations of these in our minds. Thinking is a kind of mental manipulation. What we manipulate is not objects themselves, but representations of them. Bruner's theory describes the development of three ways of representing objects, situations or concepts in our minds. Bruner called these 'modes of representation'.

Modes of representation: enactive, iconic and symbolic

The **enactive mode** of representation means representing an object or situation by means of actions – i.e. body movements.

For example we can represent cutting paper with scissors by remembering the sequence of movements we make. Sometimes when people are talking about how to do things, they reproduce the physical actions involved. If you try to explain to someone how to toss a coin or throw a frisbee, it is difficult to resist making the movements involved. The enactive mode uses actions which are the same, or nearly the same as those involved with the object, situation or skill they represent.

The **iconic mode** of representation means representing an object or situation by means of mental pictures (an icon is an image, portrait or statue), or remembered sounds or even smells. For example, someone who is deciding the best route to take when driving across town may visualise the junctions and landmarks they will pass. The iconic mode uses sensory images, sounds or smells which resemble those associated with the real situation they represent.

The **symbolic mode** of representation means representing an object or situation by means of something else which (even though it does not resemble the object) stands for the object or situation. The type of symbols we most often use in thought are words – but anything can be a symbol, as long as it is made to stand for something else.

Enactive	Objects or situations are represented by actions or memories of actions
Iconic	Objects or situations are represented by mental images
Symbolic	Objects or situations are represented by arbitrary symbols e.g. words

Figure 2.7: Bruner's modes of representation

For example the word 'vegetable' is a symbol for a group of allegedly edible plants. The word has nothing in common with what it symbolises. The word is not edible, not good for you and does not contain fibre. The word 'vegetable' occurs in two quite different forms – one is the printed word you see on this page, another is the sound you make when you say the word.

Another example of a symbol is the use of a red triangle on a map. This is used to represent a youth hostel, even though none of these are actually red or triangular. Other map symbols are partly iconic, for example the symbol for a camp site is a picture of a blue tent.

Bruner suggests that adults use all three modes of representation, but in childhood these modes are acquired in the following order:

Enactive mode: this is the mode used in the first 18 months of infancy. This period corresponds to most of Piaget's sensorimotor stage.

Iconic mode: this is acquired from around 18 months.

Symbolic mode: this is acquired at around 6- or 7-years-old – corresponding to the start of Piaget's operational stages. The acquisition of this mode of representation increases the child's ability to deal with abstract concepts and hypothetical situations.

The key difference between this and a stage theory is that when each mode is acquired the previous modes are not lost. A child aged 8 will use enactive and iconic and symbolic modes.

PRACTICAL Activity

Decide which of the following are examples of enactive, iconic and symbolic representation.

1. Repeating 'left over right and right over left' to yourself when tying a reef knot.

2. Someone miming drinking from a glass.

3. Humming the signature tune of a TV programme to yourself, to remind you to set the video.

4. A toddler reaching up towards a dish of tasty ice-cream on the table, then looking round, wagging his finger, and walking away.

5. Using a piece of twisted ribbon to communicate your concern for breast cancer sufferers.

6. Trying to remember what ingredients to buy in a shop by visualising the bits floating in a steaming casserole of goulash.

Study 2.7

Aim Bruner and Kenney (1966) wanted to find out at what age children began to use the symbolic mode of representation.

Method Children aged from 3 – 7 years were shown a board divided into nine squares. On each square was placed a plastic beaker. The beakers were of different sizes and widths, with the tallest beakers at the back and the widest on the left.

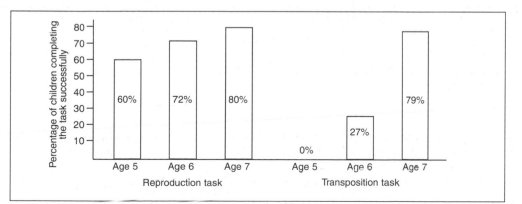

Figure 2.8 Bar chart showing percentage success rate for children aged 5, 6, and 7 on two tasks

Each child was asked to look at the arrangement of beakers. Then the child was given two tasks. The first was called the reproduction task. The researchers mixed the beakers up and asked the child to put them back the way they had been to start with – in other words to reproduce the original arrangement. The researchers recorded the resulting arrangement of beakers.

This was followed by the transposition task. The researchers showed each child the correct starting arrangement, then removed the beakers, and asked the child to replace them in a mirror image of the original arrangement. They placed the first beaker in position. The researchers recorded the resulting arrangement of beakers.

Results The results showed that most children of 5 years and older correctly reproduced the original arrangement. However few children under 7 could manage the transposition task, while most 7-year-olds could.

The reproduction task was designed so that it could be done by using iconic representation: the child forms a mental picture of the arrangement and then copies it, using the beakers. However, the transposition task cannot be done like this because the transposed arrangement does not look like the original arrangement.

Conclusion The study supports the view that children on average begin to acquire the symbolic mode of representation at around 7 years old.

This task required the ability to mentally transform the visual memory, probably using some verbal rule such as 'the thin ones go on the right, and the tall ones at the back' – in other words symbolic representation.

Bruner's explanation for children's increased capacity to deal with abstraction

As children get older, they are more able to use abstract concepts. Abstract concepts exist only as ideas – not as actions or physical, perceivable things. The first of Bruner's modes of representation (the enactive mode) does not enable children to use abstract concepts, because it represents actions. The second mode (iconic) can be used to represent concrete situations. Only the third mode – the symbolic mode – enables abstract concepts to be represented and used. Abstract concepts are almost always represented using symbol systems – such as language.

Examples of abstract concepts mentioned earlier in this chapter included repression and validity. People can use and understand such concepts by defining them using language, and by giving examples and illustrations. Validity could be defined as a property a test has if it succeeds in measuring what it is intended to measure. The concept can be illustrated by showing someone an IQ test item which is not valid (perhaps because it tests knowledge rather than intelligence). However we could never communicate validity with gestures (enactively) or by getting a piece of validity for them to look at.

The child's acquisition of the symbolic mode of representation – including language acquisition – is what makes abstract thinking possible.

2.4 Implications for education: summary

The approaches of Piaget, Vygotsky and Bruner have different implications for educating children.

Piaget's theory implies that in order to learn and develop, children need opportunities to explore their world for themselves. One assumption behind this is that the concepts a child needs are aspects of the real world waiting to be discovered. The concepts of colour and number for example are 'out there' available for every child. A second assumption is that the child has an inbuilt tendency to learn (through the process of adaptation).

The implications for education are:

1. Early years education should be child-centred. The child's own interest and stage of cognitive development should determine what the child learns. The view that all children of the same age should learn the same things is mistaken, because some will be ready for learning things which others are not.

2. The role of educators is not to teach, but to provide opportunities to make discoveries, by providing appropriate educational play materials, encouragement, stimulation and support.

Vygotsky's view was rather different. He assumed that the concepts a child needed to learn are not 'out there' in the real world, but are invented by cultures. For example, a scientific concept such as 'gravity', while it corresponds to what we can observe is essentially a human invention.

The implications for education are:

1. Education should focus on transmitting cultural knowledge from adults to children. It should be determined by the culture, not the individual child.

2. The role of educators is to instruct, teach and to shape children's thinking. Adults take the lead in cognitive development.

Bruner's view included features of Piaget's and Vygotsky's theories. Like Piaget he recognised the importance of development through adaptation. However his concept of scaffolding indicates that he felt the role of adults was more active and instructional.

2.5 Sample questions

SAMPLE QUESTION 1

(a) Identify Bruner's three *modes of representation*.
     (AO1 = 3)   *(3 marks)*

(b) A child is travelling in the back seat of a car, watching a television screen. He comments on what he sees to his mother, who is driving. At one point he says, 'The big cloud is lonely, isn't it Mum?'

     Decide which of Piaget's stages of intellectual development best fits the child's comment.

     Justify your answer.
     (AO1 = 2, AO2 = 3)   *(5 marks)*

(c) Piaget developed a number of tests of cognitive development. Evaluate Piaget's use of *two* of these tests. Refer to empirical evidence in your answer.
     (AO1 = 5, AO2 = 7)   *(12 marks)*

SAMPLE QUESTION 2

(a) Describe *one* way of testing whether or not a child has achieved *object permanence*.
     (AO1 = 4)   *(4 marks)*

(b) Using an example, explain what Bruner meant by scaffolding.
     (AO2 = 4)   *(4 marks)*

(c)   Describe Piaget's approach to children's learning and compare it with Vygotsky's approach.

(AO1 = 6, AO2 = 6)   (12 marks)

QUESTIONS, ANSWERS AND COMMENTS

SAMPLE QUESTION 1

(a)   Enactive, iconic and semantic.

Comment: 2 marks – one each for the first two modes named. The third answer 'semantic' is wrong – it should be 'symbolic'.

(b) The boy will be in the preoperational stage because when he says 'The cloud is lonely', that is animism, which is typical of that stage. Animism is when the child thinks an inanimate object i.e. the cloud has feelings.

Comment: 3 marks. 1 (AO2) mark for correctly identifying the stage. 1 (AO2) mark for recognising the example of animism, and one (AO1) mark for describing animism.

Two other marks were available for recognising that the child also showed egocentrism – in assuming that his mother could also see the cloud on the TV screen – and describing it.

(c) One test Piaget used was his 'three beakers' test. He got two beakers full of water and asked a child if there was the same amount of water in each beaker. The two beakers were the same. If the child said 'Yes', he poured one of the beakers into another beaker which was taller, so the water did not fill it. Then he asked if one beaker was fuller than the other. This was a test of conservation. Piaget found that children aged 7 years and over could do this, and so must be in the stage of concrete operations. However Vygotsky said that this was not a fair test because the child might not have understood the question. The child might have judged on how far up the beaker the water came, which is intuitive judgement. Another problem is that by asking the same question twice, the child might have thought the researcher wanted a different answer the second time – otherwise why ask again?

A second test Piaget used was to take two balls of plasticine the same size and ask a child if they were the same. Then one of the balls was rolled out into a sausage shape. The child was then asked whether there was the same amount in each piece of plasticine. If the child said 'Yes' then it showed they had conservation. This was a fairer test than the three beakers test because children are used to playing with plasticine.

Comment: 5 marks (AO1 = 3, AO2 = 2)

This answer includes several errors and confusions. It illustrates how easy it is to make a complete mess of describing something which seems quite simple – a conservation experiment.

The first mistake was to say that the beakers are full to start with. They are not, but they both contain equal amounts. The second mistake was the description of the second question, '. . . he asked if one beaker was fuller than the other'. This does not test conservation at all. In fact the first and second questions are the same – the ideal version is 'Is there the same amount of water in these two beakers, or is there more in one than the other?' The candidate fails to get across what conservation actually is.

The candidate attempts to criticise the test – although wrongly cites Vygotsky – and gains two (AO2) marks for identifying two criticisms – though these are not well analysed.

The conservation of mass test is described better, although the attempt at evaluation, 'This was a fairer test . . .' is not convincing.

The candidate scores 3 (AO1) marks for description of tests. It is quite easy to score all 5 AO1 marks by accurate descriptions of two tests. As commonly happens, this candidate has lost most marks because they have included very little evaluation or analysis.

A better answer would have chosen two different tests – instead of two tests of conservation. For example a conservation test and a test of egocentrism such as the mountains test would be ideal. Evaluation would include detail of criticisms such as the idea that improved, more child-relevant versions of Piaget's tests show children acquiring abilities earlier than Piaget thought. These would be supported with evidence of studies such as those by Rose and Blank (1974) and Hughes (cited in Donaldson 1978). A judgement could also be made about whether these criticisms mean that Piaget's test were without value, or merely capable of improvement.

2.6 FURTHER READING

Introductory texts

Flanagan, C. 1996: **Applying psychology to early child development**. Hodder and Stoughton, London.

Lee, V. J. and Das Gupta, Prajna (Eds) 1995: **Children's cognitive and language development**. 5th Ed. The Open University/Blackwell, Milton Keynes/Oxford.

Schaffer, D. R. 1993: **Developmental psychology: childhood and adolescence**. 3rd Ed. Brooks/Cole, Pacific Grove, CA.

Smith, P. K., Cowie, H. and Blades, M. 1998: **Understanding children's development**. 3rd Ed. Blackwell, Oxford.

Specialist sources

Bukatko, D. and Daehler, M. W. 1992: **Child development: a topical approach**. Houghton Mifflin, Boston.

Crain, William 1992: **Theories of development.** 3rd Ed. Prentice-Hall International, Englewood Cliffs, NI.

Donaldson, M 1987: **Children's minds**. Fontana Press, London.

Hetherington, E. M., Parke, R. D. and Locke, V. O. 2003: **Child psychology: a contemporary viewpoint**. 5th Ed. updated. McGaw Hill, Boston, MA.

Messer, D. and Miller, S. (Eds) 1999: **Exploring developmental psychology: from infancy to adolescence**. Arnold, London.

Piaget, J. 1952: **The origins of intelligence in children**. International Universities Press.

Sutherland, P. 1992: **Cognitive development today: Piaget and his critics**. Paul Chapman Publishing.

Thomas, R. M. 2000: **Comparing theories of child development**. 5th Ed. Wadsworth, London.

Van der Veer, R. and Valsiner, J (Eds) 1994: **The Vygotsky reader**. Blackwell, Oxford.

Vasta, R., Haith M. M. and Miller, S. A. 1999: **Child psychology: the modern science**. John Wiley & Sons, Chichester.

Vygotsky, L. S. 1978: **Mind in society**. Harvard University Press, Cambridge, MA.

3

Moral development

3.1 Introduction

Moral behaviour and moral cognition

When psychologists talk about moral behaviour, they mean behaviour which a reasonable person might judge to be good or bad. An example of good behaviour is a person helping a young child to learn to read. On the other hand, you might regard somebody deliberately upsetting another person by teasing them as immoral behaviour. Psychologists, however would define moral behaviour as behaviour which has some moral content, good or bad. When the word 'morality' is used by the media and in everyday conversation, it often refers to sexual morality. However morality actually refers to a wide range of issues including breaking promises, helping people, killing, stealing, telling the truth and so on.

You might expect a chapter on moral development to be all about how children acquire morally acceptable and morally unacceptable behaviour. In fact this chapter is not about how children learn to help others, tell the truth and stop tormenting their siblings. Most of the moral development included in this chapter is the development of moral understanding or moral judgement – the child's developing ability to think about moral issues – which is also known as **moral cognition**.

Moral cognition means thinking about morality, and the morality of particular actions. One example is of a person wondering whether it is right or wrong to tell a lie to get a friend out of trouble. Another example is of a person trying to decide on how a thief should be punished.

3.2 Piaget's work on moral development

Jean Piaget (1896–1980) is best known for his work on cognitive development (see Chapter 2). However his earlier work in psychology focused on the development of moral cognition. The theory he produced was rather limited in scope, but provided a starting point for Lawrence Kohlberg, who developed a more extensive and detailed theory.

Piaget's research

Piaget (1932) investigated several aspects of moral development, including:

1. children's judgements of wrong-doing and punishment

2. children's understanding of telling lies

3. children's understanding of rules.

He investigated these topics by using informal interviews with young children he knew, and by observing and questioning children during play.

1. CHILDREN'S JUDGEMENTS OF WRONGDOING AND PUNISHMENT

Study 3.1

Aim Piaget (1932) wanted to find out how children's moral judgements changed as they got older. In the same study he also investigated children's views of punishment.

Method Piaget used a method of **moral comparison** (sometimes called a *moral dilemma technique*). He studied several children of different ages. He read out two stories, in each of which a child had done something wrong or naughty. In one story the child was intentionally naughty, but caused little damage. In the other story the child unintentionally caused quite a lot of damage.

In this way Piaget manipulated two variables:

A: Whether or not the child was intentionally naughty

B: The amount of damage caused

Here is an example:

John's story

A little boy called John is in his room. He is called to dinner. But behind the door there was a chair, and on the chair there was a tray with 15 cups on it. John could not have known that there was all this behind the door. He goes in, the door knocks against the tray, bang go the 15 cups and they all get broken.

Henry's story

Once there was a little boy whose name was Henry. One day when his mother was out he tried to get some jam out of the cupboard. He climbed up onto a chair and stretched out his arm. But the jam was too high up and he could not reach it and have any. But while he was trying to get it he knocked over a cup. The cup fell down and broke.

After reading these two stories, Piaget asked the child which boy was naughtier, and why. Piaget also asked other questions, such as how each child should be punished.

Results Piaget found that children under 10-years-old based their judgements on the amount of damage, and did not take intentions into account. They said that John was naughtier. They tended to recommend harsh punishments.

Children, aged around 10 years and over, took intentions into account, and said that Henry was naughtier. They tended to recommend more limited punishments, which related to the type of wrongdoing.

Conclusion Piaget concluded that from about 10-years-old children are able to think for themselves about moral issues, and also able to take several factors (damage, intentions) into account when making moral judgements. Piaget based his stage theory of moral development on this and other studies.

PRACTICAL Activity

1. Try out a pair of stories like Piaget's on children aged from 4 to 8. In one story, make the child's intentions good, and the level of damage high. In the other story make the child's intentions bad, and the level of damage low.

You will have to write the stories so that they fit the child's world today. For example, things like stealing jam from a cupboard might be replaced by stealing choc ices from the freezer. Use your imagination, but make sure what you write relates to what children know and understand.

2. Notice that if you combine two variables – such as intentions (good and bad) and damage level (high and low) – there are four possible combinations; not just the two Piaget used. Decide what should happen in the two missing stories.

3. What problem might have arisen if Piaget had asked children to compare four stories instead of two?

EVALUATIVE COMMENT

One criticism of Piaget's method is that the task of comparing two stories makes a large cognitive demand. The child has to remember both stories in order to make a comparison. This alone might make the task more difficult for younger children. The differing memory abilities of younger and older children could be a confounding variable in this study. If so, it is possible that Piaget's moral comparison technique led him to underestimate the moral understanding of younger children. This is similar to the general criticism made of Piaget's tests in Chapter 2 – the design of the tests led to an underestimation of children's abilities at a given age.

Another criticism is that Piaget's stories only featured two of the possible four combinations of intentions and damage, so his manipulation of variables was not systematic.

Sharon Nelson (1980) designed a similar moral judgement task, which avoided some of the problems with Piaget's method.

Study 3.2

Aim Nelson (1980) wanted to find out whether knowledge of a person's intentions influenced the moral judgement of very young children.

Method Instead of telling each child two stories, Nelson told one simple story to a sample of 3-year-olds. There were four different versions of this story, but each child only heard one of them. As in Piaget's study, there were two variables:

A: Whether or not the outcome of the action was intended

B: Whether the action described had positive or negative consequences

In each story a child throws a ball towards his friend. Because there are two variables to be manipulated, there are four versions of the story. These are shown in Figure 3.1 below.

	Story	Intention	Consequences
Version 1	A child is angry with his friend and throws a ball towards the friend. The ball hits the friend on the head and makes the friend cry.	Bad	Negative
Version 2	A child sees that his friend has nothing to play with and throws a ball towards the friend. The ball hits the friend on the head and makes the friend cry.	Good	Negative
Version 3	A child is angry with his friend and throws a ball towards the friend. The friend catches the ball and plays with it.	Bad	Positive
Version 4	A child sees that his friend has nothing to play with and throws a ball towards the friend. The friend catches the ball and plays with it.	Good	Positive

Figure 3.1: The manipulation of two variables in Nelson's design

After telling one of the versions of the story, Nelson asked each child to rate how good or bad the actor's behaviour was. 'Actor' means the child who throws the ball.

Results As expected, children tended to rate the actor whose behaviour had a negative consequence as more naughty than if there was a positive consequence. However, they also rated the actor whose intentions were good as better than an actor whose intentions were bad. In fact, despite the different consequences, the child in version 2 whose motive was good was judged to be better than the child in version 3 whose motive was bad.

Conclusion Young children are able to take account of both intentions and consequences when making moral judgements, and sometimes view intentions as more important than consequences. This contradicts Piaget's findings that children only begin to take account of intentions at around 10-years-old.

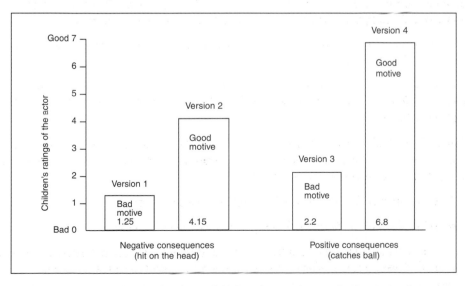

Figure 3.2: Bar chart showing children's ratings of the actor's goodness in four versions of the story

2. CHILDREN'S UNDERSTANDING OF TELLING LIES

Piaget (1932) asked children about telling lies, and asked them to judge how naughty different lies were. He found that as children grow up, their understanding of lying changes. Younger children believe that a lie is a statement which is false, and the more inaccurate, the naughtier it is. For example the statement, 'That tree can play the piano', would be judged to be a naughtier lie than, 'I can play the piano' (if this was false).

Older children understood that a lie was a false statement intended to deceive. The more serious the deception, the naughtier the lie. The statement, 'That tree can play the piano' would not be seen as a lie, because nobody could be deceived by it. However, older children would judge the statement , 'I can play the piano' (if false) to be a lie.

Piaget's findings were consistent with his moral comparison study described above. Older children were able to take more than one factor into account in their understanding of lying. They considered

(i) whether the statement was false, and

(ii) whether it was intended to deceive

Here is another example:

A little girl opened the door of her house and there was a person with long hair standing there. The little girl thought it was a lady, so she told her mother that there was a lady at the door. But really it was a man with long hair. Did the little girl tell a lie?

A young child is likely to answer that the little girl did tell a lie – because she made a false statement. An older child is likely to answer that the little girl did not lie, because her false statement was mistaken and not intended to deceive.

3. CHILDREN'S UNDERSTANDING OF RULES

Piaget (1932) observed and interviewed children as they played marbles. He asked them several questions including: 'What are the rules of this game? Where do rules come from? Can you change the rules if you like?'

He noticed that up to about 5 years, children rarely use rules in play – although they may know something about them.

By about 6-years-old, children are able to follow rules in play. They see these rules as fixed, and do not question them. In practice however, they do not always follow the rules.

By about 10 years, children understand that rules exist because people agree to them, and that rules can be changed by general consent. However, they tend to be more conscientious in applying the rules than younger children.

Piaget's stages of moral development

On the basis of his studies, Piaget divided moral development into the following stages. The ages indicated are for the average child.

1. PREMORAL JUDGEMENT: BIRTH TO 5 YEARS

The child makes no meaningful moral judgements. In other words the child is unaware of moral issues. For this reason, many people think it is wrong to punish or blame very young children for undesirable behaviour. At around 4 or 5 years, the child starts imitating rule-bound behaviour i.e. following rules.

2. MORAL REALISM: 5 TO 9 YEARS

In this stage a child's view of morality is based mainly on what parents do to control and modify behaviour. The child does not have his or her own personal morality, but accepts and reflects the moral controls of others. The child's judgement is strongly influenced by objective facts – such as the amount of damage done. The child is not able to take into account subjective factors, such as a person's intentions.

The child also understands rules, and has a very rigid attitude towards them. Rules are seen as laws which must not be broken (in other words as moral absolutes), rather than as agreed conventions which can be flexible to suit circumstances. This stage is sometimes called 'the morality of adult constraint' or the **heteronomous** stage.

During this stage the child's view of punishment is expiatory. **Expiatory punishment** means the belief that a person has to pay for wrongdoing. The child is not concerned with making a punishment match the type of wrongdoing, and is likely to suggest a harsh punishment. For example, a child who had listened to the story of Henry described on page 65, commented, 'Throw him in the bin!'

Children at this stage also seem to believe in **immanent justice**. Immanent justice is the belief that unpleasant events which happen by chance after wrongdoing are actually punishments. So if a child steals a bicycle and then falls off it, the accident is seen as a punishment.

3. MORAL RELATIVISM: 10+ YEARS

In this stage a child has his or her own internalised moral beliefs. He or she is able to see things from other people's points of view, and is able to take account of more than one factor (e.g. the damage done and the intention) in judging wrongdoing. By the age of 10, children understand that rules exist because people agree to them, and that rules can be changed by general consent.

This stage is sometimes called 'The morality of co-operation', or the **autonomous stage**. In this stage the child becomes aware that conduct can be judged from several points of view, and that there may not be just one view of what is good or bad.

The child's view of punishment includes the idea that a punishment should not be harsh and should somehow match the wrong done. Piaget calls this **punishment by reciprocity**. For example an older child who had listened to the story of how Henry tried to steal jam commented, 'Don't let him have any sausages for two weeks'.

Factors influencing moral development

Piaget believed that a child's progress through these stages depended partly on their cognitive development. For example, before a child can grasp the importance of a person's intentions when judging their behaviour, one must be able to see the other person's point of view. The egocentric child is unable to do this. **Egocentrism** is a term used by Piaget to mean a child's inability to see a situation from another person's point of view. Similarly, the ability to take both intentions and consequences into account when judging wrongdoing requires the ability to de-centre. To de-centre means to be able to take two or more factors into account when judging a situation. (Piaget's theory of cognitive development is described in Chapter 2.)

Piaget also believed that a child's moral development was influenced by equal-status contact, i.e. interactions with peers. These interactions – typically in play situations – often lead to disagreements and conflicts and so provide the child with experience of moral issues and the need for rules. In attempting to solve such problems the child has to think for him- or herself, and so develop moral relativism.

Parents are also likely to be a major influence on moral development, particularly in achieving

Factor	Comment
Cognitive development	The child must be able to de-centre so as to take intentions into account
Equal-status contact	Provide experience of moral conflicts
Parents	Provide authority and rules – but may inhibit moral relativism

Figure 3.3: Piaget's view of factors influencing moral development

the stage of moral realism. Parents provide authority and impose rules. However, according to Piaget, parents may make it more difficult for a child to progress to the stage of moral relativism, by continuing to insist on the child accepting their view of morality.

Some parents believe that a child's moral development consists of being taught 'the difference between right and wrong'. Piaget makes clear that children progress beyond this crude and simplistic knowledge in the stage of moral relativism when they develop a morality of their own. In this stage children are able to recognise that their parents often fail to follow the rules they themselves lay down.

Piaget's stage theory – summary

There are two main themes in Piaget's theory. One is a trend from external control (relying on parental authority for moral judgements) towards internal control ((being able to think for yourself on moral issues). The other is a trend from judging actions on the basis of their objective consequences towards judging them on the basis of more subjective criteria, such as the actor's intentions.

	Stage of moral realism	Stage of moral relativism
View of wrongdoing	Naughtiness is judged by the amount of damage done	Naughtiness is judged by intentions as well as by consequences
View of justice and punishment	Belief in immanent justice. Punishment is expiatory – to pay for wrongdoing	Reciprocal punishment, designed to match wrongdoing. Recognition that other people have rights
View of lies	Lying means saying something which is false	Lying means saying something which is false with the intention to deceive
View of rules	Seen as fixed, set by external authority	Rules can be changed, by general consent

Figure 3.4: A summary of the main features of Piaget's stages of moral realism and moral relativism

PRACTICAL Activity

1. Sort the following statements according to whether they fit Piaget's stage of moral realism or the stage of moral relativism.

(a) Peter wasn't really naughty because he did not mean to trip the other boy up.

(b) Peter was naughty because he made the other boy fall over and he got a nose bleed.

(c) The other boy should be allowed to stamp on Peter's foot to pay him back.

(d) Peter should be kept in for the rest of the afternoon, so he knows he should be more careful in future.

(e) You can never wear shoes indoors because your Mum tells you off.

(f) it is OK for Michael to have a start in the race, because he's only little.

2. According to Piaget's theory, how would children in different stages answer the following question?

If you came indoors because it was raining, but when you came in it stopped but you did not notice, and told your mother it was raining, would that be telling a lie?

(a) The child in the stage of moral realism would say . . .

(b) The child in the stage of moral relativism would say . . .

3. Decide which of the following is an example of (i) expiatory punishment, (ii) punishment by reciprocity and (iii) immanent justice.

(a) Tara makes a big fuss when it is time for her bath. It takes so long that Tara's father misses his favourite TV programme. Tara's sister suggests she should be punished by not having a bedtime story that night.

(b) Ceri's mother has promised to take him to a swimming pool with big waterslides. In the morning, Ceri keeps shouting while his mother is trying to talk on the phone. She warns Ceri that he must behave well, or they will not go to the pool. When they are ready to set off for the pool, the car will not start. Ceri thinks this has happened because he was naughty.

(c) Sofia hears a news item about children stealing mobile phones. Her father asks her how the thieves should be punished. She replies, 'You must take all of their toys and break every one.'

Evaluation of Piaget's theory of moral development

IS THE THEORY SUPPORTED BY EVIDENCE?

Hoffman (1970) confirmed that younger children see rules as moral absolutes, believe in immanent justice, and judge the wrongness of acts according to the consequences rather than intentions. Lickona (1976) found a positive correlation between level of moral judgement and cognitive development, as Piaget had suggested. Lickona also found that children take intentions into account more as they get older, and that a belief in immanent justice and expiatory punishment declines with age. These findings are consistent with Piaget's theory.

However, Judith Smetana (1981, 1985) found that 3-year-olds showed a strong respect for moral rules – earlier than Piaget had claimed.

Laupa and Turiel (1986) found that 6- to 10-year-olds are capable of questioning parental authority – they believe that parents are justified in making and enforcing rules about moral issues such as stealing, but not in imposing conventional rules e.g. about children helping with housework. This conflicts with Piaget's view that children of this age regard parental authority as the standard by which they make moral judgements.

Harris et al. (1976) found that children who have opportunities to interact with their peers tend to show greater sophistication in moral thought than children who have few such opportunities. This is consistent with Piaget's view of the importance of equal-status contact with peers. However, Kugelmass and Breznitz (1967) found that children reared in an Israeli kibbutz (who have plenty of opportunities for interactions with peers) are no more morally sophisticated than similar children growing up in a family group in a city. This conflicts with Piaget's views of the influence of parents and peers.

Constanzo *et al.* (1973) told stories to children aged 6, 8 and 10 years. In different versions of the stories a boy empties a box of toys on the floor. In the 'good intention' version he does this so as to sort them out. In the 'bad intention' version he does it to make a mess. The boy's mother, who does not know about his intentions approves of his action in some versions of the story, and disapproves in others. The researchers found that 6-year-olds judged the boy to be naughty when his mother disapproved – regardless of his intentions. The older children in the study took intentions into account more when judging the action. This partly supports Piaget's view of young children being unable to take account of intentions and being strongly influenced by the responses of others (especially parents). However the fact that 8-year-olds were found to take account of intentions suggests that Piaget underestimated the moral judgement of this age group.

Nelson (1980), in Study 3.2, found that children as young as 3 years were able to take intentions into account. This strongly contradicts Piaget's theory. First it demonstrates that children are able to make meaningful moral judgements at an age when Piaget suggested they were in the pre-moral stage. Second it demonstrates that children can take intentions into account much earlier than Piaget claimed.

HOW COMPLETE IS PIAGET'S THEORY OF MORAL DEVELOPMENT?

Piaget did not study moral development much beyond 11 years. Other researchers including Kohlberg and Eisenberg found further stages of moral development beyond this age.

HOW EFFECTIVE WAS PIAGET'S EMPIRICAL RESEARCH?

Piaget studied very few children (mainly his own and his friends' children), so his theory cannot be said to be based on the evidence of a representative sample of children.

His study methods tended to lead him to underestimate children's understanding. As noted above, his use of the moral comparison technique has been superseded by improved techniques developed by Nelson, Kohlberg and others.

PIAGET'S CONTRIBUTION

Piaget laid the foundations for the study of the development of moral cognition, including both theory and research technique. This generated a large body of later theory and research, most notably from Lawrence Kohlberg.

REFLECTIVE Activity

In Chapter 2 it was pointed out that researchers have often found that children were able to demonstrate abilities at an earlier age than Piaget claimed. Nelson's study seems to be another example of this. Why should children show a greater ability on Nelson's moral comparison task than Piaget's task described on page 68?

3.3 Kohlberg's work on moral development

Lawrence Kohlberg (1927–87) made a major contribution to the study of moral development during the last century. This contribution included both a theory and extensive research. Like Piaget, he studied the development of moral reasoning – that is the ability to think about moral issues. He was more interested in how people's moral thinking developed – rather than their moral behaviour.

Kohlberg's use of the moral dilemma technique

Like Piaget, Kohlberg wanted to get participants to make and explain moral judgements. As described above, Piaget used a technique of moral comparison in which the participant had to compare the morality of two children in different stories. Kohlberg developed a different technique. He used a single story which featured a **moral dilemma**.

A moral dilemma is a situation in which a person is faced with a choice, but whichever alternative they choose, they will have to do something which could be considered immoral. For example, your best friend asks you to tell other people that he is ill, when in fact he is taking a day off work to watch a tennis match. You promise to do this. Later the friend's boss telephones you about a serious problem which has arisen at work, and asks you if you know where your friend is. You have to choose between telling the truth (in which case you will break your promise to your friend), or keeping your promise (in which case you will have to tell a lie). Both alternatives involve an immoral action, but you have to choose one of them. This kind of dilemma often occurs in real life.

One of the stories Kohlberg used was the 'Heinz' dilemma:

> **In Europe, a woman was near death from a special kind of cancer. There was one drug that the doctors thought might save her. It was a form of radium that a druggist in the same town had recently discovered. The drug was expensive to make, but the druggist was charging ten times what the drug cost him to make. He paid $200 for the radium and charged $2,000 for a small dose of the drug. The sick woman's husband, Heinz, went to everyone he knew to borrow the money, but he could only get together about $1,000 which is half what it cost. He told the druggist that his wife was dying and asked him to sell it cheaper or let him pay later. but the druggist said: 'No, I discovered the drug and I'm going to make money from it.' So Heinz got desperate and broke into the man's store to steal the drug for his wife. Should the husband have done that?**
>
> **(Colby _et al._ 1983)**

In this story the moral dilemma facing Heinz is between two unacceptable behaviours:

- to steal, or

- to fail to help save his wife.

Notice that there is no easy way out. Although children may be taught that they should never steal, and always help other people in need, circumstances often occur in which it is impossible to avoid acting immorally. The issue then becomes one of deciding which is the lesser wrong.

Kohlberg would read this story to each participant and then ask them whether Heinz was right to do what he did. He also asked them to explain or justify their answers, and to suggest suitable punishments.

Study 3.3

Aim Kohlberg (1963) wanted to find out how children's moral judgement changed as they grew up.

Method He studied 72 boys from middle- and lower-class families in Chicago. The sample studied were aged 10, 13 and 16 years. He interviewed each boy, first reading out a story featuring a moral dilemma and then asking the child to make and explain judgements of the actions described in the story. These judgements were recorded. Each interview lasted about an hour and featured nine different dilemma stories.

Results Kohlberg found differences between the responses of younger and older participants. Younger participants were more likely to make judgements based on the likelihood of rewards and punishments, while older participants were more likely to refer to the actor's intentions and the importance of being accepted by society.

Conclusion Kohlberg concluded that moral judgements became more sophisticated during adolescence. He identified different levels of moral judgement which were revealed by the participants' statements. He developed these into a stage theory of moral development (see below).

REFLECTIVE Activity

Suggest two reasons why it might not be justifiable to generalise Kohlberg's findings from this sample of participants.

Kohlberg's stages of moral development

Following his (1963) study, Kohlberg divided the development of moral reasoning into three levels:

the preconventional level

the conventional level

the post-conventional level.

Each level contained two separate stages of development, giving six stages altogether.

He assumed that these stages were followed in an invariant and irreversible sequence. You might think that a stage theory like this implies that development is determined by **maturation**, i.e. genetically-programmed, in the same way that motor development during the first year of life appears to be. However, although Kohlberg described moral reasoning as developing over time, this is not a maturational theory. He did not believe that a person moved from (say) Stage 2 to Stage 3 because of some genetically-programmed growth. In terms of the **nature/nurture debate**, Kohlberg did not believe that **nature** alone determined moral development.

Neither did he believe that **nurture** alone determined moral development. In other words, he did not believe that progress through the stages was determined purely by instruction or social learning from parents and others.Instead, Kohlberg believed that progress through stages resulted from individuals thinking about moral problems and situations. This is very similar to Piaget's view that moral and cognitive development occurs by active self-discovery. However, Kohlberg did believe that this progress was influenced by the child's social environment. For example, a child's thinking would be stimulated by coming across a moral dilemma, listening to other people's opinions, and by experience of taking a variety of social roles (e.g. being a team captain). Kohlberg also believed that a child's development of moral reasoning was helped if they grew up in a social environment which allowed discussion and tolerated disagreement instead of being authoritarian.

KOHLBERG'S LEVELS AND STAGES

LEVEL 1 Pre-Conventional morality: around eight to 12 years
This means a kind of moral thinking children use before they get the idea of morality as a matter of convention, of something agreed by a society. In this level children's moral thinking is based on understanding how to keep out of trouble and getting what you want.

Level 1 includes two stages:

Stage 1: punishment and obedience orientation
What is wrong is what is punished. People do the right thing simply to avoid punishment. Moral

rules are seen as fixed, and the individual can do nothing to change them. This is similar to Piaget's stage of moral realism. A typical response of a child at this stage to the Heinz dilemma would be: 'Heinz can steal it because he asked first. He will not get punished' (Rest 1973).

Stage 2: instrumental hedonism orientation
In this stage, children begin to recognise that different people might have different moral opinions. People choose what to do according to what brings rewards. Doing things for other people might be good – provided they reward you. Moral behaviour may be seen as a fair exchange of favours. **Hedonism** is the belief that what is pleasurable is morally good. A typical response would be: 'He might steal the drug if he wanted his wife to live, but he does not have to if he wants to marry someone younger and better-looking' (Kohlberg 1963).

LEVEL 2 Conventional morality: Around 13 to 16 years
A convention is an agreed arrangement. Conventional morality is not so much seen as a fair exchange of favours, but more like a socially-agreed system of behaving which benefits most people in the long run. For example, if everyone agrees to obey the rules, and nobody cheats society will be a better place.

Level 2 includes two stages:

Stage 3: 'good boy/girl' orientation
Good behaviour is what pleases others, doing what people approve of – even if it does not bring immediate rewards. Judgements of behaviour are really judgements of character. A typical response would be: 'Heinz was a good man for wanting to save her' (Kohlberg 1963).

Stage 4: the morality of authority and maintaining social order
At this stage, the individual becomes more concerned with how society (not just friends and family) will judge them. Morality is about obeying authority and conforming to norms of accepted behaviour. Being good means doing one's duty and obeying the law, otherwise order will break down. A typical response would be: '. . . if everyone did as he wanted to do, set up his own beliefs as right and wrong, then I think you would have chaos' (Colby *et al.* 1987b).

LEVEL 3 post-conventional morality: early adulthood onwards
In this level the individual can question the moral values of the society they live in. They become aware that their society's laws and norms may not be the best. They can develop their own moral values and conscience make judgements. Morality is internalised – that is based on strongly-held beliefs.

Level	Stage	Description
Preconventional	1. Punishment and obedience orientation	Bad behaviour is whatever is punished
	2. Instrumental hedonism orientation.	Good behaviour is whatever brings rewards
Conventional	3. 'Good boy/girl' orientation	Good behaviour is what pleases others
	4. The morality of authority and maintaining social order	Being good means doing one's duty and obeying the law
Post-conventional	5. Morality of contract, individual rights and democratically accepted law	Everybody has rights, and laws can be changed by agreed processes
	6. Morality of individual principles of conscience	An individual's moral principles are more important than conventional rules or laws

Figure 3.5: Kohlberg's levels and stages of development

Level 3 includes two stages:

Stage 5: morality of contract, individual rights and democratically accepted law
Moral judgement is more flexible than in Stage 4. Laws are not just accepted unquestioningly. There could be bad laws which restrict reasonable rights. Laws can be changed by agreed democratic procedures – for example by a government after complaints from the public. All individuals have rights. A typical response would be: 'Usually the moral and legal standpoint coincide. Here they conflict. The judge should weight the moral standpoint more heavily but preserve the legal law in punishing Heinz lightly' (Kohlberg 1976).

Stage 6: morality of individual principles of conscience
Right and wrong is defined on the basis of an individual's self-chosen ethical principles. The law may conflict with one of these principles, but the principles are more important than the law. This is the kind of moral belief which people are sometimes prepared to die for.

PRACTICAL Activity

Assigning statements to stages:

Once Kohlberg had identified these six stages of development, he was able to use them to analyse the moral statements made by participants. Each statement made by a participant would be assigned to the stage it seemed to fit into best. You can see how this works by trying it for yourself. Write the stage number (1 to 6) in the box after each statement.

Note that the statements are responses to several different moral dilemmas.

Statement	Stage number
I would not fight in a war, because I believe that it is never right to kill people – under any circumstances	
People should be polite to each other, because it pays off in the long run. My Mum says she'd stop buying me sweets if I was rude:	
It's quite simple; Heinz shouldn't have stolen the drug, because that's theft and it's the law you see. If he got away with it, then others would do the same thing.	
Well, they shouldn't do it. Maybe you could get away with it, I don't know. But I wouldn't do it because my Dad would half murder me if he found out.	
You can't really blame him, because he was trying to help. Most people would actually think better of him for doing it.	
Technically what he did was against the law, but a lot of reasonable people might do the same thing. Maybe they should change the law.	

Figure 3.6

A scoring manual (Colby *et al.* 1983) was produced as a guide for assigning statements to stages and deciding what stage of development a person had reached.

Evaluation of Kohlberg's stage theory

DOES MORAL DEVELOPMENT PROCEED THROUGH SIX DISTINCT STAGES?

Turiel (1978, 1983) argued that moral development did not take place in distinct stages, but instead was gradual and **continuous**. The fact that people tend to think differently as they grow up does not mean that they have progressed from one stage to another, merely that they are gradually becoming more sophisticated. This implies that Kohlberg (and Piaget before him) has imposed stage boundaries on development without any convincing evidence that these boundaries exist. A problem for these stage theories is that participants commonly produce a range of statements from two or more stages at the same interview. If moral development progressed though stages you might expect all a person's moral statements to belong in one stage.

Kohlberg stopped using Stage 6 to analyse participants' responses in 1975. This was partly because very few participants ever produced statements which fitted this stage. A new edition of his scoring manual, (Colby *et al.* 1987a) removes this stage altogether.

DOES MORAL REASONING DEVELOP THROUGH AN INVARIANT AND IRREVERSIBLE SEQUENCE OF STAGES?

Kohlberg and Kramer (1969) carried out a longitudinal study in which teenagers were tested at three-year intervals to observe their progression through the stages. Most of the participants either moved on one stage or stayed at the same stage. These findings are consistent with the theory. However some participants skipped a stage (i.e. progressed to the next stage but one) and some went back a stage.

Study 3.4

Aim Walker (1989) wanted to test Kohlberg's claim that moral reasoning develops in an invariant and irreversible sequence of stages.

Method 233 participants were studied, of both sexes and ranging in age from 5 to 63 years. The longitudinal study was carried out over 2 years.

Participants were asked to respond to hypothetical dilemmas, and their responses were scored according to Kohlberg's stages.

Results Six per cent of participants scored at an earlier stage after 2 years than they had at first. This suggests that a small proportion of participants went back to an earlier stage (reversing). Thirty-seven per cent of participants (including 62% of the children) showed a change to the next stage (progressing). However no participants missed out a stage.

Conclusion The data broadly supported Kohlberg's view of an invariant and irreversible sequence of stages.

ARE KOHLBERG'S STAGES UNIVERSAL?

Kohlberg argued that the sequence of development he described would be found in all cultures. He and other researchers carried out cross-sectional and longitudinal studies in rural Mexico, Turkey, Taiwan, Israel, Kenya, the Bahamas and India. The evidence shows that moral development tends to be more advanced in urban areas, such as Chicago and Taiwan, and slower in rural areas of Mexico and Turkey. Despite these differences, Kohlberg claimed that the same sequence of development was shown in all the cultures, even though the rate varied (Snarey 1985).

IS KOHLBERG'S THEORY CULTURALLY BIASED?

Despite Kohlberg's cross-cultural studies, his theory has been criticised as reflecting western culture. This criticism implies that the theory may not be an accurate description of moral development in all cultures. Kohlberg's stages focus on an individual's behaviour in relation to social rules. Western culture values individual freedom and choice. Some Asian cultures value the good of the group (especially the family) more highly than the good of the individual. Dien (1982) pointed out that Kohlberg's stages do not reflect this moral viewpoint.

The fact that Kohlberg found that people from cities tended to be more advanced in moral reasoning than people from rural areas could be because city populations around the world tend to be more westernised. If so, their performance could simply reflect their cultural similarity to Kohlberg and his fellow workers, rather than a greater sophistication than people from rural areas.

IS KOHLBERG'S THEORY BIASED AGAINST WOMEN?

Gilligan (1982) pointed out that Kohlberg's stages were derived from interviews with males, and that they do not accurately describe moral development in females. Since Kohlberg's early studies used only male participants, this is a reasonable criticism. However, when Walker, de Vries and Trevethan (1987) used Kohlberg's technique to compare moral judgements made by males and females, they found no differences. This suggests that the claim of a bias against women may be mistaken.

DOES KOHLBERG'S THEORY PLACE TOO MUCH EMPHASIS ON JUSTICE?

A wide range of moral issues arises in everyday life. Summarising moral development into a series of stages runs the risk of concentrating on some aspects of moral thinking at the expense of others. Gilligan (1977) argued that Kohlberg's theory focuses on justice and ignores caring for others.

Issue	Comments
Does moral development proceed through six distinct stages?	Stages do not appear to be distinct, so moral development may be gradual and continuous.
Is the sequence of development invariant and irreversible?	In a small minority of cases only, individuals appear to skip stages or to go back one stage.
Are the stages universal?	The pattern is similar in a wide range of cultures, but development is typically more advanced in urban than rural communities.
Is the theory culturally biased?	It tends to focus on western values of individuality and choice.
It the theory biased against women?	Not according to the evidence.
Is there too much emphasis on justice?	Other aspects of moral thinking are also important.

Figure 3.7: Evaluation of Kohlberg's theory — summary

Shortcomings of the moral dilemma technique

ECOLOGICAL VALIDITY

One criticism of Kohlberg's technique is that participants were questioned about hypothetical dilemmas – in other words about situations which they might not have experienced themselves – such as the Heinz dilemma. More valid data might result if participants were questioned about situations they had experienced. By using stories to elicit moral statements, Kohlberg's technique lacked ecological validity. In contrast, Gilligan (1977) used a similar technique in which pregnant women who were considering having abortions were interviewed about the real dilemma they faced.

Walker, de Vries and Trevethan (1987) used the moral dilemma technique with a large sample of children and adults. Each participant was questioned about three of Kohlberg's moral dilemmas and one real-life dilemma the participant had experienced for themselves. Sixty-two per cent of participants reasoned at the same stage in the hypothetical and real-life situations. Of the remaining 38% about half reasoned at a higher level about the real-life dilemma, and half at a lower level. This suggests that ecological validity is not a problem for Kohlberg's use of the moral dilemma technique.

CONTENT VALIDITY

One risk of the moral dilemma technique is that it might not measure what it is supposed to measure. Kohlberg (1963) was worried that his original scoring method focused too much on the judgements participants made rather than the reasoning behind it. Because of this and the results of his study with Kramer in 1969, he revised his theory and his scoring method to produce a modified scoring manual with more emphasis on reasoning (Colby et al. 1983).

PREDICTIVE VALIDITY

For the dilemma technique to have predictive validity, you might expect participants' moral behaviour to be consistent with their moral judgement. In other words, you might expect people to act in a real situation as they said they would act when questioned about a moral dilemma.

Kohlberg (1975) found that consistency increased as individuals progressed through the stages. In a study of cheating, he found that 70% of young people assigned to the pre-conventional level cheated although they said it was wrong, while 55% of those in the conventional level did so. Only 15% of those in the post-conventional level showed this inconsistency. This suggests that the moral dilemma technique lacks predictive validity except for those individuals in the post-conventional level.

However, this criticism is based on a mistake. It assumes that moral thinking correlates with moral action. The following example shows that this is an unreasonable assumption: a skilled confidence-trickster tricks old people into giving money to a bogus charity he has set up. He succeeds because of his sophisticated understanding of moral issues – he knows how to make his victims feel guilty. A person can use their moral understanding to help them act in anti-social, immoral ways as well as pro-social, moral ways.

SUBJECTIVITY AND RELIABILITY

Another problem is that allocating statements to stages is subjective. The researcher has to make a judgement as to whether a statement belongs to stage 3 or stage 4. This is often difficult to do, so there is a risk that the process is unreliable. To avoid this criticism, Kohlberg asked several researchers to rate a sample of the statements, and then checked to see how many of the ratings differed. He found that inter-rater reliability was high.

Issue	Comments
Low ecological validity	The dilemmas were hypothetical – not real life. However this turns out not to make much difference to results.
Low content validity	Difficult to assess – but the revised scoring method is widely accepted.
Low predictive validity	Only a problem if you assume that sophisticated moral cognition should lead to good behaviour.
Involves subjective, unreliable judgements	High inter-rater reliability found.

Figure 3.8: Shortcomings of the moral dilemma technique – summary

3.4 Alternatives to the theories of Kohlberg and Piaget

Eisenberg's model of levels of prosocial reasoning

Much of the work carried out on children's moral understanding was restricted to examples of wrong actions – typically of anti-social behaviours such as theft and telling lies. In fact we also make moral judgements about right actions.

Nancy Eisenberg (1983) studied the development of moral reasoning, using examples of **prosocial behaviour**, such as helping. This kind of behaviour is also called **altruistic behaviour**. Eisenberg used a dilemma technique similar to Kohlberg's, except that the dilemma was about whether to help another person when this involves some disadvantage to the helper. This requires a participant to judge the relative importance of serving one's own interests and helping others.

Study 3.5

Aim Eisenberg-Berg and Hand (1979) wanted to find out how children's prosocial moral judgement changed as they grew up.

Method Children ranging from pre-school to secondary school age were interviewed using stories such as the following:

One day a girl named Mary was going to a friend's birthday party. On her way she saw a girl who had fallen down and hurt her leg. The girl asked Mary to go to her house and get her parents so that they could come and take her to a doctor. But if Mary did, she would be late to the party and miss the ice-cream, cake, and all the games. What should Mary do?

Each child's responses were recorded.

Results The researchers found that pre-school and nursery school children were most likely to answer **hedonistically**, i.e. to consider one's own interests more than the needs of others. In the story above, they are likely to say that the most important thing is to get to the party in time to enjoy all the treats. In contrast, secondary school children are likely to answer **empathically** i.e. to consider the needs of others as more important, and report that they would feel guilty if they did not help someone in need.

Conclusion During childhood, children show a progression from moral judgements based on hedonism towards those based on empathy. The researchers identified a sequence of five stages in this development.

EISENBERG'S LEVELS OF PROSOCIAL REASONING.

The table in Figure 3.10 shows the five levels of prosocial reasoning described by Eisenberg.

As children get older their thinking becomes less hedonistic and more empathic.

PRACTICAL Activity

Assign the following statements to Eisenberg's stages. In each case, write the stage number in the box following the statement.

Statement	Stage number
She ought to help really, because she wouldn't want to be left alone if she was hurt. Maybe she could get a lift to the party afterwards.	
The girl isn't too badly hurt if she can still talk. If she's still there when Mary comes back, she could help her then.	
Supposing she didn't help. Mary couldn't enjoy the party knowing that she had not helped someone who was in trouble.	
Mary could help, and then when she is late for the party she can say why and everyone will say what a hero you are.	
Mary should help the girl because maybe her parents are rich and she will get a reward.	

Figure 3.9:

Level	Description
1. Hedonistic (self-centred)	Helping is likely only if it will benefit oneself.
2. Needs-oriented	Helping depends on how strong the needs of others are e.g. it is more likely if the other person shows signs of distress. Otherwise children show little sign of sympathy, or guilt for not helping.
3. Approval-oriented	Helping is likely if other people will see it as praiseworthy.
4. Empathic/self-reflective	Some evidence of sympathy is shown, and of guilt for not helping. Some signs of awareness of duties and principles. A transition stage between levels 3 and 5.
5. Strongly internalised	Helping is justified with reference to the child's own values, sense of responsibility, and recognition that not helping will lead to loss of self-respect.

Figure 3.10: Eisenberg's levels or stages of prosocial reasoning

REFLECTIVE Activity

It is reasonable to expect that different stage theories of moral development would show similarities. Theories which conflict tend to undermine the credibility of at least one theory. Compare Eisenberg's five stages with Kohlberg's stage theory to see whether there are more similarities than differences.

Evaluation of Eisenberg's theory

1. The fact that some similarities exist between this theory and those of Piaget and Kohlberg could be taken as support for the validity of the theory. For example, all three theories show a development with age from a concern about the consequences of actions towards a concern with internalised moral beliefs.

2. Eisenberg's work is valuable in that it considers the morality of prosocial behaviour – previously ignored by researchers.

3. Eisenberg's stage theory is supported by cross-cultural studies featuring children from several nations. Boehnke et al. (1989) found a similar pattern of development in German, Italian and Polish children as Eisenberg found in American children.

However there are strong cultural similarities between Europe and America. In contrast, Tietjen (1986) found that children from the Miasin people of Papua New Guinea tend to reason at Level 2 (needs-oriented reasoning) well into adolescence and adulthood.

Gilligan's ethics of care: differences between boys and girls

Carol Gilligan (1977, 1982) claimed that theorists such as Freud and Kohlberg suggested that women were on average less advanced in moral reasoning than men. Gilligan questioned that this implied inferiority. She argued that women's moral judgements are not less advanced than men's, but that women tend to think differently about moral issues. If this is true, it could explain why women score less well on a scale derived from males.

GILLIGAN'S THEORY OF FEMALE MORAL DEVELOPMENT

Her theory suggests that women have a greater interest than men in relationships and caregiving, and as a result, females develop a **morality of care** and responsibility while males develop a **morality of justice**. This view is plausible because it is consistent with traditional gender stereotypes which see women as caring and men as tough-minded and assertive.

- The morality of care refers to a tendency to think about the effects of actions on the feelings and needs of others, on relationships and on the prevention of harm

- The morality of justice refers to the tendency to think about whether or not society's rules have been broken, and about appropriate punishment.

Gilligan felt that the morality of justice was similar to Kohlberg's stage 4. She explained that statements about the needs of other people tended to be assigned to Kohlberg's Stage 3, (the 'good boy/girl' orientation), while statements about justice tended to be assigned to Stage 4, (the morality of authority and maintaining social order). If true, this could explain why women might score lower on Kohlberg's stages, because caring statements are more likely to be assigned to Stage 3, and rule-bound statements more likely to be assigned to Stage 4. Gilligan pointed out that Kohlberg's theory was based on research with male participants only, and implied that if his earlier research had included female participants, Stages 4 onwards would have included some features of a morality of care.

Gilligan's three levels of moral development

Study 3.6

Aim Gilligan (1977) wanted to find out whether the moral judgements of women showed similar levels of sophistication as those found by Kohlberg in men.

Method She carried out unstructured interviews with 29 pregnant women who were all considering having abortions. This is an example of a real-life moral dilemma. She assumed that the women's responses to this issue would reveal different aspects of a morality of care. She recorded the women's responses and analysed them into different levels.

Results Gilligan found that the women produced higher-level statements when talking about the abortion issue than they did on Kohlberg's dilemmas.

Conclusion Gilligan identified three stages in the development of a morality of care in women.

Gilligan concluded that statements at her Levels 2 and 3 demonstrated that a morality of care could involve the kind of principles which Kohlberg identified in the post-conventional level. In other words, the morality of care is not restricted to a conventional level, and so moral judgements in women can be just as sophisticated as those in men.

Level	Description
Level 1 Self-interest	Women who made statements suggesting they would do what was best for themselves were assigned to this stage.
Level 2 Self-sacrifice	Statements suggesting that a woman was willing to put the welfare of others before their own interests were assigned to this stage.
Level 3 Non-violence	Statements emphasising the importance of not hurting others were assigned to this stage.

Figure 3.11: Gilligan's three levels in the development of a morality of care

Evaluation of Gilligan's work

IS GILLIGAN RIGHT TO CLAIM THAT KOHLBERG'S METHOD OF MEASURING MORAL UNDERSTANDING IS BIASED AGAINST WOMEN?

Most studies (e.g. Walker 1984) using Kohlberg's method show no difference in the sophistication of moral judgements made by women compared with men.

ARE THERE SEX DIFFERENCES BETWEEN WOMEN'S AND MEN'S MORAL JUDGEMENTS?

Most research has failed to find evidence of sex differences in moral judgements, and Gilligan's view of sex differences in moral thinking is not widely shared.

For example, Walker *et al.* (1987) interviewed participants of both sexes, using hypothetical dilemmas and a real-life dilemma the participant had experienced. Responses were scored according to Kohlberg's stages, but also according to Gilligan's two moral orientations. The researchers found no significant correlation between sex and orientation. In fact participants of both sexes used both orientations. They also found that responses to hypothetical and real-life dilemmas were similar.

Psychoanalytic explanations of moral development

Sigmund Freud (1856–1939) produced psychoanalytical explanations for a wide range of behaviour and experience. His theory of moral development is not really about moral cognition, but more about how children acquire moral rules and the motivation to act morally. In other words it is a theory about the psychological development on which moral behaviour is based.

Freud (1961) believed that children acquire an awareness of morality during the **phallic stage** of **psychosexual development** – at around 4- to 6-years-old. During this stage, the child acquires the third and final component of personality – the **superego**.

The role of the superego

Freud suggested that the self or personality has three components. The **id** (also known as the pleasure principle) included instinctual energies or drives such as sex (also known as **libido**), dominance/aggression and self-preservation. The id provides motivation for action – it seeks gratification of a person's wants and desires. To grasp Freud's idea of the id, it is useful to think of the behaviour of a baby. A baby cries immediately it is uncomfortable or hungry, demanding instant satisfaction of its needs. It cannot delay its actions until a more convenient time. One result is frequent nappy-changes. Imagine how it would be if adults were like this. According to Freud, the more controlled behaviour of adults is due to the fact that they have developed two more components of the self – the **ego** and the **superego**.

Freud claimed that children begin to gain conscious control over their behaviour as the ego develops. The ego (also known as the reality principle) is the part of the self which is able to take account of what is happening around us. The ego can use this information to decide whether or not to take an opportunity to satisfy the needs of the id.

Carol sees an opportunity to release aggressive energy

For example, Jason is at the cinema with his girlfriend. He is annoyed by another man sitting behind him, who frequently makes silly remarks about the film they are watching. Jason's id happens to be overflowing with dominance/aggression at the moment. Jason's ego sees this as an opportunity to release some of this aggressive energy. He could turn round and say 'Listen pal, are you going to shut up, or shall I give you a smack?' Jason's ego also takes into account other factors in the situation, such as how big and strong the other man is, and whether showing dominance/aggression will impress his girlfriend.

This example illustrates that the ego makes it more likely that Jason will not act impulsively, but will consider the consequences. If the other man looks weak, and his girlfriend is easily impressed by tough guys, Jason will take the opportunity to release some aggressive energy.

Freud called the third part of the personality the superego (also known as the morality principle). The superego is the part of the personality which influences us to act in ways we find morally acceptable. It can be thought of as a set of moral principles guiding action. This component

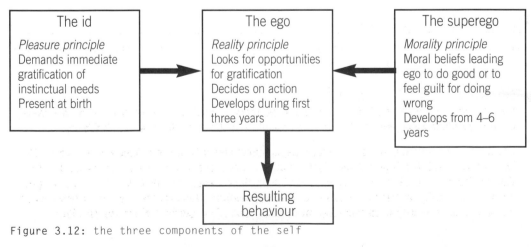

The id	The ego	The superego
Pleasure principle Demands immediate gratification of instinctual needs Present at birth	*Reality principle* Looks for opportunities for gratification Decides on action Develops during first three years	*Morality principle* Moral beliefs leading ego to do good or to feel guilt for doing wrong Develops from 4–6 years

Resulting behaviour

Figure 3.12: the three components of the self

contains two parts – the ego-ideal which tends to lead us to perform good actions, and the conscience, which tends to prevent us performing actions we think wrong.

Some students get the impression that the superego dominates the other two components of the self, but Freud did not believe this. The role of the superego is to influence our actions according to our moral beliefs, but it is the ego which finally decides on any action. However, the superego can punish the ego for wrongdoing by inducing feelings of guilt.

The diagram above shows the three components of the self, indicating how the id and ego can both influence the ego, which decides on action.

PRACTICAL Activity

A 4-year-old girl has a baby brother whom she dislikes. One day she is left alone with the baby for a few minutes. She pinches the baby's cheek hard enough to make him cry.

1. How might the id have contributed to this behaviour?

2. How might the ego have been involved?

3. Think of one reason why the little girl does not have a superego.

4. If the little girl did have a superego – how might she have felt, following her action?

CONFLICT BETWEEN COMPONENTS OF THE SELF

Sometimes the components of the self operate without internal conflict. For example, if a woman wants to have sex with a man who is her regular partner, the man is willing, and the situation convenient, there is no conflict between the instinctual desires of her id (libido), and the contents of her superego.

However, conflicts do occur. For example, imagine you are very thirsty but have no money. You pass a refreshment stall stacked with chilled bottles of drink. There are few people around, and the stall attendant is reading a newspaper. It would be easy for you to take a drink without paying for it.

Your id's drive for self-preservation motivates you to take the drink. Your ego recognises that there is little risk involved in taking the drink, but your superego includes the belief that it is wrong to steal. Whether you go ahead and steal the drink will depend on several factors, such as how strong your motivation is (how thirsty you are) and how strong your conscience is.

REFLECTIVE Activity

Think of two examples of your own – one situation in which the components of the self are unlikely to conflict, and another situation in which they are.

EVALUATIVE COMMENT

Freud's view of a self divided into three components is useful, because it explains the inner conflict or discomfort people often feel in real-life situations such as sexual infidelity.

However, there is no empirical evidence that the components Freud describes actually exist. The facts about child development on which Freud's theories are based can be checked. It is true that babies seem unable to delay gratification of their wants, and that infants gradually gain control over bodily functions and the expression of emotion. However the idea of components of the self is just one way of interpreting those facts, and other interpretations are possible.

HOW THE SUPEREGO DEVELOPS

Freud's explanation of development during the phallic stage is very strange. It is based on the assumption that children in the phallic stage have sexual feelings towards their opposite sex parents. The word 'phallic' comes from the Greek word 'phallus', meaning an erect penis.

The explanation assumes that at around 4 to 6 years old, boys experience what Freud called the **Oedipus complex** and girls experience the **Electra complex**.

THE OEDIPUS COMPLEX

According to Freud, a boy begins to feel sexually attracted to his mother during the phallic stage. However, he realises that this puts him in conflict with his father, to whom he feels hostile. The boy experiences a conflict between his desire for his mother and his fear that his father will cut his penis off. Freud called this the Oedipus complex. Boys resolve this conflict by suppressing their desire – becoming unaware of it – and identifying with their father. **Identification** means becoming like his father, including acquiring the father's set of moral beliefs. In this way the child **internalises** moral rules or standards. At the same time the boy acquires a superego. Aggression which would otherwise have been directed towards the boy's father is directed towards the self – in the form of feelings of guilt. To avoid this self-punishment, the boy is motivated to act according to his moral beliefs.

THE ELECTRA COMPLEX

Freud's explanation for moral development in girls is rather different. Girls experience the Electra complex – a sexual attraction towards the father and a rivalry with the mother. However the girl's fear of castration is much less than that experienced by boys. Since a girl does not have a penis, she will assume that her mother has already punished her by cutting it off. As a result, the girl has less to fear than a boy, and will not identify with her mother as strongly as boys identify with their father. The result of this (according to Freud) is that girls and women are morally weaker than boys and men.

This idea of the moral inferiority of women was quite widespread (among both men and women) when Freud was young. For example it was assumed that if a young woman experienced sex before she was married (and so before she was under the control of a man), she would be unlikely to be able to control her sexual appetite. Men, being morally stronger were assumed to be able to keep control of their sexual appetites. As a result it was acceptable for men to be sexually promiscuous before marriage, but not women. This is an example of a **double-standard**, where there is a different set of rules or expectations for each sex. Today, people are likely to reach exactly the opposite conclusion to Freud's. If men are more sexually promiscuous than women, this suggests they are morally weaker rather than stronger.

Evaluation of Freud's theory of moral development

DOES MORAL DEVELOPMENT TAKE PLACE BETWEEN 4 AND 6 YEARS OF AGE?

Freud's claim that the conscience emerges by 6-years-old is not supported by other psychologists, such as Piaget and Kohlberg. Their work demonstrated that moral development is only just beginning at this age, and continues over a much longer period.

DOES FEAR OF PARENTS LEAD TO BETTER MORAL BEHAVIOUR?

Freud's theory predicts that children who are afraid of their parents are likely to develop stronger superegos. However there is plenty of evidence to suggest that parents who use a very punishing approach to child rearing tend to have children who often misbehave and rarely show guilt (Brody and Shaffer 1982). Possibly children who are over-controlled by parents lack opportunities to develop and practise self-control.

ARE GIRLS MORALLY WEAKER THAN BOYS?

Hoffman (1975) reviewed previous research in which children were given the opportunity to break rules. Little difference was found between boys and girls, although girls were found to be slightly more able to resist temptation. This does not support Freud's theory of sex differences in superego strength.

Gilligan (1982) argued that Freud's view of moral development was biased by unjustified assumptions about male superiority.

ARE PARENTS THE MAIN AGENTS OF MORAL DEVELOPMENT?

Freud's theory implies that for the superego to develop the child must grow up with two parents – a same-sex parent and an opposite-sex parent. Yet many children aged 4 to 6 only have contact with one parent. There is no evidence that these children fail to develop morally, e.g. fail to develop a conscience.

There is plenty of evidence that children's moral behaviour is influenced by other people, in addition to parents, such as their peers. For example, Bandura et al. (1963) found that children imitate the aggressive behaviour of other adults.

It is possible that in the past parents were more important in communicating moral values to children than they are today. For children growing up in a developed nation today there are more sources of ideas and examples (especially in the mass media), and more opportunities to think about moral issues. Children might therefore be more likely to think for themselves, rather than accepting a ready-made morality provided by parents or by the teaching of a religion.

IS THE RESOLUTION OF THE OEDIPUS/ELECTRA COMPLEX THE MAIN PROCESS INVOLVED IN MORAL DEVELOPMENT?

Freud's account of the Oedipus and Electra complexes are largely discredited. There are other far more plausible explanations of how children identify with parents and acquire the ability to act morally. These include social learning theory, which argues that behaviour is acquired by learning from selective reinforcement and discouragement, and by modelling, in which children observe and imitate the behaviours of others.

Issue	Comments
Does moral development take place between 4 and 6 years?	Other theories suggest that the main development takes place later than this.
Does fear of parents lead to better moral behaviour?	Evidence shows the opposite.
Are girls morally weaker than boys?	Evidence conflicts with this view.
Are parents the main agents of moral development?	Parents are important, especially during early years, but other adults, peers and the media also play a part.
Is the Oedipus/Electra complex the key process?	This is implausible, and there are alternative more plausible explanations.

Figure 3.13: Evaluation of Freud's theory of moral development

3.5 Moral behaviour and moral cognition

Most of the theories discussed in this chapter have been theories of moral cognition. Freud's theory alone is about how children acquire the motivation to act morally.

You might expect that moral cognition would correlate strongly with moral behaviour. For example a child who believes it is wrong to cheat should be less likely to cheat than a child who believes that cheating is acceptable. People do tend to behave in ways that are consistent with their beliefs.

Surprisingly however there is considerable evidence that children's moral beliefs and behaviours are often inconsistent. Hartshorne and May (1928–30) studied 10,000 children aged between eight and 16 years. They investigated their moral beliefs, and put them in situations where they were tempted to lie, steal or cheat. They found that the children's moral behaviour was quite inconsistent. For example the same children would cheat in some situations but not in others. This finding is similar to the findings of research on the consistency between attitudes and behaviour. Whether people act consistently or not seems to depend partly on the circumstances. Hartshorne and May also found that stated beliefs did not correlate with behaviour. For example, a certain proportion of children who cheated, stated that cheating was wrong. The same proportion of children who did not cheat also said that cheating was wrong. However other studies have found that as children get older there is increasing consistency between moral beliefs and moral behaviour (Kohlberg 1975; Blasi 1980).

However, it is important to remember that researchers such as Piaget and Kohlberg who studied moral cognition did not aim to study actual moral beliefs. Instead they studied moral understanding. In fact Kohlberg became dissatisfied with his original method of analysing moral statements because he believed that it focused too much on the actual judgements made rather than the reasoning behind those judgements. It would be a mistake to assume that a person with a more sophisticated level of moral understanding would necessarily behave in a more morally correct way.

3.6 Sample questions

SAMPLE QUESTION 1

(a) Briefly outline the role of the superego in moral behaviour.
     (AO1 = 2)   *(2 marks)*

(b) Explain the difference between *moral realism* and *moral relativism*. Illustrate your answer with an example of each.
     (AO1 = 2, AO2 = 4)   *(6 marks)*

(c) Discuss psychological theory and research into differences in the moral development of boys and girls.
     (AO1 = 5, AO2 = 7)   *(12 marks)*

SAMPLE QUESTION 2

(a) Read the three statements made by three different people, and decide which of Eisenberg's levels of prosocial reasoning each statement belongs to.

   (i) I donate blood every year because I think people who are lucky enough to be healthy owe it to less fortunate people to help out.

   (ii) it is a good idea to be nice to people because then they have to be nice back to you.

(iii) I would go out of my way to give a friend a lift back home, because people appreciate that sort of thing. I like my friends to think well of me.
(AO2 = 3) (3 marks)

(b) Outline the main features of a psychoanalytic theory of moral development.
(AO1 = 5) (5 marks)

(c) Evaluate Piaget's contribution to the study of moral development.
(AO1 = 5, AO2 = 7) (12 marks)

QUESTIONS, ANSWERS AND COMMENTS

SAMPLE QUESTION 1

(a) The superego is the moral part of the self. It tells the ego what to do in cases where there is a moral dilemma.

Comment: 1 mark – for a rather vague account of the relationship of the superego and ego. A better answer might refer to the two components of the superego, pointing out that the ego-ideal tends to influence the ego to perform good actions, while the conscience punishes the ego by feelings of guilt for wrongdoing.

(b) Moral realism is a stage in Piaget's theory of moral development in which a child judges wrongdoing just by the outcome. For example a child would say a boy was naughtier if he broke four plates than if he broke one plate. Moral relativism is the next stage. The difference is that the child can now take intentions into account as well. For example, if a boy broke four plates accidentally he would not be judged as being as naughty as a boy who broke one plate on purpose.

Comment: 6 marks – 2 AO1 marks for factually correct information (stages in Piaget's theory, plus correct order). 4 AO2 marks, 1 each for explaining each stage and 1 each for appropriate examples.

(c) Kohlberg found that, while most people fit into the conventional level of moral development, women are more often in Stage 3, while men are more often in Stage 4. This suggests that girls do not develop as quickly or as far as boys.

Gilligan criticised this and said that Kohlberg was wrong. This was because his research participants had all been boys, so his Stages were biased. Gilligan did an enormous amount of research with women and found that they have a different way of moral thinking than men. She called this the morality of care, which means that women think about how other people feel when they make moral judgements. She said that men do not have this. Instead men have a morality of justice, which is more concerned with deciding the rights and wrongs of a situation and deciding the correct punishment. Gilligan found three stages in the development of female morality. These were: self interest, self-sacrifice and non-violence. She showed that the later stages were just as highly developed as the morality of justice was in men.

One piece of research she did was to test women who were about to have abortions. They made judgements about the rights and wrongs of doing this.

Comment: 7 marks (AO1 = 5, AO2 = 2)

This answer does some of the things the question requires, including referring to theory and evidence. The stages of Gilligan's theory of the morality of care are correctly identified, and there is a brief reference to relevant research.

However the question asks the candidate to 'Discuss', which usually means presenting two sides of an argument. Here the candidate has given a one-sided answer which implies that Gilligan was right. In fact Gilligan's view of a sex difference in moral judgement has been challenged.

Sample questions, answers and comments

There was some inaccuracy too, notably the claim that Gilligan 'did an enormous amount of research'. AO1 marks were awarded for factual details of theory and research. AO2 marks were awarded for the evaluation made of Kohlberg's work. The small number of AO2 marks shows that the candidate has concentrated on description at the expense of discussion.

A better answer would have criticised Gilligan's view of sex differences and bias, and perhaps cited a study whose findings conflicted with this.

A discussion of Freud's account of sex differences in morality due to developments in the phallic stage would have provided more opportunities to score marks. Freud's view that women are morally weaker than men is easy to criticise.

3.7 FURTHER READING

Introductory texts

Bukatko, D. and Daehler, M. W. 1992: **Child development: a topical approach**. Houghton-Mifflin, Boston.

Schaffer, D. R. 1993 **Developmental psychology: childhood and adolescence**. 3rd Ed. Brooks/Cole, Pacific Grove, CA.

Smith, P .K., Cowie, H. and Blades, M. 1998: **Understanding children's development**. 3rd Ed. Blackwell, Oxford.

Specialist sources

Crain, William 1992: **Theories of development**. 3rd Ed. Prentice-Hall International, Englewood Cliffs, NJ.

Eisenberg, N. and Mussen, P. H. 1989: **The roots of prosocial behaviour in children**. Cambridge University Press, Cambridge.

Hetherington, E. M., Parke, R. D. and Locke, V. O. 2003: **Child psychology: a contemporary viewpoint**. 5th Ed. updated. McGaw Hill, Boston.

Messer, D. and Miller, S. (Eds) 1999: **Exploring developmental psychology: from infancy to adolescence**. Arnold, London.

Thomas, R. M. 2000: **Comparing theories of child development**. 5th Ed. Wadsworth, London.

Vasta, R., Haith M. M. and Miller, S. A. 1999: **Child psychology: the modern science**. John Wiley & Sons, Chichester.

4

Exceptional development

4.1 Introduction

Mothers and fathers of newborn babies are usually thrilled at the arrival of what they see as a little miracle. They marvel at their special child and wonder at every developmental milestone, such as the first word and first step. Despite this early wonder, most of us turn out to be rather less special than our parents first thought we were. In fact, many of us turn out to be quite ordinary and unexceptional. There are however, some children who defy the description 'ordinary', either because they have particular talents or abilities, or perhaps because they do not show abilities and behaviours that most of us take for granted. Whatever their condition, they are different to the vast majority of children and for that reason might merit the description 'exceptional'. In this chapter the emphasis shifts to focus on unusual aspects of child development, with consideration of disorders like autism and, rather less unusually, learning difficulties like dyslexia. At the other end of the spectrum there will be an analysis of giftedness and how this too can bring with it many difficulties, simply because such children are so different to most other children.

4.2 Autism

Defining and determining autism

According to The National Autistic Society, autism is defined fairly generally as a 'complex life long disability which affects a person's social and communication skills'. The extent to which a sufferer's social and communication skills are affected is indicated by the description of autism in the Diagnostic and Statistical Manual (DSM) IV for mental disorders. In DSM IV autism is referred to as a **pervasive mental disorder**, suggesting that such children show severe and extensive developmental deficits with disturbances in almost every aspect of functioning, including relationships, thinking and language. The term autism stems from the Greek word 'autos' meaning 'self' and perhaps for this reason autism has been described as 'a mental disorder characterised by self-orientation' (Flanagan 2000).

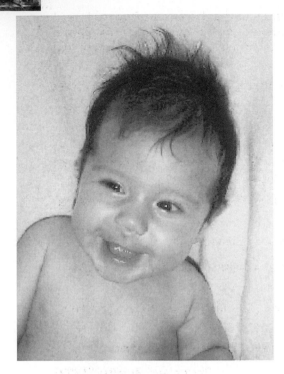

Will this baby turn out to be an exceptional child?

PRACTICAL Activity

Think about what Flanagan means by the term 'self-orientation'. Make a list of behaviours that you think would demonstrate 'self-orientation'. These would be behaviours that indicate a child is self-focused or self-absorbed. Now read on to the description of behaviours typically demonstrated by a child with autism. Tick these behaviours or symptoms off against the list you made.

Estimates of the frequency of autism vary considerably, but recent findings suggest that it occurs in at least one in 1,000 people (Happe 1999). The disorder is usually identified before 30 months of age and, although relatively rare, it is four or five times more common in males than females (Ritvo *et al.* 1989). Autism was identified by Kanner (1943) and Asperger (1944), and Asperger's syndrome is often referred to as a mild form of autism. Occasionally some sufferers (known as **autistic savants**) exhibit phenomenal intellectual ability or artistic talent, such as the ability to perform feats of mental arithmetic or the ability to produce minutely detailed images from memory. More frequently however, sufferers of autism show general intellectual impairment, and many have an IQ test score of below 70 points (Prior and Wherry 1986), which is the determining level for diagnosis of mental retardation according to DSM IV.

According to Kanner (1943), autism is characterised by five types of behaviour: poor communication; poor social interaction; preference for routine; preference for objects rather than people; occasional extreme ability or special talent. For diagnostic purposes clinicians have reorganised and refined Kanner's original characteristics into three groups, each containing a number of specific behaviours.

THREE CATEGORIES OF BEHAVIOUR USED IN DIAGNOSIS OF AUTISM

- Deficits in social interaction

  There is a marked lack of responsiveness to other people with impaired use of non-verbal behaviours such as eye contact and facial expression. Sufferers prefer objects to people and avoid games and joint activities with other children. Autistic children seem unable to engage in pretend play and show a profound lack of empathy

- Deficits in communication

  Sufferers often show absence of, or severely restricted speech, with a reluctance to initiate or participate in any conversation. Any language is often repetitive and stereotypical, for example where the child repeats a word or sound over and over (**echolalia**)

- Repetitive and stereotyped behaviours

  Children have limited interests and will become preoccupied with and attached to unusual objects e.g. rocks, keys, etc. Routine and ritual are extremely important and deviations from routine can precipitate violent temper outbursts. Repetitive behaviours such as head banging and rocking back and forth are quite common.

In addition to these three main groups of symptoms, autistic children may show additional symptoms such as insensitivity to pain, abnormal responses to sensory stimuli, inappropriate emotional expression and movement disturbances, for example, lack of motor control and fidgetiness.

For a diagnosis of autism to be made, children are expected to show at least six target behaviours from across the three major categories.

PRACTICAL Activity

Read the descriptors of autistic children in the quotations given below and compare them with the three main behavioural categories outlined above. Decide which category of behaviour each descriptor relates to.

> **He . . . collected objects such as bottle tops, and insisted on having two of everything, one in each hand.**
>
> **. . . a child seems apart or aloof from others, even in the earliest stages of life.**
>
> **If speech is present, it is almost never used to communicate except in the most rudimentary fashion . . .**
>
> **Mothers often remember such babies as never being 'cuddly', never reaching out when being picked up . . .**
>
> **. . . autistic children are said to be obsessed with the maintenance of sameness.**
>
> **Carson and Butcher (1992)**

Causes of autism

Given that there are many and varied symptoms of autism, and that some autistic children show high levels of cognitive functioning whilst others are quite severely impaired, it is difficult to identify a single cause of autism. Three main types of theory about the cause of autism have

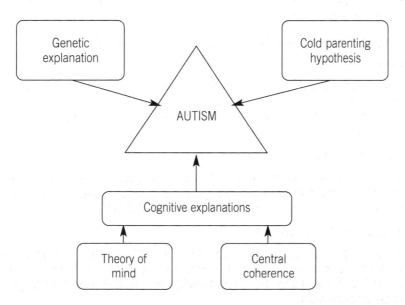

Figure 4.1: Explanations for autism

been proposed, although the most prevalent contemporary view is a cognitive explanation known as **theory of mind**.

THE COLD PARENTING HYPOTHESIS

The 'cold parenting' hypothesis originally proposed by Kanner (1943), suggested that what might be an innate disorder in the child would be aggravated by the behaviour of a cold, unresponsive mother or **refrigerator mother**. In 1967 Bettleheim was partially successful in treating some cases of autism at the Orthogenic School of the University of Chicago. Since the treatment which seemed to alleviate some of the problems in some autistic children revolved around a programme of warm acceptance and reinforcement, it seemed possible that the mother's cold behaviour might have been responsible for the autistic behaviour in the first place.

In some ways, particularly in their reluctance to engage in social interaction and communication, the behaviour of children with autism appears similar to that of emotionally neglected or abused children. Bettleheim noted how autistic behaviour was like the withdrawn and hopeless behaviour demonstrated by survivors of World War II concentration camps. This observation led some mental health professionals to conclude that autism could have been a consequence of child abuse. However, whilst not denying that early socialisation probably does affect later social behaviour, there is ample evidence to suggest that cold parenting is not a causal factor in the disorder. McAdoo and De Myer (1978) found no significant differences in the personality traits shown by parents of autistic children and parents of children suffering from other developmental disturbances. They also found that mothers of autistic children had fewer psychological problems than mothers who were being treated for mental health difficulties. Cox *et al.* (1975) showed that parents of autistic children are no less warm or less responsive than other parents.

EVALUATIVE COMMENT

Bettleheim's theory that autism was a result of cold and unaffectionate behaviour on the part of the parents is not really testable. A child who is emotionally withdrawn and has severely impaired communication would be a very difficult child to parent. Perhaps having such an unrewarding, difficult child to look after in itself causes a parent to be less affectionate. Thus it is very difficult to demonstrate any cause and effect relationship between parental behaviour and behavioural outcomes for the child. Powell (1999) concludes that any coldness in the parents' behaviour is more likely to be caused by the behaviour of the autistic child than vice versa. Whilst perhaps not intended, Bettleheim's explanation for autism had profound negative effects on parents of autistic children who were made to feel responsible for their child's condition.

THE GENETIC THEORY

Concordance studies are often used to determine the extent to which a condition is inherited and involve calculating the percentage likelihood of someone suffering from a disorder if they have a relative who is also a sufferer. Folstein and Piven (1991) reported a concordance rate for autism of between 2 and 3% for siblings, which is much higher than the frequency of autism in the general population. This indicates a substantial genetic component. However, the strongest evidence for genetic factors in autism comes from twin studies, some of which indicate that the concordance rate for **monozygotic** (identical) twins is as high as 96%, with a concordance rate for **dizygotic** (fraternal or non-identical) twins similar to that of ordinary siblings (Folstein and Piven 1991). Although concordance rates vary from study to study, Rutter *et al.* (1999) are convinced that autism has a strong genetic component and that several different genes may be involved.

Study 4.1

Aim Ritvo *et al.* (1985) set out to determine the likelihood that autism was inherited.

Method Forty twin pairs were examined for symptoms of autism. Of these, 23 were monozygotic (identical) twins, and 17 pairs were dizygotic (non-identical or fraternal) twins. Ritvo *et al.* calculated the concordance rate for the two sets of twins, establishing the mathematical chance of one twin having the disorder if the other twin also had autism.

Results Twenty-two of the 23 monozygotic pairs were found to be concordant (96% concordance rate), whereas only four of the dizygotic pairs were concordant (23% concordance rate).

Conclusion Whilst this seems to be extremely strong evidence for the genetic basis of autism, it should be remembered that dizygotic twins are no more similar genetically than ordinary siblings who typically show only a 2% concordance for the disorder. This suggests that environmental factors might also have some influence on autism, since the environment for twins is likely to be more similar than it is for ordinary siblings.

EVALUATIVE COMMENT

The suggestion that autism has a genetic cause is consistent with findings showing a link between autistic symptoms and other genetic disorders. For example, it has been found that approximately 10% of children with autism have a chromosomal abnormality known as *Fragile-X syndrome* (Bee 1989). Autism has also been associated with other genetic disorders such as *Tourette's syndrome* and *Phenylketonuria (PKU)*, which if left untreated leads to severe mental impairment. Comings and Comings (1991) noted that sufferers of Tourette's syndrome and autism share many symptoms, including obsessive and ritualistic behaviours, adherence to routine and stereotypical movements.

REFLECTIVE Activity

Imagine you are the parent of an autistic child. What would it be like to be told that the child's impairments and difficult to manage behaviours are genetic? Would you be relieved that the disorder was nothing to do with your parenting? Would knowing the disorder is inherited make you more or less likely to try to change your child's behaviour? Would you feel better able to cope with the child or not?

The theory that autism is inherited might be supported by biological evidence for differences in brain structure or brain chemistry between autistic people and non-sufferers, although biological differences in themselves do not necessarily confirm that a disorder is inherited. In one study using a **double blind** procedure Leboyer *et al.* (1992) found that injecting patients with naltrexone, a drug that blocks the activity of the body's natural opiates or **endorphins**, dramatically reduced autistic symptoms. This and similar findings have led to the suggestion that abnormally fluctuating levels of the body's own endorphins could be responsible for the symptoms of autism (Kalat 1992).

Happe (1999) suggests that although certain areas of the brain have been implicated as responsible, it is likely that, given the pervasive nature of autism, any differences in brain anatomy or function between people with autism and non-sufferers will be fairly substantial and non-localised. Recent neurological research has variously focused on cerebellum size (Courchesne 1991), overall brain enlargement (Piven *et al.* 1995), cerebral blood flow abnormalities (Ohnishi *et al.* 2000) and the functioning of specific structures like the amygdala (Baron-Cohen *et al.* 2000), but a clear link between brain abnormalities and autism has yet to be established.

COGNITIVE EXPLANATIONS

Theory of mind

The social and communication deficits observed in people with autism suggest that sufferers do not understand the world from the point of view of others. For example, if someone asks, 'Can you open the door?' we would normally assume they want to come in and would open the door for them, whereas an autistic person might just answer 'Yes', as if responding to a request for information. This everyday example illustrates a profound lack of ability to understand another person's point of view or intention. The apparent failure of people with autism to understand that other people, or indeed themselves have a mental state was proposed by Frith (1989). Frith proposed that people with autism seriously lack the ability to mind-read, in short, they lack a **theory of mind**.

PRACTICAL Activity

If you know two young children you can try the following activity to see whether they have a theory of mind. First show the two children a tube of sweets, letting them have a couple each. Then send one of the children out on a pretend errand. Whilst this 'stooge' child is out of the room, remove the sweets from the tube and hide them somewhere, then put a pencil inside the tube and replace the lid. When the 'stooge' child returns ask the other child what the 'stooge' child thinks is in the tube. Does the answer show that the child understands what the 'stooge' child knows and does not know? If so, then the child has a theory of mind. Ordinarily children over 4 years succeed at this task because they understand that the 'stooge' child would still think the sweets were in the tube. However, in a study like this, known as the 'Smartie Test', Perner *et al.* (1989) found that 80% of children with autism gave an incorrect answer.

Study 4.2

Aim Baron-Cohen *et al.* (1985) set out to demonstrate differences in mind-reading ability between children with autism, Down's syndrome children and ordinary children.

Method Children observed a scenario involving two puppet dolls, Sally and Ann. As the scenario developed Sally left her ball in a basket and went out. Whilst Sally was out, Ann moved Sally's ball from the basket to the box. Children were then questioned about where Sally would look for the ball when she returned. The correct answer 'Sally will look in the basket' requires an understanding of what Sally knows, or more importantly, what she does not know. The sample of autistic children ranged between 6 and 16 years of age with a mean verbal age of 5½ years, the Down's syndrome children were approximately the same chronological age but had lower verbal ability and the ordinary children had a mean age of 4½ years.

Result The researchers recorded the percentage of correct answers for each group of participants. The Down's syndrome group and the ordinary children gave the correct answer 85% of the time, whereas the children with autism gave the correct answer on only 20% of the trials.

Conclusion The autistic group's understanding of the scenario was fundamentally different to that of other two groups of children. Specifically, children with autism were much less able to put themselves in Sally's place and understand the way she represented the situation in her mind, supporting the view that children with autism do not have a theory of mind.

The **theory of mind** hypothesis (Baron-Cohen *et al.* 1993) accounted neatly for the highly selective nature of deficits in autistic children who are severely debilitated at tasks requiring an understanding of another person's mind (mind-reading), and yet largely unaffected in ability to perform many cognitive tasks. Leslie (1987) extended the theory of mind hypothesis proposing that there is an innate **Theory of Mind Mechanism (ToMM)** which is normally fully mature by about two years of age. According to Leslie, biological damage, either before or shortly after birth might interfere with the development of this mechanism and so lead to the cognitive impairments typically seen in children with autism.

EVALUATIVE COMMENT

What theory of mind could not explain was the exceptional ability often demonstrated by people with autism. Accounts of 'autistic savants' are often presented in literature and there are some fascinating cases of people with autism who can perform amazing mathematical feats or play any tune from beginning to end after hearing it just once. At a more general level, it is not unusual to see a child with autism complete a complex jigsaw at incredible speed, even with the puzzle upside down. Critics of the theory of mind hypothesis argue that it is an incomplete account of the cognitive processing in autistic people since it explains only the deficits and not the tendency to display special abilities.

Central coherence

Frith (1989) elaborated on the theory of mind hypothesis, proposing that both the deficits and exceptional skills shown in autism can be explained through a lack of **central coherence**. Central coherence is the tendency to process information for its general meaning rather than for the specific meaning of each element. For example, when we are presented with a story we process the overall meaning of the content rather than recall exactly the word for word content. Similarly, when listening to a piece of music we notice the melody and sing along to the tune rather than identifying every single note on each individual instrument. Thus, in any normal processing situation, we take account of the context and the purpose of the activity, processing for general meaning or gist and do not get sidetracked by minute details which are often of little overall consequence. Everyday use of central coherence can be easily demonstrated in the activity below.

PRACTICAL Activity

Complete each sentence given below by choosing the appropriate words in brackets.

The father was delighted to see his long lost . . .   (son/sun)

Carrie hungrily ate the juicy, ripe . . .   (pair/pear)

The car stopped suddenly as he put his foot on the . . .   (break/brake)

Of course, this task should present no difficulties for most people because they use the context of the sentence to decide which of the two words is correct. In other words, when we perform this task we use central coherence and make use of our general understanding of the world to help us.

If, as Frith proposes, people with autism lack central coherence, this would account for many detail-focused autistic behaviours and the apparent inability of people with autism to understand events and information in terms of global meaning and significance. For example, an autistic person might be able to identify and reproduce every note from a piece of music but would not be able to say whether it was a 'jolly' or a 'sad' piece.

A number of investigations confirm the tendency for people with autism to process without central coherence and detail-focused processing has been demonstrated in perceptual, visuo-spatial and verbal-semantic tasks.

1. Lack of perceptual central coherence has been shown in the decreased tendency for autistic people be fooled by visual illusions which rely on the surrounding context, for example, the Titchener circles illusion.

An interesting effect of lack of perceptual central coherence was demonstrated by Hobson *et al.* (1988) who found that autistic children seem to process faces through analysis of individual features rather than analysis of the whole. Since interpretation of emotional expression depends

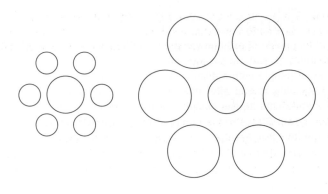

Figure 4.2: The Titchener circles: most people perceive the middle circle on the right to be smaller than the middle circle on the left, but people with autism tend to perceive the two middle circles as the same size

largely on the overall look of the face, Hobson's finding could account for the inability to determine emotional expression that is so typical of autistic people.

2. Visuo-spatial processing and central coherence

Study 4.3

Aim The role of central coherence in visuo-spatial processing was investigated by Shah and Frith (1993).

Method A group of people with autism and a control group were presented with a visuo-spatial block task of the type used in the Wechsler intelligence test. Participants were required to use a number of small patterned blocks to produce a geometric design.

Results The autism group performed exceptionally well in the block task, completing the puzzle satisfactorily and in less time than the control group.

Conclusion The inferior performance of the control group was attributed to their tendency to focus on, and be distracted by the final overall pattern, leading them to ignore the small elements of the component cubes which must be attended to if the problem is to be solved. Participants with autism on the other hand demonstrated a lack of central coherence, focusing on the detail rather than the whole. Whereas this would normally be a disadvantage, it was helpful for this task.

3. Central coherence in verbal-semantic processing is illustrated in the practical activity on page 97 and has been demonstrated in a number of studies. Memory research indicates that people with autism do not use meaning in memory tasks in the same way that other people do. For example, Hermelin and O'Connor (1967) showed how autistic people could recall lists of unconnected words just as well as they could recall sentences, whereas control groups fared much better with sentences than unconnected words. As Happe (1999) points out, this and findings from other verbal studies seem to indicate that reading a sentence may, for people with autism, be like reading a set of unconnected words.

Happe (1999) suggests that central coherence is best seen in terms of cognitive style or style of thought and as a continuum where some people are very strong on central coherence and

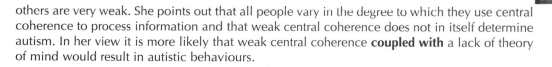

others are very weak. She points out that all people vary in the degree to which they use central coherence to process information and that weak central coherence does not in itself determine autism. In her view it is more likely that weak central coherence **coupled with** a lack of theory of mind would result in autistic behaviours.

REFLECTIVE Activity

It is interesting to think about central coherence as a general cognitive style. Are you a person who prefers to focus on detail, tending to forget the broader picture, or are you someone who thinks mostly in global terms and prefers not to spend too much time looking at finer detail? Think about different jobs that people do – accountant, supermarket manager, teacher, painter and decorator. Are some jobs more suited to people who show low central coherence and others more suitable for people who are high in central coherence?

EVALUATIVE COMMENT

Cognitive explanations for autism are not really explanations of cause as they merely elaborate on the precise nature of the cognitive differences between people with autism and non-sufferers. Whilst knowing exactly what information processing deficits and special talents are involved in autism is interesting, it remains for further research to determine the cause of these differences in processing.

Treatment of autism

DRUG THERAPY

Haloperidol has been used to treat the stereotypical movements and fidgetiness typical of autism. As a major tranquilliser also used in the treatment of schizophrenia, haloperidol is not recommended for treatment of autism unless a child's behaviour is unmanageable through other means (Sloman 1991). Fenfluramine, which acts to increase the activity of serotonin and decrease dopamine levels, has been used to increase attention span and decrease hyperactivity, but beneficial results are not consistent. Recent drug trials have involved the use of a synthetic hormone, secretin, thought to alleviate symptoms of autism and lead to improved language skills. However, Chez *et al.* (2000), using a double-blind procedure, found there to be no significant improvement in the group treated with secretin when compared to a placebo group. Drugs are generally given to control the symptoms of autism and are not in themselves a cure.

BEHAVIOUR THERAPY

Various behavioural techniques based on either operant or classical conditioning have been used to treat children with autism.

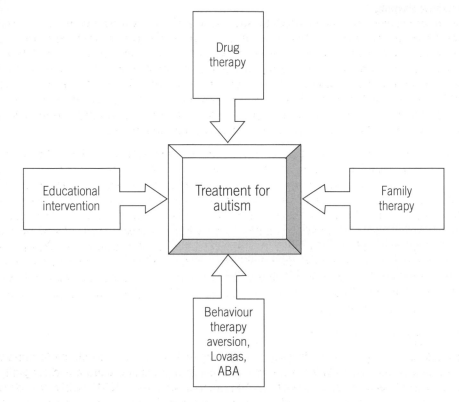

Figure 4.3: A summary of treatments for autism

Study 4.4

Aim Wolf *et al.* (1964) carried out a case study of a young boy with autism who had problems with verbal and social behaviour and engaged in self-destructive head banging behaviour.

Method The researchers monitored and documented the boy's progress as he underwent a **behaviour shaping** programme. A particular problem was his refusal to wear glasses without which his sight would not develop normally. The behaviour shaping programme was instituted involving a sweet as a reward, first for inspection of a toy, and then for inspection of the spectacle frames. Each time the child had to hold the frames nearer to his face for the reward, and finally he was rewarded only if the frames were on his head.

Result Through reward for successive approximations to the desired behaviour the child eventually learnt to wear his glasses.

Conclusion Operant conditioning techniques in the form of behaviour shaping can be used to successfully condition desired behaviour in children with autism.

1. Aversion therapy

Lovaas (1977) used electric shocks as an aversive stimulus in the case of extreme head banging behaviour in a 7-year-old boy with autism. The boy who had been diagnosed as severely mentally retarded was normally restrained for 24 hours a day to avoid injuring himself. After just a few sessions of aversion therapy the maladaptive behaviour ceased. Whilst there are obvious ethical issues related to the use of electric shocks in therapy it could be argued that the therapeutic procedure was necessary if it led to a reduction in self-injurious behaviour.

2. Behaviour shaping

Positive reinforcement has been used to successfully shape desired behaviour in children suffering from autism, most notably in what is known as the **Lovaas technique** for eliciting communication or language through the use of operant conditioning. Lovaas *et al.* (1967) used behaviour shaping principles, rewarding successive approximations to desired language in children with autism. Using food as positive reinforcement the child would be firstly rewarded for making eye-contact, then for any speech sound, then for particular vowel or consonant sounds and finally for the desired word or phrase. Although time-consuming this technique has been used frequently, both by therapists and parents of children with autism.

Recently the technique has been 're-invented' as **applied behavioural analysis (ABA)** which is used extensively in the USA. The key differences between ABA and the original Lovaas method are the intensity of application and the rigorously structured approach. Using ABA, children with autism undergo long periods of behaviour therapy, sometimes with several trainers working in shifts so that the child is being treated more or less continuously. New skills or behaviours are taught using direct instruction, repetition, and what is known as the 'hand over hand' method to keep the child's attention. Reinforcers can be social praise, edible treats or some other tangible reinforcer such as a toy. Incorrect or undesired behaviour receives a monotone 'no' from the trainer. Desired speech can also be taught through imitation of mouth movement and ABA can form part of a **token economy** programme. Although it is very popular with many parents there is much controversy about its success.

EVALUATIVE COMMENT

Many people consider aversion therapy and shaping techniques to be unethical because they involve control and manipulation. Leaving aside the ethical debate, there are other problems with the use of behavioural techniques to treat autism. As Gross (2001) points out, children treated using these methods are not magically transformed into 'normal' children and their behaviour often regresses once the treatment stops. Nevertheless, such approaches to treatment might enable children with autism and their parents to live easier lives than without the treatment, and for that reason alone, might be considered successful.

FAMILY THERAPY

Although some children with autism have been helped with behavioural treatments, one problem with these treatments is that any benefits tend to be lost when the treatment stops. Thus a child who has shown improved communication with a therapist in an institutional or therapeutic setting might revert to their original behaviour when they return to their family. Because behaviours learnt in a therapeutic context are not often generalised to other situations, efforts are made to encourage families of children with autism to be involved in the therapy themselves and impressive results have been found in projects that involve parents (Rutter 1985). Using contracts to clarify desired behaviour and outline the precise techniques that should be used to bring this about, parents can become actively involved in the implementation of the therapy.

EDUCATIONAL INTERVENTION

In an extensive study of socially unresponsive and behaviourally disturbed children with autism, Bartak and Rutter (1973) found that children following a structured therapy focused on formal schooling showed much improvement over children placed in play therapy programmes.

Stapleton (2001) summarises specific teaching strategies that might be effectively used with children with autism. These include the following:

- Presenting information in the concrete rather than the abstract and use of visuo-spatial materials where possible

- Presenting information in asocial contexts e.g. using computers to teach rather than teachers

- Organising classroom layout so that different areas become associated with different activities, allowing the child to feel in control of what happens when

- Making the environment predictable, giving the child a sense of routine and sameness

- Adopting a multi-sensory approach using all the five senses rather than just visual or auditory

- Providing opportunities for the child to share understanding with others

- Teachers learning from the student about how they can learn best and what are the best teaching strategies to use.

In an attempt to encourage symbolic play in children with autism, Christie and Wimpory (1986) devised a sensory therapeutic technique known as **communication therapy with synchronised music (CTSM)**. CTSM involves prolonged verbal interaction between the child and a familiar adult who imitates the child's vocalisations and actions. Sessions are accompanied by improvised music from a skilled musician in an effort to encourage turn-taking and social timing. This technique been shown to increase symbolic functioning and pretend play in children with autism.

PRACTICAL Activity

Summarise the four approaches to treatment of autism using a table. Try to think of one strength and one weakness for each approach. For example, a strength of family therapy might be that the family feel they have some control over what happens and that they can be effective in managing their child's behaviour.

4.3 Learning difficulties

The term 'learning difficulties' is used to mean that, either a child has significantly greater problems in learning than the majority of children of a similar age, or that the child requires different educational facilities to those normally provided because of some disability. Three main categories of learning difficulty are given in Diagnostic and Statistical Manual of Mental Disorders 1994.

Reading disorder	Usually referred to as dyslexia this accounts for 80% of all learning difficulties. Approximately 3–5% of the population suffer from dyslexia. Most estimates suggest that it affects boys more than girls.
Mathematical disorder	Dyscalculia is the mathematical equivalent of dyslexia and is thought to affect around 1% of the population. Dyscalculia is not generally recognised until a child is about 8-years-old.
Disorder of written expression	A very rare disorder in which writing skills are well below the norm for an individual of a particular age.

Figure 4.4: The three main categories of learning difficulty (DSM IV)

Defining and determining dyslexia

Snowling (1987) defines dyslexia as ' . . . a disorder manifested by difficulty in learning to read despite conventional instruction, adequate intelligence and socio-economic opportunity. It is dependent on fundamental cognitive difficulties which are frequently of constitutional origin'.

Letter reversal or rotation – the letter 'd' may be shown as 'b' or 'p'
Missing syllables – 'famel' for 'family'
Transposition of letters – 'brid' for 'bird'
Problems keeping place when reading
Problems pronouncing unfamiliar words

Figure 4.5: Features of dyslexic reading and spelling

From this and other definitions it is apparent that for a diagnosis of dyslexia to be made, we must be sure that there is no other explanation for the child's problems. In practice, psychological assessment usually involves testing both general intelligence and literacy skill. Where there is a significant discrepancy between literacy and intelligence this is taken as evidence of a specific learning difficulty.

According to DSM IV there are three criteria for the diagnosis of dyslexia:

- Reading achievement as measured by standard tests is substantially below that expected for a person's age, measured intelligence and education

- The reading difficulty significantly interferes with academic achievement or daily living activities

- The reading difficulty is in excess of that usually associated with any sensory deficit that might also be present.

The disorder affects the ability to recognise and process written symbols causing a number of learning difficulties in sufferers. In addition to having problems with spoken and written language, children with dyslexia often have difficulty performing mathematical functions, organising and ordering their work, and thinking in a logical way to enable planning ahead. Boder (1971) distinguishes between **dyseidetic** or surface dyslexics who read laboriously sounding out familiar as well as unfamiliar letter combinations, and **dysphonic** or whole-word dyslexics who can recognise a limited number of whole words by sight but have great difficulty analysing the component sounds of non-recognised words.

EVALUATIVE COMMENT

It has been suggested that the concept of dyslexia is now so widely applied to such diverse learning problems that it has become meaningless. Although having a label should allow the child access to specialist resources it might also have negative effects. Whittaker (1982) suggests that the label is unhelpful and leads to low expectations and possible limiting of effort on the part of the child, the family and teachers.

Causes of dyslexia

BIOLOGICAL EXPLANATIONS

Some studies into the origins of dyslexia have suggested a genetic component. Family research indicates that individuals have a greater likelihood of suffering from dyslexia if one or both parents have the disorder and Owen (1978) reported a concordance rate for monozygotic (identical) twins of 100%. Most other twin studies have reported lower rates of concordance, for example, Plomin et al. (1994) found monozygotic twins to be 70% concordant, whereas dizygotic twins were 40% concordant. Attempts to specify the mechanism for inheritance of dyslexia using genome scanning to identify the precise location of a dyslexia gene have led to the suggestion that a gene located on chromosome 18 is 'probably a general risk factor in dyslexia, influencing several reading-related processes' (Fisher et al. 2002). Fisher et al.'s results

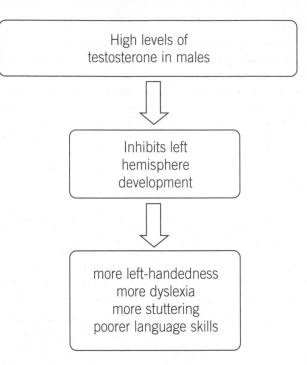

Figure 4.6: Is there a link between testosterone and dyslexia? (Geschwind and Galaburda 1985)

were based on combined analysis of two genome scans using large samples of UK and US families.

Carlson (1994) reports a number of studies showing that brain abnormalities may be responsible for cases of dyslexia. Postmortems of people with a history of dyslexia show that they have abnormalities in the planum temporale, part of Wernicke's area (see *Introducing psychology* (Pennington 2000) Chapter 2). In comparison to non-dyslexics whose cells are arranged in regular columns, the cells of people with autism show irregular arrangement. Scanning techniques have also confirmed that the planum temporale on the left side of the brain is much smaller in people with dyslexia than in non-sufferers.

Geschwind and Galaburda (1985) hypothesised that several behavioural and medical conditions, including dyslexia, are more prevalent in males due to increased levels of testosterone which inhibits development of the left side of the brain.

Study 4.5

Aim Geschwind and Behan (1984) set out to discover a link between left-handedness and dyslexia.

Method A group of left-handed people and a group of right-handed people were assessed for various behavioural and clinical conditions including learning difficulties and immune disorders such as diabetes and rheumatoid arthritis.

Results The left-handed participants were 10 times more likely to have specific learning disorders and 2½ times more likely to have immune disorders.

Conclusion The researchers suggested a causal link between left-handedness, dyslexia and disorders of the immune system, due perhaps to suppressed development of the left hemisphere.

COGNITIVE EXPLANATIONS

Children with dyslexia have consistently been found to have problems with processing speech sounds or phonemes. Such **phonological deficits** affect a child's ability to discriminate between speech sounds and the ability to articulate sounds clearly. Since learning to read involves matching written letters to speech sounds, it is not surprising that children who have trouble processing phonetic information also have problems learning to read. Stackhouse (2000) conducted a longitudinal study of children with speech difficulties and found that their level of auditory discrimination at 4 years was related to reading ability at 5 years, and again at 6 years. Stackhouse concluded that children with phonological disorders are most at risk of dyslexia and has noted that adults with dyslexia perform poorly on tests of articulation even though they have no obvious speech problems.

Study 4.6

Aim Bryant and Bradley (1985) reported the results of a longitudinal study testing the effects of phonological or sound awareness on subsequent reading ability.

Method Four hundred children who were not yet able to read were tested for memory, verbal intelligence and a phonological task. The phonological task involved listening to four spoken words, three of which were the same in some way, and identifying the odd one out. Sometimes the three similar words began with the same letter (alliteration) and sometimes they sounded the same (rhyme). Four years later, at the ages of 8 or 9 years, the children were tested again on the original task and those who could read were also assessed for their reading ability. Controlling for differences in intelligence the researchers correlated performances between the original measures and the tests aged 8 or 9 years.

Results Children who performed poorly on the original phonological awareness test were those who were finding reading difficult. Interestingly, there was no link between poor performance at the original test and other abilities such as mathematics.

Conclusion Reading ability is closely linked to the ability to distinguish sounds suggesting that dyslexia may be due to poor phonological awareness.

EVALUATIVE COMMENT

Short-term memory deficits have been observed in children with dyslexia and may be linked to their poor phonological awareness. However, studies using non-verbal stimuli tend to indicate that short-term memory in children with dyslexia is not significantly different to that of non-sufferers. For example, Holmes and McKeever (1979) found that poor readers and normal readers were no different at recalling faces but that the poor readers were significantly worse at a word recall task. This has led Bancroft (1995) to suggest that dyslexic poor performance at short-term memory tasks may be due to limited reading experience in contrast to the experience of a control group of average readers. Following this line of argument, Bancroft suggests that it is difficult to determine whether poor reading ability as seen in cases of dyslexia is a consequence of the disorder or, indeed, a cause of it.

BIOLOGICAL AND COGNITIVE EXPLANATIONS COMBINED

Children with dyslexia have sometimes been found to experience problems in visual perception tasks, leading to suggestions that a **visual perceptual deficit** might partly explain the disorder. Stein and Talcott (1999) found that people with dyslexia are much slower to recognise movement changes in a visual dot display than non-sufferers, with participants who had the poorest reading and spelling ability performing least well at the movement detection task. Stein and Talcott have proposed that dyslexia may be linked to defects in large nerve cells known as magna cells, which form part of the visual pathway from the retina to the visual cortex. The defect may explain why people with dyslexia have problems identifying written letters and words. Stein and Talcott's work has led to the development of a controversial and much disputed biological explanation for dyslexia, **magnocellular theory**.

EVALUATIVE COMMENT

There is really no consensus about what causes dyslexia although there is a widely held belief that at least a predisposition to the disorder is inherited. The debate about dyslexia neatly illustrates the different psychological perspectives in psychology. Note how cognitive explanations tend to focus on specifying the precise nature of the information-processing deficit, whilst the biological explanation focuses on the genetic and neurological mechanisms that might be involved. Although the existence of opposing views might be looked upon as profound disagreement, these two viewpoints are best considered as complementary rather than contradictory.

Treatment of dyslexia

Since children with dyslexia have such a potentially wide range of difficulties and the level of difficulty each child experiences is quite individual, approaches to remediation can also vary considerably. Selikowitz (1998) has summarised useful strategies in three categories:

PRACTICAL Activity

Contact someone who has a child at primary school and ask to have a look at the child's school books. Explain to the parent that you are interested in ways of teaching children to read, write and spell and they probably will not mind. Look at the way the child is being taught to form letters and whether the child is making any mistakes. Then try to remember what it was like when you learnt to read and write. Many of you will recall trouble with shaping letters and getting similar letters confused.

Hornsby and Shear's (1976) Alpha-to-Omega scheme is an example of a highly structured multi-sensory approach that has been particularly successful in treating dyslexia. The pupil is taught step-by-step, beginning with single letter sounds linked to letter names and letter shapes. Pupils then progress to learning single syllable words followed by complex multisyllabic words. Teaching drills are multi-sensory using sight and hearing to write and read. Other techniques include the 'whole word' approach and LOOK, COVER, WRITE, CHECK (Snowling 1985).

Spelling difficulties	For phonetic errors the child should be taught how to break words down into constituent parts matching the sound to the written symbol. For lexical errors (e.g. confusing 'brake' for 'break') use tasks to encourage visual memory for whole words.
Reading difficulties	Use structured phonic schemes e.g. alpha-to-omega and Orton-Gillingham-Stillman, where sounds are taught first, and then words.
Writing difficulties	The child should be taught to sit and hold the pen correctly. Writing should be approached in three stages, firstly using completely separate letters, then using precursive letters (letters with tails that will lead eventually to joined writing) and finally, using cursive or joined-up writing.

Figure 4.7: Techniques for overcoming the difficulties of dyslexia (Selikowitz 1998)

Dyscalculia and other learning difficulties

Dyscalculia is a learning difficulty affecting mathematical performance. Sufferers frequently have normal or advanced language skills but experience problems with mathematical processes such as addition, subtraction, and dealing with money. People with the disorder often have a poor sense of direction, poor map reading skills and problems with abstract concepts like time. Specific mathematical deficits include substitutions, reversals and omissions. Remedial recommendations include making maths relevant, for example, giving the child responsibility for counting out the right number of question sheets for the class. Maths problems should be written on large squared paper to keep numbers properly aligned and the pupil should be encouraged to write down the rules for a new theory or process.

Dyspraxia involves problems with fine and/or gross motor co-ordination leading to problems with physical activities in subjects like science and physical education. Many people with dyspraxia have poor understanding of mathematical concepts and experience problems understanding symbols. Pupils are encouraged to write on alternate lines and benefit from a multi-sensory approach to teaching.

Dysgraphia is a disorder of writing which can involve the physical aspects of writing, for example, pencil grip and angle. It might also involve poor spelling and difficulties transferring thoughts to paper. Use of computers has helped people with dyspraxia considerably but other useful strategies include use of a tape recorder to record ideas and the option of oral reporting in examinations.

4.4 Gifted children

Defining and determining giftedness

Many people would consider Arran Fernandez to be an exceptional child. He has certainly demonstrated unusual mathematical ability for his age, but is he gifted? According to Bee (1992) giftedness might be defined as '. . . very high IQ (above 140–150), but may also be defined in terms of remarkable skill in one or more specific areas, such as mathematics or memory'. Bee's definition illustrates the problematic nature of defining giftedness as she essentially offers two alternatives: generally high intelligence or outstanding skill in a very specific area.

REFLECTIVE Activity

Think of someone you know who you believe is gifted, and consider them in relation to Bee's definition. Would you say the person you have chosen is exceptionally intelligent in a general way, or do they have a clearly identifiable skill that sets them apart from other people?

Historically we have identified people like Darwin and Mozart as gifted because they have made exceptional contributions to science or the arts. Taking this definition, it would be unlikely that most of us would know anyone gifted so perhaps it might be sensible to include in a definition of giftedness the 'potential for excellence'.

The notion of potential as a factor in giftedness raises the question of how to test for that potential ability and leads to the use of IQ scores in determining giftedness. Most educationalists regard children with a high IQ as gifted. However, Robinson (1981) argued for a distinction between the 'garden variety gifted' who have high IQs between 130 and 150 but no exceptional ability in a specific area, and the 'highly gifted' with exceptionally high IQ and/or extraordinary skill in one or more areas.

Arran Fernandez who passed his GCSE maths when he was five

Study 4.7

Aim Terman (1925–59) began a longitudinal study of a group of highly intelligent children in 1921 with the aim of investigating long-term outcomes.

Method 643 10-year-olds, with an average IQ score of 151 on the Stanford-Binet intelligence test were identified and systematically studied for over 30 years. They were assessed for intelligence, physical and motor ability, language skills, motivation and their key life achievements were recorded.

Results Follow-up assessment at age 35 years showed that the high level of intelligence had been maintained. Sixty-eight per cent of the sample were graduates and many were outstanding in their chosen field. In 1959, when the participants were 48 years old 71% were in professional or managerial positions and their average income was substantially higher than the average for college graduates.

Conclusion Terman concluded that giftedness stems from the ability to make sensitive and appropriate judgements in all manner of problem solving situations and that this ability can be captured in an IQ score.

EVALUATIVE COMMENT

Terman seems to have suggested that IQ is stable over time and can be used to predict who will show remarkable achievement. However, although Terman's extensive study yielded much interesting and informative data, the results require cautious interpretation. First, the promising children were selected by their teachers and these same teachers were involved in the early assessments of their ability. Second, most of the sample came from white, middle-class families and so experienced above average nutrition and an encouraging social environment, both of which may have contributed to their life-long outcomes. Third, there was no comparison of outcomes for a control group of children with average IQs. According to Winner (1998), Terman's study has led to a belief that all highly intelligent children are happy, well-adjusted and have hugely successful lives. As we shall see this may not always be the case.

The idea that giftedness can be determined from a single IQ score rests on the assumption that it is possible and meaningful to determine a person's intelligence using an IQ test, in itself a controversial issue. Leaving aside the validity of IQ testing, it is of greater present concern to ask whether or not a single test or a number of separate tests should be used to determine giftedness. Many researchers have suggested that giftedness is not a unitary phenomenon that can be determined from a single IQ test score.

The idea of multiple talents led to recognition amongst the US educationalists that children could be seen as gifted if they showed exceptional ability or potential in any/or a combination of the following domains: general intellectual ability; specific academic aptitude; creative or productive thought; leadership; visual or performing arts; psychomotor ability.

Gardner's theory of **multiple intelligences** (1983) acknowledges that all normal individuals can be expected to achieve a measure of competence in at least six separate areas. Ultimate achievement will vary from person to person according to factors such as heredity and environment. Whilst every normal person possesses a unique blend of these intelligences, gifted individuals tend have superior ability in one domain. Gardner's view of domain specific giftedness is very different to the original broad construct IQ approach of Terman.

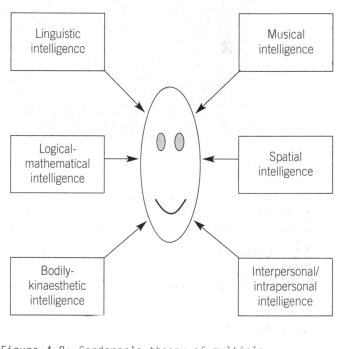

Figure 4.8: Gardener's theory of multiple intelligences

PRACTICAL Activity

Look at the names of the famous people below, each successful in their chosen field. Now rate them for intelligence on a scale of 1–5 referring separately to each of Gardner's multiple intelligences. You will have six ratings for each person. Do your ratings confirm that it is possible to be exceptional in some areas and fairly ordinary or even quite poor in others? How does this activity relate to the idea of giftedness as either a broad intellectual ability or a special talent?

David Beckham

Sir Paul McCartney

Tony Blair

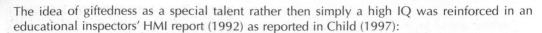

The idea of giftedness as a special talent rather then simply a high IQ was reinforced in an educational inspectors' HMI report (1992) as reported in Child (1997):

> **The majority of educationalists working in this field accept criteria which include general intellectual ability, specific aptitude in one or more subjects, creative or productive thinking, leadership qualities, ability in creative or performing arts and psychomotor ability. The term 'very able' is intended to refer broadly to the top 5% of the ability range in any of these areas, while the term 'exceptionally able' refers to that tiny minority . . . functioning several years beyond their age group.**

Renzulli (1986) suggested a three-ringed model of giftedness according to which giftedness should be characterised not just by ability, but also by additional factors such as motivation and task commitment. A study by Bloom (1985) seems to bear this out. Bloom identified 25 high achievers under the age of 25 years and investigated the background to their achievement. Extensive interviews revealed that although their special talents had been recognised at an early age, they had reached their exceptional level of achievement only after years of intensive hard work and practice. Critics of Renzulli's emphasis on motivation and determination as key factors in giftedness point to the many cases of academically gifted but underachieving children, those children whose extreme ability does not translate into eventual academic achievement.

MATHEMATICAL GIFTEDNESS

Exceptional ability in the mathematical domain is usually determined by a checklist such as Straker's (1983) *Mathematics for Gifted Pupils*, which specifies a number of characteristics. Taken together these ways of thinking demonstrated by mathematically gifted children might be seen as a more general ability to think in the abstract rather than the concrete.

Ability to grasp the essence of a problem at once
Ability to generalise mathematical material rapidly and with ease
Tendency to skip over intermediate steps in a procedure or logical argument
Preference for an elegant rather than merely functional solution
Ability to reverse the train of thought e.g. working backwards from a solution to a formula
Ability to recognise and remember relationships and principles in a problem rather than the specific details

Figure 4.9: Checklist for the mathematically gifted

MUSICAL GIFTEDNESS

Musical intelligence is the ability to use a fundamental set of musical elements, such as pitch, tone and rhythm. Whilst it is perhaps quite easy to recognise musical intelligence in an individual, it is very difficult to define. Rooted in emotion and pleasure and often associated with intense experience, music and musical talent do not lend themselves easily to assessment. One attempt to measure musical intelligence is the Bentley Test for Music (1966) which involves assessment of four areas: pitch discrimination, tonal memory, rhythmic memory and chord analysis.

Case histories of mathematically or musically gifted people often indicate that, although they have a predisposing ability and are aware of it, the fulfilment of their talent arises from a single momentous event or what Gardner (1983) refers to as a 'crystallising moment'. For example, the composer Debussy (1812–1918), although a competent young musician, showed no interest in composition until he was introduced to the work of Wagner. Inspired by Wagner's opera, Debussy went on to realise his creative potential through composition.

EVALUATIVE COMMENT

Cases such as Debussey's seem to support the 'talent' view of giftedness, suggesting that giftedness is almost accidental. This explanation for giftedness contrasts sharply with the view that gifted children achieve highly only as a result of years of regimented and intense instruction or '*hot-housing*'. Howe (1999) argues that the 'talent' account of giftedness as an innate potential is unsupported by the evidence, and that exceptionally able children achieve as a result of their early experience, opportunities, training and practice. Furthermore he points out that those people who achieve exceptional things are often doggedly determined, persistent and hardworking.

Giftedness and information processing

Gifted people have been found to have specific information processing strategies. They learn quickly, transfer knowledge and skills to new situations with ease, are very aware of their own cognitive ability (**meta-cognitive awareness**), and process information flexibly. Sternberg (1988) proposed a theory of intelligence which can be used to explain the differences between gifted and non-gifted individuals and to determine ways of identifying giftedness. According to Sternberg intelligence has three components:

Is exceptional musical talent the result of an innate predisposition or the product of many years of instruction and practice?

- **Componential Intelligence** consists of what is normally measured in IQ tests, for example remembering facts and procedures and being able to adapt them to solve problems. Five aspects of componential intelligence have been identified:

1. Metacomponents – higher order executive processes used in planning and decision making. Metacognitive ability includes awareness of one's own ability and understanding of what cognitive strategies are effective. According to Bee (2000), gifted children seem to have a keen awareness of their own cognitive skills and what they do and do not know.

2. Performance components – processes involved in carrying out a cognitive task, for example, perceiving elements of the problem and making a response.

3. Knowledge-acquisition components – processes involved in acquiring knowledge, for example, choosing what is relevant and what is irrelevant, or combining information in an integrated and meaningful way with previously stored information. This ability to acquire and organise knowledge equates to insight, which is much more evident in the problem solving ability of the gifted.

4. Retention components – the ability to recall information from memory as required. Gifted chess players have been found to have exceptional memory for moves and chess positions because they use chunking to encode the information, thus optimising the capacity of short-term memory (Chase and Simon 1973).

5. Transfer components – the ability to generalise information from one task or context to another.

• **Experiential Intelligence** refers to the ability to process information automatically and deal with novel tasks and situations – both of which would arise out of practice and experience. Gifted children show much greater ability to use automatic processing and so can use more of their conscious processing capacity to cope with novelty. Therefore, according to Sternberg, intelligence should be assessed through tasks that are unfamiliar but not totally alien to one's experience. Using such tasks Davidson and Sternberg (1985) found that gifted children were better able to deal with novel tasks alone whereas non-gifted children required extra instruction. The interplay between automatic processing and novel task demands can be understood if we take the example of a gifted reader who devotes little conscious attention to the process of reading, and so has more cognitive capacity for rapid processing of the content of the text.

• **Contextual intelligence** refers to the ability to direct intelligent activity and process information according to the demands of the situation and context. In normal circumstances a highly intelligent person would adapt his or her behaviour to 'fit in' with the demands of the situation and what other people expect. However, there might also be times when it is inappropriate to adapt to unreasonable requirements of others and therefore contextual intelligence can be used to re-shape the environment to increase the fit between it and the individual. If the individual cannot adapt and cannot shape the environment then contextual intelligence may be used to enable selection of an alternative environment.

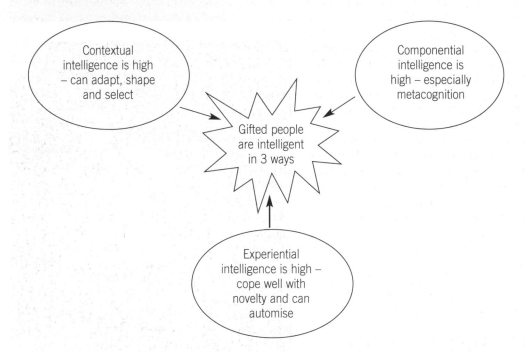

Figure 4.10: Key features of Sternberg's triarchic theory of intelligence as they relate to giftedness

REFLECTIVE Activity

Explore your contextual intelligence:

Imagine you work for a large company, a bank perhaps.

What sorts of situations would arise where you would need to use contextual intelligence?

How might you adapt to the work environment?

When would you resort to shaping rather than adapting to the work environment?

What would you do if adaptation and shaping proved unsatisfactory solutions to a problem at work?

EVALUATIVE COMMENT

Sternberg's theory provides a broad basis for understanding the complexities of gifted behaviour, offering an information processing explanation both for moderate and also high levels of giftedness. The theory also has implications for the measurement of intellectual giftedness suggesting that measures should: test the specified components and especially metacomponents of intelligence; allow for the demonstration of automatised responses in novel situations; include tasks which are context appropriate.

Social and emotional development of gifted children

Terman's longitudinal study (1925–59) emphasised the positive long-term outcomes for high achievers but not all research suggests that children identified as gifted are socially and emotionally well adjusted. Most studies of the social and emotional development of gifted children have focused on the moderately gifted, who tend to show normal or above average levels of self-esteem and no greater incidence of depression than non-gifted children. However, Winner (1998) suggests that extremely precocious and highly gifted individuals are twice as likely to suffer from emotional and social problems as ordinary children and that academically gifted girls are even more at risk. Where a child is extremely gifted with, say an IQ of 180, a 6-year-old would be on an intellectual level with an average 11-year-old and a gifted child at 11 would be similar intellectually to the average 'A' level student. It therefore follows that if gifted children are amongst their age peers, they will, of necessity, be highly unusual, and be likely to have difficulties in social adjustment.

REFLECTIVE Activity

Think about the differences between 6-year-old and 11-year-old children. What are the interests of the two age groups? What do they talk about? What do they know about the world? Considering these issues we realise just how difficult it must be for a highly gifted child to 'fit-in' with people of their own age.

Michael Jackson showed exceptional ability at a very early age. How has this extraordinary talent affected his social and emotional development?

Studies of social adjustment of highly gifted children confirm they show significantly greater incidence of feelings of isolation and rejection (Sheldon 1959 – IQ over 170) and limited social acceptance by others (Gallagher 1958 – IQ over 165). A sub-group of very high IQ children (over 170) identified in Terman's longitudinal study were reported in follow-up interviews with teachers and parents to be 'solitary' and 'poor mixers'. However, Terman suggested that this was not particularly because they had been rejected by their age peers, but rather because the children preferred to spend time alone. Terman suggested that most gifted children are fairly well adjusted but that children with exceptionally high IQs of around 180 and above can suffer severe social isolation.

Study 4.8

Aim Janos (1983) set out to compare the psychosocial development of very high IQ children and children of average intelligence.

Method Thirty-two children aged 6–9 years with IQs of over 164 were compared with 49 moderately intelligent children on measures such as academic performance, social isolation/integration, motivation, etc.

Results Janos found that the high IQ group were rated more highly for academic performance but fared less well on all the other measures.

Conclusion Very high IQ children do have problems in psychosocial development in relation to peers of average IQ. However, although the high IQ group showed greater social isolation, Janos found that the isolation was not of a clinical disturbance type, but rather simply due to absence of friends of a similar age to whom the child could relate.

The Janos study above suggests that social and emotional problems in gifted children are largely a result of their loneliness and isolation. Not surprisingly, gifted children, with their extraordinary intellectual ability, tendency to think in the abstract rather than the concrete, sophisticated moral reasoning and play interests are unlikely to find suitable companionship amongst age peers. Hollingworth (1942) argued that where exceptionally gifted children who have been rejected by children of a similar age are allowed to interact with intellectual peers, their problems of isolation and loneliness disappear.

Study 4.9

Aim Hollingworth (1942) investigated school experiences and long-term outcomes in children with very high IQs.

Method Data from various assessments of two groups of very high IQ children (over 180) were collated and analysed. Twelve of the children were studied by Hollingworth in a longitudinal study lasting 23 years. The rest of the sample consisted of 19 children studied by other researchers.

Result Children within the IQ range of 125–155 were identified as of 'socially optimal intelligence' and were well balanced, confident and enjoyed rewarding friendships with age peers. However, children with an IQ of over 160 were found to have special problems of social isolation, particularly between the ages of 4 and 9.

Conclusion Hollingworth concluded that the difficulties faced by extremely high IQ children occurred because they were so different to their age peers, but equally importantly, because the school failed to recognise and respond to their special needs. Such children, unlike children at the opposite end of the intellectual spectrum, do not disrupt the smooth functioning of the school and therefore do not appear to require any special attention. According to Hollingworth 'Society attends to that which is socially annoying'.

EVALUATIVE COMMENT

A school's failure to recognise and respond to the special intellectual requirements of a gifted child may result in underachievement because (a) the work is unstimulating and insufficiently challenging or (b) of a deliberate attempt to become more acceptable to age peers. Despite these problems, the majority of gifted children are often taught in class levels several years below their tested ability.

Giftedness as a special need

If some of the social and emotional problems that affect gifted children arise out of their school experiences it is important to consider how giftedness is managed, both in school and in society in general. Some researchers have argued that teachers often fail to understand and respond appropriately to highly gifted children, suggesting that this failure might lead not just to loneliness but also to problems such as delinquency, refusal to learn and dropping out of school (Torrance 1970). If this is correct then gifted children should be seen as having special needs in just the same way as children at the opposite end of the ability spectrum.

Three aspects of managing giftedness will be considered:

- Identification

- Special provision within the curriculum

- Extra-curricular provision.

First, however, the importance of sensitive management for gifted children can be emphasised through consideration of a longitudinal study of 15 highly gifted Australian children which showed how they often have very negative school experiences which impact on their social and emotional well-being (Gross 1993). Gross undertook a detailed and extensive investigation using analysis of school documents, observations, psychometric testing, measures of self-esteem and moral development, and interviews/questionnaires with parents. Five main findings emerged:

- Gifted children were very aware of the differences between themselves and their age peers – an awareness they found highly depressing and de-motivating

- The children knew they were disliked and rejected by other children leading to a negative effect on their self-concept

- The children faced a conflict between their need for intellectual achievement and their desire to be accepted by others, which often resulted in the deliberate sacrifice of attainment for peer acceptance

- Those who had been accelerated in school to be taught with intellectual rather than age peers scored much better on measures of self-esteem than those who remained with age peers

- Some of the children were identified as suffering from depression during the study and not every case of depression was alleviated by grade acceleration.

IDENTIFYING GIFTED CHILDREN

Teachers quite often have difficulties identifying gifted children. Most checklists for identification are more appropriate for the moderately gifted, who generally have fewer adjustment problems anyway, and tend to focus on positive rather than negative aspects of behaviour. Richert *et al.* (1982) found that exceptionally gifted children were particularly at risk of non-identification. Parents are probably better placed to be able to identify their child as gifted because almost as soon as a gifted child starts formal education they tend to hide their giftedness in order to fit in with the other children, and their special ability is often translated into 'fooling around' and generally misbehaving. Gross (1993) found that two-thirds of the sample she studied could walk independently before their first birthday, said their first word at 9.7 months on average and could read before they were 3 years old. Despite the fact that many parents were keenly aware of their child's exceptional ability before the child started school, Gross also found that they chose not to stress their child's ability to the teacher for fear of appearing 'pushy', and that those who did were often disbelieved.

PRACTICAL Activity

Ask your parents how old you were when you first walked independently and said your first word. Most children reach these developmental milestones when they are 15 months and 12 months respectively. Ask parents who have young children whether they think their child is advanced for their age, and for school-aged children whether or not they have discussed this with the child's teacher.

Whilst parents may be the key to early identification of giftedness, problems have been found to arise where parents themselves have labelled the child as 'gifted'.

Study 4.10

Aim Freeman (1979) set out to investigate the effects of parental attitude to giftedness.

Method Three groups of 70 children aged between 5 and 16 years were compared: Group 1 (gifted parentally identified GPI) had been identified by the parents as gifted; Group 2 (gifted control GC) were matched with the GPI group for intelligence, sex, school and age but had not been labelled by their parents as gifted; Group 3 (control C) were matched with GC for all variables except their IQ which was average. All participants were tested for IQ and social adjustment and parents and teachers were interviewed about behaviour and background. Parents were also asked about their own attitudes to the child and to education.

Results Parents of the GPI group rated their children as more difficult and as having fewer friends in comparison to parents of the two control groups. Teacher ratings confirmed that the GPI children had problems making friends and were more withdrawn or aggressive in class. Home investigations revealed that parents of the GPI group provided stimulating and encouraging environments, but sometimes put undue pressure on their children.

Conclusion Problems experienced by highly intelligent children were not due to their exceptional ability but were related to the way the children were handled and parental expectations.

Ruth Lawrence was a mathematical prodigy whose father was accused of 'hot-housing' and pushing her to achieve

The Freeman study appears to show it is the label 'gifted' that brings problems, rather than the giftedness per se. Labelling can have profound consequences because any label brings with it certain expectations that influence the way people treat the 'gifted' child. In addition to school experiences it is undoubtedly the case that a child's home experiences and parental beliefs will affect how they cope with their giftedness.

SPECIAL PROVISION WITHIN THE CURRICULUM

Van Tassel-Baska (1989) identified several elements essential to the success of gifted children including **acceleration** and **enrichment**. Acceleration refers to the progression of a child through school at a faster than usual pace, either through content area acceleration or, more usually, through class or grade skipping. Enrichment refers to the provision of activities and opportunities beyond the established school programme, planned with the needs and interests of a particular student or group of students in mind.

A number of studies have shown that children normally benefit from acceleration rather than suffer as a result of it. Richardson and Benbow (1990) compared a sample of 1237 accelerated children with a control group of gifted children who had not been accelerated and found that only 5% reported any negative effect of acceleration. Positive effects of acceleration were evident in **meta-analysis** data from 26 studies showing that gifted accelerated students out-performed controls academically (Kulik and Kulik 1984). Children also seem to benefit from acceleration aspirationally, motivationally and socially. Terman and Oden (1947) found that young children once rejected by older children with whom they wished to play became accepted into the older age group when they were moved up into the same class. Gross (1993) asserted that acceleration does not make children conceited and helps them avoid the anger, frustration and dismay at having to progress at a slower pace than they would like.

EVALUATIVE COMMENT

Although radical acceleration to be with children who share the same intellectual abilities appears to be a successful way to deal with the problems faced by gifted children, there is a general reluctance on the part of schools to accelerate. One argument against school acceleration is that it is unkind to deny a child ordinary childhood experiences and that, whatever their intellectual level, children need play and social experiences appropriate for their chronological age if they are to develop normally (AEP June 1998). In practice, some children are accelerated perhaps a year, or maybe occasionally two years. More frequently, children identified by schools as 'gifted and talented' are provided with extra educational experiences or enrichment to help develop their potential for greater achievement.

Study 4.11

Aim Stanley and Benbow (1983) set out to investigate the effectiveness of an enrichment programme for the mathematically gifted.

Method Children showing unusually high ability on the mathematical component of the US Scholastic Aptitude test attended a summer school where they received tuition in complex mathematical skills including university level calculus. They also had classes in languages and science.

Results Various benefits were recorded, including a more positive attitude, enhanced self-esteem and reduction in feelings of superiority. The participating children were also highly successful at gaining admission to competitive universities.

Conclusion Gifted children can benefit substantially from well-managed and appropriate enrichment programmes.

Enrichment programmes have been found to benefit gifted children only where they are designed to extend and develop the child's academic and intellectual talents. Critics of enrichment programmes point out that they are often simply 'more of the same' and have little purpose other than to keep the quick working child busy. To be of significant value, enrichment should have clear objectives, provide for excitement of learning and lead to an advancement in thinking.

EXTRA-CURRICULAR PROVISION

Lewis (1995) advocates a whole-child approach to managing gifted children in which he states that there is little point in special school programmes for gifted children if parents have no involvement in their child's special status. He stresses that the gifted children should be considered a child first and a gifted child second, thereby emphasising the importance of as normal experience as possible for the gifted child. He also asserts that gifted children should not be pressured to achieve because to do so negates any intrinsic reward or pleasure in the achievement. Finally, choice of school should be influenced by the school's attitude to giftedness.

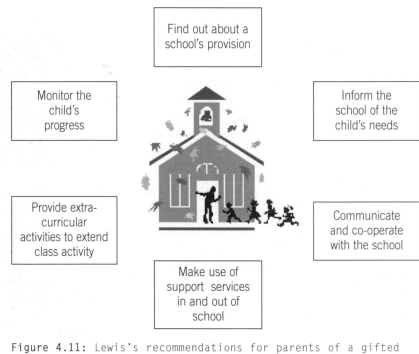

Find out about a school's provision

Monitor the child's progress

Inform the school of the child's needs

Provide extra-curricular activities to extend class activity

Communicate and co-operate with the school

Make use of support services in and out of school

Figure 4.11: Lewis's recommendations for parents of a gifted child (1995)

Lewis suggests that parents can be effective through establishing a network for enrichment and operating a mentor system. Out of school activities could include workshops and excursions, with mentoring aimed at fostering individual talent for those who were not catered for sufficiently at school. Mentors would not necessarily be teachers but would be knowledgeable and skilled individuals who could form a one-to-one relationship with a gifted child. Lewis describes the mentor as a 'specialist guide', a person with whom a child can share a deep interest or talent. Freeman (1997) argues against the use of amateur help for gifted children, asserting that it is important to train teachers to provide the level of education needed in schools.

PRACTICAL Activity

Ask people you know about whether they ever had any special tutoring when they were young. Did they, for example, have a music teacher for the piano or did they go to dancing lessons? Were they particularly good at sports and did they benefit from extra coaching at swimming, gymnastics or football? How many of the people you have talked to who had extra tuition in their chosen field when they were young have turned out to be exceptionally talented in that area? How many of them would recall their specialist tutor as a mentor and particular influence in their lives?

EVALUATIVE COMMENT

Reading about exceptional development we see that children with extraordinary talent require special consideration just as much as children with learning disabilities. Parents of any children, whether gifted or learning disabled are faced with many choices about what is best for their child. The task for psychologists is to understand the behaviour of these exceptional children so that parents, teachers and society are better able to cater for their needs.

4.5 Sample questions

SAMPLE QUESTION 1

(a) Outline *two* behaviours that might be demonstrated by a child with autism.
    (AO1 = 4, AO2 = 0) *(4 marks)*

(b) Outline and briefly discuss *one* treatment for autism.
    (AO1 = 2, AO2 = 2) *(4 marks)*

(c) Discuss at least *one* explanation for autism.
    (AO1 = 4, AO2 – 8) *(12 marks)*

(Total marks AO1 = 10, AO2 = 10)

QUESTIONS, ANSWERS AND COMMENTS

SAMPLE QUESTION 2

(a) Suggest *one* possible cause of a named learning difficulty.
    (AO1 = 1, AO2 = 2) *(3 marks)*

(b) Describe *one* study in which the cause of a learning difficulty was investigated.
    (AO1 = 5, AO2 = 0) *(5 marks)*

(c) Discuss the social and emotional effects of giftedness.
    (AO1 = 4, AO2 = 8) *(12 marks)*

(Total marks AO1 = 10, AO2 = 10)

Answer to 2(a)

One learning difficulty is dyslexia and psychologists are arguing about what causes it. A cause that seems to be important is the lack of sound awareness in recognising speech sounds. Others have said the trouble might be due to biological brain deficits.

Comment: 1 mark for knowledge of the possible cause and another mark for analysis via the reference to another possible explanation. A further AO2 mark could have been gained by further expansion on 'sound awareness'. Note that the instruction 'suggest' usually requires both knowledge and analysis.

Answer to 2(b)

One study investigating dyslexia was carried out by Bryant who followed a large number of children over a long period to see whether their language skills would be normal or not. He tested the children before they could read to see whether they were good at recognising rhymes and similar sounding words. When they went to school he tested them again and found that those who were good at sound recognition when they were young were better readers. Bryant concluded there was a link between sound awareness and reading ability.

Comment: This answer gets 3 marks out of a possible 5. The aim is incorrect and details of the method/results are somewhat limited.

Answer to 2(c)

Giftedness can bring many problems for a child and family. A study by Freeman in 1979 showed how parents treat their child differently if they had decided for themselves that the child was gifted. Parents of the children concerned had all joined the Association for Gifted Children. These children were compared with two control groups and it was found that the parent-identified children were less well adjusted than the children in the other two groups. Freeman suggested that these parents were 'pushy' parents, not allowing their children normal development.

Whether parents play a role or not there are other findings that gifted children are less emotionally secure than non-gifted children. Hollingworth suggests this is due to their being very different to normal children in their interests and abilities. This big difference means that gifted children who have to stay with children of their own age have little in common with their classmates. Terman's extensive Termites study found that children with IQs over 170 were described by teachers and parents as lonely and poor mixers, but this might be because they had no one similar with whom they could interact. One estimate from Winner suggests that gifted children are twice as likely to suffer from emotional problems as other children and girls are especially likely to have problems. Hollingworth found that social isolation caused problems for those between 4 and 9 years in particular.

One problem with much of the research on giftedness is that samples tend to be very limited. Usually they are longitudinal studies so it is simply impossible for the researchers to study many children. Because samples are so small care should be taken not to generalise the results too widely, however, when studying exceptional children it is unlikely that there will ever be a big sample because there are just so few of them. Another methodological problem in this area is the lack of a control group in some studies.

Taking the research as a whole it seems that moderately gifted children show reasonably normal social and emotional development, with only the highly gifted children at real risk of being maladjusted. The problems may not be just because they are gifted but more likely because their giftedness is not handled correctly. Gross (1993) carried out a detailed investigation revealing problems such as low self-concept and lack of motivation could be helped if highly intelligent children were moved up in school so they could be taught alongside children of the same intelligence. This seems to be a suitable option if extremely intelligent children are to avoid social and emotional problems although it did not seem to help with children suffering depression. However accelerated schooling and enrichment can bring problems and many teachers and educational psychologists do not support it.

Comment: This part of the answer is awarded 11 out of 12 marks. The answer is well organised and focused on the question. The candidate is awarded 4 AO1 marks for a good awareness of research in the area and for clearly identifying lots of examples of social and emotional difficulties. There is competent evaluation and analysis, for example, the understanding in the final paragraph that the problems may not be due just to being gifted but may also be due to the way the giftedness is managed, and the awareness about the argument over acceleration. In all 7 out of 8 AO2 marks were awarded.

Overall mark: *16/20 (AO1 = 8, AO2 = 8)*

4.6 FURTHER READING

Introductory texts

Bancroft, D. & Carr, R. 1995: **Influencing children's development**. Blackwell, Oxford.

Bee, H. 2000: **The developing child**. 9th Ed. Allyn and Bacon, Boston.

Gross, R. D. 2001: **Psychology, the science of mind and behaviou**r. 4th Ed. Hodder and Stoughton, London.

Harris, M. & Butterworth, G. 2002: **Developmental psychology: a student's handbook**. Psychology Press, Hove.

Specialist sources

Baron-Cohen, S. & Bolton, P. 1993: **Autism the facts**. Oxford University Press, Oxford.

Frith, U. 1989: **Autism: explaining the enigma**. Blackwell, Oxford.

Gross, M. 1993: **Exceptionally gifted children**. Routledge, London.

Lewis, D. 1995: **Bringing up your talented child**. Harper Collins, Sydney.

Snowling, M. J. 2000: **Dyslexia**. 2nd Ed. Blackwell, Oxford.

Stapleton, M. 2001: **Psychology in practice, education**. Hodder and Stoughton, London.

5

The behaviourist perspective

5.1 Introduction

Give me a dozen healthy infants, well-formed, and my own specific world to bring them up in, and I'll guarantee to take any one at random and train him to become any type of specialist I may select – doctor, lawyer, artist, merchant-chief, and yet, even beggar man and thief, regardless of his talents, penchants, tendencies, abilities, vocations, and race of his ancestors.   (Watson 1930: 104)

This famous quotation was made by one of the most important founding fathers of the behaviourist perspective in psychology. As you can see from the quotation, Watson took an extreme position, called **radical behaviourism**, towards learning in humans: that all learning comes from experience. For the radical behaviourist, biology or nurture has an insignificant influence on how people behave and what they do in their lives.

Not all psychologists working within a behaviourist perspective adopt such an extreme position, as we shall see later in this chapter. However, all seek to provide a theory of how learning, in both humans and other animals, takes place and how behaviour can be changed.

Watson was the founding father of behaviourism and developed a radical behaviourist approach

Learning may be defined as follows:

any relatively permanent change in the behaviour, thoughts and feelings of an organism that results from prior experience.

Note that this definition would not be acceptable to radical behaviourists such as Watson, since it refers to thoughts and feelings. Radical behaviourists were only concerned with what is observable, that is, behaviour. Since thoughts and feelings cannot be directly observed, the radical behaviourists did not regard them as a legitimate object of study by scientific psychology.

REFLECTIVE Activity

Cast your mind back over the past few weeks and bring to mind a time when you felt very emotional (happy, sad, etc.) and a time when you had to think long and hard about something. How would other people know the emotion you were feeling and how would they know you were having a long, hard think? List behaviours that you might have engaged in at these times. Talk to someone else who has carried out this activity and see if some behaviours are in common. Given your findings, why do you think radical behaviourists rejected the inner experiences of people as not amenable to scientific enquiry and research?

The behaviourist perspective represents different theories of learning to explain, understand and change human and animal behaviours. In this chapter we will consider three theoretical perspectives: classical conditioning, operant conditioning, and cognitive learning theories.

PRACTICAL Activity

To refresh your knowledge and understanding of behaviourism read Chapter 1, pages 12–14 of the AS text *Introducing Psychology* (Pennington 2002).

5.2 Assumptions of the behaviourist perspective

The behaviourist perspective, especially that of radical behaviourism, is based on four main assumptions. These are determinism, empiricism, reductionism, and environmentalism. We shall consider determinism more fully in Chapter 11 of this book. Determinism represents the view that all behaviour is determined by past events. Within the behaviourist perspective this means that knowledge of the stimulus allows the prediction of the response, or behaviour. Conversely, given the response or behaviour, then the cause or stimulus can be specified. Behaviour, whether human or other animal is controlled by external forces in the environment.

The second assumption of the behaviourist perspective is that scientific psychology must be empirical. This means only that which can be observed, recorded, measured and is overt. To quote Watson:

Psychology, as the behaviourist views it, is a purely objective, experimental branch of natural science which needs introspection as little as do sciences of chemistry and physics. It is granted that the behaviour of animals can be investigated without appeal to consciousness.   **(Watson 1919)**

This means that mental events of any kind could not be the study of empirical psychology.

EVALUATIVE COMMENT

If this extreme position were adopted today then the cognitive perspective (see Chapter 6) would not be regarded as scientific psychology. However, the cognitive perspective adopts a highly scientific approach to human thought and mental events through careful experimentation and measurement.

In the early days of behaviourism Edward Tolman used the term **purposive behaviour** to state that all behaviour is goal-directed. The use of the word 'purposive' was criticised by radical behaviourists because it seemed to acknowledge mental events as important. Tolman (1932) proposed a cognitive explanation for learning. Here, for example, when rats learn to get food in a maze they develop *cognitive maps*. This is similar to humans who know a town or neighbourhood well and can go from one point to another by various routes because they have a cognitive map of the area represented mentally.

Hence, even within the behaviourist perspective early psychologists regarded mental events or processes as essential to explain human and animal learning.

The third assumption of **reductionism** is drawn from the natural sciences. For example, the workings of a clock can be understood by reducing it to the basic, physical components of which it is made. This applies to any machine, however complex, since its workings are no more than the collection of component parts. A lawnmower can be taken to bits, reassembled and, if properly done, will work the same as before it was taken apart. In a similar way complex human behaviour is assumed by behaviourists to be reducible to simple components. In this case the simple components are stimulus–response (S–R) associations which have been learnt. For example, behaving in a friendly way to another person involves a cluster of behaviours – such as smiling, laughing, saying nice things. Each of these component behaviours of friendliness would, according to behaviourists, be learnt from the reinforcement of the S–R links.

REFLECTIVE Activity

Think of a behaviour such as going out to eat at a restaurant with friends or working on a project in a team. Break the behaviour down into component, more simple behaviours. Try to think how these component behaviours were learnt. Can you recall any reinforcement of stimulus–response links?

EVALUATIVE COMMENT

The idea that human behaviour can be reduced to simple component parts has been challenged by the humanistic perspective (see Chapter 8). Humanistic psychologists argue that people are not like machines, and that the whole is greater than the sum of the parts. This means that reducing, for example, friendly behaviour to simpler, component parts will result in the general behaviour of friendliness being lost. A machine can be taken apart and reassembled without changing how it works and functions. In contrast, human behaviour does not have equivalent physical component parts that can be separated in such a way.

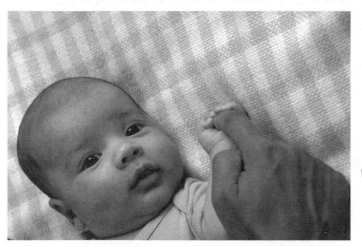

The grasping instinct in the baby is inherited, and Watson's radical behaviourism accepted a small number of physical instincts in people

The fourth assumption of **environmentalism** is that all behaviour comes from experience and that biology and genetics play a minimal role. In terms of the nurture/nature debate the behaviourist perspective comes clearly down on the side of nurture (see Chapter 11 for a more detailed

Assumption	Description	Comment
Determinism	All behaviours are determined by past events	All human behaviour is controlled by external events; this means that freewill does not exist
Empiricism	Only that which can be observed, measured and recorded should be scientific psychology	Consciousness and mental processes cannot be observed, so cannot be part of the subject matter of psychology
Reductionism	Complex human behaviour can be reduced to simple, component parts	People are not like machines; people cannot be reduced to components without losing the sense of a person
Environmentalism	Extreme view that all learning comes from experience and that heredity has no role to play	Even radical behaviourists had to admit of three innate emotions and certain reflexes as a result of heredity

Figure 5.1: The four basic assumptions of the behaviourist perspective

treatment of this issue). However, in explaining emotional reactions – the actual physical reactions of a person experiencing an intense emotion – Watson did acknowledge three innate emotions. These inherited or biological given physical responses could be found in human infants and are those of rage, fear, and love. Watson (1930) called these *basic pattern reactions* which are inherited. Any other emotion came through conditioning and learning. Watson also accepted that certain reflexes or instincts were innate and present in the newborn child. For example, the grasping reflex, as shown in the picture opposite.

EVALUATIVE COMMENT

Even with the extreme radical behaviourist position of Watson, the environmentalist assumption could not be adhered to. Innate emotional responses and certain reflex actions were acknowledged in the young human infant.

In considering these four basic assumptions of behaviourism, summarised in Figure 5.1, it is possible to distinguish between behaviourism as a method of study in psychology and behaviourism as a theory of human behaviour. With the former, the perspective advocates controlled experiments and objective observation. With the latter, behaviourism puts forward a rather mechanistic model of human behaviour. This mechanistic model pays little acknowledgement to heredity, consciousness, and explains all behaviour as resulting from conditioning. Behaviourism as a method has been and continues to be highly influential in present-day psychology. Behaviourism as a theory, as we shall see later in this chapter, has had to modify its early, extreme, environmentalist and determinist position to take account of consciousness and mental processes.

5.3 Classical and operant conditioning

Classical and operant conditioning exemplify the basic principles of learning and have been applied equally to humans and other animals. Whilst modifications have been made with cognitive theories of learning (see Section 5.5) it is important to understand the concepts underlying operant and classical conditioning. It is worth defining what is meant by the term **conditioning**. Consider the following definition:

> **conditioning involves learning associations between events that occur in an organism's environment.** **(Weiten 2002: 167)**

The association between events involves the stimulus and the response. A stimulus is that which causes us to do something and the response is the specific behaviour enacted. So, for example, if you have been conditioned to run away when you see a very large spider, the stimulus is the spider and the response is running away. Events in the past have conditioned this response. Both classical and operant conditioning are able to explain a good deal of human behaviour, as we shall see.

PRACTICAL Activity

Get together in a group of three or four and each identify a mild fear or phobia you may have (e.g. heights, spiders, snakes.). Think about how long you have had this mild fear and try to identify how it might have been conditioned for you.

Classical conditioning

Classical conditioning was the first type of learning to be studied systematically by Ivan Pavlov,

(a) Before classical conditioning

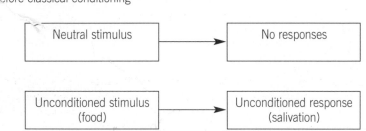

(b) During classical conditioning

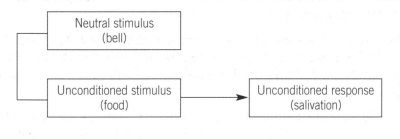

(c) After conditioning

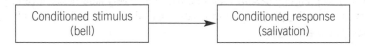

Figure 5.2: The process of classical conditioning. Initially the UCS (food) elicits the UCR (salivation), but the neutral stimulus (the bell) does not — see (a) above. During conditioning the neutral stimulus (the bell) is paired with the UCS (the food) — see (b) above. After conditioning (c) — the bell becomes the conditioned stimulus which elicits the conditioned response of salivation in the absence of food being presented

a late nineteenth-century Russian psychologist. Classical conditioning is sometimes called Pavlovian or respondent conditioning. Classical conditioning is a form of learning in which a stimulus (the conditioned stimulus) acquires the ability to cause a behavioural response originally evoked by another stimulus (unconditioned stimulus). The basic process of classical conditioning is summarised in Figure 5.2.

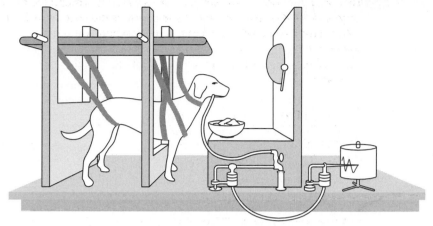

Pavlov investigated classical conditioning using the salivation reflex action of a dog when presented with food

Laboratory research on classical conditioning has tended to use simple behavioural responses. Besides salivation, behavioural responses of eye-blinks (by putting air into the eye), knee jerks, and limb flexing have been used. Conditioning of fear and fear responses have been widely studied in human behaviour. Emotional responses, including fear, have been studied when specific behavioural or physiological responses occur. In general, emotional responses appear to be very susceptible to classical conditioning, perhaps one of the most famous being the case of Little Albert, conducted by Watson and Raynor (1920).

Study 5.1

Aim Watson and Raynor conducted a study to demonstrate how classical conditioning could result in a young infant developing a fear of white rats.

Method An 11-year-old boy, called Little Albert, was presented with a white rat and at the same time a very loud noise was made by striking a steel bar with a hammer. This was repeated a number of times. Eventually the white rat was put in front of Little Albert, but in the absence of the loud noise.

Findings Initially Little Albert was unafraid of white rats. After the pairing of the loud noise with the presentation of the white rat, Little Albert showed fear of the rat. In the absence of the loud noise, the white rat alone elicited a fear response in Little Albert.

Conclusions Fear can be conditioned in a young child by pairing an initially neutral stimulus (the white rat) with an unpleasant stimulus (UCS) of a very loud noise. Five days later Watson and Raynor found that Little Albert had generalised his fear to any small white object, such as a small rabbit and a white dog.

REFLECTIVE Activity

1 Identify the CS, UCS, UCR and CR in the above study.

2 Considering ethical principles of research that psychologists should abide by, how ethical do you think this study was?

In what follows two aspects of classical conditioning will be discussed: first, application to human behaviour, and second, whether or not some pairings of stimuli and response are formed more easily than others.

Classical conditioning has been proposed as a good explanation for many human phobias or irrational fears (Merkelbach *et al*. 1991; Ost 1991). For example, a person may develop a phobia about driving a car because as a teenager one parent may have been a bad driver and scared the teenager on many occasions when they went out in the car. Munjack (1954) studied people with a phobia about driving cars and found that about half of the phobics traced their phobia back to experiences of poor driving and a car accident. Joseph Wolpe (1958) pioneered the treatment of phobias and anxiety disorders using a therapeutic technique called **systematic desensitisation**. This may be seen as the use of classical conditioning as a behaviour therapy to reduce a person's anxiety through counter-conditioning. The goal of systematic desensitisation is to weaken the association between the conditioned stimulus and the conditioned response of anxiety. If you have a phobia about dogs, for example, the association between the stimulus of a dog (CS) and fear (CR) would be weakened by first showing pictures of dogs, then real dogs at a distance, then the dogs on a leash with the owner, etc. In a sense, the association between dog and fear is unlearnt through counter-conditioning.

The second point of discussion is whether or not some pairs of stimuli and response are formed more easily than other pairings. Until research by Garcia and Koelling (1966) it was thought that any CS could be paired with a UCS to eventually produce a conditional response. For example, in Pavlov's experiments with dogs it was found that a bell, or a tune, or another sound could equally be presented with the unconditioned stimulus and eventually produce the conditional response alone. Garcia and Koelling (1996) found that taste was more effective as a conditional stimulus for learning a conditioned response to mild poisoning in rats. By contrast, pairing a bright light and a noise was more effective as conditioned stimuli for learning a conditional response to an electric shock. From this the originally neutral stimulus, which becomes the conditioned stimulus is not entirely neutral. Some stimuli will pair more quickly with a response than others.

PRACTICAL Activity

Get together with another person and identify the unconditioned stimulus (UCS), unconditioned response (UR), conditioned stimulus (CS) and conditioned response (CR) in the following scenario:

John has recently developed an allergy to dogs. If he is in the same room as a dog for 10 minutes or more he becomes mildly asthmatic. After a number of such reactions he becomes mildly asthmatic immediately upon entering a room with a dog present.

EVALUATIVE COMMENT

Pavlov's research into classical conditioning helped psychology to become more scientific and objective. Pavlov regarded animal and human behaviour like a machine. For Pavlov, humans were complicated machines, but machines that could be broken down to the simple components of stimulus, response and association. However, Pavlov did recognise that other forms of conditioning took place and were not based on pairing a conditioned stimulus with an unconditioned stimulus. The most important alternative form of conditioning is where responses are conditioned by their consequences. This is called *operant conditioning*.

Operant conditioning

Imagine that you have just handed in a psychology essay and that you worked very hard on it to the extent that you gave up going out on Friday and Saturday nights. A week later you are given your essay back by your teacher and to your delight you have been given an A+ grade.

You are very pleased with this mark and say to yourself that you will work just as hard at the next essay assignment. This is a good example of operant conditioning – your hard work has been rewarded and you will continue to work hard in the future. Operant conditioning is a type of learning in which voluntary behaviour is controlled or conditioned by its consequences. In our example, working hard at an essay in the future has been conditioned by the rewarding consequence of getting a high mark for an essay you have worked very hard on.

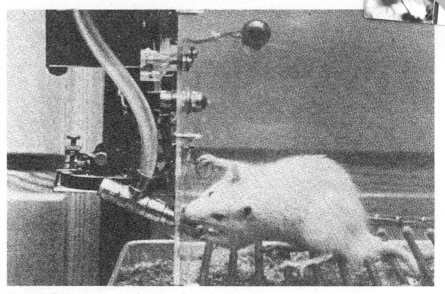

Figure 5.3: A typical example of the Skinner Box. In this version both positive reinforcement (dispensing of food pellet) and negative reinforcement (electric shock to the floor) are studied

B. F. Skinner (1953) developed research methods for the experimental analysis of behaviour, and stated that the principles of operant conditioning could be applied to both human and animal behaviour. To study behaviour experimentally Skinner developed the **Skinner Box**, an example of which is shown in Figure 5.3 above. Typically a hungry rat would be placed in the box and the experimenter would condition the animal to press a lever. Because lever-pressing is not normal rat behaviour the first step is to *shape* the behaviour. To do this the experimenter would reward (issue food from the dispenser) if the animal came close to or touched the lever. Once this had been done a few times the rat would have to actually press the lever to obtain food. Once the rat had learnt that food appeared as a consequence of pressing the lever, the rat would continue to press the lever to receive food. Here the rat has operated on its environment to obtain a reward; as a consequence lever-pressing has been learnt or conditioned as a behaviour.

REFLECTIVE Activity

Consider the hungry rat in the Skinner Box. Skinner brought a scientific approach to every aspect of his work. How then, might you define a 'hungry rat'? How would you know it was hungry? A hungry rat (or any other animal) is motivated to find food to reduce sensations of hunger. Do you need to use an internal concept like motivation to explain learning or conditioning?

Reinforcement of an operant behaviour is key to conditioning taking place. Without a reinforcement the rat may only press the lever by accident and not again. If you had not gained an A+ grade for your essay, in our imaginary example, you would not have been reinforced and may, as a consequence, not work so hard in the future. Skinner derived the **law of acquisition** from his basic experiment. This states:

> **that the strength of an operant behaviour increases when it is followed by a reinforcing stimulus.**
> **(Schultz and Schultz 2000: 234)**

EVALUATIVE COMMENT

Notice in this definition of the law of acquisition that no mention is made of any type of inner event such as motivation or inner state such as pleasure or satisfaction. You might feel joy or pleasure in our imaginary essay example when getting a high grade. However, Skinner only wanted to make reference to observables, and inner feelings or states are not observable. In this sense Skinner carried on with the radical behaviourist tradition established by Watson.

Notice also in this definition that the reinforcer is also called a stimulus. So whilst behaviourists talk about the strength or conditioning of a stimulus–response (S–R) link, with operant conditioning the stimulus (reinforcer) comes after the response. In classical conditioning it is the other way round.

Reinforcement can be of two types – positive reinforcement and negative reinforcement. A **positive reinforcement** occurs when a behaviour (response) is strengthened because it is followed by a rewarding stimulus. This is generally how people normally think of reinforcement – as positive and associated with inner mental states such as good, satisfying, pleasurable. By contrast, a **negative reinforcement** occurs when a behaviour (response) is strengthened because it is followed by the removal of an aversive (painful) stimulus. The word 'negative' is often a source of confusion and often associated with punishment. However, negative reinforcement is reinforcing of a behaviour and punishment stops a behaviour. Negative reinforcement strengthens a response, and punishment weakens or stops the response.

PRACTICAL Activity

Get together with another student and consider the following. Decide which is an example of positive reinforcement, which negative reinforcement and which punishment.

1. You drive your car at 60 m.p.h. in a 50 m.p.h. speed limit and receive a speeding fine when the police stop you.

2. You receive a £100 cheque as first prize in a competition that you have entered.

3. You tidy up your bedroom so that you will not be nagged by your parents.

4. A rat presses a lever in a Skinner Box and terminates an electric shock.

Negative reinforcement occurs in two ways, first by escape learning. Here a behaviour is reinforced through escape from an aversive situation – this is (d) above. The second is by avoidance learning. Here a potentially aversive situation (being nagged by parents) is avoided by behaving in a certain way (tidying up your bedroom). Figure 5.4 summarises the types of reinforcement and punishment in operant conditioning.

EVALUATIVE COMMENT

Skinner (1974) regarded operant conditioning as applying to all animals, including humans. However, recent research has shown that there are biological limitations imposed on conditioning (Shettleworth 1998). The present view is that the basic laws of learning are universal across species. However, specific instincts, resulting from evolution, may affect the learning of a particular type of animal. For example, some animals have an instinctive aversion to certain kinds of taste. Animals must quickly learn what food is poisonous and what is safe to eat. Evolution will favour animals that quickly learn what not to eat (Garcia 1989). Hence, biology and evolution need to be taken account of in the operant conditioning of animals.

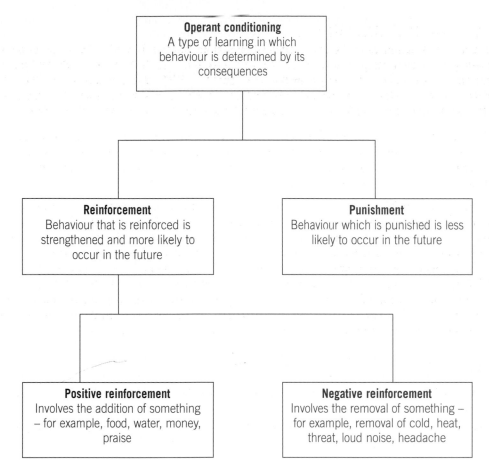

Figure 5.4: Key concepts in Skinner's operant conditioning

5.4 Key concepts

In considering classical and operant conditioning we have come across a number of key concepts that will be explored further here. These include stimulus, response and reinforcement. To complete the picture we also need to consider punishment and the extinction of behaviour.

Stimulus

The concept of stimulus takes a number of forms. In classical conditioning there is the unconditioned stimulus (the food presented to the dog), a neutral stimulus (the bell before it is paired with the food – UCS) and the conditioned stimulus (CS). The conditioned stimulus was once a neutral stimulus. Note that in all these three types of stimuli in classical conditioning the stimulus occurs in time before the response (salivation in Pavlov's dog experiments).

We also saw, with the Watson and Raynor (1920) classical conditioning study whereby Little Albert was conditioned to fear a white rat, that classical conditioning applies to humans. What Watson and Raynor (1920) went on to demonstrate with Little Albert was the ideas of *stimulus generalisation* and *stimulus discrimination*.

After Little Albert had been conditioned to fear a white rat it was found that he also showed similar fear responses (crying, trying to escape) to other small, white, furry objects. For example,

Little Albert also showed the same fear responses to a rabbit, a small white dog, a Santa Claus mask (white hair and beard), and even to Watson's white hair. This is known as stimulus generalisation and may be defined as follows:

> **stimulus generalisation occurs when an organism that has learnt a response to a specific stimulus responds in the same way to new stimuli that are similar to the original stimulus.**   **(Weiten 2002: 172)**

REFLECTIVE Activity

Think about some mild fear you might have or a situation that makes you mildly anxious. What range of situations cause such a response? That is, how widely does generalisation occur?

The other side of stimulus generalisation is stimulus discrimination. For example, would you expect Little Albert to show a fear response to a small brown dog or a white polar bear? The answer would probably be no since these two stimuli bear little resemblance to the small white rat.

Stimulus discrimination may be defined as follows:

> **stimulus discrimination occurs when an organism that has learnt a response to a specific stimulus does *not* respond in the same way to the new stimuli that are similar to the original stimulus.**   **(Weiten 2002: 174)**

Generally, the less the new stimulus resembles the original stimulus the more discrimination will occur.

Stimulus generalisation and stimulus discrimination can equally be applied to operant conditioning. For example, a pigeon conditioned to peck at a red circle will, once conditioned, peck at a range of different colours of red circles. The pigeon can also be conditioned to peck at a particular type of red circle by only reinforcing pecks at a particular colour of red circle.

Response

In both classical and operant conditioning the response is the actual behaviour that takes place. In classical conditioning the response is normally automatic and not under the control of the organism. For example, it is difficult not to salivate if you are hungry, and see and smell nice food. Hence, the behavioural response in classical conditioning is said to be *elicited*. By contrast, in operant conditioning the behaviour is under the control of the organism, is not normally automatic or involuntary, and may not be a behaviour that the organism has made before. In operant conditioning, then, the response is said to be *emitted*.

EVALUATIVE COMMENT

The behaviourist perspective, in the form of classical and operant conditioning, only regards observable behaviour as the province of scientific enquiry. When Watson and Raynor conditioned Little Albert to fear a white rat they made behavioural observations and recordings of Little Albert's response to the white rat after conditioning. The feeling of fear in Little Albert was not of scientific interest because it is not objectively observable. This would be true of any emotion – the behaviourist would look solely for behavioural responses. In humans the use of language would also be taken as a behavioural response.

Reinforcement

Skinner made an important distinction between reward and reinforcement. Whilst these two terms are often used interchangeably, they should not be so used. For Skinner a reinforcement strengthens or makes more likely repetition in the future of the behaviour. A reward may or may not strengthen a behaviour. Rewards such as prizes, money, praise, etc., often do strengthen behaviour, but may not necessarily do so. Also, rewards often do not immediately follow behaviour, whereas for Skinner, reinforcement does immediately follow the response. Reinforcers, by definition, always strengthen a behaviour.

REFLECTIVE Activity

Cast your mind back over the past few months and think of three or four different rewards that you have received. Have each of these rewards encouraged or made you repeat certain behaviours? When people think they are giving you a reward, is it rewarding to you?

SCHEDULES OF REINFORCEMENT

Operant conditioning, as has been outlined so far, involved reinforcement of the lever-pressing behaviour of the rat in the Skinner Box every time the rat pressed the lever. However, it is possible to vary the reinforcement schedule either through the number of lever presses or over time. Four different schedules of reinforcement have been investigated: fixed ratio, variable ratio, fixed interval and variable interval. A ratio schedule is where the rat must press the lever a certain number of times before food (reinforcer) is issued. A fixed ratio is where, for example, reinforcement would be given after every 10 or 20 presses of the lever. A variable ratio schedule of reinforcement is where reinforcement is given on a variable basis, for example, after 5, 10, 8, 12, 14 presses of a lever. With a variable ratio a regular pattern does not exist. An interval schedule reinforces behaviour according to time and not the number of lever presses that take place. A fixed interval schedule of reinforcement might be, for example, issuing a food pellet after every 20 seconds, regardless of how often the lever is pressed. A variable interval schedule of reinforcement is where a reinforcer is issued at variable times, for example, after 10, 20, 25, 15, and 30 seconds. This is summarised in Figure 5.5.

	Fixed schedule	Variable schedule
Ratio schedule	Fixed ratio	Variable ratio
	Reinforcement given every X times as behaviour is emitted. For example, every 10 lever presses.	Reinforcement given after variable times behaviour is emitted. For example, after 8, 12, 18, 15 lever presses.
Interval schedule	Fixed interval	Variable interval
	Reinforcement given after every fixed time period. For example, after every 20 seconds.	Reinforcement given after variable periods of times. For example, after 20, 40, 35, 50, 30 seconds.

Figure 5.5: Different schedules of reinforcement

PRACTICAL Activity

Discuss the following with another student and decide what schedule of reinforcement each represents:

1   In a factory, being paid £10 for every 10 items produced.

2   Playing a slot or fruit machine and winning sometimes.

3   Surfers waiting for the 'big wave' to surf on.

4   Getting paid every week on Friday.

Given these four schedules of reinforcement it is of interest to know which strengthen behaviour most. In the Skinner Box it is found that ratio schedules produce faster lever-pressing than interval schedules, whilst variable schedules (either ratio or interval) usually result in the behaviour occurring in a more steady way.

EVALUATIVE COMMENT

People who are addicted to gambling may become so because playing fruit machines, or playing roulette, provides rewards (winning) on a variable ratio schedule of reinforcement. However, not everybody who plays a fruit machine becomes a gambling addict. Hence, it would seem reasonable to infer that other factors also need to be present. For example, an addictive personality type may be more susceptible to becoming addicted to gambling than other personality types.

Punishment

Punishment acts to decrease the likelihood that a behavioural response will occur. Punishment occurs in many aspects of our lives – getting a fine for speeding, not being allowed out by parents when a child does something wrong, being sacked from a job for being dishonest. Punishment can be divided into two basic types. One type is where something happens which is aversive – a fine for speeding or not being allowed out. The other type is where something is taken away – losing your job for dishonesty or having your clothes allowance (if you have one) taken away.

EVALUATIVE COMMENT

Punishment can be effective in decreasing the strength of a behaviour or the likelihood that it will be repeated in the future. However, when parents punish children for naughty behaviour the child may not know which behaviour is being punished. This may especially be the case, in both humans and animals, if the punishment is delayed and does not immediately follow the naughty or incorrect behaviour.

Extinction and spontaneous recovery

Extinction of a behaviour occurs when the behaviour ceases to be emitted. In operant conditioning removal of the positive reinforcer usually results, after a period of time, in the behaviour being extinguished. However, with negative reinforcement, behaviour is less readily extinguished and may take a considerable period of time to become so.

Spontaneous recovery can also occur. This is where a previously learnt behaviour recurs but in the absence of any new reinforcement.

Study 5.2

Aim Williams (1959) attempted to extinguish tantrum behaviour in a 21-month-old infant using the principles of operant conditioning.

Method Whenever the child threw a tantrum, the parents refused to respond to the screams and crying of the infant (previously they had sat with and comforted the child until he fell asleep, i.e. reinforcing the tantrum behaviour).

Results As can be seen from Figure 5.6, the tantrum behaviour extinguished quickly over a number of nights when the child was put to bed (solid line). Figure 5.6 also shows spontaneous recovery of tantrums and that this was extinguished also.

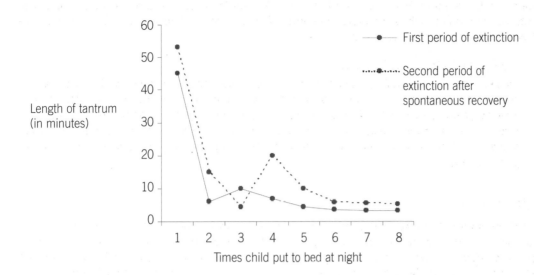

Figure 5.6: Extinction of tantrum behaviour using operant conditioning principles. The broken line shows spontaneous recovery of tantrum behaviour after the initial extinction period. Adapted from Williams (1959)

Conclusions Operant conditioning techniques can be effective in changing unwanted and unnecessary behaviour in children. To do so the reinforcers have to be recognised, and then withdrawn.

5.5 Observational and imitative learning

Consider the following scenario. John, a young teenager, is out with a group of friends in a shopping centre. One of the friends notices that a woman shopper has accidentally dropped her mobile phone and is walking off without noticing this. One of John's friends, Linda, picks up the mobile phone and returns it to the woman. The woman is very grateful to Linda, thanks her very much, and buys her an ice-cream from a nearby shop. John and his friends observe all this. If a similar incident occurred in the future it is likely that John would help out a shopper in a similar way. Why is this? John has received no direct reinforcement in this at all. It is Linda who has had her behaviour reinforced through being bought an ice-cream and being treated nicely by the woman shopper. However, John has observed Linda being reinforced for her helpful behaviour. Through **observational learning** John has learnt that if he behaves in helpful ways to people then he too might be rewarded and have his behaviour directly reinforced.

Observational learning plays an important part in how we interact with and behave towards other people. Albert Bandura (1965, 1969) developed these ideas into what is called **social learning** theory.

REFLECTIVE Activity

You will have come across social learning theory when studying for the AS psychology in the Gender section of Unit 1. To refresh your knowledge of social learning theory read Chapter 4, pages 105–109 of the AS text *Introducing psychology* (Pennington 2002).

In the above scenario John has learnt through what is called **vicarious reinforcement**. This means that he has observed someone else, in this case Linda, obtain reinforcement for behaving in a certain way. John has observed and memorised this. Hence, John has the ability to perform helpful behaviour in the future, but only under the right conditions. John then, has to decide in any future situation whether or not helping is likely to lead to reinforcement. For example, if John was on his own in a shopping centre, saw someone drop their mobile phone and also saw a group of young men pick up the phone and make off, he is hardly likely to help. To help in this situation might result in punishment rather than reinforcement.

Bandura (1967) recognised that neither classical nor operant conditioning could account for all learning in humans. He also recognised that people's cognitions or how they thought and stored information in memory played a central role in observational learning. This represents a major shift away from the fundamental principles of radical behaviourism. With social learning theory or observational learning, cognitions are central and essential.

For John, in the above scenario, Linda acts as a model. The most relevant aspects of the model's behaviour, and ones memorised by the observer, are called modelling cues. Models can be of two sorts, broadly speaking: live models (the model is physically present) or symbolic models (people in films or television or novels and cartoon characters). Symbolic modelling is regarded as important in cultures where media such as television and films are widely available.

Observing a model's behaviour and its consequences serves an attention-focusing function. Cheyne (1971) showed that children showed better acquisition or memory of a model's behaviour when the model was either reinforced or punished than where there were no apparent consequences for the model.

Study 5.3

Aim Spiegler and Weiland (1976) conducted a study to investigate the attention-focusing function on an observer of reinforcing or punishing consequences for a model.

Method Participants were given a short story to read about a student's response to cuts in education at her school. There were three versions of the consequences for the student: praise for raising the issue; punishment where she was told off, and no consequence; and told her views would be taken into account.

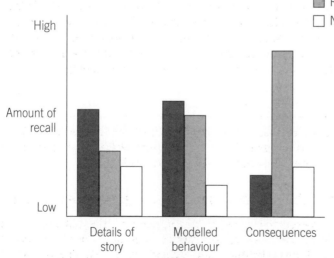

Figure 5.7: Recall of three aspects of the story depending upon punishing, reinforcing or no consequences for the model. Note that the observer recalls high levels of details of the story and the behaviour of the model when the model is punished. Adapted from Spiegler and Weiland (1976)

Results Figure 5.7 depicts three sets of results from this study. First, details of the story were best remembered where the symbolic model was punished. Second, the behaviour of the model was best recalled when there were reinforcing or punishing consequences. Third, the consequences of the model's behaviour were best recalled when they were reinforced and least recalled when they were punished.

Conclusions These results lead to three conclusions. First, people learn more than shown in imitation of behaviour from observation. Second, both reinforcing and punishing consequences of the model's behaviour enhance acquisition of the behaviour by the model. Third, where a punishment is observed the behaviour of the model is acquired, but may not be imitated by the observer.

Observing another person being told off or punished may result in the observer acquiring the behaviour that was punished. However, the observer is unlikely to perform the behaviour because the consequence would also be punished

EVALUATIVE COMMENT

The findings from this experiment highlight a very important difference between observational learning and operant conditioning. In operant conditioning, punishment extinguishes the behaviour. However, in observational learning, observing a model being punished results in the observer acquiring and memorising the behaviour. Whether or not the observer will actually perform the behaviour will depend on the situation. Hence, when observing a model behaving, acquisition of the behaviour by the observer is equally effective when there are observed consequences of the behaviour for the model (either reinforcement or punishment).

PRACTICAL Activity

With a small group of students or friends, pick a television programme or film that you have all recently seen. Recall the behaviour of two or three of the actors or actresses. Do all the behaviours recalled have consequences (reinforcement or punishment)? It is likely that most behaviours recalled will have them?

5.6 Limitations of the behaviourist perspective

As we have seen, the behaviourist perspective consists of a number of different theories of learning. On their own, neither classical conditioning, operant conditioning, nor observational learning can explain all aspects of human learning and behaviour. Whilst proponents of

Sample questions, answers and comments

classical and operant conditioning have attempted to apply principles to both animal and human behaviour, it does seem clear that animal behaviour can be better explained. Nevertheless, classical conditioning has enjoyed applications to human behaviour. For example, in understanding how people acquire fears and phobias, and in the world of advertising; operant conditioning has been successfully used to treat people with fears and phobias. So whilst each has rather a narrow approach to the range of behaviours studied, classical conditioning explains how we acquire a phobia, and operant conditioning helps a person to get rid it.

The limitations of operant conditioning are that mental and emotional events are ignored as an object of study. This is a major shortcoming since we often regard the difference between humans and other animals to be to do with consciousness, reflective thought and recognition of how emotions affect how we behave. Skinner regarded emotions as responses to behaviour and not causes of behaviour. As such Skinner thought that behaviour could only be changed by reinforcement or punishment, and not by analysing emotions, as is done in the psychoanalytic perspective.

Another limitation of classical and operant conditioning is that most of the research has been conducted on animals such as rats, pigeons, dogs, etc. It is assumed that the principles of learning identified in these animals can be equally applied to humans. This is a mistake for two reasons. First, human behaviour is more complex, and second, humans are conscious beings who can think about how to behave, rather than mechanically respond to a stimulus or reinforcement or punishment. This leads to the more philosophical limitations of the behaviourist perspective which is that it is deterministic and allows of little or no free will for humans (see Chapter 11 for a detailed treatment of the free will-determinism debate).

The final limitation of the behaviourist perspective to be considered here is that it ignores or undervalues the contribution of heredity to explaining and understanding behaviour. Behaviourists do not regard instinctive behaviour as featuring in any important way in human behaviour.

5.7 Sample questions

SAMPLE QUESTION 1

(a)   Outline what is meant by the terms 'stimulus' and 'reinforcement' in the behaviourist approach.
(AO1 = 4)   *(4 marks)*

(b)   Explain how classical conditioning can account for the acquisition of fear in a person.
(AO1 = 2, AO2 = 2)   *(4 marks)*

(c)   Discuss at least *two* limitations of the behaviourist perspective in psychology.
(AO1 = 4, AO2 = 8)   *(12 marks)*

Total AO1 marks = 10   Total AO2 marks = 10   Total = 20 marks

QUESTIONS, ANSWERS AND COMMENTS

SAMPLE QUESTION 2

(a)   Outline what is meant by operant conditioning and briefly explain how it can be applied to human behaviour.
(AO1 = 2, AO2 = 2)   *(4 marks)*

(b) Explain two assumptions of the behaviourist approach.
(AO1 = 2, AO2 = 2)   (4 marks)

(c) Discuss how observational and imitative learning provide a better explanation of some types of learning. Refer to examples of human behaviour in your answer.
(AO1 = 6, AO2 = 6)   (12 marks)

Total AO1 marks = 10   Total AO2 marks = 10   Total = 20 marks

Answer to 2(a)

Operant conditioning is a theory developed by Skinner, a behaviourist psychologist. It deals with stimulus–response theory, which means that a stimulus in the environment causes a response in the organism. The association between the stimulus and response can be strengthened by reinforcement. If the association is positively reinforced it will become stronger and the behaviour repeated.

Operant conditioning can be applied to how a child gains gender identity. Reinforcement for appropriate gender-role behaviour will come from those closest to the child, such as parents.

Comment: This answer would gain 3 of the 4 marks available. The description of operant conditioning is adequate, but could have been improved by mentioning punishment, and also that the response has to be emitted before it is reinforced. The application to gender identity is appropriate, but a specific example of a behaviour would have helped.

Answer to 2(b)

Two assumptions of the behaviourist approach are that it is reductionist and only regards behaviour as scientific. Behaviourists assume that all behaviour, human or animal, can be reduced to S–R links and reinforcement. How consciousness can be reduced to this is not clear. Behaviourists state that since only behaviour and not mind can be observed, then only behaviour can be studied.

Comment: Two assumptions have been correctly identified, so a mark for each would be awarded. A further mark would be given for explaining how reductionism applies to humans and other animals. The answer is a little confused over the second assumption so only 3 marks overall for this answer.

Answer to 2(c)

Operant and classical conditioning only deal with how a stimulus from the environment causes a response in the organism. They do not see any mediating variable and do not take into account subjective experiences. Observational learning may offer a better explanation of some behaviour as we are all influenced by those around us. We may observe a behaviour but it does not necessarily cause a response in an organism. We observe something and then we imitate or copy the behaviour, to see what the response is and whether or not it is reinforced. In this way we can choose how we want to act.

This can be seen in gaining gender identity. A boy may copy his father's behaviour, imitate what he does, but if he imitates his mother's response he may get a negative response and not act that way again.

This can also be applied to moral development. A child may copy aggressive behaviour and be punished for it and not do it again.

Social learning theory tried to integrate mental processes into learning. Imitation in the laboratory was tested by Bandura to see if children imitated aggressive behaviour. Children who watched aggression being reinforced displayed more aggression themselves. Those who watched aggression being negatively reinforced displayed less aggressive behaviour. This shows that we learn by observation, which is different and better for understanding people.

Comment: This answer demonstrates a clear understanding of observational and imitative learning. The opening paragraph also points out a shortcoming of the classical and operant conditioning, so earns an AO2 mark. Towards the end of the first paragraph the answer is confused, since the observer should already know whether the behaviour would be rewarded or not if performed. In observational learning you do not wait to see if reinforcement follows. There is an expectation in the first place. The two examples of gender identity and moral development are appropriate – but not well developed. Mention of social learning integrating mental processes is correct, and the short description of the experiment gains a mark. Overall, good understanding demonstrated but not enough discussion given to score highly. This answer would gain 7 out of the 12 marks available (AO1 = 4, AO2 = 3).

Total marks for question 2 = *13 out of 20 (AO1 = 8, AO2 = 5).*

5.8 FURTHER READING

Introductory texts

Hill, G. 2001: **A level psychology through diagrams**. Oxford University Press, Oxford.

Pennington, D. C. 2003: **Essential personality**. Chapter 7. Hodder & Stoughton, London.

Weiten, W. 2002: **Psychology: themes and variations**, 5th Ed. Chapter 6. Wadsworth, London.

Specialist sources

Nye, R. D. 2000: **Three psychologies: perspectives from Freud, Skinner and Rogers**. 6th Ed. Chapter 2. Wadsworth, London.

Ryckman, R. 2000: **Theories of personality**. Chapters 15, 16 and 17. Wadsworth, London

Schultz, D. P. & Schultz, S. E. 2000: **A modern history of psychology**. 7th Ed. Chapters 9, 10 and 11. Harcourt College Publishers, Fort Worth, **TX**.

6

The cognitive perspective

6.1 Introduction

Pause from your studies for a moment. What thoughts are you conscious of? In looking round you what are you paying attention to? Or it may be that you are recalling from memory some exciting event in which you were involved in a few days ago. From this it is evident to yourself that you have thoughts and that you are conscious about what you are thinking. In many ways this ability of people to be conscious about their thoughts distinguishes us from other animals. Given this it is hardly surprising that psychologists regard our thoughts, or more generally our mental processes, as a legitimate area of study. Such psychologists are called cognitive psychologists and work within a **cognitive perspective**.

PRACTICAL Activity

Refresh your knowledge and understanding of cognitive psychology which you studied at AS level by reading Chapter 1, pages 16–19 of the AS text *Introducing psychology* (Pennington 2002). Additionally, you would have studied at least one topic in cognitive psychology at AS level. Look through the relevant chapters (Chapters 9, 10, 11 and 12) of *Introducing psychology* to refresh what you learnt then.

We take computers for granted these days. Cognitive psychologists liken our mental processes to software operations in a computer

Cognitive psychology has been the dominant perspective in psychology since the 1960s and 1970s. The use of a computer metaphor applied to human mental processes provided and still provides a model for investigating human mental functions. The word *cognition* comes from the Latin *cognoscere* which means to apprehend in the sense of getting the meaning of, understanding and recognising (not to catch as in 'the police apprehended a criminal'). However, as we shall see in this chapter, cognitive psychologists also need to take motivation, emotion and other human aspects into account in developing theories of cognition.

Cognitive psychology may be seen as being made up of three different but interlinking areas, as shown in Figure 6.1. These are human experimental psychology, which investigates and develops theories about memory, attention, problem-solving and language. The use of a computer analogy in terms of artificial intelligence and computer simulation are different (see Section 6.6.) as well as cognitive neuroscience which looks at how damage to the brain affects cognitive processes. These three areas interlink because all are concerned with human (and sometimes animal) **cognitive processes**.

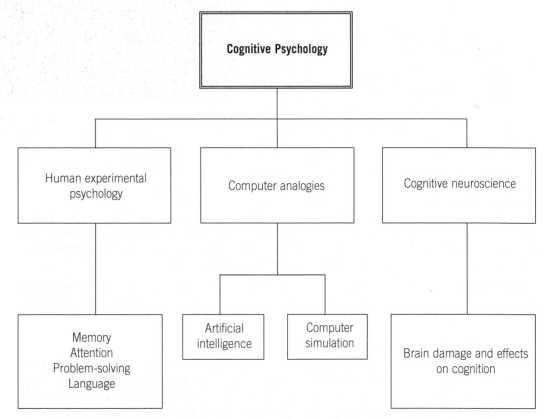

Figure 6.1: Cognitive psychology may be regarded as being made up of three interlinking areas: human experimental psychology, computer analogies and cognitive neuroscience

6.2 Development of cognitive psychology

The seeds of cognitive psychology date back to the times of the Ancient Greeks, over three thousand years ago. The Ancient Greeks were interested in how we gained knowledge of the world. The seventeenth-century philosopher René Descartes defined human existence through his famous phrase *cogito ergo sum*, which means 'I think, therefore I am'. For Descartes thinking or thought was the defining aspect of being human. The empiricist philosopher, John Locke, proposed that simple ideas came from observation and experience, and that complex ideas result from mental manipulation of simple ideas. However, it was not until the late 1900s that attempts were made scientifically to investigate human thoughts and feelings.

Early introspection

If we are to study consciousness we must use introspection and introspective reports

(Farthing 1992)

This quotation from a relatively recent book on consciousness applies as strongly today as it did over 100 years ago when Wilhelm Wundt established the first scientific laboratory in psychology. **Introspection** is a method of investigating conscious thought and mental processes by asking people verbally to report on what they are conscious of thinking and feeling. Wundt trained his assistant to introspect in a particular way and to analyse sensations, images and emotional reactions into component parts. Essentially Wundt tried to break down conscious

The influential philosopher John Locke claimed that simple ideas resulted from experience, and that complex ideas resulted from combining and changing simple ideas

thoughts and feelings into smaller and smaller parts or elements. Wundt then saw the task of psychology as discovering the laws of connection of how these elements were organised. For example, Wundt proposed a tri-dimensional theory of feelings based in three dimensions: pleasure–displeasure, tension–relaxation and excitement–depression.

From this you can see that Wundt may be regarded as an early cognitive psychologist. However, because his method of introspection was subjective and not scientific, the use of introspection in scientific psychology did not re-emerge for well over 50 years.

EVALUATIVE COMMENT

The shortcomings of Wundt's version of introspection are that there is no objective way of resolving differences between different observers. Also, disagreements cannot be resolved by repeated introspections – as Wundt had hoped. Finally, Wundt claimed that higher mental processes could not be investigated by introspection – only simple sensations and feelings. As a result Wundt limited the scope of psychology. Modern cognitive psychology regards all mental processes as a legitimate area of study.

Influence of early cognitive psychologists

Edward Tolman (1932) was a behaviourist who proposed a cognitive explanation for learning based on *purposive behaviour*. Tolman rejected Thorndike's law of effect and hence rejected one of the key principles of behaviourism (see Chapter 5) that learning resulted from reward or reinforcement. Tolman conducted much of his research on rats running in simple mazes to get food. Tolman showed that rats, after running the same maze a number of times, develop *cognitive maps* of the maze. This is much the same as a person knowing the roads and streets of the town or city in which he or she lives. People with a cognitive map of where they live can use a number of routes to get to the same destination. Tolman is regarded as a forerunner of modern cognitive psychology, introducing the idea of an intervening variable between stimulus and response (see Section 6.4 for the mental processes of the organism as intervening variables).

In 1960 George Miller founded the Center for Cognitive Studies at Harvard University. Miller rejected behaviourism and instead seized upon similarities between computers and how the mind works. Miller did not regard the shift to cognition as representing a revolution in psychology, but a process of gradual change, which was taking place elsewhere in psychology. Researchers at the Center for Cognitive Studies studied aspects of human mental processes now commonly associated with cognitive psychology. These included language, memory, attention, thinking and cognitive development in children.

Finally, Ulric Neisser published a highly influential book in 1967 called *Cognitive psychology* which attempted to define this new field of psychology. As a result Neisser became known as the 'father' of cognitive psychology. Just 19 years later Neisser was critical of the way cognitive psychology had developed. He thought it should be applied to practical problems and not be obsessed with laboratory experiments which had questionable ecological validity. Together Miller and Neisser were of paramount importance in the development of modern cognitive psychology.

Chomsky and psycholinguistics

Skinner's radical behaviourist (see Chapter 5) view of human language was that it was learnt solely from experience. Also, Skinner (1957) claimed that speech was not the expression of ideas (mental events) but the emission of verbal responses. This means that all speech, for Skinner, results from the control of a stimulus in the external environment. Chomsky (1959) demonstrated the inadequacy of this account of language. Chomsky argued two important points. First, that certain aspects of language are inherited and not learnt from experience. Second, that to explain how we can say a sentence that we have never heard before requires the mind to have internalised rules of grammar. Some of these internalised rules of grammar, according to Chomsky, are inherited and others learnt. Skinner's inability to explain adequately one of the defining features of human beings – language – was a turning point for behaviourism. Chomsky emphasised essential cognitive aspects to language and speech. As such he contributed to the development of modern cognitive psychology.

PRACTICAL Activity

In a small group review what has been said about Tolman, Miller, Neisser and Chomsky. Identify and discuss each of their different contributions to the development of modern cognitive psychology.

6.3 Assumptions of the cognitive approach

Seven main assumptions can be seen to underlie or provide the foundations for the cognitive approach in psychology. These are as follows:

1. That mental processes can be studied scientifically.

2. That mental processes can be regarded as information processing.

3. That the mind operates in a similar way to a computer allowing a computer analogy to throw light on cognition.

4. That introspection can be a valid scientific method of studying cognitive processes.

5. That aspects of the organism, including conscious and unconscious thought, act as mediational processes between stimulus and response.

6. The brain, particularly damage to parts of the brain, affect cognitions and cognitive processes.

7. That the findings and methods of cognitive psychology can be applied to other areas of psychology such as child development, abnormal psychology and applied areas such as sport and the law.

In this section we will look at four of these assumptions in more detail. The subsequent sections will look at mediational processes, information processing and computer analogies separately.

Scientific study of mental processes

Mental processes, such as memory, attention, problem-solving and reasoning, are studied by cognitive psychologists by extensive use of laboratory experiments.

REFLECTIVE Activity

Read back over your notes or the appropriate chapter(s) in the AS text *Introducing psychology* (Pennington, 2002), and identify the extent to which the empirical research in the topic areas of perception and attention, remembering and forgetting, and language and thinking uses the laboratory experiment.

The extensive use of laboratory experiments in cognitive psychology is similar to the behaviourist approach. However, there are two important differences. First, the vast majority of laboratory experiments in cognitive psychology use people as participants. In the behaviourist approach, animals such as rats and pigeons are commonly used. Second, cognitive psychologists use the findings of experiments to *infer* mental processes. The use of the word *infer* here reflects the fact that mental processes cannot be observed, but measures can be taken that allow cognitive psychologists to be confident of what is going on mentally. An experiment by Sternberg (1966) illustrates this.

Study 6.1

Aim To determine whether or not people retrieve information from a list by scanning all information, in sequence, until they come across the piece of information they are looking for.

Method Participants were asked to memorise a list of words of different lengths. Following this participants were asked to say whether or not the words they had learnt were on two other lists of words. With these two lists, one was twice as long as the other.

Findings Participants took longer to identify words they had learnt from the longer list compared to the shorter list.

Conclusions Because participants take longer to recognise words not on the longer list, they must be scanning the list in a sequential, rather than a random way.

Modern introspection

Farthing (1992) regards the use of introspection and introspective reports by people as essential to the study of consciousness. Contemporary cognitive psychology remains uncertain about the value of introspection for shedding light on cognitive processes.

Modern introspection falls into two categories. First, methods that ask people to reflect and report on their experiences (thoughts and feelings). This is called **retrospective phenomenological assessment** because of the focus on reporting experiences (phenomenology). Second, methods which ask people to 'think aloud' whilst solving a problem (Ericsson and Simon 1980). This approach views verbalisations as the products of mental processes which as such may justifiably be interpreted.

Some cognitive psychologists believe that verbalisation of what a person is thinking and feeling whilst looking at a painting, for example, throws light on cognitive processes

REFLECTIVE Activity

Have a go at each type of introspection. For the 'think aloud' approach select a problem to solve (this may be a crossword clue, or other type of puzzle). Get a tape recorder and attempt to solve the problem by verbalising everything that comes into your head. For the other, phenomenological approach, look at something in your surroundings, for example a picture or another person, and try to report into a tape recorder what you think and feel.

With the phenomenological type of introspection, attempts have been made to quantify the reports and conduct statistical analyses. This is an attempt to make the reports more objective and appropriate for scientific analysis.

However, some psychologists have questioned whether or not a person can have access to higher mental processes, particularly those to do with making judgements and decisions. An influential paper by Nisbett and Wilson (1977) entitled 'Telling more than we can know' stated, with evidence, that we do not have access to our thought processes. Nisbett and Wilson (1977) showed that often introspective reports did not reflect mental processes but a person's beliefs about something.

EVALUATIVE COMMENT
Modern introspection employs different methods of achieving introspective reports from people. However, there is still controversy over the scientific value of such reports, and whether they really do reflect mental cognitive processes.

Cognitive neuropsychology

Over the past 20 years cognitive psychologists have become interested in how damage to different parts of the brain affects both behaviour and cognitive functions. Essentially, it was realised that people who suffered cognitive deficits, such as loss of speech or inability to read the printed word, could provide insights into cognitive functioning in normal people. One of the most well researched areas in **cognitive neuropsychology** is around reading and writing. For example, cognitive psychologists think that there are a number of different pathways in the brain by which the written word becomes translated into speech. This is evidenced by some brain-damaged patients reading aloud the written word by translating each letter of the word into an

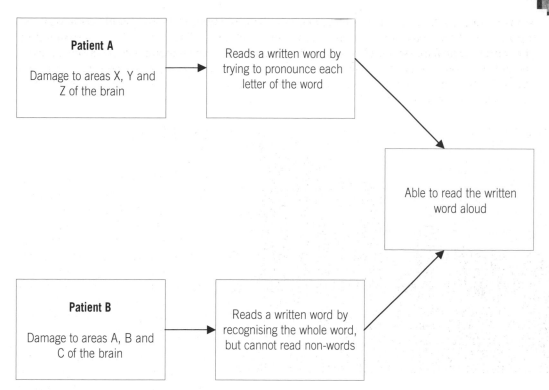

Figure 6.2: Two different ways in which patients with damage to different areas of the brain read aloud the written word

appropriate sound. Patients with damage to different parts of the brain can only read aloud the whole word, and have difficulty pronouncing non-words. In this case it seems that reading takes place because the whole word is recognised rather than trying to pronounce the whole word from its constituent letters (Ellis 1973). This is shown in Figure 6.2.

Cognitive neuropsychology assumes that any cognitive system (reading, writing, speaking, etc.) is made up of a number of component parts which are called *modules* (Marr 1982). Each module, it is claimed, has a distinct function and together these modules perform a larger scale function. Another assumption is that these modules are located in different parts of the brain. This means that damage to a specific part of the brain will not destroy the larger scale function of, for example, reading or speaking or writing, but will destroy some of the component modules that make up the function of, for example, reading aloud. Hence, the example given earlier of two different brain-damaged patients is understood in terms of different modules having been destroyed by the damage to the brain.

EVALUATIVE COMMENT

Cognitive neuropsychology is a complex area of study and one requiring psychologists with high levels of skills and knowledge about the brain. The idea of 'modules' in the brain is useful but in reality brain damage can be quite extensive, and it is not always clear exactly which parts of the brain have been damaged. Hence, it is difficult to be certain about damage to specific areas of the brain and the resultant deficit in cognitive functioning for the person.

Influence on other areas of psychology

The theories, concepts and research methods of cognitive psychology have been readily applied to other areas of psychology. For example, in child development how a child comes to know about and understand the world around them has been extensively investigated by psychologists such as Piaget, Vygotsky and Bruner. In looking at exceptional child development (see Chapter 4) learning difficulties such as dyslexia reflect cognitive impairments.

PRACTICAL Activity

Get together with three or four others studying A level psychology. Go over what each of you have covered in Module 4 on Child Development. Identify those aspects of child development which are to do with cognitive development.

Another influence of cognitive psychology is in the area of ageing. Here psychologists are interested in, for example, how memory may differ in very old age, and how attention in the elderly differs from younger people. Knowing about normal human memory helps understand memory impairments that may come from degenerative diseases associated with old age, such as dementia and Alzheimer's disease.

Applied areas of psychology have also benefited from cognitive psychology. For example, criminological psychology and the cognitive interview, abnormal or atypical psychology, and various types of cognitive therapies used to treat people.

Cognitive psychology may be seen as a core or central topic in psychology, where its theories, concepts and research methods have influenced and informed numerous other areas of psychology, as shown in Figure 6.3.

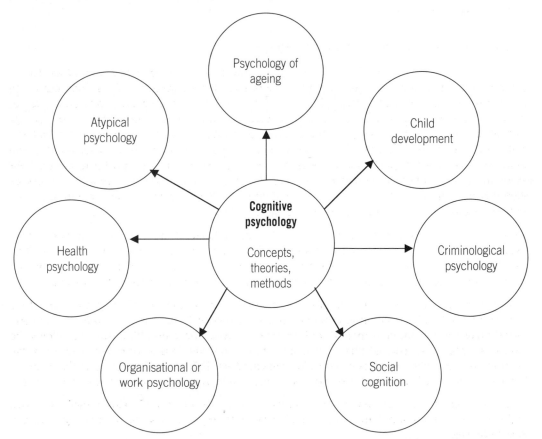

Figure 6.3: Cognitive psychology as a central or core area which influences other areas and applications of psychology

6.4 Mediational processes

The radical behaviourist approach (see Chapter 5) is only interested in observable behaviour and objectivity. The emphasis on reinforcement of stimulus–response links deliberately ignores mental processes within the organism. Cognitive psychologists, and cognitive behaviourists such as Tolman, regarded it as essential to look at mental processes of the organism and how these influence behaviour. Instead of a simple S–R linkage, the **mediational processes** of the organism are given central attention. Without an understanding of the mediational processes that occur in the mind of the person, it is argued, psychologists cannot have a proper

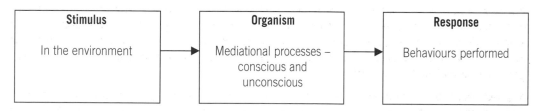

Stimulus	Organism	Response
In the environment	Mediational processes – conscious and unconscious	Behaviours performed

Figure 6.4: Cognitive psychologists place mediational processes at the centre of interest to understand human behaviour (the SOR model of cognition)

understanding of behaviour. In this section we will consider conscious and unconscious human mediational processes and individual differences. We will also consider the question of whether or not animals can think.

Conscious and unconscious processes

Consciousness is still regarded as one of the great mysteries of mind (Young and Block 1995), since it is not clear how the physical brain causes us to be conscious. **Consciousness** is the awareness we have of both stimuli in the environment, stimuli from our body and states of mind. Consciousness may also be seen to involve different levels – alert and awake, asleep, altered states of consciousness, hypnotic states. Some people when experiencing an altered state of consciousness describe being overwhelmed by stimuli – internal and external – and being conscious of too much at once. *Attentional processes*, which you may have studied at AS level, limit the amount of information that we are conscious of at any one time. In a different way memory allows vast amounts of information to be stored so that at any one time we are conscious of a limited amount of information and feelings.

Research has shown that if a person is aware that attempts are being made to condition certain aspects of behaviour, conscious awareness of this can prevent conditioning taking place. This sets human beings apart from other animals. Hence conscious thought mediates between stimulus and response, and may at times prevent the stimulus from causing the response.

Consciousness serves two main purposes in relation to cognition: monitoring and controlling (Kihlstrom 1984). The monitoring function allows the person to keep track of the environment, their behaviour and internal mental and emotional states. The controlling function allows the person to plan and control their behaviour, based on the information received from the environment and internally. Hence consciousness mediates behaviour through controlling how to behave and monitoring that the behaviour is appropriate in a particular social situation or context.

At a conscious level, your perceptions, thoughts, memories of previous experiences, feelings, and even mood at that particular time, are all aspects of cognition that mediate between stimuli and responses.

REFLECTIVE Activity

Think of a social situation which is familiar to you, in a café or at the pub with friends, for example. Think about how you normally behave, and then try to identify a time when you behaved differently. What mediational or cognitive processes might have been different this time to explain your behaving differently from normal?

Cognitive psychologists have also recently shown an interest in unconscious mental processes. These are not the irrational, instinctive unconscious processes of Freud (see Chapter 7). Instead it may be better to use the term **non-conscious** (Kihlstrom *et al.* 1992). Most human mental processes – memory, attention, for example – occur at a non-conscious level. We saw in Section 6.3.2 that attempts by introspection are made by cognitive psychologists to find out more about non-conscious processes.

Research in the area of **subliminal perception**, which may be regarded as non-conscious information processing, shows that we can be influenced by stimuli we cannot see or hear consciously. While the effects of subliminal perception studies have been shown to be small (Krosnick *et al.* 1992; Greenwald *et al.* 1991) they do show that mediational processes can and do operate at a non-conscious or unconscious level.

Individual differences

Perhaps the most important individual difference with respect to cognition and mediational process is that of intelligence. Sternberg (2001) characterises intelligence as how well people learn from experience and adapt to the world in which they live. Additionally, and importantly, Sternberg (2001) also links intelligence to people's understanding and control of their cognitive processes. In particular the processes of problem-solving, reasoning and decision-making.

A cognitive and information processing view of intelligence has been put forward by Deary (2000). In this view individual differences in intelligence are seen as differences between people in the rate of processing of simple information. For example, consider the two lines, where it is obvious that one line is longer than the other. Cognitive psychologists have found that more intelligent people need to see the picture of the two lines for a shorter period than less intelligent people to judge which is the longer line.

Intelligence, however it is determined and measured, may act as a mediational process because of its influence on the speed with which information is taken in and processed by the person. Highly intelligent people seem to process information more quickly and hence will respond more quickly to a stimulus.

Other types of individual differences that affect cognitive or mediational processes include **need for cognition** (Cacioppo and Petty, 1982). Need for cognition refers to the level of thought a person gives to a task, message or problem. People who score high on the need for cognition scale think deeply about a problem and have a need to understand the world around them more than those who score low on the scale. People who score high on need for cognition enjoy thinking and reasoning and may have good access, through introspection, to their cognitive processes. Need for cognition is a mediational process because it influences how fully a person may or may not process information in forming a response. Figure 6.5 gives some items for the Need for Cognition scale of Cacioppo and Petty (1982).

Can animals think?

Dog lovers often use the phrase 'he understands every word I say' to indicate that their pet is conscious of what is being said. Research by Kemp and Strangman (1994) showed that around 40 per cent of the general population regard animals as possessing consciousness. Animal

1.	I really enjoy a task that involves coming up with new solutions to a problem.	Agree/disagree
2.	I only think as hard as I have to. *	Agree/disagree
3.	I find little satisfaction in deliberating hard and for long hours. *	Agree/disagree
4.	I would prefer a task that is intellectual, difficult and important to one that is somewhat important but does not require much thought.	Agree/disagree
5.	I prefer to think about small, daily, projects rather than long-term ones.	Agree/disagree
6.	Learning new ways to think does not excite me very much. *	Agree/disagree

Figure 6.5: Agreement with 1, 4 and 5 scores towards need for cognition: disagreement (those with an asterisk) with 2, 3 and 6 scores towards need for cognition

psychologists have attempted to look at the cognitive capabilities of the organism in the S–O–R model of cognition. Some research (Cook 1993) has shown that some animals do respond to colour photographs of familiar objects. Other research has shown that laboratory animals display mediational processes such as the coding and organisation of abstract symbols (Wasserman 1993).

However, psychologists sometimes argue that whilst animals may show evidence, solely on the basis of behavioural responses, of cognitive processes, these are not similar to those operating in human beings (Baum 1994).

PRACTICAL Activity

In groups of three or four, consider a number of different animals, for example, dogs, cats, monkeys, rats and mice. Discuss, for each type of animal, what behaviours might show evidence of consciousness and cognitive processes. Do you think there is a major difference between the mental processes of people and those of other animals? Discuss your answers to this question.

Some psychologists argue that since animals do not possess a language like human beings, then they cannot think. We tend to regard thought as some kind of internal language and believe that we think using language. Animals do have communication systems but whether or not any of these systems constitutes a language has been an issue of long-standing interest in psychology.

EVALUATIVE COMMENT

How do we know that we think? Probably because we say so and are conscious of having thoughts and can communicate this using language. Animals cannot do this, hence any inference about animal cognition can only come from observing behaviour. Hence, we can probably never really know if animals think, and whilst pet owners may believe their dog understands every word said, it is highly unlikely to be the case.

6.5 Information processing

At the very heart of the cognitive approach is the idea of information processing. This characterises the approach and makes it different from other approaches such as behaviourism and humanism. The environment (external or internal to the person) provides stimuli through the senses. These stimuli are inputs which can be transformed, stored and retrieved using various mental or cognitive processes. Information is stored in and retrieved from memory. It is transformed through thinking and reasoning to solve a problem. This information processing model is depicted in Figure 6.6.

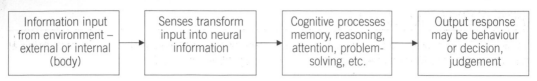

Figure 6.6: The information processing approach which characterises cognitive psychology

The information processing model of cognitive psychology does present a mechanistic view of the mind. This is because it is seen to be governed by rules but likened to a computer. We will look at the computer analogy in more detail in Section 6.6. Information processing models of different cognitive processes, such as memory and attention, are usually represented by flow charts. The use of flow charts, such as that of memory given in Figure 6.7, assumes that mental or cognitive processes follow clear sequences. There are two views about this – the **serial processing** view of early cognitive psychology, and the more recent parallel processing or connectionist view of contemporary cognitive psychology.

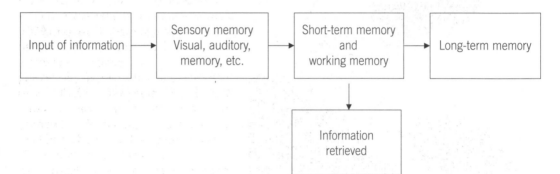

Figure 6.7: An information processing model of memory. Adapted from Atkinson and Shiffrin (1971)

The classical view

Cognitive psychologists first adopted the idea of information processing as a model to explain human cognitive processes. In the early days it was assumed that each of the stages in a flow diagram, such as that shown in Figure 6.7, had to be completed before moving onto another stage. This classical view, known as the **serial processing** model also assumes that the stimuli or information impinging on the person is processed in an automatic way by that person. This rather passive view of information processing is conceptualised as *bottom-up* information processing. That is information processing is entirely dependent on the stimulus input of information through the senses. However, it is easy to show that the knowledge a person holds and expectations a person has influence perception and what is attended to and remembered. This is called *top-down* processing. The well known psychological example of the young woman/old woman ambiguous figure demonstrates top-down processing well. Look at Figure 6.8(a) – what do you see? If you look for an old woman you can see one, and if you look for a young woman you can see one. By contrast the figures shown in 6.8(b) and 6.8(c) are relatively unambiguous. Hence, with an ambiguous picture, what you expect to see or are looking for, you usually do see. Translating this idea more widely to interpreting human behaviour, it is often the case that an example of behaviour is ambiguous and needs interpreting. Hence, expectations and pre-judgements often strongly influence the meaning you give to what somebody has done.

PRACTICAL Activity

The concepts of bottom-up and top-down information processing were covered at AS level. If you did not study this at the time read pages 234–9 of the AS Text, *Introducing psychology* (Pennington 2002).

Figure 6.8: The young woman/old woman ambiguous figure. You can see either depending upon what you are looking for

6.5.2 The connectionist view

A number of problems have been identified with the classical or serial information processing view. First, serial processing is too slow to account adequately for human information processing. The one-step-at-a-time approach of serial information processing does not reflect how the brain and interconnection of neurons seem to work (Dawson 1998). For example, Posner (1978) showed that people can perform extremely complicated information processing tasks in a fraction of second. This does not seem to square with a serial processing explanation. Second, studying how the brain works and how networks of neurons in the brain operate does not show step-by-step serial processing of information. Instead, it is much more likely that **parallel processing** of information is taking place. Parallel processing means that a number of steps or operations in an information flow diagram are operating at the same time. Also, parallel processing refers to the idea that the same information is being processed at the same time in different parts of the brain.

The parallel processing model has been developed into a *connectionist network* which at its simplest has three types of information processing units – input units, hidden units and output units. An example of a simple connectionist network is shown in Figure 6.9. Input units receive stimuli or information from the environment. Hidden units detect and process patterns and features of the input units. Finally, output units encode information for the response. Notice in Figure 6.9 that there are many interconnections between all three types of units, hence the name connectionist networks.

EVALUATIVE COMMENT

The connectionist view of information processing has a number of advantages over the serial processing view. First, connectionist networks represent better what goes on at a physical level in the brain between neurons. Second, connectionists assumed that the architecture of cognition, how cognitive processes are structured, is like that of the brain. Third, connectionist

networks explain how people can perform complex information processing tasks in very short periods of time measured by milliseconds. Finally, connectionist networks have been successfully applied in understanding how knowledge is represented in the mind and how information is organised in long-term memory (Smolensky 1995).

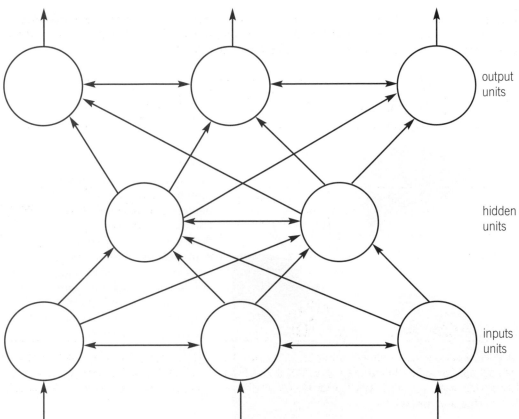

output
units

hidden
units

inputs
units

Figure 6.9: A simple connectionist network showing the three types of units — input, hidden and output. Direction of arrows indicates flow of information

6.6 Computer analogies

Of fundamental importance to the development of cognitive psychology was the use of a computer as an analogy for the human brain. The computer was being developed at about the same time that cognitive psychology was becoming established as a legitimate area of scientific, psychological, inquiry. Likening the human mind and its operations to a computer and how it works through information processing has, and remains, a powerful analogy for cognitive psychology. In what follows we shall explore the computer analogy more fully, then look at how psychologists have used the computer to simulate human mental abilities, in artificial intelligence and areas of application.

The computer as human mind

The parallels between how computers process information and how humans process information are very compelling, as the following quotation demonstrates:

Computers take a symbolic input, recode it, make decisions about the recoded input, make new expressions from it, store some or all of the input, and give back a symbolic input.

(Lachman *et al.* 1979)

This is very similar to how the human mind processes information. Humans code information, remember it, make decisions based on it, change their internal levels of knowledge, and turn all this into a behavioural output. This is shown in Figure 6.10.

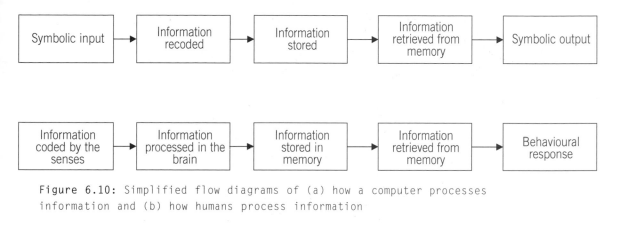

Figure 6.10: Simplified flow diagrams of (a) how a computer processes information and (b) how humans process information

PRACTICAL Activity

Consider the topics of face recognition and making a decision about what film to go and see at your local cinema. For each attempt draw a flow diagram starting with the input information and finishing with a response (recognising a face correctly and which film to see). Can you identify any differences that might exist between you and a computer for these two cognitive tasks?

The computer analogy of human cognitive processes can be seen to work because of five key areas of similarity. These are to do with coding, channel capacity, span of apprehension, central processing unit and information store. Both computers and humans as information processors have these in common. Coding is fundamental to both how computers work and human information processing. All communication systems use some form of *coding*. For example, a telephone translates our voice into an electrical signal, transmits it to another telephone, where it is decoded back into a voice. How the brain represents a picture, for example, is through coding the information into electrical impulses. The Ancient Greeks, such as Aristotle, and Plato, believed that a picture was literally copied into our mind and not coded.

Channel capacity is the idea that any system which channels or communicates information has an upper limit on the amount of information it can deal with at any one time. Even with fibre optics, there is a limit to the amount of information that can be transmitted at any one time, but this is very large indeed. In human attention, people seem able only to attend properly to one message at a time. Channel capacity in humans is, it seems, much less than computer systems. *Span of apprehension* refers to how much information can be taken in at any one time. How much information can be taken in at any one time depends on how the information is arranged, as shown in Figure 6.11. The span of apprehension can be increased if information is organised in ways which make it easy to apprehend. This is the same with computers, but there are fewer constraints here.

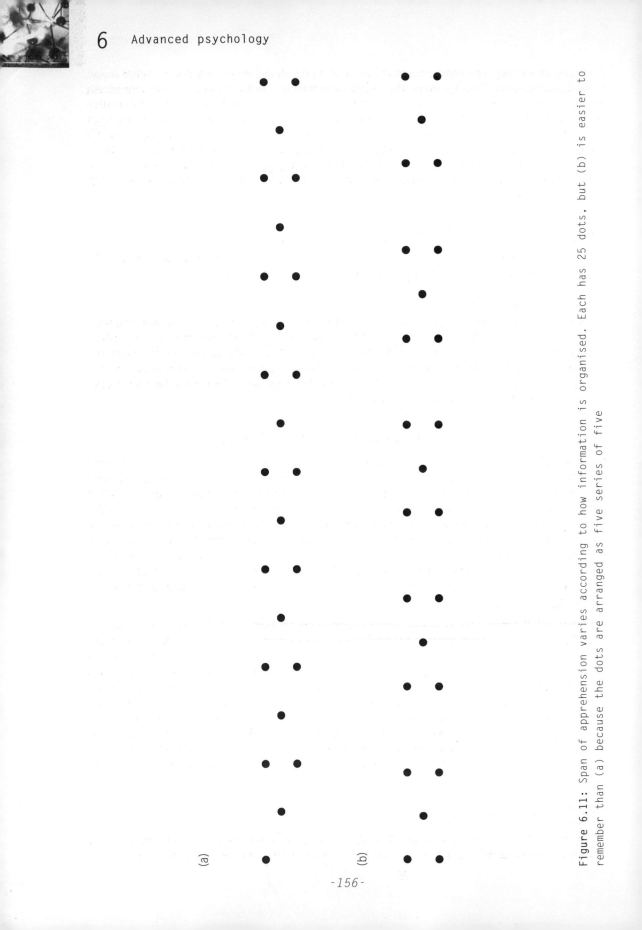

(a)

(b)

Figure 6.11: Span of apprehension varies according to how information is organised. Each has 25 dots, but (b) is easier to remember than (a) because the dots are arranged as five series of five

A *central processing unit* manipulates information which is what both computer systems and mental processes do. Finally, information is stored in memory. With computers a random access memory (RAM) system is used. In humans information is stored in the memory in an associative or network form. Both computers and humans store information and reference information from memory. One important difference is that computers do not 'forget' in ways that people do. If a computer stores information it can be retrieved, and only fails to do so if the computer is faulty or the memory capacity has been exceeded. In humans, forgetting is a common occurrence, for which there are numerous explanations (see the AS Text *Introducing psychology*, Chapter 10, Pennington 2002).

REFLECTIVE Activity

Think about other ways in which computers provide a good analogy for human cognition. Think about, for example, languages in each, damage to each – virus in a computer versus illness in a person.

EVALUATIVE COMMENT

There are some shortcomings with the computer analogy. These include representing humans as, in the end, mechanical devices which operate in an entirely predictable way. Also, information stored in the memory in a computer can be transferred to another computer. In contrast, human memory built up over a lifespan cannot be 'downloaded' to another person (or computer) in the same way. Finally, in what sense can a computer be said to be aware and conscious in the way people are conscious beings?

Computer simulation and artificial intelligence

Computer simulation and artificial intelligence are different. Computer simulation is concerned with attempting to simulate human cognitive processes on a computer. The aim of computer simulation is to make computers perform the same information process in the same way as that of humans. To do this a psychological theory is first needed about how humans perform the cognitive task. If a computer performs in indistinguishable ways from humans, including making the same types of errors, then it can be said that a computer simulation has been achieved. Attempts to simulate human cognitive processes, such as making judgements and decisions, may help psychologists understand the shortcomings of a theory. A computer simulation may differ from how a human works and this may provide valuable insights into shortcomings of a psychological theory.

Artificial intelligence (AI) is about getting computers to perform tasks that we regard as requiring intelligence. Here there is not necessarily any attempt to simulate human intelligence. AI may have as one of its aims the attempt to understand human intelligence, but it is primarily concerned with producing machines that behave intelligently, regardless of whether this reflects human intelligence. One area of AI that has developed greatly over recent years is that of *expert systems*. Expert systems, such as systems for medical diagnosis, are attempts to develop intelligent systems dealing with complex problems that exist in the world. Artificial intelligence has also produced computers that play chess to grand master (international) standards. AI also has a key role to play in the development of robots where vision, movement and three-dimensional perception are all programmed into the computer in order for the robot to 'see' and move around in its environment.

PRACTICAL Activity

Get together with two or three other people. Think about science-fiction films which have portrayed intelligent computers (for example HAL in *2001*) or advanced robots (such as R2D2 in the *Star Wars* series of films, or the

Terminator). Discuss the extent to which you think they simulate human beings and try to identify a number of differences as well. Do you think these machines are aware and conscious in the same way as people? Whatever you answer, how can you be sure of what you are claiming?

6.7 Limitations and strengths of the cognitive approach

The cognitive approach in psychology has both limitations and strengths; overall the strengths outweigh the limitations and make it one of the dominant perspectives in psychology both today and for the foreseeable future. In what follows we shall consider five main limitations and five main strengths.

The five main limitations are that the cognitive perspective is mechanical, is often more interested in mental processes than behaviour, tends to be theoretical and abstract, involves experiments that lack ecological validity, and has until recently ignored affect and human emotion. Because of the use of the computer analogy human beings are depicted as little more than machines (hardware and software) with the result that the image of people is rather mechanical and lacking in essential humanity. Human attributes, like consciousness and self-awareness, which distinguish people from animals remain major problems or mysteries for cognitive psychologists.

Some critics accuse cognitive psychologists of being too narrow in their theoretical and empirical treatment of people. There is too much focus on detailing and understanding mental processes, such as memory and attention, and not on behaviour. Ironically, this criticism is almost exactly the opposite of that made of the behaviourist perspective. This leads on to the limitation that cognitive psychology tends to be seen as highly theoretical and abstract, and in some ways loses sight of the whole person whilst theories of memory and attention are developed and tested. The dominant empirical approach in cognitive psychology is the laboratory experiment. The danger here is that abstract or technical experiments are conducted that do not readily generalise or relate to how people think and act in the 'real' world. Finally, until recently, cognitive psychologists had paid little attention to emotions and how emotions can affect cognitive processes such as memory and attention. Recently research has turned to look at how cognitions and emotions interact in everyday life, for example how cognitions play a role in stress and emotional responses (Lazarus 1991).

The five key strengths of the cognitive perspective are that it is scientific and objective, looks at mental characteristics of human beings, has practical applications, is important in other areas of psychology (see section 6.3.5) and assumes that the mind is the brain (See the mind–brain debate in Chapter 11). The behaviourists refused to study mental events because they regarded behaviour as objective and measurable because only overt behaviour is observable. Cognitive psychologists have clearly demonstrated that a scientific, mainly laboratory approach, can be applied to cognitive processes. Theory, hypotheses, and empirical investigation all characterise the scientific approach of the cognitive psychologist (see Chapter 10 for more on the scientific approach in psychology). Practical applications have been made to the treatment of people suffering certain mental disorders, such as anxiety and depression, using for example, Ellis's (1989) rational-emotive therapy. Rational-emotive therapy requires people to think logically and rationally and attempts to minimise irrational and illogical thinking. Another therapeutic approach is that of cognitive therapy (Beck 1991). In a similar way to rational-emotive therapy, attention is given to the way a person's cognitions about themselves and the world are distorted. Cognitive therapy has been used successfully to treat depression, anxiety disorders and eating disorders (Beck 1991). With anxiety disorders attempts are made to get the person to believe that they are over-emphasising the feared event, and under-emphasising their abilities to cope and adjust to life.

Applications of cognitive psychology have also been made to criminology. For example, the cognitive interview (Geiselman *et al.* 1985) is built upon certain basics of what is known about human memory. Basically, attempts are made in the cognitive interview to provide cues and the context of the crime to help trigger memories of the event. Also, the person interviewed is asked to state everything that he or she can remember about the event and to attempt to describe the event from the point of view of another person. Research has demonstrated that the cognitive interview produces more correct detail than other interview techniques (Geiselman *et al.* 1986).

6.8 Sample questions

SAMPLE QUESTION 1

(a) Describe what is meant by mediational processes in cognitive psychology.
    (AO1 = 4)   *(4 marks)*
(b) Explain how the concept of information processing applies to human thought.
    (AO1 = 2, AO2 = 2)   *(4 marks)*
(c) Discuss the use of computer analogies to help understand human behaviour.
    (AO1 = 4, AO2 = 8)   *(12 marks)*

Total AO1 marks = 10 AO2 marks = 10 Total = 20 marks.

QUESTIONS, ANSWERS AND COMMENTS

SAMPLE QUESTION 2

(a) Identify and outline two assumptions of the cognitive approach in psychology.
    (AO1 = 4)   *(4 marks)*
(b) Explain the idea of mediational processes in cognitive psychology.
    (AO1 = 2, AO2 – 2)   *(4 marks)*
(c) Discuss at least two limitations of the cognitive approach. Refer to at least one other perspective in your answer.
    (AO1 = 4, AO2 = 8)   *(12 marks)*

Total AO1 marks = 10 AO2 marks = 10 Total = 20 marks.

Answer to 2(a)

Two assumptions of the cognitive approach are that thought and mental events in the mind can be studied scientifically and damage to the brain can help understand cognition. The latter is called cognitive neuropsychology and looks at how damage to particular areas of the brain affect what a person can remember or attend to.

Comment: Two assumptions are correctly identified, so 1 mark is awarded for each. The second assumption to do with cognitive neuropsychology is expanded on so a third mark here. Some extra detail about the first assumption is needed to score the full 4 marks available. So 3 marks awarded overall.

Answer to 2(b)

Mediational processes are those that go on between stimulus and response and refer to mental processes within the organism. The organism may be human or another animal. In the human, mediational processes are to do with levels of thought and memory and may occur at both a conscious

Sample questions, answers and comments

and non-conscious level. If at a conscious level the person should be able to report on them, but would not be able to report to a psychologist if at a non-conscious level.

Comment: A good answer that would score the full 4 marks. The idea of mediational processes is well understood and seen to refer to both humans and other animals. The kinds of mental processes that are included are detailed correctly.

Answer to 2(c)

Two limitations of the cognitive approach are that people are seen to be like machines and that emotions have not been studied. Because the cognitive approach likens humans to computers then they are seen to be no more than a collection of mechanical processes involving hardware and software. The hardware in the analogy is the actual physical body and the software is the mind and its mental processes. This is a limitation because people are more than machines and have human qualities such as conscience, self-awareness and free will which machines do not have. In many ways the cognitive approach is like the behaviourist approach in that both approaches regard human behaviour as predictable and determined. This is unlike the humanistic perspective which regards humans as conscious, free to choose and wanting to self-actualise all the time. These are not mechanical concepts and could not be applied to computers.

Cognitive psychologists have not paid much attention to emotions, and again have missed what it is to be human. Machines do not have emotions; only people do. Also emotions can affect cognitive processes. For example, if you are very stressed out you will not be able to think straight. Or if you have taken a mind-altering drug such as LSD you may think differently and see the world in a different way. Hence, emotions are important in cognition but are also unique to humans.

Comment: A reasonably good answer with two limitations correctly identified and two other perspectives referred to in the response. The limitation of people as machines is developed well and given good discussion, showing good knowledge and analysis. The limitation concerning emotions is correct, but not developed as fully as the first limitation. Overall, this answer would attract 9 out of the 12 marks.

The answer to question 2 would score 16 out of 20 marks, and overall represents an excellent answer to the question.

6.9 FURTHER READING

Introductory texts

Parkin, A. J. 2000: **Essential cognitive psychology**. Chapter 1. Psychology Press, Hove.

Specialist sources

Schultz, D. P. & Schultz, S. E. 2000: **A history of modern psychology**. 7th Ed. Chapter 15. Fort Harcourt College Publishers, Worth TX.

7

The psychoanalytic approach

7.1 Introduction

The psychoanalytic perspective in psychology includes a number of different theories, and in this chapter we will consider those of Sigmund Freud, Erik Erikson and Melanie Klein. These theories have three important principles in common. First, they regard mental processes or thought as occurring both at a conscious and unconscious levels. Unconscious mental processes are not directly accessible to consciousness so techniques such as dream analysis and free association are used in an attempt to understand the unconscious. Second, all regard early childhood experiences, particularly with parents, as important and vital influences on the adult personality. In particular, how the young child handles conflict and unpleasant experiences will be reflected in how the adult handles periods of stress and trauma. Third, these theories are concerned with how the adult is able to adjust to life and the difficulties and challenges life presents to everybody. People who are able to adjust well to changing circumstances will function effectively. People who do not adjust to change may experience anxiety and suffer from, for example, depression. This means that the psychoanalytic perspective is concerned to explain and treat people who suffer mental disorder.

REFLECTIVE Activity

Think about the earliest childhood memory that you can recall. At what age do you think this relates to and what is the memory about? Most people can go back to about the age of 4 or 5 years, but rarely earlier.

7.2 Freud's approach to personality

Sigmund Freud's theories and therapy have had a profound influence on the development of psychology, particularly in the treatment of various types of abnormal behaviours. Whilst Sigmund Freud regarded himself as a scientist, psychologists today would not agree with this since he did not conduct empirical research or experiments. Furthermore, most of his concepts and ideas refer to unobservable mental events.

REFLECTIVE Activity

You will have studied some of the basic ideas of Freudian theory when you took the AS Psychology in the Approaches section of Unit 1. To refresh your knowledge of psychoanalysis read Chapter 1, pages 9–11 of the AS text *Introducing psychology* (Pennington 2002).

Id, ego and superego

Freud's model of the mind consists of three types of mental processes or structures, the id, ego and superego. The **id** is the most primitive part of the mind, to quote Freud:

Sigmund Freud developed a theory of personality that attempted to explain how childhood experiences were of vital importance to the adult personality

It contains everything that is inherited, that is present at birth, that is laid down in the constitution.

Freud (1933/1940)

The id operates according to the pleasure principle and has no concept of reality. The id's most important driving forces are the sex (life) instinct and the aggressive (death) instinct. These instincts create wishes at an unconscious level, which result in tension or anxiety if not fulfilled. For the id, the ideal state is absence of tension or anxiety. This is achieved through wish-fulfilment. The fulfilment of a wish reduces tension; this tension reduction is pleasurable. So, for Freud, the pleasure principle is concerned with the absence of tension, rather than the receiving of something pleasurable. This is shown in Figure 7.1.

The **ego** operates according to the reality principle and is largely conscious and in touch with the outside world (reality). The ego, in contrast to the id, uses logical reasoning and common sense. The ego also employs various defence mechanisms (see the next section) to cope with the unreasonable, and instinctive demands of the id. The ego gives a person a sense of their own identity and needs to be strong to cope with id demands.

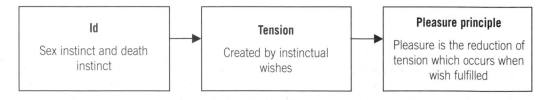

Id Sex instinct and death instinct	Tension Created by instinctual wishes	Pleasure principle Pleasure is the reduction of tension which occurs when wish fulfilled

Figure 7.1: The id and how the pleasure principle works

The **superego**, according to Freudian theory, develops around the age of 4–5 years during the phallic stage of psychosexual development (see Section 7.3.3). The superego is made up of two systems: a person's conscience and the ideal self. The conscience can punish the ego through causing feelings of guilt. Hence, if the ego gives in to id demands, the superego may make the person feel bad through guilt. The ideal self is an imaginary picture of how you ought to be, and represents career aspirations, how to treat other people, and how to behave as a member of society. Behaviour which falls short of the ideal self may be punished by the superego through guilt. If a person's ideal self is of too high a standard, then whatever the person does will represent failure. The ideal self and conscience are, according to Freud, largely determined in childhood from parental values and how you were brought up. Figure 7.2 summaries Freud's concept of the superego.

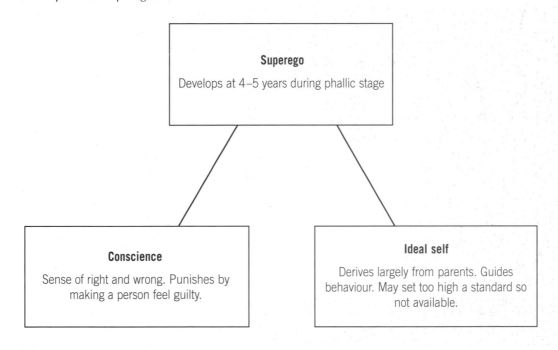

Figure 7.2: The two components or processes within Freud's concept of the superego

EVALUATIVE COMMENT

The ideal self and the conscience of a person can be seen to come about through both classical and operant conditioning (see Chapter 5). The rewards and punishments that parents give to a child when the superego is developing will have long-lasting effects for the individual. This may be why a person's sense of guilt and ideal self do not change much throughout life.

Defence mechanisms

In order to deal with conflict (which may be internal or with other people and hence external) and problems in life, Freud stated that the ego employs a range of **defence mechanisms**. Defence mechanisms operate at an unconscious level and help ward off unpleasant feelings or make good things feel better for the individual. There are a large number of defence mechanisms; the main ones are summarised in Figure 7.3. In what follows we shall consider four in more detail: repression, projection, reaction formation and sublimation.

Defence mechanism	Description	Example
Repression	Unconscious forgetting. Disturbing thoughts not allowed to become conscious.	Aggressive thoughts from the id remain unconscious.
Reaction formation	Behaving in ways directly opposite to unconscious impulses, feelings.	Behaving in a friendly way to someone that you dislike.
Displacement	Transferring impulses and feelings to an originally neutral or innocent target.	Scapegoating where a social group is wrongly blamed, e.g. the Jews.
Projection	Attributing one's own unacceptable impulse or feeling onto another person.	Saying somebody else is frightened of the dark when you actually are.
Rationalisation	Also known as intellectualisation. Remove the emotional content of an idea or event by logical analysis.	Coping with the death of someone close to you by intellectual analysis.
Identification	Behaving in a similar way to someone you regard as a role model.	Son imitating father in the garden with toy wheelbarrow.
Sublimation	Redirection of threatening impulses to something socially acceptable.	Use of aggressive impulses in a sport such as boxing.

Figure 7.3: Examples of defence mechanisms used unconsciously by the ego

The defence mechanism of **repression** is of fundamental importance within Freud's theory of personality. Repression is an unconscious mechanism employed by the ego to keep disturbing or threatening thoughts from becoming conscious. Repression is a widely used defence mechanism and one used by everybody, according to Freud. Thoughts that are commonly repressed are those that would result in feelings of guilt from the superego. Examples, include thoughts of aggression or hostility against another, sexual fantasies and childhood memories from the psychosexual stages of development. In particular, memories from the Oedipal complex (see Section 7.3.3). In the Oedipal complex aggressive thoughts about the same sex parent for the 4- to 5-year-old child are repressed. There has been recent research on repression.

Study 7.1

Aim Boden and Baumeister (1997) used a questionnaire to investigate individual differences in memory for emotional events.

Method The repressive coping style questionnaire (Weinberger *et al.* 1990) was given to a large number of people; at the same time participants were asked to recall details about emotional events in their lives.

Results Participants scoring as 'repressors' i.e. use the defence mechanism of repression, were less able to recall details of emotional events than non-repressors.

Conclusions Use of a repressive coping style in everyday life has the consequence that both positive and negative emotions are less well remembered.

Projection is when an individual attributes their own thoughts, feelings or motives to another person. Thoughts most commonly projected onto another are ones that would cause guilt. For example, aggressive and sexual fantasies or thoughts. Newman *et al* (1997) have shown that individuals actively suppress thoughts that have undesirable characteristics and see other people as possessing such characteristics and not themselves.

Reaction formation is where a person behaves in the opposite way to which he or she thinks or feels. For example, Freud claimed that men who are prejudiced against homosexuals are making a defence against their own homosexual feelings. Adams *et al.* (1996) demonstrated reaction formation when homophobic men showed sexual arousal to viewing homosexual behaviour between two men.

Sublimation was regarded by Freud as a highly positive mechanism of defence and one which benefited society. In sublimation sexual and aggressive thoughts and feelings are channelled or redirected in socially acceptable behaviour. For example, these energies could be sublimated into work and become dedicated to their career. Freud thought that all art and literature resulted from sublimation of the sexual instinct. Here instinctual sexual energy is converted into love of beauty and expression.

Freud regarded sublimation of the sexual instinct to result in art and literature

EVALUATIVE COMMENT

Defence mechanisms operate at an unconscious level in the mind. As such they are not observable and all that can be scientifically studied is behaviour. Hence, a link has to be made between behaviour and defence mechanisms to provide evidence of a defence mechanism. Recent research by experimental psychologists has seen a renewed interest in defence mechanisms and their measurable effects.

Unconscious mental processes

Freud distinguished between conscious, preconscious and unconscious mental processes. **Unconscious** mental processes take place without our being directly aware of them. However, for Freud, unconscious thoughts have the greatest influence on how we consciously think and feel, and how we behave. The **preconscious** contains thoughts and feelings that a person is not currently aware of, but which can easily be brought to consciousness. This is what we mean in our everyday usage of the word 'memory'. For example, you are presently not thinking about your mobile telephone number, but now it is mentioned you can recall it with ease. Mild emotional experiences may be in the preconscious but sometimes traumatic and powerful negative emotions are repressed and hence not available in the preconscious. The **conscious** is that which you are aware of at any time and this may be to do with thoughts and feelings. For example, you may be feeling thirsty at this moment and decide to get a drink.

Freud applied these three systems to the id, ego and superego. Here the id is regarded as entirely unconscious, whilst the ego and superego have conscious, preconscious, and unconscious aspects. Freud also regarded the mind to be like an iceberg, where the greatest part is hidden beneath the water or unconscious. This is shown in Figure 7.4.

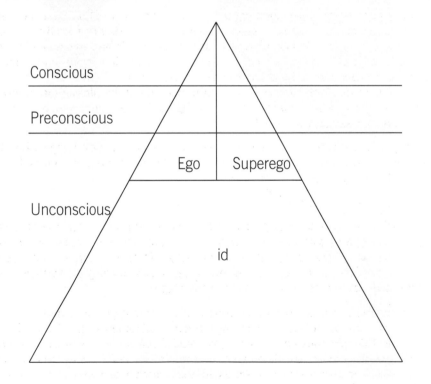

Figure 7.4: The id, ego and superego in relation to conscious, preconscious, and unconscious mental systems

EVALUATIVE COMMENT

By definition the unconscious is hidden. This makes it a difficult concept for many psychologists to accept because it is not possible directly to investigate the unconscious and its claimed effects on our conscious thoughts and awareness of feelings.

7.3 Freud's psychosexual stages of development

One of Sigmund Freud's lasting contributions to psychology has been the recognition that early childhood (the first five years of life) strongly influences and determine the adult personality. Positive childhood experiences can have ego-strengthening effects, whilst negative experiences may play a role in psychological disorders in older teenage and adult life. Freud proposed that all children go through five stages of development, three of which occur before the age of 5–6 years. These are called **psychosexual stages** of development since they represent how the sexual instinct results in strong sexual urges in the young child.

EVALUATIVE COMMENT

Freud's concept of sexual urges in the young child needs to be taken in the wider context of the life instinct, than the more narrow interpretation that we, as adults, may place on the idea of sexual urges. It may be more appropriate to think of pleasurable bodily experiences in the young child as what Freud meant by sexual urges. However interpreted these do originate from the sexual instinct and impulses from the id.

7.3.1 The oral stage

The **oral stage** of psychosexual development occurs in the first year of life. Here the area of the mouth (lips, tongue, mouth) becomes associated with pleasure due to feeding. The mother's breast (or bottle) becomes the first object of desire for the infant, since feeding reduces uncomfortable feelings of hunger. Feelings of hunger create tension in the infant; removal of tension, as we saw in Section 7.2.1, is experienced as pleasure by the id. For Freud the mother becomes the first emotional attachment for the child, because of the pleasure from feeding she gives the infant. As the first line object of the infant the mother becomes a model for all future love relationships as a teenager and adult.

The oral stage was sub-divided into two sub-stages: oral passive and oral aggressive. The oral passive stage occurs first and pleasure is gained from sucking at the breast. The oral aggressive stage is marked by biting or grabbing at the breast.

PRACTICAL ACTIVITY

Get together with two or three other people that you know well. See if you can describe oral passive and oral aggressive behaviours in each other. Oral passive behaviours are, for example, being accepting of others, being gullible, speaking kindly of people. Oral aggressive behaviours are, for example, having a 'biting' wit, being sarcastic, being over-critical of others. Do you think such behaviours are a result of the oral stage?

Freud thought that the infant could become *fixated* at the oral stage. By fixation is meant that the infant does not move on fully to the next stage, but instead remains 'stuck' or unable to 'give up' the oral stage. This may happen, according to Freud, because of very negative experiences of breast feeding or discomfort associated with feeding. Someone fixated at the oral stage may be very clingy and over-dependent on others as an adult. Such a person may also have a need for approval and love from others all the time.

The anal stage

The **anal stage** typically occurs during the second year of life as the child gains control of anal muscles during toilet training. Freud said that in the anal stage the child gains pleasure from retention and expulsion of faeces. The child learns that he or she can please or defy the parents. The parents are trying to toilet train the child and the child can comply and use the toilet instead of defecating in the nappy, or the child can defy the parent by either retention of faeces or defecating in the nappy.

EVALUATIVE COMMENT

Most people find these claims ridiculous upon first reading. However, if you observe children of this age, the experience of defecating does seem to be emotionally very powerful. A rare, but recognised, abnormality in young children is the hoarding of their faeces or stools in their bedroom drawers, for example. However, in a few years the anal region is associated more with dirtiness and disgust than pleasure.

As with the oral stage, the anal stage was seen to fall into two sub-stages: the anal expulsive and anal retention. In the former, which comes first, the child enjoys expulsion or elimination. Symbolically, Freud regarded this as not caring for the parents – trying to 'eliminate' them. In the second sub-stage, the retention and then expulsion symbolically represents the child giving the parents a gift. Towards the end of the anal stage retention outweighs elimination pleasure and the child is then toilet trained.

Fixation at the anal stage may come about because of conflict-ridden or inconsistent toilet training. The personality characteristics resulting from fixation at this stage include those of orderliness, parsimony (miserliness) and obstinacy. The **anal personality** is characterised by somebody who is excessively tidy, does not give to others and is mean with money, and will stick to their opinion even when it is obvious it is wrong to do so.

EVALUATIVE COMMENT

Fisher and Greenberg (1977) looked at numerous correlational studies of these three characteristics of the anal personality. The evidence does show that these three characteristics go together and are present in some adult personalities. The strongest pairing was found to be between orderliness and meanness. However, studies reviewed by Fisher and Greenberg (1977) have failed to support the claim that the anal personality results from difficulties during toilet training. Freud's observation that the characteristics of orderliness, parsimony and obstinacy go together seems to be correct, but the claim that the anal personality results from fixation at the anal stage has not been supported empirically.

The phallic stage and Oedipal conflict

Roughly between the ages of 3–6 years the main object of the sexual instinct moves from the anal region to the genital region. In boys it is the penis and in girls, the clitoris that becomes the source of pleasure.

EVALUATIVE COMMENT

Freud's theory of psychosexual development was regarded as sexist because the stage was named after the male sexual organ – the phallus – when it covered both males and females. Notice that the next section of this chapter deals with the genital stage which has no connotations of gender.

Because the superego has yet to develop, according to Freud, boys and girls discover that playing with their genitals is pleasurable. This is what Freud called childhood masturbation.

Also, children are not inhibited from playing with their genitals in front of other people. Adults may find this embarrassing, but young children seem to find this good fun!

The most important aspect of the phallic stage is the **Oedipus complex**. This is one of Freud's most controversial ideas and one that many people reject outright. The name of the Oedipus complex derives from Greek myth where Oedipus, a young man, kills his father and marries his mother. Upon discovering this he pokes his eyes out and becomes blind.

In the young boy, the Oedipus complex or more correctly conflict, arises because the boy develops sexual (pleasurable) desires for his mother. He wants to possess his mother exclusively and get rid of his father to enable him to do so. Irrationally, the boy thinks that if his father were to find out about all this, his father would take away what he loves the most. In the phallic stage what the boy loves most is his penis. Hence the boy develops castration anxiety. This is the Oedipal (generic term for both Oedipus and Electra complexes) conflict. The Oedipal conflict is resolved in the young boy by repressing or 'giving up' his desire for his mother and identifying with his father. The consequence of this is that the boy takes on the male gender role, and adopts an ego ideal and values that become the superego.

For girls, the Oedipus or Electra complex is less than satisfactory. Briefly, the girl desires the father, but realises that she does not have a penis. This leads to the development of penis envy and the wish to be a boy. The girl resolves this by repressing her desire for her father and substituting the wish for a penis with the wish for a baby. The girl blames her mother for her 'castrated state', represses her feelings and identifies with the mother to take on the female gender role.

EVALUATIVE COMMENT

The Oedipus complex for girls has been heavily criticised because it is based on the absence of something that the male possesses – a penis. In Freudian theory, women are regarded as having a weak superego. This lack of a balanced view of male and female psychosexual development has, rightly, been regarded as chauvinistic and reflecting the male-dominated and patriarchal society in which Freud lived. Karen Homey, a psychoanalyst, has suggested that men suffer from 'womb envy' and the inability to bear children. (See also the film _What Women Want_)

Latent and genital stages

Following the phallic stage and the 'resolution' of the Oedipal complex, the child enters a latency period through to the onset of puberty. It is called a latency period because no further psychosexual development takes place, and whilst the sexual drive does not develop, it is present during this stage. However, Freud thought that all or most sexual impulses and urges were heavily repressed during the latent stage and sexual energy could be sublimated towards school work, hobbies and friendships.

The final stage of psychosexual development is the **genital stage**. The genital stage starts at puberty and the sexual instinct is directed to heterosexual pleasure, rather than the self-pleasure during the phallic stage. For Freud, the proper outlet of the sexual instinct in adults was through heterosexual intercourse. Fixation and conflict might prevent this with the consequence that sexual perversions may develop. For example, fixation at the oral stage may result in a person gaining sexual pleasure primarily from kissing and oral sex, rather than sexual intercourse.

EVALUATIVE COMMENT

Freud's emphasis on psychosexual development was too narrow since other forms of development, such as social, emotional and intellectual, are also important during childhood. Developmental psychologists do not regard sexual development as of prime importance. Additionally, the mother–child attachment in terms of providing trust and security is seen as critical to child development. Difficulties in interpersonal relationships in adult life may come

from insecurity of attachment to the mother. In turn, difficulties in interpersonal relationships may result in sexual problems, rather than the other way round with Freud.

7.4 Freud's use of case studies

Freud pioneered the use of case studies in psychology and demonstrated how detailed accounts of a person's mental life illuminates Freudian concepts and ideas. It is incorrect to criticise Freud for selecting middle-class Victorian women for his case studies and psychoanalytic treatment. Throughout Freud's 20 volumes of writing, 133 cases are mentioned (Storr 2001). However, only six are developed into full accounts; seven if you include Freud's self-analysis which appears in his book *The interpretation of dreams*. The six case studies he writes about at length are as follows:

- Judge Schreber
- Dora
- Rat Man

- Little Hans
- Wolf Man
- Unnamed female of 18

Of these, Judge Schreher was dead, and Freud used his autobiography to make psychoanalytic interpretations. With Little Hans, Freud conducted the analysis through the father, and Freud only ever met Little Hans once. Freud saw the other four people personally over varying lengths of time.

Freud did not use case studies in an attempt to prove his theories and concepts of psychoanalysis. His case studies were written for three main reasons. First, he wanted to show how psychoanalytic concepts applied to a real person's mental life: that is, to give practical demonstrations of his theories and ideas. Second, he aimed to appeal to a wider audience than other psychoanalysts in an attempt to spread the word about psychoanalysis and make it accessible to interested people. Third, he wanted to show how psychoanalysis could help treat, and to some extent, 'cure', a person suffering from some kind of mental disorder or dealing with the difficulties of everyday life.

Psychosexual stage	Age	Primary concerns	Conflicts
Oral	0–18 months	Feeding and dependency	Feeling hungry and poor feeding experiences
Anal	2–3 years	Toilet training – expulsion and retention of faeces	With authority – parents Anal personality – orderliness, parsimony, obstinacy
Phallic	4–6 years	Oedipus/Electra complex – desire for opposite sex	Conflict with same sex parent parent until identification takes place
Latency	7–11 years	Repression of sexual instinct and urges	Sublimation of sexual instinct to schoolwork, hobbies, friends
Genital	12+ years	Heterosexual intercourse as adult	Sexual perversions may develop if fixated at earlier stage

Figure 7.5: The five psychosexual stages of development suggested by Sigmund Freud

EVALUATIVE COMMENT

Case studies can be of scientific value if conducted in certain ways – see Chapter 3 of *Introducing psychology* (Pennington 2002). Freud did not take notes at the time he was seeing a client; instead he made notes in the evening of the day he had seen the client. Freud usually saw five to six clients a day and did not make notes during the consultation. He wrote up his notes in the evening which may have caused confusion of case therefore increasing the possibility of error. Selective memory might have been a problem since Freud may only have recalled material consistent with his theory and concepts.

In what follows we shall look at three of Freud's case studies: Little Hans, Dora, and the Rat Man.

Little Hans

The case of Little Hans (Freud, 1909/1977) was called 'Analysis of a phobia in a five-year old boy' by Freud. Hans suffered from a phobia of horses: he feared they would bite him or fall down in the street and 'make a row'. Freud interpreted the horses as symbolising Hans' father and the fear of being bitten as representing the Oedipal complex that Little Hans was going through. The fear of being bitten Freud interpreted as representing the castration anxiety resulting from Little Hans's sexual desire for his mother. The castration anxiety comes about because Little Hans thinks his father would castrate him if he found out about Little Hans's sexual desire for his mother.

Little Hans's father, whose name in real life was Max Graf, acted as his son's analyst and interpreted, following Freud's instructions, the boy's sexual interests, where babies come from, and his feelings for his parents. These interpretations were all made in relation to the Oedipal complex and the conflicts this produces.

REFLECTIVE Activity

Try to imagine yourself as this 5-year old little boy. Your father is talking to you about sex, sexual desires for your mother and hostile feelings to the father. Just how much sense do you think that Little Hans could make of all this? How much might Little Hans have accepted because of lack of understanding?

In reading the case study, what Little Hans is reported as saying does not confirm these Oedipal interpretations. In fact, Little Hans was more frightened of his mother who, for example, threatened to have his 'widdler' (penis) cut off if he kept touching it. She also threatened to abandon him.

Shortly after the time Freud spent with Little Hans's father on the case, Little Hans's parents got divorced. Freud failed to mention this important fact.

EVALUATIVE COMMENT

Whilst Freud used the Little Hans case to highlight his theory of the Oedipal complex, other simpler explanations for Little Hans's phobia exist. His parents did not get on and his mother threatened him with castration and abandonment. All this must have been deeply unsettling for Little Hans. What does need explaining is why Little Hans feared horses. One account is that his mother was cruel to his baby sister and Little Hans associated the screams of his sister with horses 'making a row' when they fall down. Little Hans had witnessed a horse falling down next to him in the street.

Dora

Dora (Freud, 1905/1977) was an 18-year-old woman referred to Freud by her father following a suicide note that Dora had written. Dora suffered from a number of 'hysterical' or neurotic symptoms including headaches, shortness of breath, a nervous, persistent cough that led to loss of voice, and depression. Dora's father said to Freud that her symptoms could be traced back to an incident when she was 16 years of age. Dora's parents were friendly with another family, called the 'Ks' in Freud's case study. In fact, at the time, Dora's father was having an affair with Frau K. The incident when Dora was 16 was, according to Dora, when the two families were on holiday in the Alps. Dora was out walking by a lake with Herr K when he made sexual advances towards her. Dora said that she slapped his face and ran away. Herr K denied the event and Dora's father believed him.

When in psychotherapy with Freud, Dora said that Herr K had made another sexual advance to her recently, and this seemed to precipitate the suicide note. Dora felt in some way she had not been believed by her father about Herr K's advances because of his own guilt at the affair he was having.

Freud was forceful in his interpretations to Dora. For example, her rejection of Herr K's advances Freud interpreted as a reaction formation (see Section 7.2.2) where in fact Dora is really in love with Herr K. Freud also interprets some of Dora's symptoms as love for Herr K. For example, Freud establishes that her loss of voice only occurs when Herr K is away on business. Since he is away her voice is of no use since she is not able to speak to the man she really loves. At one point Freud also says that Dora has sexual (lesbian) desires for Frau K and is in love with Freud as well!

EVALUATIVE COMMENT

In some ways it is a mystery why Freud published this case study since it seems to be a failure – he did not cure Dora. He used it to highlight the ego's use of defence mechanisms and how Oedipal conflicts from the age of 5 years were present in an 18-year-old woman. Freud in a sense betrayed Dora, just as her father had failed to believe her, because he assumed that 18-year-old women would respond to an older man's sexual advances. Dora took control; finding the relentless sexual interpretations unacceptable she broke off the psychoanalysis. Critics have regarded Freud's approach to this young woman was unsympathetic and aggressive.

PRACTICAL Activity

Get together with a group of two or three other people. Discuss how you think Dora might have felt about Freud's interpretation. Take into account the complex situation with the two families.

The Rat Man

The Rat Man (Freud, 1909/1979) who real name was Ernst Lanzer, came to see Freud when he was 29 years of age. He displayed numerous obsessive-compulsive behaviours and had obsessive, and fearful, thoughts about rats. The onset of these obsessive thoughts about rats seemed to be when he was on military training and heard an officer describe a particularly nasty torture using rats. This consisted of putting hungry rats into a bucket and tying this to the buttocks of a person. The torture consisted of the rats eating into the person through the anus. To ward off this image and thoughts that it might happen to his father, girlfriend and other people he was fond of, the Rat Man engaged in obsessive-compulsive rituals.

Freud interpreted these thoughts and obsessive behaviours as resulting from the mixture of love and hate that he felt for his father. Unconsciously, Freud said, the Rat Man hated his father and wished to torture him with rats. Any thought of this would cause the Rat Man to experience unbearable feelings of guilt and fear. The obsessive-compulsive behaviours helped to reduce the fear and feelings of guilt. Freud treated the Rat Man for about a year, after which he said that the treatment had 'led to the complete restoration of the patient's personality, and to the removal of his inhibitions'. In short, Freud claimed to have cured him of his phobia of rats and obsessive-compulsive tendencies.

EVALUATIVE COMMENT

Freud made no mention of the Rat Man's mother throughout the case study. As with the other two case studies we have considered, Freud focused on the father and the Oedipal complex, and omitted the mother. With the Rat Man, the mother was a dominating and controlling figure in his life. For example, even at the age of 29 years, he had to get her permission to see Freud, and she controlled all his money. Also, Freud did not mention the fact that the Rat Man had experienced the death of his older sister when he was four years old. Hence, a domineering mother and childhood feelings of abandonment might offer a simpler explanation for his phobia and compulsive behaviours.

7.5 Post-Freudian theories

Numerous theories within a psychoanalytic perspective have been developed since Freud's original ideas. Some theories have developed the idea of unconscious mental processes more fully. For example, Carl Jung (Storr 2001) thought that each person had two types of unconscious – the personal and the collective. The collective unconscious contains memories from our ancestors (see Steven 2001, for introduction to Jung). Other theories developed the idea of the ego and became knows as ego theories – in what follows we shall consider the ego psychology of Erik Erikson. Yet other theories were staged broadly within the Freudian tradition, most notably Freud's youngest daughter, Anna, and Melanie Klein. We shall consider Melanie Klein since she developed the idea of the death instinct more fully and centrally in her theory. Other psychologists rejected the overwhelming importance of the unconscious and sex instinct and focused on conscious thought and experiences. These became known as the humanistic psychologists (see Chapter 8).

Erik Erikson

Erikson adhered to the Freudian structure of the personality in terms of id, ego and superego, and the existence of strong instinctual forces. He also regarded development as occurring in stages, but instead of Freud's psychosexual stages, Erikson (1963) proposed that development takes place over the lifespan of the person. Erikson stated that **psychosocial development** was most important, even more so than psychosexual development. By using the term 'psychosocial development', Erikson saw the greatest influence on psychological development to be the interactions of the child, teenager, and adult with other people. These are parents, brothers and sisters, friends and peers, teachers and other significant people in a person's life. Erikson's view of psychosocial development over the lifespan of an individual was also concerned with the development of the ego and different strengths that the ego gains, or should gain, from each of the developmental stages. As well as other people, Erikson also emphasised the importance of culture and society on a person's development.

According to Erikson (1968) psychosocial development took place in eight stages, with the first occurring in the first year of life and the last in old age. For Erikson, each stage is marked by a critical point or crisis that the individual has to go through and resolve. Successful resolution of the crisis provides the ego with a basic strength. Failure to resolve the crisis means that the ego lacks the strength associated with any one stage. Figure 7.6 identifies each stage, the age at which it occurs, the nature of the crisis and ego strength.

From Figure 7.6 you will see that the first psychosocial stage of development is that of trust versus mistrust and that the important relationship is with the mother. The ego strength of hope results from a basic feeling of trust from this stage. Hence, the mother–child relationship is of fundamental importance to whether the child will trust others and the world in which he or she lives (see Chapter 1 of this book for more on attachment).

Stage	Rough age	Psychological crisis	Description of the crisis	Ego strength	Important relationships
1	0–1 yrs	Trust vs mistrust	Learns to feel comfortable and trust parents' care; or develops distrust of the world	Hope	Maternal person
2	1–3 yrs	Autonomy vs shame	Learns sense of competence by learning to feed oneself, play alone, use toilet; or feels ashamed and doubts own abilities	Will	Parents
3	3–5 yrs	Initiative vs guilt	Learns to use own initiative in planning behaviour; or develops sense of guilt over misbehaviour	Purpose	Basic family
4	5–11 yrs	Industry vs inferiority	Learns to meet demands imposed by school and home responsibility; or comes to believe he or she is inferior to other people	Competence	Family, neighbours, teachers
5	11–18 yrs	Identity vs identity diffusion	Acquires sense of identity in terms of beliefs, vocation, etc.; or fails to achieve identity	Fidelity	Peers, ingroups and outgroups
6	18–40 yrs	Intimacy vs isolation	Engages in successful intimate relationship, joint identity with partner; or becomes isolated	Love	Friends, lover
7	40–65 yrs	Generativity vs stagnation	Helping others, allowing independence to children; or self-centred and stagnant	Care	Spouse, children
8	65 onwards	Integrity vs despair	Reaps benefits of earlier stages. Develops acceptance of temporary nature of life; or despairs over ever being able to find meaning in life	Wisdom	Spouse children, grandchildren

Figure 7.6: Eight stages of psychosocial development proposed by Erickson (1950). Table shows the 'crisis' at each stage, the successful outcome for the ego, and the social relationships of prime importance at each stage

PRACTICAL Activity

In a group of four or five, consider and discuss each of the psychosocial stages in Figure 7.6. You might want to look at how each one applies to yourself, your parents or siblings.

Erikson's theory differs from Freud's in three important ways. First, Erikson focuses on relationships with people, whilst Freud's main concern is with unconscious effects of the sex instinct. Second, Erikson considers what can strengthen and weaken the ego, whilst Freud is more concerned with the conflicts the ego has to resolve between the id and superego. Third, Erikson's theory presents a much more positive and optimistic view of the human condition. By contrast, Freud presents a view of human beings locked in perpetual conflict.

Erikson studied other cultures and individuals to provide evidence for his theory. For example, he studied the Sioux and Yurok American Indians (Erikson 1963), and analysed Ghandi, a leader of the Indian Congress movement, from a psychosocial perspective (Erikson 1969).

Melanie Klein

Melanie Klein developed a particular psychoanalytic perspective called **object relations theory** (Klein 1964). This theory takes intimate relationships as its central concern, in particular how young children develop relationships with significant other people as they develop. The term *object* comes from Freud's claim that an instinct has an aim and an object – the object is usually a person, but not always. Hence object relations theory is about how the two most important instincts – life (sex) and death (aggression) – affect psychological development and how a person interacts with other people. Klein's (1932) theory paid particular regard to the death or aggressive instinct and its consequences. Klein subscribed to Freud's idea of the id, ego and superego, and to the importance of unconscious mental processes.

Klein differed from Freud in that she thought that the newborn was not pure id (as Freud thought) but contained a primitive ego. This primitive ego also has a number of primitive defence mechanisms that it can use – the most important being that of *splitting*. Klein says that in order for the baby to cope with feeding at the breast as a positive experience on one occasion and a negative experience at another time, the breast is 'split'. The 'good breast' exists when there is a positive experience, and the 'bad breast' whenever there is a negative experience. Hence, one part – object, of the mother, the breast, is split into two objects, one good, one bad. Klein says that the young baby does this with many things, and one of the early developmental tasks is to combine the good and bad into one object (Klein 1975).

Klein also differed from Freud by stating that the child goes through two developmental positions (she did not like the word *stages*) in the first year of life. The first is called the 'paranoid-schizoid position', and the second, the 'depressive position'. In contrast to Freud, Klein claimed that the superego was formed at the end of the second position, i.e. at about one year of age. Freud claimed the superego to be formed around the fifth year of life.

Klein also developed and pioneered a form of psychoanalysis for young children. This she achieved through analysis of a child's play. Klein would give a young child a box of toys to play with. These included little people, cars, lorries, etc. At each session Klein would ask the child to play with the toys. She would note down the play and make interpretations. For example, if the child repeatedly ran a toy person over with a lorry Klein might interpret this as the child symbolically hating or wanting to get rid of a parent.

In many ways Klein's object relations theory adheres closely to most of Freud's theory. Whilst Freud recognised the death or aggressive instinct later in his theoretical development, Klein saw it as central from the outset. In Klein's theory the life and death instincts produce unconscious conflict in the individual. This is then reflected in the nature of the relationship with other people.

REFLECTIVE Activity

Read back over the sections on Erikson and Klein and for each make two headings – one 'similar to Freud' and the other 'different from Freud'. List similarities and differences from Freud for each of Erikson and Klein's psychoanalytic perspectives.

7.6 Limitations of the psychoanalytic approach

In evaluating the contribution of the psychoanalytic perspective to psychology it is important to consider both limitations of the perspective as well as strengths. Psychoanalysis, particularly Freudian theory, has been likened by some psychologists to a religion (Fine 1990). This means that it depends on whether or not a person believes in the fundamentals – unconscious, repression, sex instinct, etc. A religion is not built upon scientific facts and testability of hypotheses derived from a theory. Hence, likening psychoanalysis to a religion means that some regard it as not scientific. This is a major limitation of psychoanalysis, as many critics have pointed out (Eysenck 1990; Fisher and Greenberg 1996). Concepts such as repression, the Oedipal complex and psychosexual stages of development are difficult to subject to scientific examination because testable hypotheses cannot be derived. If a testable hypothesis cannot be derived from a theory, then according to Popper (1963), a theory is not scientific. It is also problematic that one behaviour can have numerous Freudian interpretations – some of which are directly opposite to each other. For example, imagine someone saying that they strongly dislike another person. In Freudian interpretations this could mean either that they do dislike the person or that the defence mechanism of reaction formation is operating. In which case, the expressed emotion is really the opposite at an unconscious level. That is, the person really likes the other person! In the world of Freudian interpretations both may be equally valid, but how would you go about deciding scientifically which is the true interpretation?

PRACTICAL Activity

In a small group, consider the Freudian ideas of unconscious, repression and the Oedipal complex. For each discuss how you might go about scientifically investigating each. First, derive a hypothesis and second, devise a suitable empirical investigation. Third, decide if possible, what evidence would refute the hypothesis. All three steps are required for an investigation to be scientific (see also Chapter 12 of this book).

Another limitation of the psychoanalytic perspective is that case studies are open to numerous different interpretations. Different interpretations may result from a different theoretical perspective (for example, Freudian and Erikson's ego psychology) or differences within one perspective. The latter is possibly more problematic since if two Freudian psychologists disagree over interpretation of the same case, there is not an objective way of supporting one and rejecting the other interpretation. Interpretations in psychoanalysis are, in the end, subjective and may depend on what behaviours and thoughts of the person are selected to interpret in the first place (Powell and Boer 1995).

REFLECTIVE Activity

Consider one of the case studies of Freud outlined earlier in this chapter. Now think of the case from another psychoanalytic perspective, for example, Erikson's theory of psychosocial development. Each produces different interpretations – can you see any way of testing the validity of each?

Another limitation is that the effectiveness of psychoanalysis as a therapy has not been demonstrated. Eysenck (1952) examined thousands of case histories of people who underwent psychoanalytic therapy. He (1952) concluded that psychoanalytic therapy did not significantly help people suffering from neurotic disorders to recover. Eysenck found that over 70% of people who suffered from neurotic disorders but received no treatment of any kind recovered. In contrast, two-thirds of those treated to completion by psychoanalysts were cured or much improved. It may be that psychoanalytic therapy is effective for some types of people and not others, but recent research has not demonstrated the effectiveness of the therapy (Stunkard 1991).

Other limitations are that psychoanalysis is regarded as too deterministic and fatalistic when explaining human behaviour (see Chapter 11 for more on determinism). This means that the theory provides an unfolding sequence of psychosexual stages, that are pre-determined in some way. Another limitation is that Freudian theory of female psychosexual development has not been carefully worked out and is based on male development. Finally, Freudian theory regards the sexual instinct and its psychological effects as central and of overriding importance to psychological functioning. This has been at the expense of other importance influences, such as social and other people, particularly the mother.

On the positive side, the psychoanalytic perspective has, and continues to be, a major influence in psychology. In particular its influence has been most profound in the clinical area, and with the development of therapies to treat psychological disorders. The psychoanalytic perspective has also provided unique insights into human psychological functioning, particularly the characterisation of a person with internal conflicts, at both conscious and unconscious levels, that may result in psychological distress. Also, early childhood experiences are an important basis for later adult psychological functioning. These have greater acceptability now, than in the early days of psychoanalysis.

7.7 Sample questions

SAMPLE QUESTION 1

(a) Describe two defence mechanisms in Freudian psychoanalysis.
   (AO1 = 4)   *(4 marks)*
(b) Using an example, explain what is meant by unconscious mental processes in the psychoanalytic perspective.
   (AO1 = 2, AO2 = 2)   *(4 marks)*
(c) Discuss at least *one* strength and *one* weakness of Freud's use of case studies. Refer to one case study in your answer.
   (AO1 = 4, AO2 = 8)   *(12 marks)*

Total AO1 marks = 10 Total AO2 marks = 10 Total = 20 marks

QUESTIONS, ANSWERS AND COMMENTS

SAMPLE QUESTION 2

(a) Describe *one* psychosexual stage of development in Freudian theory.
   (AO1 = 4)   *(4 marks)*
(b) Discuss *one* way in which Erikson's theory differs from Freudian theory.
   (AO1 = 1, AO2 = 3)   *(4 marks)*
(c) Discuss at least *one* strength and *one* limitation of the psychoanalytic perspective. Refer to at least one other perspective in your answer.
   (AO1 = 5, AO2 = 7)   *(12 marks)*

Total AO1 marks = 10 Total AO2 marks = 10 Total = 20 marks

Answer to 2(a)

One stage is the oral stage. This occurs first of the three psychosexual stages and is to do with the feeding of the baby. The oral stage occurs in the first year of life and there may be fixation at this stage. This means that the adult will have an oral personality – enjoying eating chocolate and talking a lot.

Comment: Correctly identifies one of the three psychosexual stages and correctly describes when it occurs. Mentioning fixation and consequences scores a mark, but answer needs to be a little more precise and detailed to score the full marks. This answer would get 3 out of 4 marks.

Answer to 2(b)

One way in which Erikson's theory differs from Freud's is that Freud concentrated on the id and the unconscious whilst Erikson concentrated on the ego and the conscious. This means that Freud was interested more in the conflicts of the mind, and Erikson the things that make an ego stronger. Both were psychoanalysts though.

Comment: Correctly identifies a difference, although Erikson did not really focus entirely on the conscious as given in the answer. Also difference, as a consequence, in conflict and ego correct. Good answer, but more detail and more clarity to get full marks. This answer would get 3 out of the 4 marks available.

Answer to 2(c)

The psychoanalytic approach was first developed by Freud. He focused a lot on the early experiences of childhood, believing that these could have a great impact on the adult personality. Most of the time Freud studied adults which led to findings obtained in retrospect. This can sometimes lead to incorrect memory of what actually happened at a younger age.

Freud used clinical interviews or case studies and it is not always right to generalise the findings from one unique individual to a 'general law' of the population. This leads psychoanalysis to be seen as unscientific, just like the humanistic approach. The humanistic approach was criticised for having vague terminology, something that psychoanalysis suffers from as well.

Not being scientific enough has been seen as a weakness of the approach since it makes it difficult to prove something wrong. Psychoanalytic theories always seem to be able to explain the behaviour studied. Behaviourism is a very scientific approach, focusing on external events and reinforcement. It can be distinguished from psychoanalysis because it ignores the unconscious, which is the main focus of psychoanalysis.

However, both had had great impact in abnormal psychology. Psychoanalysis is often used to identify the cause, and the behaviourist approach on the shaping of behaviour by reinforcement and punishment. Behaviourism is more effective in treating the disorder.

Freud was criticised for having an unrepresentative sample when developing his ideas about psychosexual stages in childhood. The focus on sexuality might have occurred because of the sexual repression in the Victorian era. It has also been claimed that Freud emphasised those aspects of case studies that support his theory. This is shown in the case study of Little Hans.

Freud's theory of personality and unconscious experiences allowed psychologists to describe mental problems such as phobias and depression.

Comment: This answer demonstrates a good grasp of Freudian psychoanalysis and mentions both strengths and weaknesses. There is reference to two other perspectives in the answer – humanistic and behaviourist. The essay is not that well structured and deals with strengths and limitations more as a list than within a coherent essay plan. Some more details would help clarify certain aspects of the essay. For example, the third paragraph dealing with psychoanalysis not being scientific enough would benefit from one or two specific examples to highlight the point. Nevertheless, this was a good attempt with little inaccuracy/confusion and some useful discussion. This would get 9 marks out of the 12 available.

7.8 FURTHER READING

Introductory texts

Hill, G. 2001: **A Level psychology through diagrams.** Pages 16, 158/9, 161, 216. Oxford University Press, Oxford.

Pennington, D. C. 2003: **Essential Personality.** Chapters 3, 4 and 5. Arnold, London.

Storr, A. 2001: Freud: **a very short introduction.** Oxford University Press, Oxford.

Specialist sources

Ryckman, R. M. 2000: **Theories of personality.** 7th Ed. Chapters 2, 3, 4, 6 and 7. Wadsworth, London.

Nye, R. D. 2000: **Three psychologies: perspectives from Freud, Skinner and Rogers.** 6th Ed. Chapter 2. Wadsworth, London.

Freud, A. 1986: **The essentials of psychoanalysis: the definitive collection of Sigmund Freud's writing.** Penguin Books, Harmondsworth.

Breger, L. 2000: **Freud: darkness in the midst of vision.** John Wiley & Sons, New York.

8

The humanistic perspective

8.1 Introduction

REFLECTIVE Activity

Pause for a minute from reading and studying and look around you. Consider all the things you can see – objects and other people. If someone else is present consider your feelings for this person. If you are in a familiar place what thoughts and feelings do you have for some of the physical objects around you? Finally, focus on your own state of awareness – what are you feeling at this particular moment and are you happy with your present state of conscious experience?

The above activity goes to the very heart of what **humanistic psychology** is about. Humanistic psychology or **humanism** places great importance on the unique aspects of human experience, and values the subjective feelings and conscious thoughts of the person.

PRACTICAL Activity

Refresh your knowledge and understanding of humanistic psychology, which you studied at AS level, by reading Chapter 1, pages 14–16 of the AS text *Introducing psychology* (Pennington 2002).

Humanistic psychology makes three key assumptions about human beings. First, that each person can exercise free will and hence has control over what they think and feel, and how they behave. Second, that each person is a rational and conscious being, and not dominated by unconscious, primitive instincts. Third, that a person's subjective view of the world is of greater importance to understanding that person than objective reality. These three assumptions characterise the humanistic perspective in psychology and are the foundations for numerous different theories within this perspective. In what follows we shall consider the person-centred approaches of Carl Rogers and Abraham Maslow.

8.2 The person-centred approaches of Rogers and Maslow

Two of the most influential and enduring theories in humanistic psychology that emerged in the 1950s and 1960s are those of Carl Rogers (1951, 1961) and Abraham Maslow (1962, 1970). Both theories regard people as basically good and that human nature is positive, not bad or evil. Both theories view people as active, creative and constantly seeking to express themselves. Additionally, and most importantly, people seek personal growth and may suffer psychologically if they are not able to grow and change in a positive way throughout their life. Because of this focus on the person and his or her personal experiences and subjective perception of the world the humanists regarded scientific methods as inappropriate for studying people.

EVALUATIVE COMMENT

Humanistic psychology is called the 'third force' in psychology after psychoanalysis and behaviourism. Humanistic psychology rejected the behaviourist approach which is characterised as deterministic, focused on reinforcement of stimulus–response contingencies and heavily dependent on animal research (see Chapter 5). Humanistic psychology also rejected the psychoanalytic approach because it also is deterministic, with unconscious, irrational and instinctive forces determining human thought and behaviour. Both behaviourism and psychoanalysis are regarded as dehumanising by humanistic psychologists (De Carvalho 1991).

The person-centred approach

The person-centred approach is so called because, as we have seen above, humanistic psychologists place a person's subjective experience and subjective point of view at the very centre of their theories. This approach to understanding people can be traced back over 200 years to philosophers such as Jean-Jacques Rousseau, Friedrich Nietzsche and Søren Kierkegaard. Broadly speaking these philosophers developed a type of philosophy called **existential philosophy**. Existential philosophers ask very fundamental questions about what it is to be human, such as 'What is the meaning of life?' Existential philosophers are concerned with personal responsibility for actions, and the need people have to exert free individual choice. In the twentieth century Martin Heidegger developed **phenomenology**. This is a method used to examine human experience and how people should live their lives (Heidegger 1927). Basically, these philosophers state that each person has to find the meaning of his or her life from within rather than from the

Humanistic psychologists, such as Carl Rogers and Abraham Maslow, regard each person as unique and focus on subjective experiences of the person

external world. This is very much the basic idea within humanistic psychology, particularly the theories of Rogers and Maslow.

Both Rogers and Maslow regarded personal growth and fulfilment in life as a basic human motive. This means that each person, in different ways, seeks to grow psychologically and continuously enhance themselves. This has been captured by the term **actualisation** or **self-actualisation** which is about psychological growth, fulfilment and satisfaction in life.

REFLECTIVE Activity

Think back over the past few weeks and identify an experience you found pleasurable and fulfilling. Also identify an experience that you found unpleasant and unfulfilling. Was the positive experience one you had personally worked towards and hence exerted free will over? With the negative experience, how are you going to make this positive in the future? Positive experiences and negative experiences promote personal growth. Fulfilment or actualisation come from positive experience that you have chosen to work towards.

Carl Rogers

Carl Rogers originally entered religious training in his early twenties, and as a result developed an interest in psychology. He qualified as a clinical psychologist and throughout his life was equally committed to psychotherapy and the development of psychological theory. In 1963 he founded the Centre for the Studies of the Person, in California. He was active as a humanistic psychologist until he died at the age of 85 in 1987.

Carl Rogers was an important influence in humanistic psychology and developed a form of therapy called person-centred therapy

In considering the work of Carl Rogers we will look at person-centred theory (Rogers 1951, 1961, 1980) both in terms of the key theoretical ideas and his approach to therapy. The key ideas are those of the fully functioning person, self-worth and positive regard, the self-concept and congruence/incongruence. We will look at each in turn.

THE FULLY FUNCTIONING PERSON

In common with other humanistic psychologists, Rogers believed that every person could achieve their goals, wishes and desires in life. When they did so self-actualisation or self-fulfilment took place. For Rogers (1961) people who are able to self-actualise, and that is not all of us, are called **fully functioning persons**. This means that the person is in touch with the here and now, his or her subjective experiences and feelings, and continually growing and changing. In many ways Rogers regarded the fully functioning person as an ideal and one that people do not ultimately achieve. It is wrong to think of this as an end or completion of life's journey; rather it is a process of always becoming and changing. Rogers identified five characteristics of the fully functioning person which are shown in Figure 8.1.

For Rogers, fully functioning people are well-adjusted, well-balanced and interesting to know. Often such people are high achievers in society,

Characteristic of fully functioning person	Description
1. Open to experience	Both positive and negative emotions accepted. Negative feelings are not denied, but worked through.
2. Existential living	In touch with different experiences as they occur in life; avoiding prejudging and preconceptions.
3. Trust feelings	Feelings, instincts and gut-reactions are paid attention to and trusted.
4. Creativity	Creative thinking and risk-taking are features of a person's life. Person does not play safe all the time.
5. Fulfilled life	Person is happy and satisfied with life, and always looking for new challenges and experiences.

Figure 8.1: Five characteristics of the fully functioning person as seen by Rogers (1961)

business and social life. In many ways western society values and prizes such people.

EVALUATIVE COMMENT

The fully functioning person, as conceived by Rogers, represents an ideal state, and probably one that is never achieved by any person. Critics may claim that the fully functioning person is a product of western culture and represents an individualistic and selfish approach to understanding what human beings are about. In other cultures, such as eastern cultures, the achievement of a group of people may be valued more highly than the achievement of any one person.

SELF-WORTH AND POSITIVE REGARD

How we think and feel about ourselves, our feelings of **self-worth** are of fundamental importance both to psychological health and to the likelihood that we can achieve goals and ambitions in life. Self-worth may be seen as a continuum from very high to very low. For Rogers (1959) a person who has high self-worth, that is, has confidence and positive feelings about him- or herself, faces challenges in life, accepts failure and unhappiness at times, and is open with people. A person with low self-worth may avoid challenges in life, not accept that life can be painful and unhappy at times, and will be defensive and guarded with other people.

Rogers believed feelings of self-worth developed in early childhood and were formed from the interaction of the child with the mother and father. As the child grows to be a teenager and adult, interactions with significant others affect feelings of self-worth. Significant others include teachers, friends, family and more intimate relationships. Early influences on a child's feelings of self-worth can influence how future interactions with people and achievements are perceived. For example, a teenager with low self-worth who does well in an examination may say that it is due to the questions being easy rather than to do with the teenager's ability and the fact that he or she studied hard for the examination. The consequence of this subjective perception is that feelings of low self-worth are perpetuated.

Rogers viewed the young child as having two basic needs: positive regard from other people and positive self-worth. **Positive regard** is to do with how other people evaluate and judge us in social interaction. Rogers made a distinction between *unconditional positive regard* and *conditional positive regard*. Unconditional positive regard is where parents, significant others (and the humanistic therapist as we shall see later) accepts and loves the person for what he or she is. Positive regard is not withdrawn when the person does something wrong or makes a mistake. The consequences of unconditional positive regard are that the person feels free to try new things out and make mistakes, even though this may lead to getting it wrong at times. People who are able to self-actualise are more likely to have received unconditional positive regard form others, especially their parents in childhood. *Conditional positive regard* is where positive regard, praise and approval, depend upon the child, for example, behaving in ways that the parents think correct. Here the child is not loved for the person he or she is, but on condition that he or she behaves only in ways approved by the parent(s). At the extreme, a person who constantly seeks approval from other people is likely only to have experienced conditional positive regard as a child.

EVALUATIVE COMMENT

In most people's lives, and early childhood, both types of positive regard are likely to be experienced. It is the relative balance between the two that determines the extent of a person's positive or negative feelings of self-worth Also, either type of positive regard is preferential to negative regard where a person can do nothing right from another person's view. If a person has experienced considerable unconditional positive regard he or she may avoid and not wish to develop a friendship with someone showing only conditional positive regard.

REFLECTIVE Activity

Think about two people in an intimate relationship. Now consider Figure 8.2 where one person may show the other either conditional or unconditional positive regard, as may the other person. What do you think the relationship between the two people may be like for each of the three different relationships shown in Figure 8.2?

Which relationship(s) do you think might be successful and which not successful? In which relationship are the individuals likely to self-actualise?

		Person A	
		Unconditional positive regard	Conditional positive regard
Person B	Unconditional positive regard	1. Unconditional – unconditional relationship	2. Unconditional – conditional relationship
	Conditional positive regard	3. Unconditional – conditional relationship	4. Conditional – conditional relationship

Figure 8.2: Different types of positive regard – conditional and unconditional – in a relationship between two people

SELF-CONCEPT AND CONGRUENCE/INCONGRUENCE

For Rogers, the **self-concept** has two aspects. The first is self-worth, which we have already considered. The second is our *ideal self*, which is our conception of how we should be in all aspects of our life, work, relationships, feelings of fulfilment, etc. A person's ideal self may not be consistent with what actually happens in life and the experiences of the person. Hence, a discrepancy or difference may exist between a person's ideal self and actual experience. This is called *incongruence*. Where a person's ideal self and actual experience are consistent or very closely aligned a state of *congruence* exists. Rarely, if ever, does a total state of congruence exist; all people experience a certain amount of incongruence, as shown in Figure 8.3.

When incongruence is high the person may find it difficult to adjust and live a happy life. High incongruence would reflect many aspects of a person's life differing greatly from their ideal. When incongruence is low, or congruence is close, then a person is likely to be satisfied and fulfilled with life.

A person with a high level of incongruence may suffer psychological distress, and may find it difficult to adjust and live effectively in society.

CLIENT-CENTRED AND PERSON-CENTRED THERAPY

Having looked at Rogers's concepts of the fully functioning person, self-worth and positive regard, the self-concept and congruence /incongruence, you may begin to see what Rogerian therapy tries to achieve. Someone with low self-worth, and a high degree of incongruence may have developed this state of mind because of the absence of unconditional positive regard. Rogers (1959) called his

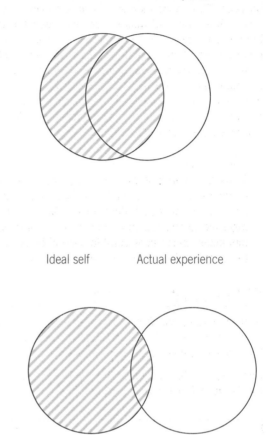

(a) Ideal self   Actual experience

(b) Ideal self   Actual experience

Figure 8.3: Different levels of incongruence between a person's ideal self and actual experience. In (a) incongruence is low, and in (b) it is high

therapeutic approach client-centred or person-centred therapy because of the focus on the person's subjective view of the world. Rogers regarded everyone as a 'potentially competent individual' who could benefit greatly from his form of therapy. Person-centred therapy operates according to three basic principles that reflect the attitude of the therapist to the client, these are:

1 The therapist is congruent with the client.

2 The therapist provides the client with unconditional positive regard.

3 The therapist shows empathetic understanding to the client.

The purpose of Rogers' humanistic therapy is to increase a person's feelings of self-worth, reduce the level of incongruence between ideal and actual self, and help a person become more of a fully functioning person. The three principles given above, and described in more detail in Figure 8.4, are designed to help achieve these goals of therapy.

Principle of client-centred therapy	Description
1. Therapist congruent with the client	The therapist is real, genuine and non-defensive towards the client. Genuineness reflects harmony and trust towards the client.
2. Therapist provides unconditional positive regard	The client is valued and accepted in all ways for what he or she thinks, feels or says. This makes the client feel safe to be open to the therapist.
3. The therapist shows empathy towards the client	The therapist does his or her best to understand the subjective experiences and perceptions from the point of view of the client. At the same time the therapist should not get bound up in the emotions of the client.

Figure 8.4: The three principles of genuineness (congruence), unconditional positive regard, and empathy, on which Rogerian therapy or counselling are based

Later in his career Rogers moved away from one-to-one therapy and became more involved with group counselling. He developed what he called *encounter groups* in which people could feel safe and free to express feelings and explore problems in their lives. An encounter group would be facilitated by a Rogerian therapist and operate according to the three principles described in Figure 8.4.

EVALUATIVE COMMENT

Sexton and Whiston (1994) reviewed a large number of research studies that had been conducted to find out just how effective Rogerian therapy or counselling is for people. They found that generally the three principles of therapy did result in positive personality changes and successful outcomes for clients. However, they also reported that success was not inevitable and that much may depend on the personality of the client. It was found that clients who became very involved in the therapeutic process saw their therapists as more helpful than clients who were more detached from the process. The problem with most of these studies is that effectiveness is based on what clients say rather than any objective measure of better functioning and adjustment to life. Another criticism of these studies is that there is not usually a long-term follow-up of clients.

PRACTICAL Activity

In a group of three or four people, discuss problems with conducting research on the effectiveness of Rogerian therapy. Consider the following questions. Why might the research affect the therapy itself? What problems are there with relying on what clients say have been the benefits of therapy? Why is it important to follow-up clients two/three years after therapy?

Abraham Maslow

Abraham Maslow was born in 1908 in New York. As a child and teenager he was shy and socially introverted. Initially he studied law, but psychology interested him more and he undertook a PhD with Harlow (who conducted the famous research on attachment in monkeys). Maslow rose to fame later in his career, in the 1960s and 1970s, when his theory of human needs and the concept of self-actualisation became highly influential. Maslow remained shy with people throughout his life and disliked public speaking. He died in 1970 after suffering poor health for a number of years.

In what follows we shall consider Maslow's theory of motivation and hierarchy of needs and, his concept of self-actualisation. We shall also look at Maslow's research on the health personality and research measuring potential for self-actualisation.

Human motivation and hierarchy of needs

Maslow (1970) stated that human motivation is based on people seeking fulfilment and change through personal growth. Maslow characterised the human condition as one of 'wanting' – meaning we are always seeking and desiring something. Maslow conceptualised these 'wantings' or needs into a hierarchy of five needs. These five needs are made up of basic or **deficiency needs** and **growth needs**.

Abraham Maslow had a profound influence on psychology through his theory of hierarchy of needs and self-actualisation

EVALUATIVE COMMENT

Maslow's hierarchy of needs contrasts with the psychoanalytic approach which characterises people as avoiding conflict and wanting absence of tension (see Chapter 7). Maslow's theory also contrasts with the behaviourist approach (see Chapter 5) which ignores drives or needs and explains behaviour as a result of external (reinforcement and punishment) and not internal forces.

Maslow (1970) conceptualised needs as of five types: physiological needs, safety needs, belonging and love needs, self-esteem needs, and self-actualisation needs. These are traditionally represented as a pyramid, where the basic needs must be met before moving upwards to the top of the pyramid. This is shown in Figure 8.5.

Physiological needs are strong, basic needs deriving from biology that relate directly to the survival of the individual. Safety needs include needs for security, protection and stability, and, more importantly, freedom from fear. Belongingness and love needs reflect the assumption that we are social animals and need to be with people and loved by some. Self-esteem needs are to do with self-respect and regard from other people. Self-actualisation needs are to do with realising full potential. The first four needs are deficiency needs, and it is only when these are satisfied, according to Maslow, that the person can attempt to satisfy the self-actualisation need.

PRACTICAL Activity

In a group of three or four, get each person to list their goals in life in terms of self-actualisation needs. Then come together and discuss how, in our society, the four deficiency needs can be satisfied. Identify ways in which each of the deficiency needs can fail to be satisfied.

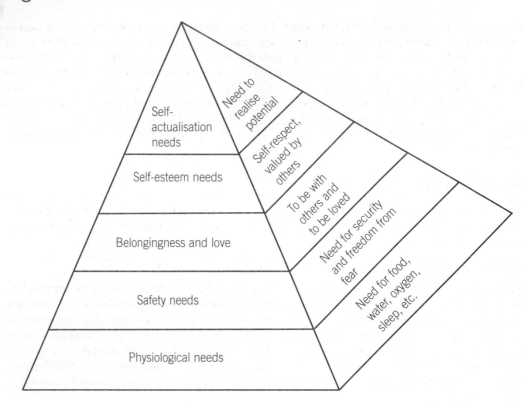

Self-actualisation needs

Need to realise potential

Self-esteem needs

Self-respect, valued by others

Belongingness and love

To be with others and to be loved

Safety needs

Need for security and freedom from fear

Physiological needs

Need for food, water, oxygen, sleep, etc.

Figure 8.5: Maslow's hierarchy of five human needs. Progression to the top of the pyramid can only be achieved with the fulfilment of lower needs

A person may progress upwards in the hierarchy if all is going well with his or her life, such as a good job, many friends, a nice home, and a rewarding intimate relationship. However, events can come along in life that push a person back down the hierarchy. For example, losing your job may threaten the very basic physiological needs and safety needs.

EVALUATIVE COMMENT

Maslow's hierarchy of needs oversimplifies human needs and behaviour. The four deficiency needs do not have to be fully satisfied before moving to self-actualisation needs. If this is the case just what level of satisfaction of a need is required before moving up to the next need? Also, human behaviour may be partially satisfying a number of needs at the same time. Only in conditions of extreme poverty and deprivation is a person motivated solely by physiological needs.

Self-actualisation

The growth need of self-actualisation (Maslow 1962) refers to the need for personal growth that is present throughout a person's life. In a sense, for Maslow, a person is always 'becoming' and never remains static in these terms. In self-actualisation a person comes to find a meaning to life that is important to them. The growth needs include, for example, those of striving for goodness, helping others, seeking truth and justice, and striving to create beauty and order. Notice that these needs are not solely to do with personal satisfaction with a positive contribution to the development of the society in which we live, and support and help for others.

Maslow (1962) believed that some people actually fear self-actualisation since it brings about duties and responsibilities for the individual. The idea that some people fear being their best or reaching their potential, Maslow called the **Jonah complex**. For males the Jonah complex shows itself as a wish to avoid responsibility or a belief that success does not bring social recognition (Hoffman 1974). For females the Jonah complex is said to show itself as a reluctance to use intellectual abilities and fear of being successful in a career. Crawford and Marecek (1989) have criticised the idea that females fear success. They say that females are often, wrongly, judged against male norms of competition and winning. Hyland (1989) argues that females do not display a Jonah complex if judged against female norms. These norms include making friends and socialisation.

REFLECTIVE Activity

Think about your own successes and disappointments in life. Are there goals or activities that you would really like to do but fear that if you try you may not achieve them? Try to identify what the fears are about – you may well find, as is often the case, that such fears are unfounded.

MASLOW'S RESEARCH ON THE HEALTHY PERSONALITY

Maslow (1970) conducted extensive, but not very scientific, research on people he categorised as self-actualisers. Maslow defined self-actualisers as people who are fulfilled and do the best for their ability. This is subjective and does not guarantee that a person Maslow categorises as a self-actualiser would be so categorised by another psychologist. Maslow stated there were three pre-conditions for a person to self-actualise. These are absence of restraints, no or little distraction from deficiency needs, and a good knowledge of yourself. From this Maslow identified what he claimed were characteristics of self-actualisers. These are summarised in Figure 8.6.

Characteristic	Explanation
Accurate perceptions	Correct and realistic understanding of reality. Able to tolerate uncertainty and ambiguity.
Accepting of others	Accept own strengths and shortcomings and those in other people. Not threatened by others.
Spontaneous and simple	Straightforward, but often unconventional. High ethical and rural standards.
Problem-centred	Oriented to tasks and challenges in the world rather than dealing with their own problems.
Autonomous	Able to be independent of the social context and culture in which they live. Self-contained.
Creative	Able to think in new ways and produce original ideals, works of art, etc.
Sense of humour	Spontaneous sense of humour that does not get a laugh at someone else's expense.
Democratic	Friendly and considerate of other people regardless of sex, race, colour, age, etc.
Detached	Similar to autonomous, but able to put aside own feelings and emotions.
Private	Have a need to spend times in solitude, reflection and privacy.

Figure 8.6: Ten characteristics that Maslow (1970) identified with self-actualisation

Maslow also introduced the idea of *peak experiences*. These are feelings of ecstasy or a deep and satisfying sense of fulfilment that causes a feeling of timelessness. Some people may regard a peak experience as religious or mystical, other people may regard it as of major significance in their life. Peak experiences often happen spontaneously and are not that frequent in life. Generally, during a peak experience the person experiences an absence of deficiency needs. Peak experiences may change a person's life.

EVALUATIVE COMMENT

Maslow did not adopt a rigorous, scientific, approach to identifying self-actualisers in his research into the healthy personality. He interviewed people he thought were self-actualisers and made his own judgements on the characteristics of these people. More objective measures of personality were not used, and self-actualisers were not compared with non-self-actualisers. Maslow's research ignored people with psychological disorders and hence did not really identify what prevents people from self-actualisation. Nevertheless, the research has provided valuable insights into the higher achievements of people.

MEASURING SELF-ACTUALISATION

Shostrum (1963, 1977) developed a standardised personality questionnaire to measure self-actualisation. This is called the *Personal Orientation Inventory* (or POI for short). This consists of 150 fixed-choice items, some of which are shown in Figure 8.7.

The results of scoring the questionnaire reveal the extent (high or low) to which a person self-actualises in their life. Research has shown that, for example, people who score low on self-actualisation experience poor interpersonal relationships (Sheffield *et al.* 1995). Also, creative thinking has been shown to be associated more with high self-actualisers (Runco *et al.* 1995).

Sample items from Shostrum's personal orientation inventory
Time competence scale
1. (a) I strive always to predict what will happen in the future.   (b) I do not feel it necessary always to predict what will happen in the future.*
2. (a) I prefer to save good things for future use.   (b) I prefer to use good things now.*
3. (a) I worry about the future.   (b) I do not worry about the future.*
Self-oriented scale
4. (a) My moral values are dictated by society.   (b) My moral values are self-determined.*
5. (a) I feel guilty when I am selfish.   (b) I do not feel guilty when I am selfish.*
6. (a) I am bound by the principles of fairness.   (b) I an not absolutely bound by the principles of fairness.*
7. (a) I feel I must always tell the truth.   (b) I do not always tell the truth.*

Figure 8.7: Sample items from Shostrum's (1963, 1974) personal orientation inventory. Select one of the two statements. The starred (*) statement scores towards high self-actualisation

EVALUATIVE COMMENT

Maslow's theory of motivation, hierarchy of needs, and concept of self-actualisation has been highly influential in psychology. Maslow's ideas have been applied to the field of organisational psychology in an attempt to understand what motivates people to work (apart from money) and what gives satisfaction at work. The concept of self-actualisation has enjoyed widespread acceptance and more rigorous, scientific research has been conducted. Self-actualisation has also been applied to atypical or abnormal behaviour to help understand people's fears and anxieties.

On a more critical note, Maslow's theories have been criticised as culture-specific, representing white, middle-class North American values. Maslow has also been criticised for paying too much attention to healthy people and not enough to those who have psychological disorders.

Rejection of scientific psychology

We have seen with the humanistic theories of Carl Rogers and Abraham Maslow that, of central concern to both, are the subjective, conscious experiences of the individual. The humanistic psychologists argued that objective reality is less important than a person's subjective perception and subjective understanding of the world. Because of this, Rogers and Maslow placed little value on scientific psychology especially the use of the psychology laboratory to investigate both human and other animal behaviour.

The humanist's view human beings as fundamentally different from other animals mainly because humans are conscious beings capable of thought, reason and language. For humanistic psychologists research on animals, such as rats, pigeons, or monkeys, held little value. Research on such animals can tell us, so they argued, very little about human thought, behaviour and experience.

Humanistic psychologists rejected a rigorous scientific approach to psychology because they saw it as dehumanising and unable to capture the richness of conscious experience. In many ways the rejection of scientific psychology in the 1950s, 1960s and 1970s was a backlash to the dominance of the behaviourist approach in North American psychology. Today many of the ideas and concepts of humanistic psychology have been scientifically investigated by other psychologists. We saw this earlier in this chapter with the measurement of self-actualisation. Many of the insights of Rogers and Maslow have been put on a more scientific footing over the past twenty years or so.

8.3 Humanistic psychology

In considering the person-centred approaches of Carl Rogers and Abraham Maslow a number of key themes or concepts are present in both theories. These are the concepts of individual experience, promoting personal growth, free will and holism. These found concepts are defining features of humanistic psychology more generally. In what follows we will look at each in turn more closely.

Individual experience

William James (1890) was one of the founders of modern psychology and put forward the view that the correct study of human beings should be to do with how they adapt to their environment and how conscious experience helps with this. James regarded conscious experiences as an essential feature of human beings and allow people to adapt to a complex environment. For James, consciousness is a continual flow of thoughts, feelings and sensations that cannot be divided up or broken down into component parts. He coined the phrase 'stream of consciousness' to encapsulate this idea.

The development of humanistic psychology in the mid-twentieth century maintained William James's idea of consciousness, but went further by considering the uniqueness of each person's experiences. This focus on individual experience was underpinned by three important principles. First, individual experience is unique to each person and cannot be repeated. Attempts can be made to reconstruct an experience, but the reconstruction can never be the same as the original experience. Second, to understand a person and in what ways a person is well-adjusted and poorly adjusted to life, the humanistic psychologist needs to try to see things from that person's perspective. This is called being empathetic with another. It entails trying to experience things as if you were the other person. Whilst it is impossible to experience fully as another person does, attempts can be made to enter into another person's way of thinking or feeling. Third, the individual experience of a person, which involves subjective perceptions and feelings, are to be seen as valid. This means that experience is valued for what it is and how the person reports it. For humanistic psychologists, the experience of a person is not questioned or challenged, but attempts are made to understand it.

REFLECTIVE Activity

Think of somebody you know well and somebody you know but as a distant acquaintance. Think of some particular situation or behaviour each has engaged in. Now try to put yourself in 'their shoes' over the situation or behaviour. How much does your own experience, subjective perceptions, interfere with this empathetic exercise? In the end you can only see another person from your perspective, but can try to understand where they are coming from.

The focus on the uniqueness of individual experience led to a 'counterculture' in the 1960s (the hippies). Here Eastern religions and meditation became popular because of the centrality of awareness of your experiences as well as 'mind altering' drugs such as LSD, which gave a person an altered or different experience of the world.

Promoting personal growth

Our consideration of Rogers and Maslow has shown that both these humanistic psychologists regard personal growth as an essential part of what it is to be human. Personal growth with Rogers occurs with the fully functioning person (see Section 8.2.2) and with Maslow through satisfaction of deficiency needs to allow for growth needs to be satisfied. Both theories talk about self-actualisation, which is the realisation of a person's full potential. In looking at what may help promote personal growth it will be instructive to consider the other side of the coin – what stops self-actualisation?

Rogers (1959) used the word *threat* to represent a person's perception of conflict and incongruity within a person's self-concept. Conflict may be threatening to how we think of ourselves because our sense of continuity and wholeness as a person may be threatened. This may come about due to a relationship breakdown, death of a loved one, or loss of job or career. In such circumstances, Rogers said that defensive processes such as denial and distortion may be employed by the person to ward off the anxiety resulting from the threat to our self-concept, and feelings of self-worth and self-esteem. When this happens to a normally well-adjusted person we may say that they are 'not themselves'. In such circumstances, a fragmental self-concept supported by defence mechanisms will prevent personal growth. The attention of the individual is inwards and towards the threat and conflicts – dealing with the negative – rather than outward and dealing with the positive.

On the other side of the coin we may ask what events, circumstances or situations actually promote personal growth. For Maslow and the hierarchy of needs, the four deficiency needs (see Figure 8.6) would need to be satisfied to allow self-actualisation. Research using standardised measures of self-actualisation has shown, for example, that absence of psychological disorders, relationship difficulties, and drug dependence, fosters self-actualisation and hence personal growth (Daniels 1988). Self-actualisers are more likely to be open to experiences and accepting of those experiences. They are also more likely to recognise a peak experience and use such experiences to enhance personal growth (Thomas and Cooper 1980).

Csikszentmihayi (1990) has developed a theory of *flow*. Flow is where a person becomes so involved in an activity that nothing else matters or intrudes on consciousness. Flow experiences occur in a wide range of situations – during both physical and mental activities. Stein *et al.* (1995) showed that students who played sport and were in a flow experience showed more enjoyment, concentration and satisfaction that students who were in bored or anxiety states. Flow experiences lead to personal growth because the person will want to improve at the activity and increase the challenges. So if you have feelings of intense involvement with an activity this helps with other activities and means that you grow through setting more and more challenges for yourself.

Free will

The humanistic theories of Rogers and Maslow rejected the deterministic approaches of psychoanalysis and behaviourism. In part, this rejection was because the humanists regarded individuals as possessing **free will**. We will consider the free will – determinism debate more fully and generally in Chapter 11, but now we will consider the idea of free will in relation to humanistic psychology.

REFLECTIVE Activity

Consider three or four actions or behaviours you have engaged in over the past week, for example, going to the cinema, going out with friends, and going to the shops to buy some clothes. For each think about whether or not you freely chose to do these things or whether you did them to please other people. If the latter what might have happened if you had said 'no'?

Free will does not mean that an individual has the freedom to do anything that he or she pleases or wishes to do. Free will has to be considered alongside personal responsibility and the rules (laws and unwritten rules) of the society in which a person lives. Whilst you are, in a sense, free to behave anti-socially and break laws, there are consequences for behaving in such ways. The consequences may be seen to be of two types: external and internal. External consequences include the punishment (imprisonment, etc.) of the law for acting illegally. Internal consequences are to do with the self-punishment or guilt that may follow from behaving in anti-social or illegal ways. Hence, whilst a person may be free to think about engaging in any kind of behaviour (whether good or bad), there are strong constraints operating internally and externally which stop most people behaving in these undesirable ways. Humanistic psychologists place great emphasis on making people accept and take responsibility for their actions. Rogers (1977), for example, states that the person-centred approach raises potential issues to do with power, control and decision-making. The person-centred approach places control and free will in the hands of the individual and that responsible behaviour is required of individuals, groups and organisations.

Should a person be held responsible for all actions that he or she engages in? Should it be assumed that a person exercises free will in every aspect of life? These are difficult questions that do not have clear-cut answers. For example, a murderer may be judged insane and hence not be held accountable for the dreadful deed of killing another person.

PRACTICAL activity

Read through the newspapers of the last few days and identify behaviours where the person was held to be responsible and had freely chosen to behave in such a way. Also identify behaviours where the person was not held responsible. In the latter case list the reasons for not holding the person responsible and not freely choosing to behave in such ways.

Holism

'The whole is greater than the sum of the parts'. This statement sums up the Gestalt approach to psychology. Gestalt psychology developed during the 1930s and 1940s through the work of psychologists such as Kohler and Wertheimer. This approach to psychology argued that perceptions, problem-solving and learning, could not be broken down into parts or 'actions' as with physics or chemistry. Humanistic psychology adopts a holistic approach to personality and behaviour and was influenced by the Gestalt school of psychology in this respect.

Humanistic psychologists saw the behaviourists as attempting to break down or reduce behaviour to 'elemental' stimulus–response (S–R) contingencies. They saw psychoanalysts, such as Sigmund Freud, attempting to break down personality into parts such as the id, ego and superego, and conscious, preconscious and unconscious (see Chapter 7). This analytic approach of behaviourism and psychoanalysis borrowed the reductionist or atomistic (reducing matter to its constituent atoms) of physical and biological science. Humanistic psychologists adopted **holism** as an essential principle in their approach. Holism avoids attempts to reduce personality to smaller elements and regards it as essential to consider the person and behaviours in a holistic way.

An important influence on the development of the person-centred approaches of Rogers and Maslow was **organismic theory** (Goldstein 1939). The organismic or holistic viewpoint treats the individual, in terms of both mind and body (see Chapter 11) as a unified and organised whole. This means that to understand a person, both biological and mental processes have to be taken together in a holistic way. The main proponent of organismic theory was Kurt Goldstein, who was an eminent neuropsychiatrist in the first half of the twentieth century. Goldstein worked with brain-injured soldiers during World War I. He stated that to understand and help soldiers with physical brain damage, the psychological consequences also had to be considered. Hence, the soldier has to be understood as a whole, with both mind and body (in this case the brain) unified. Goldstein stated that the person is a single entity and what happens in any part, psychologically or physically, affects the whole.

Organismic theory attempts to discover the principles by which the whole person functions, and assumes that each person is motivated by one overriding drive: that of self-actualisation. This single drive provides purpose and unity to the total or whole life of the person. Finally, organismic theory studies one person in detail and in a holistic way, rather than study a large number of people from only selected perspectives.

Abraham Maslow, as we have seen, studied healthy people from an holistic perspective, and attempted to show that peak experiences help people feel more integrated and complete or whole as a person. Carl Rogers used person-centred or client-centred therapy to treat the whole person using the approach of unconditional positive regard.

8.4 Limitations of the humanistic approach

The humanistic approach to understanding the person provides an optimistic and positive view of human nature. Critics, however, have argued that this optimism has been unrealistic since human behaviour can be very negative and destructive.

REFLECTIVE Activity

Read a Sunday newspaper and look for articles that present people as good and other articles that present people as bad or negative. List the negative and destructive behaviours that you have identified, and the positive good behaviours. To what extent do you think humanistic psychologists are unrealistically optimistic about human nature?

In what follows, we shall consider a number of limitations of humanistic psychology, and conclude by considering strengths and contributions made to the development of psychology. There are three main limitations: lack of empirical research, lack of comprehensiveness and vagueness of key concepts or terms.

Whilst humanistic psychologists reject a scientific approach it is nevertheless important to ascertain the extent to which key concepts and claims are supported by research. One limitation is that humanistic psychology has not generated a great deal of empirical research. However, there have been, as we have seen, more recent attempts to measure concepts such as self-actualisation through standardised questionnaires. Curiously, the empirical research that does exist has been conducted by psychologists who are often not humanistic in their outlook, but wish to put some of the valuable insights of humanistic theories onto a more scientific footing.

Some critics argue that the humanistic approach is not as comprehensive as, for example, that of psychoanalysis or behaviourism. In some ways this may seem like a strange criticism to make since, as we have seen, humanistic psychology deals with the whole person. The criticism about comprehensiveness is to do with the strong emphasis and focus on one main drive, motive, or need: that of self-actualisation. This focus on self-actualisation is regarded as a limitation because other drives, particularly biological and instructive ones, play a much less central role than may be considered appropriate.

Finally, some of the key concepts and terms have been seen as vague or poorly defined. Terms such as self-actualisation, the fully functioning person, and peak experiences, whilst providing valuable insight into human behaviour, need precise definition. Precise definition allows empirical research to be undertaken so that its validity to understanding human behaviour can be investigated. It may be because of the vagueness of these terms that little empirical research has been generated from the humanistic approach.

On the positive side, the strengths of the humanistic approach are that a positive image of the human condition is promoted and the person is viewed as a whole. Also, the approach has made valuable applications through therapy and counselling, to education and learning, and to understanding relationships between people. For example, Rogers's person-centred theory was relevant to education to support student learning. Unconditional positive regard by the teacher towards the student plays a key role here, and allows the student to reach their potential.

8.5 Sample questions

SAMPLE QUESTION 1

(a) Outline the person-centred approach of Rogers in humanistic psychology.
     (AO1 = 4)   *(4 marks)*
(b) Explain why humanistic psychologists rejected the traditional scientific experimental approach.
     (AO1 = 2, AO2 = 2)   *(4 marks)*
(c) Compare the humanistic perspective with *either* the psychoanalytic or behaviourist perspective.
     (AO1 = 4, AO2 = 8)   *(12 marks)*

Total AO1 marks = 10   Total AO2 marks = 10   Total = 20 marks

QUESTIONS, ANSWERS AND COMMENTS

SAMPLE QUESTION 2

(a) In the context of humanistic psychology explain each of the following:

- promoting personal growth

- the concept of holism

(AO1 = 2, AO2 = 2)   *(4 marks)*

(b) Outline the person-centred approach of Maslow

(AO1 = 4)   *(4 marks)*

(c) Identify and discuss at least *two* limitations of the humanistic approach in psychology. Refer to one other perspective in your answer.

(AO1 = 4, AO2 = 8)   *(12 marks)*

Total AO1 marks = 10 Total AO2 marks = 10 Total = 20 marks

Answer to 2(a)

Humanistic psychology believes that every person is essentially good and wishes to establish an environment in which the person can be the 'self he/she really is' and reach their potential psychological growth. To reach personal growth the therapist aims to increase the client's self-esteem and this is done in three ways: by genuineness, unconditional positive regard and being supportive as well as having empathetic understanding.

The concept of holism is where the humanistic approach focuses on how the 'whole is greater than the sum of its parts'. Humanists see the person as generally good, and that all people can change themselves.

Comment: The answer to promoting personal growth is done within the context of therapy/counselling – this is fine. The answer demonstrates a good understanding of the key factors needed to promote personal growth. Mention of self-actualisation would have improved the answer. The answer to holism is not very good and gives little beyond stating what the word means. 3 marks overall, these for the answer to personal growth.

Answer to 2(b)

Maslow developed a hierarchy of needs in which there are four defining needs and one growth need. The growth need is called self-actualisation and can only be reached when the other four needs have been met. The four basic needs are physiological needs, safety needs, love needs, and self-esteem needs. People who meet the self-actualisation need often have peak experiences.

Comment: A good answer in which all aspects of Maslow's hierarchy of needs are correctly described. The idea of growth and deficiency needs is also mentioned, although the answer could have briefly explained what each type of need means. The answer is correct and would get the full 4 marks.

Answer to 2(c)

The humanistic approach has been criticised for being non-scientific. However, this was deliberately done, thinking that scientific attempts to study behaviour were misleading and inappropriate. Since it is unscientific it has been accused of having vague terminology (as with psychoanalysis) which makes hypotheses more difficult to test. However, Rogers did attempt to make humanistic psychology a bit more scientific by using tape recorders and invented the 'Q sort' technique in order to get more valid data in his client-centred approach.

Humanistic psychologists disagreed with behaviourist attempts to study human behaviour by the use of animals. The behaviourists used a nomothetic approach trying to establish laws of human behaviour. A limitation of the humanistic approach is that they did not establish laws of human behaviour. This was because they thought people have free will.

Another limitation of the humanistic approach is that conscious experience is difficult to understand, and can never be repeated. Hence, humanistic psychology is too subjective.

Comment: A number of limitations are correctly identified and some good discussion given to the limitation of it being non-scientific. Reference is made to another perspective – the behaviourist perspective – and some discussion given about this. Mention is made of the psychoanalytic perspective, but only in passing and not at all developed in the answer. The final paragraph is vague and not developed very well. An average answer which would attract 6 of the 12 marks available.

Total marks for question 2 = *13 out of 20 marks (AO1 = 8, AO2 = 5)*

8.6 FURTHER READING

Introductory texts

Liebert, R. M. & Liebert, L. L. 1998: **Personality: strategies and issues.** Chapter 16. 8th Ed. Brooks/Cole Publishing Company, London.

Pennington, D. C. 2003: **Essential personality.** Chapter 8. Hodder, London.

Specialist sources

Rogers, C. R. 1961: **On becoming a person**. Houghton Mifflin, Boston.

Maslow, A. H. 1970: **Motivation and personality**. 2nd Ed. Harper & Row, New York.

Nye, R. D. 2000: **Three psychologies: perspectives form Freud, Skinner and Rogers**. 6th Ed. Chapter 4. Wadsworth, United Kingdom.

Ryckman, R. M. 2000: **Theories of personality**. 7th Ed. Chapters, 11, 12, 13 and 14. Thompson Learning, Wadsworth.

9

Comparison of perspectives

9.1 Introduction

You should now be familiar with the five main perspectives in psychology – biological, behaviourist, cognitive, psychoanalytic and humanistic. You may, rightly, be asking yourself why there are so many different perspectives in psychology, whether other perspectives than these five exist, and how coherent different theories are within any one perspective. The range of perspectives in psychology reflects how difficult it is to capture a full understanding of human thought, feelings and behaviour in a single perspective. As we shall see later in this chapter, in Section 9.5, there is value in accepting and working with a range of perspectives, or theories representing different perspectives, at the same time. As you will have seen from reading each of the previous four chapters on the behaviourist, cognitive, psychoanalytic and humanistic perspectives, that each perspective has both limitations and strengths. For psychology to adopt a single perspective would, it may be argued, result in an overly narrow view of human nature and miss important aspects of what it is to be a human being. For example, the cognitive perspective is overly concerned with human thought and pays relatively less attention to emotions and actual behaviour.

Each person is a unique individual with unique experiences. Can one perspective in psychology capture all this?

In contrast, the psychoanalytic approach may be overly concerned with the unconscious, emotional life, and childhood experiences. The behaviourist perspective is overly concerned with overt behaviour and pays less attention to thoughts and feelings which may be the determinants of behaviour. The humanistic perspective focuses on the individual's subjective experiences and is less concerned with attempting to discover rules or laws that may govern human behaviour.

PRACTICAL Activity

Each of the preceding four chapters has a section towards the end of the chapter giving limitations (and strengths) of the perspective. Read each section in these four chapters and list the limitations and strengths of these four perspectives.

In what follows we shall give a brief consideration to key aspects of the biological perspective, then compare each perspective in relation to six different topics or issues. Finally, consideration will be given to the value of an eclectic approach in psychology.

The genes that are passed down from generation to generation play an important role in human behaviour

9.2 The biological perspective

The biological perspective is, broadly speaking, concerned with how our genetic inheritance, evolution of the human species and the nervous system (both central and peripheral) affect how we think, feel and behave. More particularly, the biological perspective, because of the influence of Darwin's theory of evolution and the idea of the 'survival of the fittest', looks at how well a person adapts and adjusts in life. Maladaptiveness may be seen in terms of a person suffering from psychological disorders, such as schizophrenia and depression or being aggressive towards other people. Hence, the biological perspective seeks to discover how the genes we inherit from our parents may have a role to play in these and other types of maladaptive behaviours.

The biological perspective is also concerned with understanding how our central and peripheral nervous systems, particularly the brain, affect how we think, feel and behave. Questions arise within the biological perspective such as how the brain and the mind interact and are related (see Chapter 11 for the mind-body debate). Also of interest is how the brain, a physical organ, can produce the psychological experience of awareness of things around us and consciousness. These are matters that physiological psychologists find difficult to answer.

The biological perspective also raises the issue of the relative contribution of nature (genetic, evolution, etc.) and nurture (experiences since birth) to mental abilities such as intelligence and actual behaviours (such as schizophrenia and aggression). Commonly called the **nature/nurture debate** or the debate about the relative contribution of heredity and environment (see Chapter 11).

PRACTICAL Activity

Refresh your knowledge and understanding of the biological approach in psychology by reading Chapter 1, pages 8–9 of the AS text *Introducing psychology* (Pennington 2002). You will also find it useful to look through Chapter 2 of the AS text to get an idea of the different areas covered in the biological approach – but do not go into the detail in this chapter.

A recent development in biological psychology is called **evolutionary psychology** which is defined as follows:

> **Evolutionary psychology is the study of the evolutionary origin of human behaviour patterns ... that may influence everything from sexual attraction, infidelity and jealousy to divorce.** (Coon 2002: 519)

One area that has been extensively researched within a biological/evolutionary psychology perspective is that of human mating or sexual preferences. Buss (1994) studied attitudes and behaviours of men and women across 37 different cultures towards sexual behaviour. Buss (1994) found, for example, that men compared to women are more interested in casual sex, prefer a younger partner and get more jealous over sexual infidelity on the part of the woman. By contrast, women prefer older partners, are less upset by sexual infidelity but more upset by a man becoming emotionally involved with another woman. Buss (1994) attributes these differences to mating preferences that have evolved in response to the reproductive demands placed on men and women. Generally, women are more involved in nurturing offspring and men with providing for the family, although this traditional pattern has dramatically changed in more westernised societies. Evolutionary theory explains the male concern with sexual infidelity by the female partner as to do with concern over the paternity of offspring.

EVALUATIVE COMMENT

Evolutionary psychology presents and, to some extent, justifies a traditional male and female role in the family. It has to be noted that other explanations of the findings of Buss (1994) are possible. For example, that generally speaking the male controls money and resources.

REFLECTIVE Activity

Consider the pattern of results obtained by Buss (1994) in his study across 37 cultures. Think of alternative explanations to do with, for example, social and cultural factors rather than biological factors. Given that different explanations of the same findings can be made, just how valid do you regard the evolutionary theory explanation?

9.3 Comparison of perspectives

In what follows we will compare the different perspectives in psychology from six different angles. These are: the view of human nature, personality development, atypical behaviour, the role of society, views on aggression, and methods of studying human behaviour.

View of human nature

The psychoanalytic perspective of Freud presents, perhaps, the most negative view of human nature. This sees people as conflict-ridden, dominated by instinctual demands, operating at a largely unconscious and irrational level and consistently coping with childhood repressions. By contrast, the humanistic perspective presents a positive view of human nature, whereby personal growth and the need for each person to reach their potential are the key motivating forces. With humanistic psychology people are seen to have free will (see Chapter 11) and their human nature is to be trusted. The behaviourist perspective views human nature rather like a machine. By this is meant that human behaviour is determined by reinforcement and punishment contingencies in the environment. Biological and instinctual aspects of the person are seen as relatively unimportant. The biological perspective puts human nature too much in control of genetic and physiological forces over which the individual has little or no control. To some extent the biological perspective is compatible with the psychoanalytic perspective. Finally, the cognitive perspective presents rather a neutral image of human nature. People are seen as essentially thinking, mentally conscious and logical, but how all this relates to and allows behaviour to be better understood and predicted is less clear.

Perspective	View on human nature	Similar to other perspective
Psychoanalytic	Negative, conflict-ridden, at mercy of instincts, unconscious and childhood repressions.	Biological and cognitive perspectives.
Behaviourist	Sees people as machines responding to reinforcers or punishers in environment. Little free will.	None with radical behaviourism, but cognitive with social learning theories.
Cognitive	People as conscious, logical thinkers with memory as defining human characteristic.	Psychoanalytic at a conscious level. Behaviourist with social learning theories.
Biological	Human characteristics and behaviour determined by genetic inheritance. Physiological determinants of human behaviour.	Psychoanalytic in terms of instincts.
Humanistic	Positive image where a person grows and realises potential. Freedom to act and choose.	None really, but some elements of biological and cognitive.

Figure 9.1: The differing views on human nature presented by five different perspectives in psychology

In summary, each perspective does present quite a different view or image of human nature ranging from the negative and pessimistic (psychoanalytic) to the positive and allowance of free will (humanistic). In many ways the behavioural and biological perspectives are negative in the sense that the person is seen to have little control or freedom to choose in life.

PRACTICAL Activity

In a group of three or four, select two perspectives and discuss in more detail the differing views on human nature that each presents. In doing this try to find ways in which the two perspectives have similarities in their views on human nature.

Personality development

The psychoanalytic and cognitive perspectives put forward a 'stage' approach to personality and child development. The psychoanalytic perspective typically deals with psychosexual and emotional development of the personality. In contrast, the cognitive perspective, through the work of such psychologists as Piaget, Bruner and Kohlberg, deals with cognitive development

Realising your potential is one of the most rewarding experiences you may have in life

in terms of intellectual and moral development. Both perspectives regard developmental stages as taking place in early childhood through to early teenage years with such development complete by early adulthood at the latest.

The behaviourist perspective does not put forward any kind of stage theory of development, but sees development as a continual process resulting from the action of the environment (reinforcement contingencies and punishment) in a continuous way. Behaviour is emitted, shaped and changed in a gradual way by the action of the environment.

The humanistic perspective sees personality development to do with personal growth and realisation of life goals as taking place throughout a person's life. As such the humanistic perspective sees growth as continual rather than as being in stages either in childhood or throughout life. Finally, the biological perspective sees personality development as a maturational process whereby predetermined genetic predispositions cause physical and psychological changes up to early adulthood. For example, the onset of puberty is a predetermined maturational process caused by biological factors.

Perspective	Personality development
Psychoanalytic	Psychosexual stages of emotional development. Oral, anal and phallic stages take place in first 6/7 years of life.
Cognitive	In relation to child development – Piaget and Kohlberg – intellectual and moral development occur in stages.
Behaviourist	Development as a continual process resulting in environmental (reinforcement and punishment) contingencies.
Humanistic	Development throughout life, not in stages, through personal growth and realisation of potential.
Biological	Development as a maturational process resulting from inheritance and genetic predisposition.

Figure 9.2: Views on personality development from the different perspectives in psychology

EVALUATIVE COMMENT

Freud's theory of psychosexual development (oral, anal and phallic stages) and Piaget's theory of intellectual development (sensorimotor, preoperational, concrete operations and formal operations stages) appear to be biologically determined. This is in the sense that the stages occur in one sequence and the child enters the stages at certain ages in childhood. From this we can see that stage theories of development do seem to rely on a biological genetic predisposition of some sort.

Atypical behaviour

The application of psychological theory, research and treatments to a range of atypical behaviours and abnormal psychological conditions has, by and large, been a success story over the past 50 years for psychology. The application of psychology has improved people's lives and been of benefit to society. The different perspectives explain psychological disorders and dysfunctions differently and offer different means of treating such disorders.

With the psychoanalytic perspective, psychological disorders, especially neurotic disorders, result from unconscious conflict, childhood repressions and unreasonable demands of society upon the individual. Treatment is through the so-called 'talking cure' of psychoanalysis, although 'cure' is not the key objective, but strengthening of the ego to deal with conflicting demands. Psychoanalysis as a therapy may take many years and be difficult to assess objectively its effectiveness. Behaviourism, by contrast, attempts to change the actual behaviour of a person without delving or even attempting to delve into deeper, mental causes of the dysfunctional behaviour. Treatment has been shown to be effective for anxiety disorders and phobias.

Cognitive approaches to treatment of psychological disorders have adopted a more problem-solving approach, and approaches which attempt to change the way a person thinks (Ellis 1995; Beck *et al.* 1995). For example, with depressive disorders attempts are made to change the way a person views the causes of behaviour. Typically a person suffering depression sees factors in the environment, external to themselves, as determining negative thoughts and behaviour. Cognitive therapy attempts to help the person feel more in control and change his or her way of thinking.

Humanistic psychology views psychological disorders as resulting from the stunting or prevention of personal growth and frustration, by others in society more generally, of a person self-actualising or reaching their potential. Humanistic therapy uses empathy, unconditional positive regard and acceptance towards the person in an attempt to promote personal growth and help a person self-actualise.

The biological perspective tends to use drugs to treat psychological disorders and is more aligned with the medical model of mental illness. Drug treatments are particularly prevalent with major psychotic disorders such as schizophrenia and manic depression.

PRACTICAL Activity

If you have studied the option unit on the Psychology of Atypical Behaviour, read over your notes and relate these to the five psychological perspectives. If you have not studied this option area, read a chapter on abnormal or atypical behaviour in an introductory psychology textbook you can get from your library. Then relate what you have read to these five psychological perspectives.

The role of society/culture

Psychology, almost by definition, tends to strongly focus on the individual. However, the

Perspective	Explanation of atypical behaviour	Treatment of atypical behaviour.
Psychoanalytic	Unconscious conflict, childhood repressions weak ego.	Psychoanalysis to uncover repressions, and strengthen the ego.
Cognitive	Inappropriate and negative way of thinking about self.	Change way think about self, problem-solving approach.
Humanistic	Blocking of personal growth and self-actualisation.	Unconditional positive regard to remove these blocks.
Behaviourist	Incorrect or maladaptive reinforcements/punishments.	Change behaviour by changing reinforcement and punishment contingencies.
Biological	Chemical imbalances or deficiencies, mostly in central nervous system.	Use of drug therapies as with the medical model.

Figure 9.3: Explanations and treatment approaches to atypical behaviour according to different perspectives in psychology

influence of the society and culture in which we live affects our beliefs, values, attitudes and behaviours. To some extent the differing perspectives in psychology take, or attempt to take, these influences into account.

The psychoanalytic perspective, especially Freudian theory, sees an inevitable conflict between the instinctual demands within the person and civilisation. The sexual urges and instinctual needs of the person, even if at an unconscious level, are often at odds and in opposition to the requirements of a culture or society in which the person lives. For civilisation to continue, individual needs are often subjugated or repressed. At times this may result in psychological disorder or the inability of an individual to adapt to the 'rules' or requirements of society.

By contrast, behaviourists view society, in the form of the external environment, as controlling the person, controlling its citizens. Behaviourists see society as setting up planned contingencies of reinforcement to maximise the desired and acceptable behaviours in a society. The environment, as the society, culture or civilisation, operates to control and determine the behaviours of a person.

The humanistic perspective regards society/culture as far too restrictive upon the freedom and choices of an individual. The psychological growth and ability to self-actualise are threatened by the structures of society – education, employment and the institution of marriage, for example. From this it can be seen that there are similarities between the psychoanalytic and humanistic perspectives on how society restricts and causes the individual to experience conflicts.

The cognitive and biological perspectives have less to say and take less account of the influence of society upon the person. Although, for example, the attitudes, beliefs and values that a person holds, personal cognitions we may call them, are heavily influenced by cultural or societal norms.

REFLECTIVE Activity

Think about yourself in relation to the culture/society in which you live and have been brought up in. Identify the values, beliefs, and attitudes that may have resulted from this. Then try to identify the extent to which there may be conflict between your own desires, ambitions and aspirations and those of the culture in which you live.

Views on aggression

Aggression at an interpersonal, intergroup and international level, is a major problem for humankind in the twenty-first century. Aggression even occurs when people try, and often succeed, in harming themselves – whether this be physical or psychological harm. Aggression may be defined as follows:

any form of behaviour directed toward the goal of harming or injuring another living being who is motivated to avoid such treatment

(Baron and Richardson 1994)

Because, in part, of the widespread nature of aggression across all cultures and societies in the world, each of the five main perspectives in psychology that we are considering offer an explanation of why aggression occurs.

The psychoanalytic perspective regards human aggression as instinctual and an essential, if destructive, part of human nature. In Freud's later writings admission was made of a death or destructive instinct that worked against the life or sex instinct. This leads to a pessimistic view about the future of humankind and society's ability to cope with human aggressive tendencies. For Freud, the one positive aspect was the ability that some people have to use defence mechanisms to redirect or sublimate aggressive impulses to social constructive activities such as work, art, literature, sport and relationships.

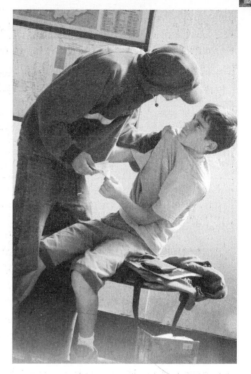

Aggression is better understood from a number of perspectives

The behaviourist perspective, even that of radical behaviourism as put forward by Skinner, acknowledges that an innate component may be present. However, the main explanations of why people engage in aggressive behaviour is seen as more to do with environmental factors such as upbringing, social circumstances such as poverty, and more generally, reinforcement contingencies that have strengthened the aggressive behavioural response to certain stimuli in the environment. Behaviourism advocates changes in the environment at a societal level in order to change people and prevent aggression.

The humanistic perspective regards aggressive behaviour as resulting from people who are not fully functioning at a psychological level – not fully functioning means that personal growth is stunted and self-actualisation not realised. To combat aggression, humanistic psychologists advocate the creation of conditions, at both interpersonal and societal levels, which will allow people to become more fulfilled in their lives.

The biological perspective very much accords with the psychoanalytic view of aggression being instinctual and something that evolved first to allow an individual to protect themselves, especially in the animal kingdom. The aggressive instinct, similar to the sex instinct, functions to ensure the survival of the species and the survival of the fittest.

The cognitive perspective has been less concerned with emotions and specific behaviours such as aggression. Nevertheless, the cognitions or perceptions that a person has about a situation that confronts them will determine how it is interpreted. If a situation is perceived to be threatening in some way then conscious thought will be given to how best to reduce the threat – this may be to remove oneself from the situation or attack (the classic 'flight or fight' response).

Perspective	View on aggression
Psychoanalytic	Aggression as instinctual and biologically given – death or destructive instinct. May be sublimated into socially constructive activities – work, art.
Behaviourist	May be some innate component, but largely determined by the environment. Factors such as upbringing, social conditions, poverty play a major role.
Humanistic	Aggression is a result of blocking of personal growth and prevention of self-actualisation. To remove aggression facilitates personal growth.
Biological	Aggression innate and instinctive resulting from benefits once provided to the individual and species for survival.
Cognitive	Perceptions and cognitions about a situation will determine whether or not seen as threatening and hence requiring an aggressive response.

Figure 9.4: Explanations of aggressions from the five main perspectives in psychology

PRACTICAL Activity

Read through today's newspaper and select a couple of articles depicting individuals or nations in an aggressive way. Use each of the five perspectives in psychology to help explain why the aggression has occurred. Does any one perspective offer a better explanation than the others? Or does each perspective provide different types of insights into explaining and understanding the aggression?

Study of human behaviour

Each of the five perspectives adopts a range of methods by which to study, research and collect evidence about human thought and behaviour. Some methods, for example, the laboratory experiment, are common to a number of perspectives; in this case, the behaviourist, cognitive and biological perspectives. In general, the more quantitative methods are characteristic of

Perspective	Methods of studying human behaviour
Psychoanalytic	Case studies. Interpretation of behaviour to unconscious motives.
Behaviourist	Laboratory experiments, often using animals such as rats and pigeons.
Humanistic	Case studies, biographies (psycho-history), subjective conscious experience.
Biological	Laboratory experiments, often using animals to investigate functions of parts of the brains. Twin studies.
Cognitive	Typically, laboratory experiments, sometimes single subject experiments and case studies.

Figure 9.5: Typical methods of studying human behaviour adopted by different perspectives in psychology

these three perspectives, whilst qualitative methods, such as case studies, are more likely to be used in the psychoanalytic and humanistic perspectives. Figure 9.5 summarises the main methods used by each of the five perspectives in psychology. From your knowledge and understanding of research methods at both AS and A2 level psychology, you should be aware that both qualitative and quantitative methods are widely used in the more scientific areas of psychology such as cognitive psychology, personality, social psychology, atypical psychology and health psychology.

REFLECTIVE Activity

Look back to one or two of the previous chapters where each perspective was considered in detail. Note the typical methods used to study human behaviour by each perspective. Why do you think such methods were adopted by each perspective? For example, why has the psychoanalytic method not made much use of the laboratory experiment, and why has the behaviourist perspective not used case studies?

9.4 Overlap and complementarity of perspectives

The comparisons that have been made between the five perspectives in relation to views of human nature, personality development, atypical behaviour, the role of culture/society, views on aggression and study of human behaviour have demonstrated that each perspective does not exist in isolation. There is overlap and a degree of complementarity of these different perspectives. In what follows we will consider just a few ways when this occurs, and you are invited to think of other ways from your knowledge of psychology and each of the perspectives.

The cognitive and biological perspectives come together in the area of cognitive neuroscience (see Section 6.3.3 of Chapter 6). Cognitive neuroscience studies the physiological (central nervous system, especially the brain) basis of cognitive functions and processes such as memory, attention, perception and consciousness.

PRACTICAL Activity

Refer back to Chapter 6 and re-read (or read for the first time if you have not already done so) Section 6.3.3 on cognitive neuropsychology. Whilst reading make note of the clear biological aspects of this exciting area of modern psychology.

We have seen earlier in this chapter that the psychoanalytic and biological perspectives have a degree of overlap and complementarity in relation to inheritance of instincts and evolution of psychological functions. Darwin's theory of evolution became an important factor in Freud's development of his theory about the sexual instinct, psychosexual development and unconscious, repressed conflicts. It is probably true to say that biological psychology has been influential in the development of the psychoanalytic perspective. However, the reverse is much less the case in that psychoanalysis has had much less or little influence on the biological perspective.

It may seem strange to say, but the psychoanalytic and behaviourist perspectives also have a degree of overlap and complementarity. Psychoanalysis provides an explanation of what is going on in the human mind, often at a largely unconscious level. Behaviourism provides an account of how we learn from experience. Thus, for example, the first psychosexual stage of development, the oral stage, will be affected by the experience the baby has of (breast) feeding. In a similar way, during the anal stage of psychosexual development, toilet training is deemed to be of vital significance. In a similar way, during the anal stage of psycholosexual development, toilet training is now considered to be of vital significance. The actual experience itself, the approach used by parents and significant others can be couched in terms of learning theory.

PRACTICAL Activity

The five different perspectives in psychology that we have considered in this chapter do offer quite different views and models of human beings and how they think and behave. These different conceptualisations exist, one could argue, because people are complex psychologically and not readily or adequately properly represented from a single perspective. Whilst modern psychology, especially in universities, adopts a strongly scientific approach (see Chapter 10), other perspectives such as the psychoanalytic and humanistic do exist and thrive to the present day. Psychologists themselves largely adopt a particular perspective and find it difficult to subscribe or operate across a range of perspectives, particularly when there are big differences such as that between behaviourism and humanism.

9.5 The Value of an eclectic approach

An eclectic approach adopts ideas, theories, methods, points of view, from a range of different perspectives in an attempt to capture better and represent the subject matter under study. In the case of psychology, taking aspects or ideas or methods from each of the five perspectives we have considered in this chapter may provide a richer, fuller, and more accurate picture of human nature and what it is to be human. Strictly speaking a proper definition of an eclectic approach is as follows:

> **An eclectic thinker is one who selectively adopts ideas from different sources and combines them in the development of a new theory.**   **(Mautner 2000: 158)**

Notice with this definition that an eclectic approach is not only about taking ideas and insights from different perspectives, but also putting these together in such a way as to produce a new theory. This new theory should, eventually, replace two or more perspectives to provide a broader, more widely applicable perspective. (See Chapter 10, Section 10.3, for a more general discussion on the nature of scientific theories and how science progresses.)

With your knowledge of psychology gained at AS and A2 levels you should be in a position to realise that psychology has not progressed, theoretically, to combine ideas from different perspectives into a new theory. The value of adopting an eclectic point of view in psychology is that human thought and behaviour does not readily lend itself to explanation and understanding from within one perspective. To some extent we have seen this in the previous section when we considered some of the complementarity of the different perspectives.

This is demonstrated in a more concrete way when considering explanations and treatments for atypical behaviour. If a treatment based upon a perspective for schizophrenia, for example, were successful it would be used to the exclusion of other therapeutic approaches. Clearly this is not the case with any of the major psychological disorders.

PRACTICAL Activity

Read back over the short section in this chapter on aggression. Discuss with others the extent to which you think one perspective provides an adequate explanation for aggressive behaviour. Identify elements of each of the five perspectives that help provide a greater understanding and fuller picture of human aggression.

9.6 Sample questions

SAMPLE QUESTION 1

(a) Explain *two* concepts within the biological perspective.
   (AO1 = 2, AO2 = 2)   *(4 marks)*
(b) Discuss *one* way in which the biological and psychoanalytic perspectives are complementary.
   (AO1 = 2, AO2 = 2)   *(4 marks)*
(c) With reference to any two issues, compare the psychoanalytic and behaviourist perspectives.
   (AO1 = 6, AO2 = 6)   *(12 marks)*

Total AO1 marks = 10 Total AO2 marks = 10 Total = 20 marks

QUESTIONS, ANSWERS AND COMMENTS

SAMPLE QUESTION 2

(a) Describe *one* similarity between the biological and psychoanalytic perspectives.
   (AO1 = 4)   *(4 marks)*
(b) Discuss the value of adopting an eclectic approach in psychology.
   (AO1 = 2, AO2 = 2)   *(4 marks)*
(c) With reference to any *two* issues, compare the behaviourist and humanistic perspectives.
   (AO1 = 4, AO2 = 8)   *(12 marks)*

Total AO1 marks = 10 Total AO2 marks = 10 Total = 20 marks

Answer to 2(a)

Both the biological and psychoanalytic approaches stress the fact that evolution and the inheritance of instincts occur in people. In evolutionary theory the sex instinct is important for the species to continue. In psychoanalytic theory the sex instinct operates at an unconscious level and is the main motive for human behaviour according to Freud.

Comment: A good answer where the similarity of instincts to both perspectives is identified. The answer then goes on to say how this is different within each perspective, thus demonstrating a knowledge of similarity and difference. Full four marks would be awarded for this answer.

Answer to 2(b)

An eclectic approach allows the best parts of the different perspectives in psychology to be selected, and the worst parts to be rejected. An eclectic approach gives a fuller and richer view of human behaviour.

Comment: This answer demonstrates a basic grasp of the value of an eclectic approach, but in the first sentence does not really express it correctly. The second sentence provides some indication of the values, but needs to go further to say in what way, using examples from different perspectives perhaps, a 'fuller and richer' view is gained. Just two out of the four marks available would be awarded for this answer.

Answer to 2(c)

The two issues that will be discussed in relation to the behaviourist and humanistic perspectives are methods of studying people and the view of each about human nature.

The behaviourist perspective makes use of the laboratory experiment using animals such as rats and pigeons. From this it is assumed that findings about how animals learn can be generalised and applied to humans. The use of animals in laboratory conditions such as the Skinner Box is artificial in itself and there may be problems with how well the findings apply to these animals in their natural environment. The behaviourist perspective is highly scientific and does not focus on an individual through the use of case studies, for example. By contrast, the humanistic perspective is against laboratory experiments and making highly scientific studies of people. Humanistic psychologists use case studies and regard understanding the subjective experience of a person as of greatest importance. Because of the focus on the individual the humanistic perspective does not try to make laws about all human behaviour.

With respect to human nature, the behaviourist perspective sees people more like machines who simply respond to stimuli in the environment. People are not seen to have free will and all learning comes from experience and reinforcement. The humanistic perspective sees people as essentially free and motivated by inner needs such as personal growth and achievement. In this respect the two perspectives are very different and have little in common.

Comment: Two appropriate issues for comparing the two perspectives are correctly identified and each understood in the context of the behaviourist and humanistic perspectives. The issue to do with methods of study is well developed and balanced with respect to each of the perspectives. Also some valuable analysis and critical comments are made. The second issue about views on human nature is dealt with less fully, but what is said is correct. More marks would have been gained here if some analysis and critical points with respect to each perspective were developed. Overall, a good answer demonstrating a good understanding of the two perspectives. This answer would be awarded 8 out of the 12 marks available, *(AO1 = 5, AO2 = 3).*

Total marks for question 2 = 14 out of 20

9.7 FURTHER READING

Krahé, B. 2001: **The social psychology of aggression**. Psychology Press, Hove.

Nye, R. D. 2000: **Three psychologies: perspectives from Freud, Skinner and Rogers**. Wadsworth, London.

Schultz, D. P. & Schultz, S. E. 2000: **A history of modern psychology**. 7th Ed. Harcourt College Publishers, Fort Worth.

10

The scientific approach

10.1 Introduction

We live in a world of science and applications of science. Just look around you and you will see televisions, cars, computers, aeroplanes, drug treatments for ill health, amongst many other benefits of the applications of science. We also live in a world of continuous change which can also be seen to be a consequence of the highly scientific world in which we live. The changes that have taken place to our world and people's lives over the past 100 years have been far greater than the changes that took place over the previous 1000 years. What has all this got to do with psychology you may ask? Many psychologists adopt a scientific approach to the study of human beings and other animals in the belief that the degree of understanding, prediction and control enjoyed in physical sciences will also become a feature of psychology. Not all psychologists agree with applying scientific procedures to the study of people, as we have seen with the humanistic perspective (see Chapter 8). Nevertheless, a scientific approach is dominant in modern psychology and an obvious feature of the cognitive perspective (see Chapter 6) which is probably the dominant research area in present-day psychology.

Psychologists look to the scientific approach for five main reasons. First, at a theoretical level the

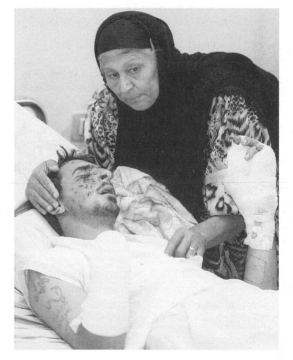

Scientific psychology may help to provide greater understanding of people's aggressiveness and so help to reduce the likelihood of war in the future

A scientific approach to health psychology may result in improving people's health and helping them to live longer, happier lives

scientific study of human and animal behaviour and mental processes will provide greater understanding and knowledge. Second, evidence and facts gathered through scientific procedures are objective and can be used to support a theory or hypothetical statement. Third, applications of a scientific approach to the study of people will bring benefits to people's lives and help them to adjust better to change and cope with trauma in their lives. Fourth, scientific procedures adopted by one psychologist or group of psychologists can be replicated by other psychologists around the world and at different times. Fifth, the study of human beings is inherently interesting and fascinating in its own right.

PRACTICAL activity

In groups of three or four, identify four or five technological benefits of science, for example, electricity and air flight. For each benefit list the positive things that it brings to people's lives. Also, for each benefit list the downsides or negative aspects and their effect on people's lives. From this you will see that science is not only about positives, but also about dealing with negative consequences. Now discuss this in relation to psychology. What might be the benefits of greater understanding, prediction and control with respect to people, and what might be the downsides?

In this chapter we will take a detailed look at what constitutes the scientific approach and how the scientific approach has been adopted by psychology. We will also consider both strengths and limitations of psychology as a science.

10.2 The nature of scientific enquiry

The word 'science' comes from the Latin word *scienta*, which means 'knowledge' and until the seventeenth century, science and philosophy were regarded as a single enterprise. What changed this were the British empiricist philosophers – John Locke (1632–1704), David Hume (1711–76) and John Stuart Mill (1806–73) – who advocated an **empirical approach** to knowledge. Empiricists believed that the only source of knowledge was that received through our senses – sight, hearing, smell, taste, etc. This was in contrast to the existing view that knowledge could be gained solely through the powers of reason and logical argument. Thus empiricism is the view that all knowledge is based on, or may be derived from, experience. At the time this was an important change being proposed and seemed to help reject prevailing superstitions (for example, belief in witchcraft and demonic possession) and irrational beliefs. The empirical approach of gaining knowledge through experience became the scientific approach and greatly influenced the development of physics and chemistry in the seventeenth and eighteenth centuries. The idea that knowledge should be gained through experience, i.e. empirically, turned into a method of enquiry that used careful observation and experimentation to gather facts and evidence. It took until the late nineteenth century for psychology to attempt to adopt an empirical and scientific approach with the first psychology laboratory being established by Wilhelm Wundt in 1879.

The subject matter, that of conscious experience, that Wundt tried to examine in his psychology laboratory was not really amenable to scientific methods. However, what is important is the idea of adopting scientific methods of enquiry in psychology. In the 1880s this was novel and controversial. In modern psychology it is viewed as both normal and a necessary part of psychology.

Scientific enquiry

The nature of scientific enquiry may be thought of at two levels: that to do with theory and the derivation of hypotheses and that to do with actual empirical methods of enquiry. We shall consider the former in the next section of this chapter, and focus on the latter in what follows.

The prime method of enquiry in science is the experiment. The key features of the experiment, whether in physics or psychology, are control over variables (independent, dependent, and extraneous), careful measurement and establishing cause–effect relationships.

Galileo (1564–1642) demonstrated that the earth was not at the centre of the universe, and that the sun revolves around the earth. This represents an early scientific approach to knowledge

PRACTICAL Activity

You will have already covered certain aspects of experiments in psychology when you studied Methods of Research at AS Level. Read over your notes or read Chapter 3, pages 56–62 of the AS text *Introducing psychology* (Pennington 2002).

In physics and chemistry, experiments carried out under laboratory conditions are regarded as providing objective knowledge that can then be applied to the real world. In physics and chemistry, human beings as scientists conduct their experiments on inert matter. There is not, in any meaningful sense, any interaction between the scientist and the object of study in the laboratory experiment. Except in very special circumstances in sub-atomic particle physics, the views and beliefs of the scientist do not interact with the object of study nor do they affect or influence the outcome of the experiment. The scientist is said to be objective and not able to influence or bias the outcome of his or her experiments. This ideal position in sciences such as physics and chemistry does not, unfortunately, hold up well in psychology.

PRACTICAL Activity

In groups of three or four, consider the stereotype of a scientist as a person wearing a white coat working in a laboratory. Identify between you the characteristics, psychological and otherwise, you associate with the stereotypical scientist. Now discuss how well or how poorly this might apply to different types of psychologists – behaviourists, psychoanalysts, humanistic psychologists and cognitive psychologists. Which appear most fit the scientist stereotype and which fit least well?

A number of important problems exist when attempts are made by psychologists to adopt scientific methods of study, most notably the laboratory experiment, for the study of human beings. The two we shall consider here are those of experimenter bias and demand characteristics of the experimental situation.

Experimenter bias (Rosenthal 1966) occurs when the beliefs, wishes, attitudes and even mere presence of the psychologists affects the experiment, or more precisely the participants (human or animal) taking part in the experiment. For example, Rosenthal and Fode (1963) demonstrated that psychologists who had been told that one group of rats had been especially bred to run round a maze fast (called 'maze bright' rats) and that another had been specially bred to be slow at running round a maze ('maze dull' rats) affected the outcome of an experiment. In reality, both groups of rats were the same and had not been bred for any special maze running ability. Nevertheless, Rosenthal and Fode (1963) found that psychologists conducting experiments with what they thought were bright and dull rats reported the so-called 'bright' rats to run mazes faster than the so-called 'dull' rats. This study demonstrates very well the effect of prior knowledge and expectations upon an experiment with animals. In the human sphere perhaps the best known experiment demonstrating experimenter bias is that of *Pygmalion in the classroom* by Rosenthal and Jacobson (1968). Here teachers were told that one group of children would be likely to do well over the school year, and that another group of children had no predictions made about them. One year later it was found, through the use of intelligence tests, that the expectations of the teachers were realised. In fact, the two groups of children were randomly formed and no known differences between the two groups had been identified. This has become known as a *self-fulfilling prophecy*.

Experimenter bias, in the form of knowledge about the purpose of the experiment and expectations, can affect the outcome. One way round this is to conduct the experiment 'double blind' where the experimenter or psychologist does not know what it is about or the hypothesis that is being tested. This does not always work because, for example, in social psychology experiments, the general attitude (friendly or unfriendly) towards a participant may influence how the person behaves in the experiment.

Demand characteristics of the psychology experiment were identified by Orne (1962). Orne said that it was wrong to regard the participant in the psychology experiment as passively responding to environmental stimuli and changes in the laboratory. Instead, the participant plays an active role and will try to guess what the experiment is really about and may try to please the experimenter by behaving or responding in ways the participant thinks the psychologist desires. The participant may also try to guess the hypothesis, and since many participants in experiments are students of psychology, this may be reasonable, and behave in ways supporting the hypothesis. Either way the participant may behave in ways which mean that the measures taken and findings of the experiment may be of little value. The above assumes that participants want to be helpful and please the psychologist. This may not always be the case and the participant may be unhelpful.

Consideration of experimenter bias and demand characteristics quite clearly point out major differences between experiments in sciences, such as physics and chemistry, and experiments in psychology. This is summarised in Figure 10.1. The important point to make is that there are limitations on adopting a scientific approach in psychology. These limitations need to be taken into account and considered in relation to any experiment using people as participants.

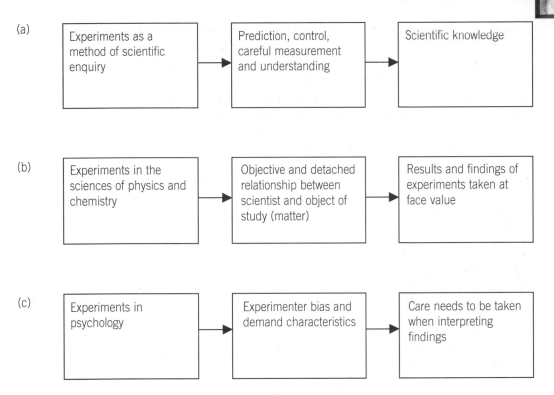

Figure 10.1: Simplified view of the scientific method of the experiment (a), and how it translates in sciences such as chemistry and physics (b), and psychology as science (c)

Common-sense

In certain ways everybody is a psychologist. This does not mean that everybody has formally to study and be trained in psychology. However, people who are successful in their lives and are able to adjust to the demands, changes and traumas that come along, have to operate as 'informal' or 'intuitive' psychologists (Heider 1958). In short, people have common-sense views of the world, of other people and of themselves. These common-sense views may come from personal experience, through socialisation as a child with the views of parents being adopted, from cultural or sub-cultural beliefs, and from numerous other sources. People have common-sense views about the causes of their own and other people's behaviour, about personality characteristics they and others possess, about what people should do and a moral code by which to lead your life, how to bring up children, and many, many more aspects of psychology.

REFLECTIVE Activity

Look through the chapter headings of an introductory text book on psychology. Can you identify any subject areas in the textbook where you do not have some kind of common-sense views and opinions? You might find that only in highly technical areas or specialised areas, for example, biological psychology, might this be the case.

The informal psychologist or lay person acquires this common-sense knowledge in a rather haphazard, anecdotal and often unsubstantiated way. Common-sense views about people are rarely based on systematic evidence, and are sometimes based on a single experience or observation. Racial or religious prejudices may reflect what seems like common-sense within a group of people. However, prejudicial beliefs rarely stand up to what is actually the case. However, people's beliefs are notoriously difficult to change (Rokeach 1960) especially when they reflect the culture in which a person lives and has been socialised into.

Common-sense, then, is an essential element people use to conduct their lives. But because it is not based on systematic knowledge, or derived from scientific enquiry, it may often be misleading, erroneous, and lead to one group of people treating others unfairly and in a discriminatory way.

Common-sense has also been called **folk psychology**. Folk psychology is the beliefs, values, attitudes and morals that are held by a culture or sub-culture. As such these aspects of folk psychology influence how people think and how people interact and relate amongst themselves and to other people outside of the culture.

There are examples of psychological theory, concepts and perspectives influencing and changing common-sense views held by people. Perhaps the most influential has been Sigmund Freud, as indicated by the following quotation from an authority on Freud:

> **Freud is often linked with Darwin and Marx as being one of the three original thinkers who have most altered man's view of himself in the twentieth century.**

> **(Storr 2001: 145)**

Whilst there is debate about the scientific status of Freudian theory (see Chapter 7) there can be little doubt that many Freudian concepts have entered everyday language. People commonly and regularly use words such as 'defensiveness', 'repression' and 'unconscious' when making common-sense interpretations of their own and other people's behaviour. These are all terms which Freud introduced to psychology.

Common-sense, then, is something which everybody uses in their day-to-day lives, guides decisions and influences how people interact with one another. However, it may at times lead to bias, error, incorrect judgements about other people, prejudiced views, etc. Since common-sense is not grounded in a scientific approach, this may seem an inevitable consequence. Alternatively, humanistic psychologists (see Chapter 8) advocate that people should trust their intuition and common-sense more, but in the context of having positive regard for other people. Psychology can, therefore, be seen to be split over the value and reliability of common-sense. The more scientific psychologists will be much more sceptical about its value, and the humanistic psychologists more positive about its value and the trust that should be placed on common-sense.

REFLECTIVE Activity

Consider each of the following perspectives in psychology: biological, behaviourist, cognitive, psychoanalytic, and humanistic. For each perspective write down what value you think it places on common-sense. Which perspective values it most and which least? Give your reasons for this.

10.3 Theory, hypothesis, evidence and replication

Is psychology a science? This simple-looking question does not have a straightforward answer, unfortunately. A number of different answers can be given depending on the view of philosophy of science that is taken. It is generally agreed that a science consists of three main aspects: an agreement over the subject matter, theories and hypotheses, and empirical, objective methods of data collection. We will look at the latter two aspects later in this section, and consider the issue about subject matter in psychology in what follows.

Thomas Kuhn (1970), a famous philosopher of science, characterised science as consisting of a unified and agreed-upon subject matter which constitutes what he calls a **paradigm**. For Kuhn a mature science is characterised by a single paradigm. If you have studied physics, Kuhn would say that Newton's laws of mechanics and electromagnetism constitute a paradigm in physics. In more detail, a paradigm consists of general theoretical assumptions, techniques of empirical enquiry and agreement amongst scientists of how to conduct empirical research. Now apply this description of a paradigm to psychology – does psychology conform to this picture? From your studies on the different perspectives in psychology – psychoanalytic, behaviourist, cognitive, biological and humanistic – you can see that there is no agreement over the general theoretical assumptions or the methods of enquiry. For example, behaviourism proposes a theory of human behaviour based on the reinforcement or punishment of stimulus–response relationships. Its method of enquiry is experimental, often using animals rather than people. By contrast, consider psychoanalysis. Psychoanalysis, at least of Freudian type, bases its theory on unconscious mental processes and conflicts deriving from the sex and death instinct. Its methods of enquiry, such as they are, come from case studies.

REFLECTIVE activity

Consider the cognitive and humanistic perspectives. Identify the basic assumptions on which theories are built for each perspective, and the typical methods of enquiry employed by these two perspectives.

By considering each of these five perspectives in relation to the description given above of what Kuhn called a paradigm, you should be able to see that there are few, if any, general assumptions in common. Also, that different perspectives foster different methods of empirical enquiry. Whilst you may think that each perspective might qualify as a paradigm in its own right, this would not reflect what Kuhn meant by a paradigm. In consequence, Kuhn (1970) did not regard psychology to be a mature science, but a *pre-science*. To become a mature science, Kuhn argued, would require the coming together of the different perspectives to become a paradigm. That is, a set of shared general assumptions common to all areas of psychology together with agreement amongst psychologists of the methods of empirical enquiry.

EVALUATIVE COMMENT

Whilst the cognitive perspective is dominant in modern psychology the other very different perspectives of psychoanalysis and humanistic psychology remain important influences in psychology. For each perspective progress occurs through greater theoretical sophistication and better developed methods of enquiry. It may be, therefore, that because of the very different way in which human beings can be thought of psychology cannot achieve the status of a mature science as defined by Kuhn. Nevertheless, psychology does adopt scientific methods in the form of theories, hypothesis testing and the collection of evidence to achieve greater understanding of people, and to make applications to help solve human problems.

Theory and hypothesis

A theory may be defined as 'a set of propositions which provides principles of analysis or explanation of a subject matter' (Mautner 2000: 563). So, for example, the propositions that all people have an innate desire to fulfil their potential, or that all men are naturally aggressive, can be characterised as theories. A theory must also be able to generate a number of hypotheses which can then be tested through empirical research. An hypothesis is a conjecture or premise which is tentatively put forward requiring empirical enquiry to determine whether it is false or supported by evidence. Hence, from the proposition that all men are naturally aggressive, a number of hypotheses can be derived. For example, a man prevented from going into a nightclub for no good reason will pick a fight with the doorman. Or, when shouted at by another man, he will fight rather than argue with the person. No doubt you can generate many more hypotheses from this theoretical statement.

PRACTICAL activity

In groups of three or four consider the theory that all people have an innate desire to fulfil their potential. Write down three hypotheses that might be derived from this theory.

These hypotheses can then be tested using scientific procedures or methods of investigation. The empirical findings may either support the hypothesis or refute it. If the former, the theory will have gained support and will be maintained. If the latter, the theory will not have been supported. However, whether the theory is rejected or maintained will depend on findings from testing other hypothesis derived from the theory. Figure 10.2 summarises what has been said above.

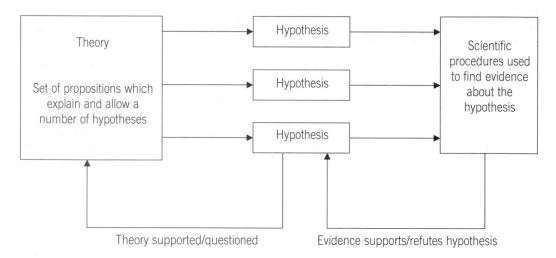

Figure 10.2: The scientific method of using a theory to derive hypotheses which are then tested using scientific methods of enquiry. Evidence may support or refute a hypothesis, which in turn has a bearing on the theory

Karl Popper (1969) argued that for a theory to be classed as scientific it must, in principle, be capable of *falsification*. Popper argued that falsification had to be the criterion not proving a theory to be true. We have seen above, that the findings of empirical research may support a hypothesis, which in turn provides support for the theory. However, this cannot be used to say that a theory is true because in the future an hypothesis derived from the theory may not be supported. This might result in the theory being rejected. Hence, for Popper, a scientific theory is one that allows hypotheses to be derived and is capable of falsification. Theories which receive empirical support will be maintained. Theories that suffer many refutations will be rejected.

EVALUATIVE COMMENT

Consider the psychoanalytic and behaviourist perspectives. It is clear that behaviourism does make testable hypotheses and produces objective evidence to support or refute the hypotheses. But how about psychoanalysis? It has often been argued that Freudian theory does not produce testable hypotheses. Kline (1984) has challenged this assertion and shown that testable

hypotheses can be drawn from Freudian theory. The problem is that whatever the findings, Freudian theory can offer an explanation and hence not be refuted. For example, consider the hypothesis: people with an anal personality will be miserly. If findings were such that some people were not, we would normally say the hypothesis has been refuted. However, a Freudian might argue that non-miserly people with an anal personality use the defence mechanism of reaction formation to turn a trait into its opposite. Thus non-miserly people do really possess an anal personality just like miserly people! Freudian explanations of behaviour typically fall into this pattern, as a consequence it is difficult to see how Freudian theory can be seen to be scientific in the way Popper describes a scientific theory.

REFLECTIVE Activity

The humanistic perspective (see Chapter 8) produces plenty of theories about people – theories about self-actualisation (Rogers), the hierarchy of human needs (Maslow), the need for unconditional positive regard (Rogers), but does not adopt scientific methods of enquiry to test these theories against objective evidence. Why do you think humanistic psychologists have largely rejected a scientific approach to psychology? Does this mean that the theories of humanistic psychologists should be rejected?

If we accept that for a theory to be classed as scientific it must produce hypotheses which are capable of being refuted, the question arises as to how a scientific theory is developed in the first place. Just how do scientists create or make up a theory?

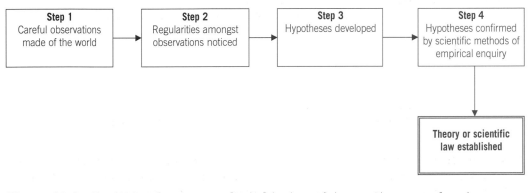

Figure 10.3: Traditional or commonly held view of how a theory or law in science is developed

The commonly held view concerning the development of a scientific theory is shown in Figure 10.3. This depicts scientists first making careful observations of the word, then noticing some kind of regularity amongst these observations. This leads to the development of one or more hypotheses. They are then confirmed by means of experiments or other scientific methods of enquiry. The hypotheses are then turned into a theory or scientific law. This is called the **inductive method** of scientific reasoning. Induction goes from the specific (observations about the world) to the general (theories and laws). However, philosophers of science such as Feyerabend (1975) have argued that science does not typically progress in such an orderly way and that human imagination and creativity have also to be taken into account. Feyerabend argues against seeing science and theory development as conforming to a prescribed order, and uses the phrase 'anything goes'. By this he means that science progresses often through adopting any methods, scientific or otherwise, and that human creativity, insight and intuition, play an important role in the development of scientific theories. In many ways and because of the radically different perspectives and range of methods employed in psychology, Feyerabend's extreme views do seem to reflect what goes on in psychology. For example, what factors do you think might influence what type of psychologist a person decides to be in his or her academic career? Why do people who study the same or similar undergraduate degree in psychology – as approved by the British Psychological Society – prefer cognitive psychology, or psychoanalysis or biological psychology?

REFLECTIVE Activity

From studying different approaches and perspectives in psychology, identify which you most enjoy studying and are interested in. Now try to identify why this is the case – are the reasons to do with scientific status, or understanding of other people, or how people are to be viewed? Compare your analysis of yourself with that of other students in your class.

Empirical evidence

(The scientific approach in psychology, as with other disciplines such as chemistry, physics and biology, attaches fundamental significance to gathering and using evidence to support or refute hypotheses and theories. However, as shown in Figure 10.5, evidence can come in many forms with only scientific evidence being admissible in the scientific courtroom of theory testing. There are at least three main features of evidence which make it scientific. First, the evidence or the data should be objective. This means that only that which is observable is admissible. Second, anyone trained in psychological or other scientific methods of empirical enquiry should be able to make the same observations and collect the same data. Third, scientific evidence in psychology comes from a number of sources.

Evidence is important in many aspects of our lives and the society in which we live. However, only certain types of evidence can be considered to be scientific

Clearly the use of the experiment in psychology, especially under laboratory conditions, is most likely to produce evidence, data and findings that we can confidently claim are objective and hence scientific. However, in psychology evidence can come from numerous other sources that meet our criteria of objectively. For example, personal records and autobiographies may produce evidence about an individual which throws light on their personality. Psychology, especially personality and psychometrics, make extensive use of questionnaires – mostly self-report questionnaires. The extent to which these questionnaires produce objective data does depend on how honestly a person answers the questions. Bias often does enter into the answers due to, for example, the person wanting to put him- or herself forward in a socially positive way (se Chapter 12 for advantages and disadvantages of different methods of research in psychology).

Raymond Cattell, a highly influential psychologist in trait theories of personality (see Pennington, 2003), suggested that evidence about a person could be obtained from three sources. The first is a person's life records which include objective data about a person (number of children, marital status, different jobs, etc.) and more subjective information gained from reports made by other people. This Cattell called *L-data* (Cattell 1983). A second source of evidence or data about a person Cattell called *Q-data*. This is data collected from questionnaires such as personality inventories and intelligence tests. Because people can fake responses to questionnaires, Cattell argued that Q-data needed to be supported by behavioural data. This comes from *T-data*, which represents objective observations of, for example, cognitive abilities through measuring such things as reaction time, ability to follow directions and memory. These three types of data suggested by Cattell (1983) are summarised in Figure 10.4.

Type of data	Description
L-data	A person's life records: certificates of educational achievement, progress in career through jobs occupied, hobbies and pastimes.
Q-data	Measurements and scores obtained from personality, intelligence, mood, etc., questionnaires.
T-data	Objective measures of behaviour and performance, for example, reaction time, memory for words, recognition of faces, etc.

Figure 10.4: Three sources of evidence or data about a person suggested by Cattell (1983)

The point of considering Cattell's suggestions for the different types of evidence or data psychologists should collect about people is that objective evidence is more elusive and harder to obtain in psychology than it is in sciences such as physics or biology. Because human beings are conscious, thinking and reasoning creatures, the collection of objective, scientific evidence presents difficulties not encountered in other sciences. Since the object of study of physics and chemistry is inert matter, then objective evidence is more readily obtained.

Replication

In psychology **replication** is most often discussed in reference to experiments. For evidence or findings to be considered scientific they must be verifiable by other psychologists. This means that other psychologists must be able to replicate the original experiment, using the same methods and procedures, and producing the same results or similar patterns of data as in the

original experiment. A psychology experiment is replicable to the extent that the method, procedure, materials used and gathering of participants are clearly and precisely described. This description may appear in a refereed journal in psychology or may be obtained directly from the psychologist who carried out the original experiment. Use of the Internet to visit websites of university psychology departments round the world is now commonly used to obtain detailed descriptions of the procedures of an experiment.

In principle, an experiment in psychology should be able to be replicated anywhere in the world and at any time. This is the criteria used in physics and chemistry. However, in psychology there are factors that question the extent to which this principle can be realised. One factor is the culture in which the original experiment and attempt at replication take place. Much of the experimental research in psychology has taken place in western cultures such as in North America and Europe. Smith and Bond (1999) review psychological research conducted in numerous cultures, and show that quite different results are often obtained from replicating the same experiment in eastern cultures. One of the variables between cultures that has been used to explain such differences in findings from the same experiment is that of individualist-collectivist (Hofstede 1980). Individualistic cultures are those which value individual achievement. Collectivist cultures are where the welfare of the group is of greater importance. Typically, western cultures are individualistic and eastern cultures collectivistic.

Methods of gathering evidence, other than the experiment, in psychology, present different problems of replication. For example, a case study on a single person conducted over a number of years simply is not replicable. Each person is unique and grows and changes with time. Whilst it is possible to replicate the procedures of a case study, each case study is a unique, qualitative, analysis of a person over a specified period of time. Field studies and field experiments can be replicated to a certain extent, but the controlled conditions of the psychology laboratory cannot easily be translated to research undertaken in real-life settings.

Can a person's private experiences be the object of scientific study?

PRACTICAL Activity

Consider the different methods of investigation you have studied in psychology including the laboratory experiment, field experiment, correlational study and case study. For each, list aspects which can be replicated and which cannot or are difficult to replicate. Then make a judgement on a 10-point scale of the degree to which each method is capable of replication (use 1 as very low and 10 as very high).

10.4 Overt behaviour and private experience

REFLECTIVE Activity

Consider the picture of the Buddhist monk meditating. There are few or no behavioural indications of what this person is thinking about. Can the private experience of a person be communicated to other people and can it be the object of scientific study?

Traditionally, a distinction is made between that which is observable as being amenable to the scientific approach, and that which is not observable as subjective and hence not open to scientific enquiry. This distinction represents on the one hand the view of radical behaviourists, as we saw in Chapter 5, that only that which can be objectively observed – overt behaviour – should be the object of study of scientific psychology. On the other hand, humanistic psychologists, as we saw in Chapter 8, place great value on private or subjective experience and are less concerned with adopting the methods of science to study people. This is a simplistic position since overt or observable behaviour is regarded as the domain of scientific psychology, and private experience as too subjective to be of scientific value.

Cognitive psychology, as we saw in Chapter 6, does attempt to investigate in a scientific way, consciousness and thought processes. Cognitive psychologists are typically interested in attention, memory, perception, language and ways in which we think. These cognitive processes certainly constitute a part of what we might call our private and conscious experience of ourselves and the world around us. However, this does not seem to fully capture what we intuitively means by the term **private experience**.

In part, the areas of study of cognitive psychology miss out some essential elements of private experience. For example, William James (1890), a founding father of psychology, talked about a 'stream of consciousness'. By this he meant the second-by-second awareness we have of the world from our various senses. My stream of consciousness as I look out of the window across a Cornish harbour whilst I write this book, is unique and private to me. Not only that, it is not repeatable, although I can try to recapture the sensations and feelings if I look out of the window again. Private experience as our stream of consciousness in this sense would not seem to be the object of scientific psychology. I can try to report on my stream of consciousness by verbalising as much as I can, but my verbalisations will only capture a small part of what I am aware of second-to-second.

PRACTICAL Activity

Sit comfortably with another person. In turn each try to verbalise all you are aware of for a couple of minutes. You may want to tape record this. From what you have heard each other say, discuss how well what the other has heard represents the actual private experiences. You should find that much has been missed out – there is simply too much going on to be able to report on it and continue to experience your stream of consciousness.

Introspectionists, such as Wilhelm Wundt and Edward Titchener, in the early development of psychology, tried to bring scientific procedures to the study of private experience. In the end they failed because of the subjective nature of the data (verbal reports) produced, and having no objective way of resolving disagreements between two or more people over subjective reports of the same external event (for example, how you think and feel in response to hearing a clock tick).

Ayer (1959), an influential philosopher of mind, makes three distinctions about the sense in which mental events may be considered to be private. First, introspective reports provide the only possible evidence for mental states. Second, each person has privileged and sole access to their private experiences. Third, introspective reports on private experiences are subjective. What this seems to indicate is that private experiences are too subjective, in their reporting through introspection, to allow scientific study. Hence overt behaviour, or behavioural (largely verbal) responses reflecting cognitive process (as used by cognitive psychologists) are objective and hence amenable to the scientific approach.

10.5 Strengths and limitations of the scientific approach

In what follows we will consider three strengths and three limitations of the scientific approach in psychology.

STRENGTHS

The first strength is that the scientific approach is objective. This means that research conducted using scientific procedures, such as the experiment, provides accurate measurement of human and animal characteristics and are replicable so that results should be repeatable if the same procedures are used. Also, the results of scientific enquiry are reliable and often generalisable to large groups or populations of people. However, we have seen in this chapter that human experimental psychology may bring with it experimenter bias and demand characteristics that do not present such problems in sciences such as physics. Psychologists need to be aware of the strengths and shortcomings of the use of experiments in human studies.

The second strength is that the scientific approach produces theories about human thought and behaviour. Scientific theories lead to the derivation of testable hypotheses. Theories stand or fall on the extent to which data and evidence support or refute hypotheses. The application of a scientific and empirical approach to psychology has meant that as a discipline psychology develops better and stronger theories, hence progressing as a science.

The third strength is that scientific psychology has enjoyed a range of applications to help solve human problems and help improve people's lives. Applied areas of psychology such as health psychology, atypical psychology and criminological psychology, which you may have studied at AS/A2 Level, are all strongly based on a scientific approach. This means, for example, that developing psychotherapies to help people with psychological disorders can be based on objective findings. This also allows the effectiveness of various different types of psychotherapies to be assessed. In relation to health psychology, the effectiveness of different stress management programmes can be evaluated. Finally, in criminological psychology, the soundness or otherwise of witness evidence can be scientifically assessed and typical human errors identified.

LIMITATIONS

The first limitation is that a scientific approach to the study of people tends to view people more as machines. This is because a scientific approach adopts a deterministic view of human thought and behaviour, looking for cause and effect in every aspect of human life. In consequence, the scientific approach fosters a view of people as, in principle, predictable, controllable, and reducible to laws and regularities of behaviour. Additionally, the scientific approach adopts a reductionist view, assuming that complex behaviour and thought can be

Scientific approach		Description
Strengths	Objective	Provides accurate measurement, research replicable, results reliable and generalisable.
	.Produces theories	Theories lead to testable hypotheses. Theories stand or fall on supporting or refuting empirical evidence.
	Applications	Applications to, for example, health psychology, atypical psychology, sport psychology, criminological psychology.
Limitations	People as machines	Deterministic and reductionist view of human thought and behaviour. Laws of behaviour–mechanistic.
	Artificiality of research methods	Experiments in psychology may lack ecological validity and suffer problems of generalisability.
	Ethical constraints	Positive value and need to have ethical guidelines for psychological research. However, constrains what can be studied scientifically.

Figure 10.5: Summary of strengths and limitations of the scientific approach in psychology

reduced to their basic, simple, component parts. This scientific 'model' of human bein gs seems to take away some essential aspect of what we consider people to be about. Humanistic psychologists would argue this and say that the whole person has to be looked at from a psychological perspective and not the parts of a person.

The second limitation is that many of the empirical methods of enquiry, especially the laboratory experiment in psychology, create artificial situations. This means that there is a lack of ecological validity and hence a problem with attempting to generalise findings to large groups of people or whole populations.

The third limitation is to do with ethical constraints that professional bodies, such as the British Psychological Society (BPS) and the American Psychological Association (APA), place upon psychological research. It is entirely right that psychological research should conform to strict ethical guidelines. This does mean, however, that certain experiments and studies which might be of scientific interest, simply (and rightly) cannot be undertaken using people as participants. In sciences such as physics and chemistry, ethical constraints still operate (for example, testing of nuclear bombs in the atmosphere), but the constraints are less. It may seem odd to cite ethical guidelines as a limitation of the scientific approach applied to psychology. However, it is important to be aware both of the vital importance of ethical guidelines for conducting scientific research, and the limitations ethical guidelines place on research conducted on people.

10.6 Sample questions

SAMPLE QUESTION 1

(a) Distinguish between common-sense and scientific enquiry.
   (AO1 = 2, AO2 = 2)   *(4 marks)*

(b) Explain the role of theory in the scientific approach.
   (AO1 = 2, AO2 = 2)   *(4 marks)*

Sample questions, answers and comments

(c)   Discuss the importance of empirical evidence and replication in the scientific approach. Refer to an area that you have studied in your answer.

(AO1 = 6, AO2 = 6)   *(12 marks)*

Total AO1 marks = 10 Total AO2 marks = 10 Total = 20 marks

QUESTIONS, ANSWERS AND COMMENTS

SAMPLE QUESTION 2

(a)   Explain why some psychologists regard the study of overt behaviour as the only way to gain knowledge about people.

(AO1 = 2, AO2 = 2)   *(4 marks)*

(b)   Explain why some psychologists might regard subjective experience as the best way to gain knowledge about people.

(AO1 = 2, AO2 = 2)   *(4 marks)*

(c)   Describe and discuss at least *one* strength and at least *one* limitation of the scientific approach in psychology. In your answer refer to at least *one* topic in psychology that you have studied.

(AO1 = 6, AO2 = 6)   *(12 marks)*

Total AO1 marks = 10 Total AO2 marks = 10 Total = 20 marks

Answer to 2(a)

The psychologists who regard the study of overt behaviour as the only way to gain knowledge about people are behaviourists. These psychologists say that everything we do and all the ways we act are caused by our learning from the environment. In effect behaviourists believe that the only way to gain knowledge is to study overt behaviour since we cannot see what goes on in our minds.

Comment: This answer is basically correct, a little repetitive in places and does not really go beyond linking overt behaviour with the behaviourist approach. 2 out of the 4 marks would be awarded. To gain more marks the answer would need to explain why overt behaviour provides a psychologist with knowledge.

Answer to 2(b)

Some psychologists, like psychoanalytic and humanistic psychologists, would say that subjective experience has its advantages. This is because our subjective experience allows us to identify with other people, share thoughts and feelings, and then come to some conclusions. Our subjective experience is important in gaining knowledge about other people because it allows us to compare experiences. Humanists like Maslow and Rogers say that subjective experience is important because it allows psychologists to help a person become fulfilled and reach self-actualisation.

Comment: This answer correctly links subjective experience to the humanistic and psychoanalytic perspectives. The use of subjective experience to identify and empathise with other people is also a useful point, as is the idea of two people sharing their experiences. This answer would attract 3 out of the 4 marks available.

Answer to 2(c)

A strength of the scientific approach is its objectivity. Psychologists using this approach make it as objective as possible at every stage of the investigation. For example, when sampling from their target population they would probably use the random sampling method. Scientific psychologists would maintain objectivity by reducing all types of bias. Objectivity would also be upheld through the elimination of demand characteristics, which could influence the results. This is where Piaget's conservation tasks are weak, since the question 'Which glass has the most water in it?' is asked twice. This leads to the demand characteristic of a different answer being required the second time.

Being objective makes the scientific approach advantageous because it allows confident generalisation. It also means that results are reliable and if an experiment were to be repeated under the same conditions, the same results will be obtained. Overall, this means that some strong conclusions can be drawn from the scientific approach.

A limitation of the scientific approach is that it is harsh and cold towards people. Because it is nomothetic it does not see people as individuals. This can link in with the topic of cognitive development. If a child is put through some scientific tests to find their level of cognitive development and find out that s/he is low on the scale, then the child's self-esteem may suffer. So the scientific approach is uncaring to those who deviate from the average. The scientific approach may be in danger of breaking the BPS guidelines of not causing harm to people.

Comment: This answer does attempt to discuss a strength and a weakness of the scientific approach, and attempts to relate the discussion to the topic area of cognitive child development. The discussion of the strength of objectivity is done reasonably well covering ideas of random sampling, demand characteristics of experiments and generalisation. The example used to highlight demand characteristics makes the point well. The limitation identified – harsh and cold towards people – is less well done and is muddled in places. Overall, this answer would attract 7 out of the 12 marks available.

Total marks for question 2 = 12 out of 20 (AO1 = 8, AO2 = 4)

10.7 FURTHER READING

Introductory texts

Bell, A. 2002: **Debates in psychology**. Chapter 5. Taylor & Francis, East Sussex, Hove.

Gross, R. 1999: **Themes, issues and debates in psychology**. Chapter 11. Hodder & Stoughton, London.

Specialist sources

Chalmers, A. F. 1976: **What is this thing called science?** The Open University Press, Milton Keynes.

Valentine, E. R. 1992: **Conceptual issues in psychology**. 2nd Ed. Chapters 1 and 7. Routledge, London.

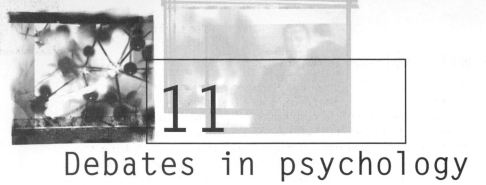

11

Debates in psychology

11.1 Introduction

Psychology has its roots in philosophy and developed from it over 100 years ago when Wilhelm Wundt established the first psychology laboratory. Contemporary psychology, as a scientific discipline, uses many methods, including the laboratory experiment to investigate human and animal behaviour. However, whilst psychology uses a sophisticated range of methods to investigate numerous topic areas – such as social, developmental, and cognitive psychology, and many areas of application such as sport, health and criminological psychology – numerous philosophical debates remain important.

The word **philosophy** comes from the Greek word *philosophia*, which means love of wisdom and the search for knowledge and truth. The method of philosophy is rational enquiry. By this is meant that logic, reasoned argument and theory are used to inquire into such issues as the nature of truth, whether or not God exists, the nature of science and many other areas of interest. Philosophy as love of wisdom and truth reflects the idea that the quest for knowledge and truth are undertaken for their own sake (for the 'love of') rather than for any obvious purpose.

Because psychology developed out of philosophy a nucleus of debates remains of central importance to this day. These are debates concerned with free will and determinism, heredity and environment, holism and reductionism, idiographic and nomothetic approaches and the mind-body debate. In this chapter we will consider each of these debates in some detail.

REFLECTIVE Activity

Think about two or three things that you are certain of as being true: that the sun will rise tomorrow, that the sky is blue (when there are no clouds!) and that the world is round. How do you know these things to be true? For example, how do you know the sun will rise tomorrow? What would it need to question the truth by which you hold these beliefs? These are just some of the issues dealt with by philosophy.

11.2 Free will and determinism

The free will–determinism debate revolves around whether or not people are free to choose how to think and behave or whether behaviour is determined and caused by factors outside of an individual's control. There are two extreme positions. First, that all thought and behaviour results from a person's free will, that is, each person has the freedom to control what he or she thinks or does. In a sense the person determines, through free choice, his or her thoughts and behaviour. Second, at the other extreme, is the position that all human thought and behaviour is determined by forces outside of a person's individual control. These forces may be biological, environmental or psychic (unconscious, for example).

PRACTICAL Activity

Consider the following: writing an essay, achieving high grades at an examination, having a dream, sneezing and catching a cold. For each of these discuss with others in a small group the extent to which you think you have free will. To what extent do you think you can control what you dream about, or decide that you will not catch a cold from a friend?

An extreme, or **hard determinism** position implies that it should be possible, in principle, to identify all causes of behaviour. As a consequence, this means that all behaviour should be predictable and able to be scientifically analysed. However, some psychologists who believe in determinism do not think it appropriate to adopt such an extreme viewpoint and put forward the ideal of 'soft' determinism. William James (1890), one of the founding fathers of psychology, believed that scientific principles should be brought to bear to the study of human behaviour. This implies an extreme determinism position akin to that of sciences such as physics or biology. However, Williams James also recognised that subjective experience is important and that our awareness of thoughts and our ability to choose what to do in many situations implied free will. This has been called a **soft determinism** position because it allows both for human behaviour to be determined, and for people to be able to exercise free will at the same time. Consciousness and self-awareness are often regarded as distinguishing human beings from other animals. In consequence, psychologists are much more likely to apply a hard determinism position to non-human animals, such as rats, dogs, cats and monkeys.

Types of determinism

At least three types of determinism may be considered to apply to human beings. These are biological, environmental, and psychic or mental determinism. **Biological determinism** includes a number of aspects; these are to do with the different functions of the brain itself, our hormone system, and genetics or heritability.

Just how much freedom to choose what to do does a person have in some situations? Here it would appear that behaviour is determined by what the gunman wants the person to do

These twins are identical and share the same genes. Genes determine physical characteristics and hence these two look alike. Genes may also determine personality, intelligence and susceptibility to mental disorder

It is well established that different parts of the brain are responsible for different behavioural and mental functions. This is what is meant by localisation of function in the brain. For example, language is located primarily in the left hemisphere with Broca's area being responsible for speech production, and Wernicke's area for understanding what people say. The hypothalamus is a small structure in the middle of the brain and has been shown to be involved in aggression and a person's sex drive. Damage to Broca's or Wernicke's areas will result in the person's language function being affected. No amount of willing or free will can restore speech production to normal if Broca's area is damaged. Similarly, an overactive hypothalamus may make a person more aggressive or experience heightened sexual feelings. The individual may be able to exert free will to control these feelings but may battle and not be completely successful. Hess (1957) found that when he stimulated certain areas of a cat's hypothalamus it behaved aggressively. By contrast, Vergnes (1975) has shown that another part of the brain, the amygdala, when stimulated, inhibits aggressive behaviour.

In a very real sense then, our brain does determine our behaviour and disorders of the brain may affect us in ways that we are unable to control, no matter how much we may try to exert our will to exercise control.

Experimental determinism is most associated with the radical behaviourist view put forward by Skinner and Watson. This states quite simply that all behaviour is under the control of two features in the external environment: reinforcement and punishment.

PRACTICAL Activity

Read Chapter 5 (pages 122 to 130). Consider how both classical and operant conditioning reflect a hard determinism position.

Environmental determinism may also seem to be a position that social psychologists subscribe to. For example, the well-known experiments of Milgram (1963), Zimbardo's (1969) prison simulation study, and Asch's (1955) line-study on conformity, all demonstrate how social forces (other people) have a strong determining influence on our behaviour.

Psychic determinism is, perhaps, best represented by Sigmund Freud's theory of the causes of our conscious thought and behaviour. Freud saw all thought and behaviour to come from the unconscious, and to be ultimately determined by two instincts: the sex (life) and aggression (death) instincts. Freud also regarded all behaviour as being *over-determined*. By this he meant that any one behaviour will have multiple causes and that to understand the behaviour the numerous causes need to be identified. For example, Freud (1900) regards all dreams as meaningful psychic events and that psychoanalysis could help unpack the true meaning of a dream. For Freud, the dream is caused by events of the previous day and unconscious childhood repressions (see Chapter 7).

Determinism and fatalism

Fatalism is the idea that all human behaviour (and thought) is predetermined and that attempts to change things are futile and a waste of effort. A **hard determinism** position would seem to support a position of fatalism. Being fatalistic may mean that a person does not bother to think about certain things, makes no attempt to influence the outcome, and passively submits to what fate may have in store. Astrology, for example, is often quoted as representing a fatalist position: the configuration of your stars at birth determines your personality, it is claimed, and what will happen to you in life. A **soft determinism** position does not support a fatalistic approach to life, neither of course, does the view that we have free will to influence events.

Free will and responsibility

Adopting the view that people have free will and can choose to do whatever they want to do, is not, at the extreme, a practical, ethical or morally acceptable position. For example, just because you do not like somebody does not allow you to go out and hit them, or in the extreme, murder the person. Just because you would like to be rich does not allow you to exercise your free will and steal millions of pounds from a bank. Living in society and engaging in relationships (friendships, intimacy or work-related) brings with it certain responsibilities. These responsibilities limit a person's freedom to act and choose what to do. Although, interestingly, these responsibilities may not limit what you think about and create fantasies about!

The limits on individual freedom are dramatically highlighted in Luke Rhinehart's (1999) classic novel *The Dice Man*. In this book the main character decides (exercises his free will) to conduct his life according to the roll of a dice. He creates acts to each of the six numbers, rolls the dice, and then carries out the act according to the number that comes up. Over a period of time the Dice Man attaches more and more extreme acts to the numbers and ends up behaving in extreme, and illegal, anti-social ways.

Humanistic psychologists (see Chapter 9) subscribe to a free will viewpoint for people, and recognise at the same time, that personal responsibility and behaving in a responsible way rightly constrains the extent to which free will can influence behaviour.

Fear of freedom

Erich Fromm, a psychoanalyst with humanistic sympathies, saw western society as causing an internal conflict for the person between freedom and helplessness. Fromm (1941) depicted people as moral beings who had to balance freedom of will with the constraints and requirements of modern society. Fromm (1941) saw this conflict as healthy and a conflict people deal with all the time. An unhealthy resolution of the conflict between freedom and moral obligation to society and other people is the renunciation of personal freedom. Personal freedom may be relinquished to authority, destructiveness (of self or others) and what Fromm called *automation conformity* (blindly following others). These ways of relinquishing personal freedom led Fromm to analyse how people became alienated and detached from society.

Fromm does not really fit into a position on the free will–determinism debate, since he talks about free will in the context of morality. Hence, the forces constraining behaviour are internal, rather than external to the person.

11.3 Heredity and environment

The debate over whether **heredity** (nature) is more or less important than the **environment** (nurture) in determining a wide range of psychological characteristics in both humans and other animals is of central and fundamental importance in psychology. As with the free will–determinism debate, the nature/nurture debate can be traced back to the philosophical roots of psychology. The French philosopher René Descartes (1596–1650) not only showed the importance of the mind-body debate (see Section 11.6 in this chapter) in philosophy, but also subscribed to what is called a **nativism** view. The nativism or innatism view states that certain human characteristics are innate. Descartes went further to claim that some aspects of knowledge, for example, our knowledge of God, is also innate. In the sixteenth and seventeenth centuries, the science of genetics and the idea of genes being passed on from generation to generation did not exist. Hence to claim that certain human characteristics and types of knowledge were innate meant that these were a given part of what it means to be human and not in need of an explanation of how they came to be passed on from parents to their children.

At the other end of the philosophical spectrum was an environmentalism or **empiricist** viewpoint. Philosophers such as John Locke (1632–1704), David Hume (1711–76) and John Stuart Mill (1806–73) put forward an empiricist position stating that all knowledge comes from or is derived from experience. Translated into the discipline of psychology the empiricist view becomes the view that human characteristics (thought, behaviour, personality, etc.) result from social and natural environmental forces that impinge on a person from birth onwards.

Philosophically, therefore, two extreme positions can be seen. The extreme view of the empiricists is that the mind is like a *tubula rasa* or blank sheet on which experience or the environment writes itself. Or, at the other extreme all human characteristics result from genetic influences or the product of heredity. As with most issues where there are extreme positions, research shows the truth to lie somewhere in between. This is what is meant by the *interactionist* position that to understand and explain human characteristics and behaviour both nature and nurture need to be taken into account. The challenge then is to attempt to show the relative contribution of both genetics and environment to psychological characteristics.

PRACTICAL Activity

Whilst studying AS psychology you might have looked at the debate about the extent to which behaviour has a genetic basis. If you did, read through the notes that you made last year, or read Chapter 2, pages 40–47 of Pennington (2002). If you did not study the biological approach at AS level read through the above reference in Pennington (2002).

What follows is a summary of some of the key points covered at AS level. We then move on to consider other types of human behaviour, and take a more detailed look at the nature/nurture debate.

The genetic basis of behaviour

The **heritability coefficient** provides a numerical figure, from 0 to 1.0, representing the extent to which a characteristic is genetic in origin. A value of 1.0 means that the trait or characteristic is determined solely by genetics, and a value of zero that genetics play no role at all and the environment is the sole determinant. Plomin *et al.* (1997) have shown that personality characteristics such as neuroticism and assertiveness have a heritability coefficient between 0.15 and 0.50. This means that both genetics and environment play a role, thus representing the interactionist position.

REFLECTIVE Activity

Consider a range of different personality characteristics such as extroversion, conscientiousness, sociability, openness, sense of humour and defensiveness. Try to identify for each, the general view in society of the extent to which each results from nature, nurture or an interaction.

The most common way of attempting to establish the contribution of nature and nurture is by using twin studies. Monozygotic or identical twins share exactly the same genetic make-up. Dizygotic or fraternal twins share 50 per cent of genes, just like ordinary brothers and sisters. The degree of similarity (physical and/or psychological) between monozygotic compared to dizygotic twins is often taken as an indication of genetic influence. Twin studies have been conducted looking at intelligence, temperament and schizophrenia and have demonstrated a clear genetic influence in each case (Gottesman 1991; Sternberg and Grigorenko 1997). However, just because a trait or characteristic has a genetic base or heritability coefficient this tells us nothing about how experience or the environment may modify the genetic potential. For example, height is a highly heritable characteristic with a coefficient typically of around 0.9. However, the average height of Europeans and North Americans has increased by over 5 centimetres between 1920 and 1970 (Van Wieringen 1978). This increase in height is due to environmental factors, such as diet, and not genetic factors.

EVALUATIVE COMMENT

Estimates of the heritability of intelligence are almost solely based on how people score on standard intelligence or IQ tests. The used of standard tests of intelligence may only capture certain aspects of human intelligence. Also, practice at these tests improves performance, thus falsely indicating a higher level of intelligence compared to those that have never completed an intelligence test (Gould 1981).

Interaction of heredity and environment

Two examples will serve to show how nature and nurture interact, demonstrating that both are vital to understanding and explaining human behaviour.

Phenlketonuria (PKU) is a rare disorder in which the body is unable to convert phenylalanine (found in dairy products) into tyrosine. If nothing is done, phenylalanine builds up in the blood and can result in the sufferer having severe learning difficulties. PKU is a genetic disorder resulting from the inheritance of a recessive gene from each parent. If detected early enough the young child can be put on a special diet low in phenylalanine (no dairy products, etc.) which will keep levels of this amino acid low and hence prevent any damage to intelligence and learning ability.

In a very different area, that of language acquisition, Chomsky (1965) argued that each person is born with an innate potential to acquire language. More specifically, he claimed that the human brain has evolved to become specialised for language. Additionally, the ease with which

The acquisition of a language is an interaction between heredity and environment. Chomsky claims that all people are born with a language acquisition device. Which language we learn depends on experience

each child learns a language, in whichever country or type of language, is evidence that a *language acquisition device* is present in the child at birth and is a result of heredity. The particular language we learn and the fluency with which we command that language comes from the environment or nurture.

The environment

The use of twin studies, particularly identical twins, in attempts to assess the relative contribution of heredity and environment is well established. Identical twins reared together are assumed, broadly, to share the same environment. However, this is a crude generalisation that does not take account of what is shared in any family environment between identical twins, fraternal twins, and brothers and sisters more generally, and what is not shared and unique. Plomin (1996) makes a distinction between *shared environments* and *non-shared environments*. It is the non-shared environments, that is, those environmental experiences unique to the sibling or twin in the family that explain differences between related individuals. For example, research has shown that identical twins reared together in the same family environment yield a correlation coefficient of 0.86, demonstrating a high degree of similarity (Henderson 1982). However, this is not a perfect correlation, a coefficient of 1.0 is needed; hence identical twins also show differences in intelligence as well. Plomin (1996) would argue that the relatively small differences in intelligence between identical twins is due to the unique experiences gained from each respective twin's non-shared environment. What this is saying is that two people cannot experience exactly the same environment as they grow from baby to teenager to adult.

EVALUATIVE COMMENT

Psychologists no longer talk about whether or not heredity or environment explain human characteristics and behaviour. Instead, research is aimed at attempting to assess the relative contribution of nature and nurture. Psychologists look to identify factors which can modify human characteristics and how enriched environmental experiences can help to realise the innate potential of many human traits.

11.4 Holism and reductionism

The holism–reductionism debate in psychology has important implications both for the nature of theories developed about human thought and behaviour, and the methods used for investigation. First we need to define each term, then relate the debate to levels of explanation in psychology.

Holism is the view that an explanation or theory based upon all the parts of the whole and the inter-relation of the parts is inadequate. In relation to human beings this means that analysing component parts such as, for example, the brain, specific cognitive processes such as memory and specific personality traits such as aggressiveness does not properly capture or do justice to the whole person. This is what Gestalt psychologists summed up in the famous phrase 'the whole is greater than the sum of the parts'. Take an everyday physical example such as a watch. A watch, whether digital or clockwork, is made up of many component parts. However, how all these parts come together to tell the time (the purpose of the watch) is missed. An alien visiting earth who had never seen a wristwatch before may be able to understand the action of all of the component parts. However, this would not tell the alien what the watch does as a whole.

REFLECTIVE Activity

Think about a couple of other complex machines such as a car and an aeroplane. If someone had never seen these before and simply observed them in a stationary position, how do you think they might come to know what each does from looking at all the component parts?

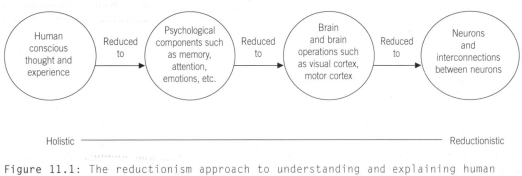

Figure 11.1: The reductionism approach to understanding and explaining human consciousness

Reductionism is the view, opposite to that of holism, that to understand human beings, psychologists have to analyse and reduce the whole into the simplest component parts. In relation to consciousness, for example, this means in order to gain an understanding and explanation, consciousness should be reduced to component psychological parts, which in turn can be reduced to physical operations in the brain, which can then be reduced to the simplest parts – neurons. This is shown in Figure 11.1.

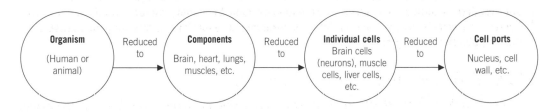

Figure 11.2: Reductionist approach in biological sciences to animal organisms

Reductionism was frequently debated in the mid-twentieth century in relation to sciences such as physics and biology. However, the roots of the debate over the extent to which whole objects or psychological characteristics such as consciousness can meaningfully be reduced to the simplest component parts date back to the development of biology in the nineteenth century. Here an organism could be reduced to a set of organs, such as the heart, brain, lungs, etc., which in turn could be reduced to individual cells. The individual cells could then be reduced further to their component parts, for example, the cell wall and the cell nucleus. This is shown in Figure 11.2.

In a similar way physics, especially with the discovery of atoms at the beginning of the twentieth century, reduced matter to the component atomic particles. Modern physics reduces atoms to sub-atomic particles.

The success science enjoyed by adopting a reductionist approach was seized upon by early psychologists and adopted as a model to apply to human thought and behaviour, and the behaviour of other animals. The reductionist approach of sciences such as physics and biology was highly influential in the development of psychology. For example, Wilhelm Wundt's use of introspection in the first psychology laboratory attempted to reduce experiences to component parts. The structuralist school of psychology, which developed in North America after Wundt, was highly influential for many years, as we shall see later in this section. Furthermore, reductionism influenced the development of radical behaviourism as put forward by Watson and Skinner (see Chapter 5). Reductionism operated here by the behaviourist assumption that all human behaviour and animal behaviour could be reduced to stimulus–response bonds that are strengthened by reinforcement and weakened or extinguished by punishment.

Levels of explanation

The idea that the whole can be reduced to its simplest component parts, that is, reductionism, when applied to human psychology, results in a number of different levels of explanation, as shown in Figure 11.3. At the highest, most holistic level, is the societal/political/sociological

	Level of explanation	Descriptions
Holistic ↑	Societal, political, sociological	Context in which a person lives and cultural context.
	Social psychological	Interactions and relationships between people.
	Psychological	Cognitive processes, emotions, motives, personality. Aspects internal to the person.
	Physical and physiological systems	Muscles, organs, skeleton, central and perpetual nervous system.
	Physiological units	Parts of the brain such as the visual cortex, frontal lobes, cerebellum.
↓ **Reductionist**	Basic physiological components	Neurons and interconnections between neurons.

Figure 11.3: Levels of explanation of human beings: from holistic to reductionist levels

context in which each individual exists. At the next level down is a social-psychological level which reflects interactions and relationships that people have with each other. Below this is the psychological level which involves cognitive processes, personality, motivation, and other aspects internal to the individual. At the next level down are physical and physiological systems such as muscles and the nervous system. Next are the physiological units such as parts of the brain – the visual cortex, cerebellum, frontal cortex. Finally, at the most basic level are the individual component parts – neurons and the interconnections between neurons. Neurons themselves can be reduced to their component parts – axon, cell body, dendrites. Finally, these component parts of neurons can be reduced to molecules and then atoms.

Some physicists (Capra, 1975) argue that a reductionist approach, both in physics and psychology, suffers from an infinite regress, that is, that one can go on reducing component parts to more basic and even more basic parts *ad infinitum*, endlessly). The same is true for higher level explanations in that higher and higher levels can be conceived of.

PRACTICAL Activity

With a group of three or four friends select a range of science and arts subjects. Continue the levels of explanation to the highest (most holistic) and lowest (greatest reductionism) that you can think of. From this exercise you should see that the levels of explanation given in Figure 11.3 represent only a band in the middle of a much wider spectrum of levels.

Reductionism and structuralism

Edward Titchener (1867–1927) developed what is known as a structuralist approach to the study of human consciousness. Like Wilhelm Wundt, Titchener (1910) believed that all conscious experience could be reduced to elementary components or sensations. Titchener stated that the subject matter of psychology is conscious experience and used a method of self-observation which he called *systematic experimental introspection*. This involved using highly trained psychologists with the aim of discovering the 'actions of the mind'. Titchener stated that psychology had three general issues to explore, as follows:

1. to reduce conscious experience to the elementary components;

2. to discover the laws by which these elementary components come together to create consciousness, and;

3. to relate these elementary components to physiological and neural processes in the senses and nervous system.

From this you can readily see the operation of reductionism in that the general state of human consciousness is reduced first to elementary sensations, and then to physiological operations.

EVALUATIVE Comment

The structuralist approach of Titchener was influential for 20 years in the early twentieth century. However, it soon became apparent that an almost infinite number of elementary sensations could be produced. Also, the approach had little practical value outside of the laboratory and introspectionist techniques are subjective. Titchener also recognised later in his life that structuralism did not help to understand thought processes. Eventually Titchener stopped referring to mental elements or atoms and moved towards a more holistic approach in attempting to understand human consciousness.

Holism and Gestalt psychology

Gestalt psychologists, such as Kohler (1887–1967), rebelled against the structuralist approach of Titchener and stated that psychological phenomena such as perception and consciousness need to be understood as a whole. The German word *Gestalt* means something like a whole, single form. The maxim that the whole is greater than the sum of the parts reflects the holistic approach. For example, Kohler (1929) applied the principles of Gestalt psychology to problem-solving in animals, such as cats and chimpanzees. Kohler argued that animal problem-solving could not always be reduced to automatic responses to stimuli (the behaviourist view) or to elementary sensations. Instead problems are often solved through *insight learning* where new ways of solving a problem are created. This related to creativity and creative thinking in humans. Gestalt psychology lacked rigorous experimental approaches, but did influence the development of cognitive psychology.

Comment on the holism-reductionism debate

In this section we have looked at different approaches of early psychologists, such as structuralism and Gestalt psychology and their positions with respect to holism and reductionism. Then, as now, psychologists generally adopt either a holistic or reductionism viewpoint. This informs both theory and methods of research. For example, the experimental and laboratory approach in various areas of psychology much more reflects a reductionism position. Qualitative methods and the experiential approaches of humanistic psychologists reflects a holistic position.

With the identification of the human genome and attempts to identify individual genes for all sorts of behaviours and psychological disorders, the reductionism approach is enjoying great favour and success. As with many things in psychology there are cycles and a return to more holistic viewpoints may become more dominant again in the future. There is no right or wrong in the holism-reductionism debate, but a philosophical view on how best to think about a person and how best to conduct enquiry into human psychological characteristics.

11.5 Idiographic and nomothetic approaches

The idiographic and nomothetic approaches in psychology are often regarded as representing opposing and conflicting positions about how best to study people. However, as we shall see later in this section, the two approaches may be seen as complementary to each other and both necessary in order to gain a fuller understanding of human beings. Allport (1937) introduced this distinction into psychology borrowing the terms from a philosopher called Windelband (1894). Windelband made a distinction between two kinds of sciences: natural sciences and moral sciences. Moral sciences, he argued, are to do with the humanities, social science and psychology. Whilst this distinction has not been seen as fundamental in philosophy, the distinction between natural science and human science is a matter of debate in psychology.

An **idiographic approach** is one that focuses on the individual and recognises the uniqueness of the person in terms of their experiences, feelings, developmental history, aspirations and motivations in life, and the values and moral code by which they live. The word idiograph is derived from the Greek word *idios* which means 'own' or private. Hence, the idiographic approach in psychology is concerned with the private, subjective and unique aspects of a person. As such the idiographic approach employs methods of enquiry which provide information about this aspect of the person. Most commonly the idiographic approach is characterised by qualitative methods of investigation (see Chapter 12 of this text, and Chapter 3 of *Introducing psychology* Pennington 2002). Qualitative methods include unstructured interviews, case studies, self-report measures, introspection and reflection, and even the psychoanalytic techniques of free association and dream analysis (see Chapter 7). The idiographic approach in psychology tends to adopt a holism perspective on the person and places great value on the conscious experiences reported by the individual. The humanistic perspective in psychology perhaps best exemplifies the idiographic approach. However, Freudian psychoanalysis can be said to adopt an idiographic approach also. Traditionally an idiographic approach has been regarded as a non-scientific approach, although this is not really the case. Scientific principles can be applied to the study of the uniqueness of the individual and the individual norms and rules by which a specific person operates and lives their life can be identified.

REFLECTIVE Activity

Think about yourself and your best friend. Identify aspects of yourself, for example, personality, social norms and religious beliefs, that are unique to each of you. Identify what psychological aspects you have in common with each other. The idiographic approach can focus on both these aspects – similarities and differences between individuals.

The **nomothetic approach** in psychology is one that focuses on similarities between people and attempts to establish general laws of behaviour and thought that can be applied to large populations of people, or indeed to all people. The word nomothetic is derived from the Greek word *nomos* which means 'law'. Hence, the nomothetic approach is most closely aligned with the scientific approach in psychology (see next section). This means that use is made of scientific methods of investigation, most notably experiments, to test hypotheses which are derived from theories about human behaviour and thought. The nomothetic approach in psychology attempts to adopt the experimental, especially through the employment of laboratory experiments, methods for theory testing used in the natural sciences of physics and biology. The nomothetic approach tends to adopt a more reductionist viewpoint and places great value on objectivity and the replication of findings from experimental research. The behaviourist, cognitive and

Approach	Key aspects
Idiographic approach	• recognises the uniqueness of the person • concerned with private, subjective and conscious experiences of the person • uses qualitative methods of investigation • exemplified by humanistic and aspects of psychoanalytic perspectives
Nomothetic approach	• attempts to establish laws and generalisations about people • concerned with objective knowledge through the use of scientific methods • uses quantitative methods of investigation • exemplified by trait approaches to personality, behaviourism and cognitive psychology

Figure 11.4: Distinguishing features of the idiographic and nomothetic approaches

biological perspectives best exemplify the nomothetic approach. However, Freudian theory also attempts to establish laws or regularities of human beings with the concepts of psychosexual stages of development, the Oedipus complex and unconscious mental processes. Freud saw these as applying to all people at all times in history. As such, Freudian theory is nomothetic in this respect. However, Freud did not use the accepted experimental methods of the natural sciences to test or find evidence for his theoretical claims. Figure 11.4 summarises the key aspects of the idiographic and nomothetic approaches given above.

Idiographic and nomothetic as conflicting approaches

Traditionally, the idiographic and nomothetic approaches are seen as conflicting together with the implication that as a psychologist you can only operate from one of these positions. That is, a psychologist is either highly scientific, employs the extensive use of laboratory experiments and gains confidence in theories about people on the basis of hard evidence and empirical support for hypotheses. Or a psychologist is not scientific and employs a range of methods, many of which are argued to be subjective, to understand and explore more deeply into the uniqueness of the individual and his or her subjective experiences. As long ago as the 1950s Cronbach (1957) identified this potential source of conflict and disagreement between psychologists about how best to go about studying and capturing the nature of human beings. If the psychologist is interested in developing theories that apply to large populations of people then the nomothetic approach seems the obvious one to adopt. If, on the other hand, the psychologist is interested in the uniqueness of a person, then the idiographic approach is the one to adopt.

In personality theory (see Pennington 2003), for example, both the nomothetic and idiographic approaches are used by different psychologists. Trait theories of personality, those theories which look at individual traits, tend to adopt a nomothetic approach, as do behaviourist approaches to personality. In contrast, humanistic and certain aspects of psychoanalytic theories adopt a more idiographic approach. Whilst it is quite reasonable to see the idiographic and nomothetic approaches as quite different and with psychologists in one camp or the other, it is also possible to think about how these two approaches may interact and be complementary to each other.

Interaction and complementarity

Cronbach (1957) recognised the distinctiveness of these different approaches and the different methods employed by each one. However, he wanted to find a way which would bring the two together and would deal with both the concern for the uniqueness of the individual whilst at the same time developing general laws about human behaviour and thought.

PRACTICAL Activity

Discuss in groups of three or four what psychologists might omit about people by adopting a purely nomothetic or idiographic approach. Discuss whether you think that both approaches are necessary to capturing a full understanding and explanation of human beings.

One attempt to create a third way by bringing the two approaches together was made by Bandura (1986) with his idea of **reciprocal determinism**. Bandura (1986) suggested that human behaviour both affects the environment and the environment in turn affects behaviour. To bring together the idiographic with the nomothetic Bandura further stated that a person's consciousness and self-awareness (idiographic) affects behaviour and the environment (nomothetic). Bandura's idea of reciprocal determinism is depicted as a triad between the person, behaviour, and environment, as shown in Figure 11.5.

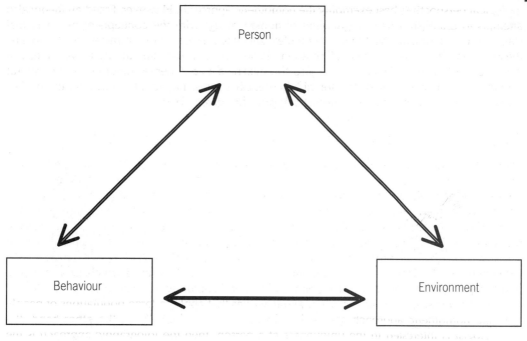

Figure 11.5: The reciprocal determinism view of Bandura (1986), whereby person (idiographic) and behaviour and environment (nomothetic) mutually influence each other

The important point about this is that Bandura takes an interactionist approach between unique aspects of the individual and laws of behaviour and the environment. The idea of reciprocal determinism also brings with it the idea that any one behaviour has a number of causes. This is similar to Freud's claim that behaviour is over-determined, that is, has numerous causes.

Comment on the idiographic-nomothetic debate

The idiographic and nomothetic approaches are often seen as determining the methods psychologists use to investigate human behaviour and thought. Crudely, the idiographic approach employs qualitative methods and the nomothetic approach employs quantitative methods. In a different way, these two approaches also have consequences for the view taken about human beings. With the idiographic approach, the unique, subjective aspects are of central interest. With the nomothetic approach, similarities between people, and laws that govern behaviour and thought are of central interest.

In contemporary psychology the idiographic–nomothetic debate is very much alive, and the distinction that is still made. Attempts, such as Bandura (1986), have been made to bring the two approaches together in an interactionist model. Unfortunately, no lasting or influential solution has been found although attempts have been made.

11.6 The mind-body debate

The **mind–body debate**, and its relevance to modern psychology can be traced back to the French philosopher René Descartes. However, discussion of which organ in the body contained the mind goes back to the Greek philosophers, Aristotle and Plato. Plato (428BC–348BC) claimed that the mind resides in the brain, whilst Aristotle (384BC–322BC) claimed that the mind was in the heart. At the centre of the mind–body debate is the problem of how the physical body relates to, or interacts with, mental states constituting the mind. Basically, as pointed out by Descartes, the physical and the mental appear to be qualitatively different with the mind or mental states being non-physical.

REFLECTIVE Activity

Pause for a moment and think about the distinction between mental and physical. If you touch yourself on your arm you touch your physical body, and at the same time you are conscious or aware of the touch. Now close your eyes and think about the last holiday that you took. No doubt you will think about, experience in the same way and be conscious of the things you enjoyed on holiday. Intuitively it does seem to make sense to say that the physical and mental are different.

Descartes attempted to show that the mind is a special kind of substance which possesses properties very different from the physical body. Descartes's solution to how these two different bodies were joined or interacted was relatively simple: he said that God ensured the mental and physical came together.

The criteria often used to distinguish mind from body are threefold. First, mind is consciousness which means that we think, imagine, perceive and reason. Second, mental states are private to the person, and that person, and nobody else, has privileged access. This means that other people cannot experience your pain if you hurt yourself or experience your thoughts about your last holiday. Another person can try to understand how you think or feel, often called showing *empathy*, but the other person cannot experience your mental states. Third, mental states show *intentionality*, that is, mental states are directed towards the same end or goal. Physical states do not have the property of intentionality.

REFLECTIVE Activity

Think about the magician Gandalf in *Lord of the rings*, or the magician in training in the Harry Potter series of books. Neither of these characters exist in reality, but, the mind can intentionally create images and associations about these fictional characters. This is something special to mental states of mind that does not have a parallel in physical states or the body.

The mind–body debate, as initiated by Descartes, puts forward a **dualistic** position in that mind and body are two separate tings, possessing qualitatively different properties.

Dualism and explanations of interaction

The dualistic position that mind and body are qualitatively different raises the problem of how the mental and the physical interact. Dualism also raises the issue of the location of the mind. Most people would answer the latter by saying the mind is somehow in the brain. This is because we tend to associate seeing, hearing, thinking and imagining as taking place inside our heads. Ryle (1963) thought it misconceived to think of the mind in this way at all, and said that mental events should be seen as dispositions to behave or in terms of publicly observable behaviour. In many ways this reflects the behaviourist view that talk about the mind is unnecessary and only observable, objective behaviour is the legitimate object of psychological study.

Attempts have been made to solve the problem of dualism and how the mind and body interact. Within the dualist viewpoint we shall consider two explanations here: occasionalists and parallelism. Malebranche (1638–1715) put forward an *occasionalist* view in which God had to intervene on every occasion a person acted. So if a person wanted to raise their arm, God would ensure that the link was made between a person's intention to raise their arm and the actual physical event of raising their arm. Leibniz (1646–1716) also argued that God was involved in joining the mental and physical but this happened on only one occasion – when God created the universe and the people in it. This is called a *parallelism* view.

PRACTICAL Activity

Discuss these two explanations of how the mind and body interact. What problems can you identify with explanations that rely on an intervention by God? For example, does God exist? Does this conception of God rely on the Christian version of creation? How does this square with Darwin's theory of the evolution of human beings?

The dualist view of mind and body presents some very difficult philosophical questions, which do not really have a satisfactory answer. Most psychologists do not subscribe to the intervention of God to ensure the two interact, but do think of the mind as in some way related to the brain.

Mind-brain identity theory

Plenty of evidence in everyday life demonstrates that the body can affect the mind, and that the mind can affect the body. Consciousness-altering drugs such as LSD and Ecstasy are chemicals that operate on the brain. These chemicals result in hallucinations, feelings of pleasure and joy, and are often associated with higher levels of consciousness.

Hence, here chemicals affect the body which in turn affects the mind and mental states in quite dramatic ways. Conversely, the mind can be used to affect body states. For example, highly trained meditation rituals in Buddhist monks enable them to keep their body heat even in extremely cold conditions. People with cancer sometimes use meditation techniques in an effort to cure themselves of the disease.

REFLECTIVE Activity

Identify two or three examples of how you think you have controlled your mind to affect your body. For example, in

Chemicals such as Ecstasy affect the body, which in turn affect the mental state of the person

running a race you may have 'willed' your body to run faster even though you felt that you had no more left. It is, however, more difficult to establish with certainty the effects of the mental on the physical.

The **mind–brain identity theory** is a monistic (as opposed to dualistic) view which says that mental states and mental events (dreaming, hoping, feeling pain, etc.) are identified with physical brain states. This theory was first proposed by Place (1956) in a highly influential essay entitled 'Is consciousness a brain process?' This resolution, or seeming resolution, of the mind–body debate has been adopted by many physiological psychologists. These psychologists attempt to identify processes and structures in the brain with mental states. Damage to certain areas of the brain can result in changes to mental states, which can be recorded using electro encephalographs. Someone who is 'brain dead' shows none of the normal electrical activity of the brain of a healthy person. Here all signs of cortical activity have ceased (that is neurons in the cortex no longer appear to be making or discharging electrical impulses), and critical life support activities are no longer controlled by the brain. People who have suffered a major brain trauma have to undergo artificial respiration, and may be on life-support machines for years.

REFLECTIVE Activity

Consider the three criteria for the mind given earlier: privacy, consciousness, and intentionality. In someone who appears from the outside to be 'brain dead', how can you know if the person is experiencing mental events? Because of the issue of privileged access, no one else, except the actual person can know. Using Ryle's (1963) idea that mental events are dispositions to behave, and since the person is not voluntarily behaving in any way is it right, do you think that no mental life exists in a 'brain dead' person?

Two or more minds in one body?

If we accept that mind and body are different, could a person have two minds? Split-brain studies (Gazzangia 1985) are so called because of research conducted on people who suffer from epilepsy and who have had the connecting tissue, called the corpus callosum, between the two hemispheres of the brain cut. It is as if the person has two brains. Does this mean that the person has two minds? Gazzangia (1970) seems to think so from evidence whereby a person, for example, angry at his wife, has tried to attack her with his left hand and at the same time protected her with his right hand. Schiffer et al. (1998) have found that disturbing childhood memories are held in the right hemisphere of the split brain.

Schizophrenia is a major psychological disorder in which a person seems to have two minds. People suffering from paranoid schizophrenia feel persecuted and constantly hear voices in their head (or mind) which constantly criticise and find fault with all that they do. In some ways it is as if two minds exist within the same person, with the one mind having distressing and debilitating effects on the person.

Whether or not split-brain studies and people suffering from paranoid schizophrenia really have two minds is a matter for debate. With the former, there are clearly links to a split, physical brain; with the latter, two different brain states are less obvious.

11.7 Sample questions

SAMPLE QUESTION 1

(a) Explain what is meant by the terms holism and reductionism.
     (AO1 = 2, AO2 = 2)   *(4 marks)*

(b) Discuss one problem with the idea of reductionism as applied to psychology and state why a holistic view may be better.

(AO1 = 2, AO2 = 2) *(4 marks)*

(c) Describe and discuss the mind–body debate in psychology. Refer to one topic in psychology that you have studied where this debate is relevant.

(AO1 = 6, AO2 = 6) *(12 marks)*

Total AO1 marks = 10 Total AO2 marks = 10 Total = 20 marks

QUESTIONS, ANSWERS AND COMMENTS

SAMPLE QUESTION 2

(a) Distinguish between the idiographic and nomothetic approaches in psychology.

(AO1 = 2, AO2 = 2) *(4 marks)*

(b) Explain what is meant by the concept of *holism* as applied to psychology.

(AO1 = 2, AO2 = 2) *(4 marks)*

(c) Describe and discuss the free will–determinism debate in psychology. Refer to one topic you have studied in psychology to illustrate your answer.

(AO1 = 6, AO2 = 6) *(12 marks)*

Total AO1 marks = 10 Total AO2 marks = 10 Total = 20 marks

Answer to 2(a)

The idiographic approach focuses on the uniqueness of the individual, studying people by the use of clinical interviews and case studies, and seeing everyone as different. This approach was widely used by psychologists such as Freud and Piaget. The nomothetic approach studies groups of people from a more general perspective, in order to find laws that can be applied to the whole population. Experimental designs are used and behaviourists lean towards this approach.

Comment: A sufficiently full answer to gain the full four marks available. The answer demonstrates a good understanding of both approaches and gives examples of methods and psychologists associated with each approach.

Answer to 2(b)

The concept of holism in psychology is to do with treating or studying the whole person. Humanistic psychologists are interested in the whole person and do not think that a person can be reduced to different parts of the brain. The Gestalt psychologists were holistic when they said that the 'whole is greater than the sum of the parts'.

Comment: An understanding of holism is demonstrated. However, the answer is a bit muddled and the contrast with a reductionist approach, whilst stated, is not clearly expressed. Correct identification of holism with humanistic and Gestalt psychology. Would get 2 out of the 4 marks available.

Answer to 2(c)

The free will–determinism debate in psychology can be explained in terms of common-sense verses a scientific approach. Free will does not see behaviour as not caused and being random, but certain actions can be taken at will. Determinism views human behaviour as influenced by external and environmental factors. The main advocate for determinism being Skinner (behaviourism). He saw behaviour as being determined by people's past experiences of reinforcement and when we see a person acting 'freely' we are unaware of the history of reinforcement.

The humanistic approach is on the free will side of the debate. Rogers was a believer in this, concentrating on the uniqueness of every individual. The whole justice system is built on the idea of free will. If we do not consider a person as having a choice over what to do, how can we hold them responsible for their actions?

Freud is seen as a deterministic psychologist because of the psychosexual stages. Freud believes in innate and predetermined sexual drives that a child goes through in order to develop a stable adult personality.

However, William James believed that if a behaviour is voluntary and in line with conscious thought, then this action or behaviour is free.

The cognitive approach focused on problem-solving and attention mechanisms and believes that these are the 'choosers' of behaviour. The attention mechanism works by remembering past experiences, and the cognitive psychologists compared this to a computer.

The idea of free will is broken by disorders such as panic, anxiety, and obsessive-compulsive disorders, where the individual loses all self-control and cannot get rid of this by will.

The debate in psychology is more likely to be between soft and hard determinism rather than free will and determinism. However, if we see them on a continuum one can ask whereabouts on the continuum different behaviours can be located.

Comment: An answer which demonstrates a good range of knowledge about the free will–determinism debate, but reads a bit like a list rather than a structured essay. Writing down an essay plan at the start and stating at the outset how the essay will answer the question would have helped produce a better structured and more flowing answer. Most of what is said is correct, but falls mostly on the descriptive rather than the evaluative side. What is said about the cognitive approach is muddled and confused. Overall a sound answer, which would gain 8 out of the 12 marks available.

Total marks for question 2 = 14 out of 20 (AO1 = 8, AO2 = 6)

11.8 FURTHER READING

Introductory texts

Bell, A. 2002: **Debates in psychology**. Taylor & Francis, Chapters 2, 3, 4 and 6. Hove, East Sussex.

Gross, R. 1999: **Themes, issues and debates in psychology**. Chapters 3, 5, 12 and 13. Hodder & Stoughton, London.

Specialist sources

Graham, G. 1993: **Philosophy of mind: an introduction**. Blackwell Publishers, Oxford.

Hospers, J. 1997: **An introduction to philosophical analysis**. 4th Ed. Chapters 5 and 6. Routledge, London.

Schultz, D. P. & Schultz, S. E. 2000: **A history of modern psychology**. 7th Ed. Harcourt College Publishers, Fort Worth.

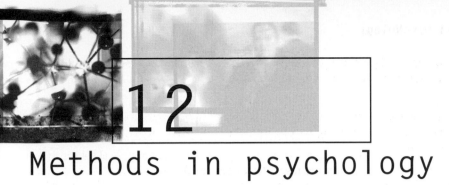

12

Methods in psychology

INTRODUCTION

Throughout its relatively short history psychology has made claims to be a science, which is reflected in one of the definitions of psychology that it is the 'scientific study of mind and behaviour'. Consequently many of the research methods used in psychology reflect a traditional view of science. According to this view, carrying out scientific research has a number of features, such as data collected in a systematic way using procedures that can be repeated by others. This is often referred to as the 'empirical approach'. Careful and accurate measurement is also a key aspect of the scientific approach. Once an effect or variable can be measured, then changes in it can also be measured. The scientific approach also emphasises the ability to replicate or repeat investigations. If an effect cannot be replicated then it is unlikely to be accepted as being worthy of serious consideration. The scientific approach in psychology has relied heavily on experiments as a way of carrying out research, but that is not to say that other research methods are not scientific. The basic idea behind experiments is that you change some aspect of a situation (the independent variable) and observe its effect on a person's behaviour (the dependent variable). The assumption is that if everything else has been kept the same then the change in the dependent variable was caused by the independent variable. However, it has to be said that the use of the scientific method and experiments in psychology has a number of critics. (See Chapter 10 for a further discussion of these issues.)

There are three main sections to this chapter. First some basic concepts and the rationale behind the use of statistics in psychological research are discussed. This is followed by a section which describes how to use different statistical tests. The final section discusses a range of issues in psychological research including the advantages and disadvantages of different methods of research.

12.1 Statistical inference

The concepts of probability and levels of significance

In our everyday life we use probabilities on a regular basis. We often talk about how likely or unlikely it is that some event will occur. For example, if the weather forecast says that there is a high probability of rain tomorrow then it means that it is likely that this will happen. In everyday life we use percentages when we are talking about probabilities. For example, if we toss a coin we might say there is a 50% chance that it will land showing a 'head' and a 50% chance that it will land showing 'tails'.

REFLECTIVE Activity

Imagine the following situation. Four playing cards are placed face down on a table and only one of them is an ace. You are allowed to turn one card over. What is the likelihood of you turning over the ace?

    (a) 20%

    (b) 25%

    (c) 50%

    (d) 75%

The answer is (b). If you got the correct answer but are not quite sure why then it might be helpful to know that the probability of turning over an ace can be calculated using the following formula:

Probability of turning over an ace =   **Number of cards that are an ace**
                                                               Total number of cards

In the activity above only one of the four cards is an ace. This means that the probability stated as a fraction is 1/4. The fraction can be converted to a decimal (0.25) and also a percentage (25%). The method for converting a percentage to a decimal and vice versa is shown in Figure 12.1.

From percentage to decimal	From decimal to percentage
1. Remove the % sign (25% = 25).	1. Move the decimal point two places to the right (0.25 = 25.).
2. Put decimal point after the number (25 = 25.0). If there is already a decimal point then go straight to the next step.	2. Remove the decimal point if there is nothing to the right of it (25. = 25).
3. Move the decimal point two places* to the left. One place would be 2.5 and two places would be 0.25. Therefore 25% is 0.25 as a decimal.	3. Add the % sign (25 = 25%).
* If there are not two numbers on the left of the decimal point then put in zeros as you go. For example, the steps when converting 5% to a decimal would be: Step 1: 5% = 5. Step 2: 5 = 5.0. Step 3: 5.0 = 0.05.	Converting .05 to a decimal would be done in the following steps: Step 1: .05 = 5. Step 2: 5. = 5. Step 3: 5 = 5%.

Figure 12.1: Percentage/decimal conversion

PRACTICAL Activity

Look at the statements below. Try and estimate how likely it is that each of the events will occur. Give each statement a value between zero (will not happen) and 10 (will definitely happen) depending on how likely you think it is to happen.

1. If you drop a book it will hit the floor.

2. You will win the lottery next Saturday.

3. It will snow on Christmas day.

4. You will have an argument with a friend before next Friday.

5. You will have an accident in a car before you retire.

6. You will eat lunch today.

7. The sun will set this evening.

8. You will break a bone in your body at some point during the next month.

9. When you roll a dice it will land showing six.

10. You will go abroad before next year.

Now divide all the values you gave by 10. So, if you answered 2 to question three then divide 2 by 10 and you get 0.2. This number represents your estimate of the probability of each event occurring.

The term 'probability' is basically a numerical value that represents the likelihood of some event happening. It is common practice to use the letter 'p' to stand for probability. In psychological research probability is measured on a scale from zero to one. Zero means that it will never happen and one means that it will definitely happen. This means that probability is expressed in decimal values, such as, 0.2, 0.5, 0.6 and so on.

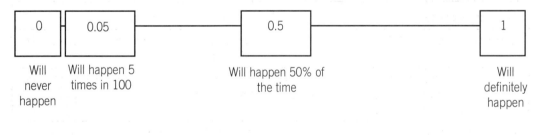

Figure 12.2: Probability as measured on a scale from 0 to 1

In psychological research we are interested in whether or not particular events or differences between a set of results occurred by chance. Imagine a friend of yours claims to have psychic abilities. She claims that when there are four playing cards, one of which is the ace of spades, placed face down on a table she can pick out the ace. In order to test out her claim you get a brand new set of cards and pick out the ace of spades and three other cards and place them face down on the table. You then ask your friend to pick out the one she thinks is the ace of spades. You repeat this procedure 100 times, each time you shuffle the cards and making sure that your friend does not see the cards as you place them face down. As we saw above, if your friend was just guessing she would probably pick out the ace in 25% of the trials. So in other words, out the 100 trials she would get the correct card 25 times purely by chance. Suppose she picked the correct card 40 times out of the 100 trials, would that be good enough evidence to assume that she had psychic abilities? We might just decide that she had been lucky. But what if she picked the correct card 80 times out of the 100 trials? This would be a very unlikely result to occur by chance, so we might conclude that your friend does indeed have psychic abilities. In other words the probability of the results occurring by chance was quite low.

Psychologists use the term 'significant' to refer to results that are very unlikely to have occurred by chance alone. But how unlikely do the results have to be before they can be considered to be significant? Psychologists use probability to decide whether or not a result is significant. The standard level of significance is usually called the '5% significance level'. If a set of results are significant at the 5% level it means that they would have occurred by chance less than five times out of a hundred. Another way of stating this would be to say that the probability of the results occurring by chance was less than 0.05. This can also be written as $p < 0.05$, where p stands for 'probability' and the symbol < means 'less than'. The symbol > meaning 'greater than' is also used at times when writing about significance levels and probability. In some situations the '1% level of significance' is used which means that the set of results would occur by chance less than once in a 100. In the same way as with the 5% significance level the 1% significance level can be written in terms of probability by using the term, $p < 0.01$. A summary of the relationship between probability and significance levels is presented in Figure 12.3.

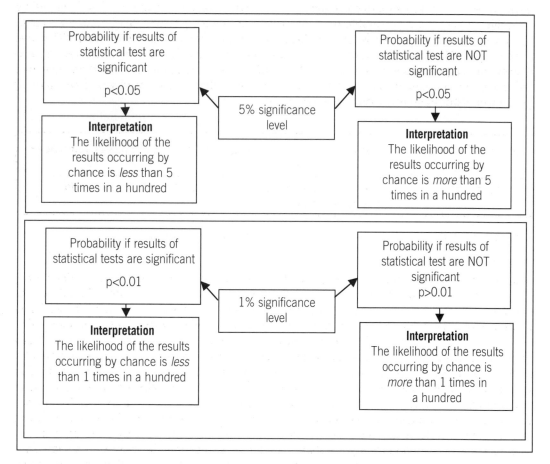

Figure 12.3: Summary of the relationship between probability and significance levels

Hypothesis testing: null and alternative hypotheses

Much of the research that is carried out within psychology attempts to follow the scientific model. This approach is referred to by several different names including, positivistic, empirical method, hypothetico-deductive, natural science based and quantitative (see Chapter 10). The

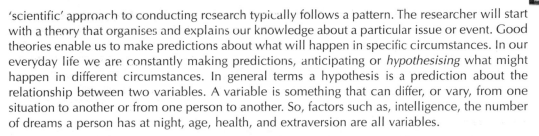

'scientific' approach to conducting research typically follows a pattern. The researcher will start with a theory that organises and explains our knowledge about a particular issue or event. Good theories enable us to make predictions about what will happen in specific circumstances. In our everyday life we are constantly making predictions, anticipating or *hypothesising* what might happen in different circumstances. In general terms a hypothesis is a prediction about the relationship between two variables. A variable is something that can differ, or vary, from one situation to another or from one person to another. So, factors such as, intelligence, the number of dreams a person has at night, age, health, and extraversion are all variables.

Using our knowledge of psychological theories of problem solving we could generate the following hypothesis, 'The level of complexity of a pattern will have a significant effect on the time taken to solve a problem'. If we wanted to we could design a study to test our hypothesis in which we had two groups. One group could be given simple problems to solve and the other could be given complex problems to solve. We could then test our hypothesis by comparing the mean times each group took to solve the problem. Hypotheses which predict that there will be a significant effect of one variable on another are referred to as 'alternative' or 'experimental' hypotheses. But we can also write hypotheses which predict that there will be no difference. For example, 'The level of complexity will have no significant effect on the time taken to solve a problem'. Hypotheses which predict that any difference, or relationship, found between two sets of results are called 'null hypotheses'. A null hypothesis states that any differences or relationships that have been found have occurred by chance.

Alternative hypothesis.	Predicts that there will be a significant difference or relationship between two sets of results.
Null hypothesis.	Predicts that there will be no significant difference or relationship between two sets of results.

Figure 12.4: Descriptions of null and alternative hypotheses

Suppose one of your friends says jokingly that for the next week every time he is driving his car and he comes to a red traffic light he will ignore it and carry on driving. Based on our knowledge of how traffic lights operate to control the flow of vehicles through roads, we know that this would be a very dangerous thing for him to do. In other words we have a theory that driving through red lights is a dangerous activity. From this theory we can generate a hypothesis which states that: 'Drivers who go through red lights will have more collisions than drivers who stop at red lights'. In this hypothesis we have turned the term 'dangerous' into something that we can actually measure and record, namely, 'collisions between vehicles'. In the process of conducting 'scientific' research we need to 'operationalise' our variables. When we operationalise a variable we develop a way in which we can measure the variable. In our example the variable in our theory that we need to operationalise is the term 'dangerous'. In our hypothesis we have defined 'dangerous' in terms of the number of 'collisions between vehicles'. Defining variables in ways that can be measured is referred to as creating an 'operational definition'.

PRACTICAL Activity

It would clearly not be ethical, or indeed sensible, to try and test our theory about driving through red lights in his car. However, there are many computer-based driving simulators that could be used in an experiment to test our hypothesis. Try to design an experiment that could be used to test the hypothesis that: 'Driving through red lights will result in more collisions between vehicles than stopping at red lights'.

Suppose you actually carried out the experiment you designed in the activity above and you get the results shown in Figure 12.5.

	Condition A: driving through red lights	Condition B: stopping at red lights
Mean number of collisions	12	0

Figure 12.5: The mean number of collisions of cars stopping and driving through red lights

In our imaginary experiment there are considerably more collisions when people drive through red lights than when they stop. This pattern of results would appear to support our hypothesis and hence the theory. The rationale of the driving study outlined above is summarised in Figure 12.6.

Aspect of research	Description
Theory	Driving through red traffic lights is dangerous.
Alternative hypothesis	There will be a significant difference in the number of collisions experienced by drivers who go through red traffic lights and those who stop at red traffic lights.
Null hypothesis	There will be no difference in the number of collisions experienced by drivers who go through red traffic lights and those who stop at red traffic lights.
Operational definition	Dangerous is defined as the number of collisions.
Results of experiment	Confirm the alternative hypothesis which is accepted and disconfirm the null hypothesis which is rejected.

Figure 12.6: Summary of main features of 'driving through red lights' research

PRACTICAL Activity

Imagine one of your friends has been playing a video game quite a lot during the past couple of weeks. He has told you that when he plays the game just before he goes to sleep he has started to have more dreams. This starts you thinking and you become interested in the relationship between playing video games and dreams. Try to write an alternative hypothesis and a null hypothesis about the relationship between dreams and playing video games.

EVALUATIVE COMMENT

One of the major features of a scientific approach is the notion that scientific statements are ones that can be disproved. According to this view it is impossible to prove something is the case, and it is only possible to disprove statements or hypotheses. Take a statement such as, 'All swans are white'. Even if all the swans we have ever seen have been white we can never rule out the possibility that sometime, somewhere we might come across a swan that is not white. This means that we can never prove that the statement is true. On the other hand, if we found a swan that was not white we would have disproved the statement. This is the basic rationale that underpins the use of a null hypothesis in research. Because we can never prove that our alternative hypothesis is true, we can only disprove the null hypothesis. This means that whenever we carry out a study where the results agree with the alternative hypothesis it does not mean that we have proved our theory to be true. We have simply failed to disprove the theory, but this is not the same as proving it.

One-tailed and two-tailed tests

Suppose we are interested in finding out if background music had any effect on people's ability to learn and recall a list of words. We could set up an experiment with two conditions, an experimental condition and a control condition. In the experimental condition participants could learn the list of words with music playing in the background and in the control condition another group of participants could learn the list of words in silence. After a period of time we could test participants' memory by asking them to write down all the words on the list that they could remember. There are two ways in which an alternative hypothesis can be written, either as a directional (one-tailed) or a non-directional (two-tailed) hypothesis. A directional hypothesis predicts the direction of the results. In other words, we might predict that the group learning in silence will recall more words than the group listening to music. When a statistical test is used with a directional hypothesis a one-tailed test is used. A non-directional hypothesis only predicts a difference but does not state which group will perform better. For example, we might predict that playing background music when people are learning a list of words will have a significant effect on the number of words recalled in a test of memory. When a statistical test is used with a non-directional hypothesis a two-tailed test is used and the group will perform better (Figure 12.7).

Type of hypothesis	Type of statistical test
Directional alternative hypothesis (One-tailed hypothesis)	One-tailed statistical test
Non-directional alternative hypothesis (Two-tailed hypothesis)	Two-tailed statistical test

Figure 12.7: The relationship between hypotheses and statistical tests

The reasoning behind the use of one-tailed and two-tailed statistical tests is fairly complex but it is basically concerned with the probability of differences occurring by chance. A directional alternative hypothesis predicts the direction of the difference, whereas a non-directional hypothesis allows for the possibility that the difference could be in either direction. In the example above, one of the directional hypotheses states that playing background music will significantly increase the number of words recalled. Assuming we are using the 5% level of significance then if the increase in the number of words recalled would have occurred by chance less than five times in a hundred then we would say that the difference was significant. However, when we are using a non-directional hypothesis because the difference could occur in either direction there is double the probability that the differences could occur by chance. In the example above there is the possibility that the differences could occur because either background music improved recall or background music made recall worse. Consequently this has to be taken into account when using a statistical test. The tables used to find out if the results of a statistical test are significant have separate sections for one-tailed and two-tailed tests. So it is important to know before you carry out your analysis whether you are using a directional or non-directional hypothesis.

PRACTICAL Activity

Which of the following hypotheses would be tested using a one-tailed test?

(a) Males and females have significantly different attitudes towards child-care.

(b) Common words are significantly more easy to recall than uncommon words.

(c) Attending therapy has a significant effect on people's level of depression.

(d) Low imagery words are significantly more difficult to recall than high imagery words.

(e) Older people have significantly more positive attitudes towards the police than younger people.

EVALUATIVE COMMENT

One-tailed tests and two-tailed tests both have their advantages and disadvantages. It is more difficult to achieve significant results with a two-tailed test than it is with a one-tailed test. But on the other hand if we are using a one-tailed test and we find a difference in the opposite direction to that which we predicted we cannot claim it is significant for that research study. As a general rule we should use one-tailed hypotheses and one-tailed tests in situations where previous research findings give us a good idea about the direction of our results.

Type I and Type II errors

Suppose we carried out an experiment to find out if children who go to nursery school have a larger vocabulary than children who stay at home. We could recruit a sample of children who attended nursery school and a sample of children who stayed at home and give them a vocabulary test. When we analyse the results we find that they are significant at the 5% level. The children who went to nursery school had a significantly larger vocabulary than children who stayed at home. In this case we would reject the null hypothesis and accept the alternative hypothesis. But we can never be absolutely certain that the results did not occur by chance, it could be the case that random or uncontrolled variables could be responsible for the differences between the two groups. For example, the children in the nursery school group may have been lucky when they guessed the answers. What we are saying when we make a statement like, 'The difference between the two conditions is significant at the 5% level' is that a set of results like this will occur by chance less than five times in a hundred. However, this still leaves open the possibility that our results did actually occur by chance. In situations where we reject the null hypothesis when, in fact the results are due to chance, we are making a 'Type I error'.

A 'Type II error' is said to have occurred when researchers fail to find any significant effect when in fact one does exist. In other words the null hypothesis is wrongly accepted. Type II errors can be the result of a poor research design, faulty sampling or random error. The relationship between Type I and Type II errors and the null hypothesis is shown in Figure 12.8.

	Null hypothesis is accepted	Null hypothesis is rejected
Null hypothesis is actually true	OK	Type I error
Null hypothesis is actually false	Type II error	OK

Figure 12.8: The relationship between null hypotheses and Type I and II errors

EVALUATIVE COMMENT

The likelihood of making a Type I or a Type II error depends on the significance level we set in our research. If we set a more stringent significance level than the standard 5% level, such as 1%, then we are more likely to make a Type II error. On the other hand if we accepted a 10% significance level then we are more likely to make a Type I error.

Positive, negative and zero correlation

A lot of research in psychology is concerned with looking for differences between groups or conditions. But sometimes psychological research is not interested in looking for differences but is more concerned with looking for relationships between variables. For example, we might be interested in finding out if there is any relationship, or correlation, between personality and behaviour. A correlation tells us something about the relationship between two variables. A positive correlation tells us that as a person's score on one variable goes up their score on the other goes up as well. For example, there is usually a positive correlation between practice and performance, the more you practise the better you get! A negative correlation tells us that as a person's score on one variable goes up, their score on the other goes down. For example, there is a negative correlation between memory and age, as a person's age increases their performance on memory tasks decreases. A zero correlation normally tells us that there is no relationship between the two variables. (See *Introducing psychology* Pennington (2002) for more on this.)

REFLECTIVE Activity

Look at the following statements:

1. People who are good at maths are usually good at music.

2. The taller people are, the bigger feet they have.

3. The more you practise playing video games the fewer mistakes you make.

4. The older I get, the less patience I have.

5. People who are good at spelling are also good at reading.

6. The more affection children receive, the less aggressive they are when they get older.

These are all examples of correlations. Decide which of these is a positive correlation and which is a negative correlation. Now try to think of other examples of positive and negative correlations from the psychological research you have covered so far.

A significant correlation tells us that a person's score on one variable is related to their score on another variable. However, we need some way of indicating how strong the relationship is between the two variables. This is done using a scale which ranges from +1 (perfect positive correlation) through 0 (no correlation) to –1 (perfect negative correlation). The number used to describe the strength of a correlation is known as a correlation coefficient (Figure 12.9).

				No relationship				
perfect	strong	moderate	weak		weak	moderate	strong	perfect

–1 –0.9 –0.8 –0.7 –0.6 –0.5 –0.4 –0.3 –0.2 –0.1 **0** +0.1 +0.2 +0.3 +0.4 +0.5 +0.6 +0.7 +0.8 +0.9 +**1**

Figure 12.9: The strength of correlation coefficients

It is important to bear in mind that the 'positive' and 'negative' signs in front of the correlation coefficients tell us the direction of the relationship. The sign tells us nothing at all about the strength of the relationship. It is the number that gives us that information. Generally speaking a correlation coefficient of less than + or – 0.3 would be considered to be fairly weak.

A person's scores on two variables such as reading and drawing tests can be plotted on a type of graph called a 'scattergram'. To construct a scattergram you need to draw two axes, a vertical one and a horizontal one, to represent scores on each of your variables. An example of a scattergram is shown in Figure 12.10.

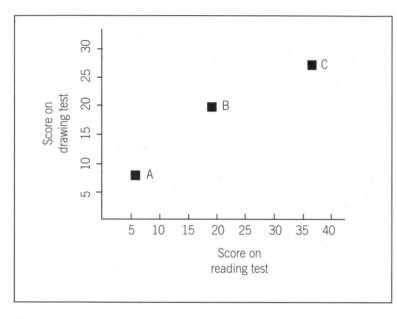

Figure 12.10: An example of a scattergram

The scattergram in Figure 12.10 shows the scores of three participants on the tests of drawing and reading. For the sake of clarity they have been labelled A, B and C, but when you draw a scattergram there is no need to label them like this. Participant A scored 6 on the reading test and 8 on the drawing test. Participant B scored 19 on the reading test and 20 on the drawing test, and participant C scored 37 on the reading test and 28 on the drawing test. Plotting the points on the scattergram is quite straightforward. Take participant B for example. If you were plotting her scores on the scattergram then you would move along the horizontal axis (reading test score) until you reached her score of 19, and then draw a vertical line. Next find her score of 20 on the vertical axis (drawing test score) and draw a horizontal line. Where the two lines cross you represent her scores by using a cross, circle, square, or some other symbol. The pattern of the points on the scattergram gives us a good indication of the strength and direction of the correlation. The patterns that are associated with a positive, negative and zero correlation are shown in Figure 12.11 below.

EVALUATIVE COMMENT

In a correlational design neither of the variables is being manipulated by the researcher. This means that it is impossible to predict which variable is having an effect on the other. All you can say is that there is a relationship between the two variables. If we find a positive correlation between reading ability and spelling ability it could be explained in different ways. For example, it could be the case that children who are good at spelling find it easier to learn how to read, but on the other hand it could be the case that children who are good at reading get more experience with words and are therefore better at spelling. So trying to decide whether being good at reading has an effect on a child's spelling ability or vice versa is not possible in a correlational design.

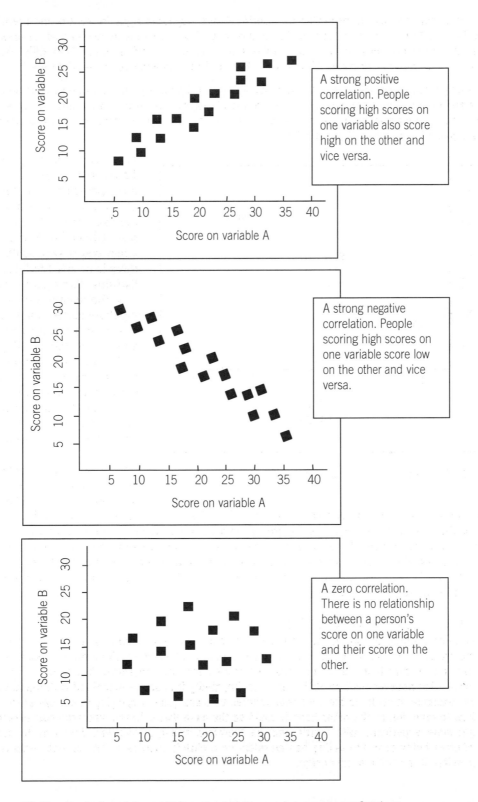

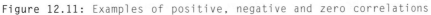

Figure 12.11: Examples of positive, negative and zero correlations

Issues to do with generalisation of findings

In psychological research we are interested in learning about large groups of people who all have something in common. We call the group that we are interested in studying our 'target population'. In some types of research the target population might be as broad as all humans, but in other types of research the target population might be a smaller group such as teenagers, pre-school children or people who misuse drugs. It is more or less impossible to study every single person in a target population so psychologists select a sample or sub-group of the population that is likely to be representative of the target population we are interested in. If the sample we select is going to represent the target population then we need to make sure that the people in it are similar to the other members of the target population. This is important because we want to generalise from the sample to target population. A simplified representation of the process is shown in Figure 12.12.

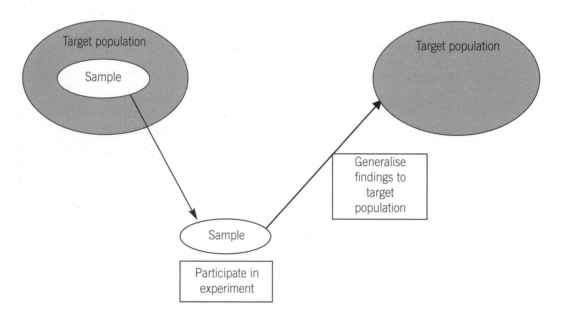

Figure 12.12: Simplified representation of the process of sampling and generalisation

Generalisability refers to the extent to which we can apply the findings of our research to the target population we are interested in. Researchers use a range of different sampling methods and some of these are more effective than others when it comes to selecting a sample that is representative of the target population.

One of the problems that can occur when selecting a sample from a target population is 'sampling bias'. Sampling bias refers to situations where the sample does not reflect the characteristics of the target population. Suppose your target population was the A level students at your school or college and you were interested in some aspect of verbal ability. If you recruited your sample from the college canteen when all the students studying A level English had a free period then you might end up with a large number of them in your sample. This would mean that your sample was biased and not representative of the target population. Consequently the generalisability of any findings based on this sample would be threatened. One of the ways in which the likelihood of sampling bias can be reduced is to use a large sample. Generally speaking the larger the sample size the less chance there is of bias.

There are many different ways of selecting a sample from a target population and they are commonly referred to as 'sampling techniques'. One of the most important sampling techniques is 'random sampling'. In random sampling every person in the target population has an equal chance of being included in the sample. This could be done using a 'lottery method' in which all the names of people in the target population are placed in a hat and the number of participants you require for your sample are drawn out. Other sampling techniques commonly used are opportunity (or accidental) sampling, quota sampling, and stratified sampling. Opportunity sampling consists of recruiting people, such as friends and family, who are at hand and are willing to participate. An example of an opportunity sample would be when a researcher interested in making a generalisation about college students takes all the participants from one class because they all happen to be available at the time s/he is doing the experiment. Stratified sampling attempts to make sure that the sample has the same proportions of whatever characteristics the researcher considers to be relevant as the population. For example, if we are sampling from a target population with equal numbers of men and women then our sample should have equal numbers of men and women. This is done by splitting the target population into men and women and then randomly selecting the participants from each group.

Sampling technique	Description
Random sampling	Every person in the population has an equal chance of being selected. The sample can be selected using random number tables.
Opportunity sampling	The sample is made up of people who were willing to take part. No effort is made to make sure that they are representative of the population.
Stratified sampling	The population is divided into groups such as men and women. Then random samples are drawn from each group to match the proportions in the population.

Figure 12.13: Summary of commonly used sampling techniques

EVALUATIVE COMMENT

Demonstrating that the results from a particular study are generalisable can often be difficult. For example, when research is carried out in a carefully controlled environment such as a psychology laboratory, then any results obtained there are very difficult to generalise to any other settings. One of the ways in which researchers attempt to ensure that their results are generalisable is to select a sample which is representative of the target population. In some cases this is not the most appropriate solution. If we are interested in developing a better understanding of the use of hand guns and street crime we might interview people who have had a particular experience and those who can describe their experiences particularly clearly. Identifying and randomly selecting a sample in this situation would be difficult. A case for the generalisability of the results could be made by repeating the research in a deliberately different setting. If the findings are similar, then the case for the generalisability of the results is strengthened. In addition, it has been argued that in psychology we are more interested in generalising the theory which produced the hypothesis for testing rather than the specific results of our study (Leary 1995).

Limitations of sampling techniques and generalisation of results

All sampling techniques have their strengths and weaknesses. Some of these strengths and weaknesses have implications for the extent to which you can feel confident about generalising the results from your sample to the population. Although random sampling is commonly seen as being the best way of avoiding a biased sample it is not without its limitations. In practice it can be extremely difficult to identify the target population and select randomly from it. For example, even if you have a relatively straightforward target population such as all the pupils at your school or college there are still likely to be difficulties in getting a random sample. You would need to get a complete list of all pupils at the school or college. But how do you deal with pupils that are ill or are on holiday? Selecting the names is fairly straightforward. You could either use some lottery method or a computer could be used to select the names at random. The next major problem would be contacting each person and getting their consent to participate. In studies that take place over a long period of time some participants may withdraw from the research (participant attrition). This can have a biasing effect on the sample since those that leave may be different in some way from the participants who remain in the study. Another problem with random sampling is that we can never be sure that our sample does have the same characteristics as the target population from which it was taken. Random sampling is unbiased in the sense that everyone in the target population has an equal chance of being selected. But there is always the possibility that the random sample may have different demographic characteristics (e.g. gender, ethnic background, age and socio-economic background) from the target population from which it is taken.

Opportunity sampling makes no effort made to ensure that the sample reflects the characteristics of the target population it is meant to represent. This means that systematic biases can be introduced into the sample. For example, if you take all your participants from one college class then they might have particular skills or expertise that makes them different from the majority of college students. This in turn means that the results cannot be generalised to the population of college students. The general advice is to avoid opportunity sampling unless there is no other way of recruiting participants. If opportunity sampling is used then you need to take considerable care both in the analysis and interpretation of the data. Nevertheless there is a lot of research that has used opportunity samples which has made a significant contribution to our understanding of a variety of social phenomena.

In some ways stratified sampling is the opposite of opportunity sampling in that it attempts to produce a sample that goes to considerable lengths to try and make sure that the sample has the same characteristics as the population. Obtaining the detailed information necessary to use the quota sampling technique is usually very difficult and in some cases more or less impossible. In practice, there are a number of ways in which stratified sampling techniques may be biased. For example, researchers could recruit participants from busy areas such as colleges, universities and city centres, where they know there will be lots of people. But a sample drawn from areas like this would under-represent those people who prefer to stay at home.

EVALUATIVE COMMENT

When deciding on a sampling technique it is important to bear in mind the reasons why the research is being carried out. In some situations it is neither possible nor appropriate to attempt to use a random sampling technique. For example, in situations where the research is investigating sensitive topics such as prostitution or drug misuse using a random sampling technique is unlikely to be possible. In reality it is more or less impossible to obtain truly random samples. Therefore it is essential when reporting any psychological research that the sampling procedure is described in detail.

Sampling technique	Strengths	Limitations
Random sampling	• Every person in the target. population has an equal chance of being selected. • Avoids systematic biases in the sample. • Findings can be generalised with a high degree of confidence.	• Identifying the target population and selecting randomly from it can sometimes be very difficult in practice. • Participant attrition can have a biasing effect on the sample. • Possibility that the sample can have different demographic characteristics be the target population.
Opportunity sampling	• Easy to recruit participants. • Participants volunteer.	• Not a representative sample. • The psychological characteristics of volunteers may not be representative of the target population.
Stratified sampling	• The sample is representative of the target population. • Avoids systematic biases in the sample. • Findings can be generalised with a high degree of confidence.	• Can be difficult to identify the strata from which to take participants. • Can be time consuming to recruit participants. • Participant attrition can have a biasing effect on the sample.

Figure 12.14: The strengths and limitations of different sampling techniques

12.2 Statistical tests

The use of non-parametric and parametric tests

There are a huge number and variety of different statistical tests. Here we are concerned with statistical tests that either assess the differences between two sets of results or assess the extent to which two sets of scores are correlated. The only exception to this is the chi-squared test, which is used in situations where participants are allocated to categories. Every statistical test has been designed to be used in particular situations with certain types of data. It is possible to divide statistical tests into two broad groups, parametric tests and non-parametric tests. Both types of test have a set of assumptions that govern when they can be used. Generally speaking parametric tests are considered to be more 'powerful' than non-parametric tests. Using a parametric test reduces the chances of making a Type I or a Type II error. Parametric tests are more sensitive to differences in the data because they use the actual scores, whereas non-parametric tests only use the rank order of the scores. Non-parametric tests are only concerned with whether or not one score is higher than another rather than the size of the difference between the scores.

As we discussed earlier in this chapter the scientific approach revolves around hypothesis testing. We pointed out the fact that it is impossible to prove the alternative hypothesis conclusively. The use of statistical tests enables us determine how confident we can be in rejecting the null hypothesis. The general procedure for using statistical tests is presented in Figure 12.15.

1. Decide on your alternative hypothesis. This is written in terms of the effects you expect the independent variable to have on the dependent variable.

2. You can then write the null hypothesis which states that any differences in the results are due to chance.

3. Decide which test to use (see Figure 12.27).

4. Calculate the test statistic.

5. Obtain critical values from the appropriate table (see Appendix 3) taking into account the degrees of freedom and whether the alternative hypothesis is directional or non-directional.

6. Compare the critical value with the calculated value.

7. Decide whether to accept or reject the null hypothesis.

Figure 12.15: Procedure to find statistical significance

EVALUATIVE COMMENT

When using statistical tests one of the factors you have to take into account is the total number of participants in the study, and also the number of participants in each condition. This is because the possibility of getting a big difference between conditions or a high correlation depends to a certain extent on the size of the sample you have used. In statistics the term 'degrees of freedom' is used as a measure of the size of the sample. It is not an easy term to explain but think about the following situation. A group of six people (N) go into a café and are shown to a table where there are six seats. The first five people are free to choose more than one seat but when they have been seated the sixth person has no choice or 'freedom' about where they sit. In other words, when five people have been seated we know where the sixth person is going to sit, so there are only five degrees of freedom (N–1). Degrees of freedom is a rather complex concept and you need not worry too much about it at this stage. In each of the statistical tests that follow you will be told exactly how to calculate the degrees of freedom.

Statistical tests of difference

SIGN TEST

The sign test (or to give it its full name, the binomial sign test) is used with related designs. In other words you have the same participants in both conditions. It could be used in the following situation. A psychologist is interested in the effect that therapy has on a person's level of depression. She asks the participants to rate their level of depression by giving a score out of 100 on two occasions, before they start treatment and again after five treatment sessions. The higher the score the more depressed they feel. Previous research has indicated that therapy is an effective way of reducing a person's level of depression. Thus a one-tailed hypothesis is used which states therapy will reduce the levels of depression experienced by people. The null hypothesis states that the therapy will have no effect on levels of depression experienced by people. The results of the study are shown in Figure 12.16.

The test statistic for the sign test can be calculated in the following way:

1. Give each pair of scores a plus (+) if the score in column B is greater than the score in column A, a minus (–) if the score in column B is lower than the score in column A, and a zero (0) if the scores are the same.

Participant	Depression rating before treatment A	Depression rating after five treatment sessions B	Direction of difference (B-A)
1	63	58	– (decrease)
2	85	22	– (decrease)
3	60	33	– (decrease)
4	75	78	+ (increase)
5	95	75	– (decrease)
6	60	60	0 (no change)
7	85	46	– (decrease)
8	80	55	– (decrease)
9	90	65	– (decrease)
10	78	72	– (decrease)

Figure 12.16: Depression rating data

2. Ignore all zeros and add up the number of the less frequent sign and call it 's'. In the table above the plus sign occurs less frequently than the minus sign, therefore $s = 1$.

3. Calculate the number of participants (N) whose score changed in either direction. In the table above one participant's scores remained the same therefore, $N = 9$.

4. Using Table 1 in Appendix 3 first decide whether you are using a one-tailed or a two-tailed hypothesis. In the example above we are using a one-tailed hypothesis. Then look across the row for $N = 9$ and compare the calculated value for s with the critical value. The calculated value for s must be equal to or less than the critical value for the difference to be significant. If s is greater than all the critical values then the results are not significant.

In the example above, for a one-tailed test and $N = 9$ s is equal to the critical value for a significance level of 0.05. This means that we can reject the null hypothesis and accept the alternative hypothesis. It would appear that the therapy does have a positive effect on people's level of depression. The pattern of results in the table above would occur by chance less than five times out of 100.

EVALUATIVE COMMENT

The sign test operates at the nominal level because it converts the raw data, which in the example above is more or less interval data, into just three categories. The categories ('+', '–' and '0') indicate whether or not there is a change and the direction of the change. Any information about the size of the change is lost. This means that participant 2 whose score decreased by 63 is considered to be the same as participant 1 whose score only decreased by 5. The test only looks at the direction of the differences. The size of the differences is not taken into account.

WILCOXON'S TEST

Wilcoxon's test (or to give it its full name, the Wilcoxon signed ranks test) is a non-parametric test that is appropriate for a repeated measures design, in other words, where you collect data from the same people in two different conditions. Consider the following example. A psychologist has been approached by a teacher who believes that children at his school are more aggressive in the playground in the morning than they are in the afternoon. A random sample of 10 pupils is selected for the study. The pupils are observed in the morning and the afternoon and their aggressive behaviour is rated on a scale of 1 to 10, 10 being very aggressive and 1 being not all aggressive. The alternative hypothesis is that there will be a significant difference in the levels of aggressive behaviour shown by children in the morning and in the afternoon. The null hypothesis is that there will be no difference in the levels of aggression shown by children in the morning and in the afternoon. The scores are shown in Figure 12.17.

Child	Morning levels of aggression A	Afternoon levels of aggression B	Difference (B-A) C	Rank of difference D	Ranks with less frequent sign
1	8	10	2	3	
2	6	5	−1	1	1
3	3	8	5	8.5	
4	3	5	2	3	
5	3	3	0		
6	7	5	−2	3	3
7	5	8	3	6	
8	6	9	3	6	
9	5	8	3	6	
10	4	9	5	8.5	
					Total (T) = 4

Figure 12.17: Aggression data

The test statistic for the Wilcoxon test is T, and should not be confused with the 't' test which is described later. Wilcoxon's T is calculated in the following way:

1. Calculate the difference between the scores of aggression in the morning and aggression in the afternoon (i.e. subtract the morning score from the afternoon score). These are the difference scores. If the morning score is higher than the afternoon score then it will be a minus score. See for example, child number 3 who scored 3 in the morning and 8 in the afternoon.

2. Rank the difference scores, giving the smallest difference a rank of 1. Ignore the sign, so participant 6, whose difference is −4 is given rank 7. Also ignore any participants where there is no difference between their scores. If there is more than one person with the same score (such as participants 1, 4 and 7) then we add the shared ranks and divide by the number of people sharing them. So in this case we have:

$$\frac{2 + 3 + 4}{3} = \frac{9}{3} = 3$$

which means that participants 1, 4 and 7 all get a rank of 3. The same principle applies to participants 8 and 9 who both get a rank of 5.5.

3. Count the number of ranks associated with minus scores and then those associated with plus scores. In the table above there are two ranks associated with minus scores and seven associated with plus scores. Add together the ranks associated with the least occurring sign, in this case it is minus. Call this value T. In the table above T has a value of 4.

4. The next stage is to find out the significance of T. First calculate the sample size (N) by counting the number of participants and subtracting those who scored the same in both conditions. In the example above there was one participant who scored the same in both conditions so N = 9. Next using Table 2 in Appendix 3 look across the row for N = 9 and find the lowest critical value which T does not exceed. For T = 4 with a sample size of N = 9 and a two-tailed hypothesis the difference between the conditions is significant at the 0.05 level (p<.05). In other words, this pattern of results would occur by chance is less than 5 times in 100. If T is greater than all the critical values then the differences between the conditions are not significant. So the results in Figure 12.17 suggest that children are more significantly more aggressive in the afternoon than they are in the morning.

EVALUATIVE COMMENT

The Wilcoxon test and the Sign test look at differences between related conditions. Whereas the Sign test only takes into account the number of differences between the conditions the Wilcoxon test also looks at the position of any differences. This means that it is more sensitive to the differences in the data. However, because it converts the data into ordinal data it is less sensitive than its parametric equivalent, the t-test.

MANN–WHITNEY

The Mann–Whitney test is designed to be used with non-parametric data and for unrelated designs, in other words when you have different participants in each condition. Suppose we want to find out the effect of mental imagery on the recall of a list of words. One group of participants were given a list of words to learn. They were simply told that they had five minutes to learn the list. The second group were given the same list of words but were told to try and create an image of the word when they were learning it. For example, if the word was 'DOG' they had to create an image of a dog in their head. One hour after they had learnt the list participants were asked to recall as many words as they could. Memory was measured by the number of words recalled. The null hypothesis for this experiment states that using mental imagery will have no significant effect on the number of words recalled from a learnt list. Since previous research has indicated that using mental imagery can improve recall a one-tailed alternative hypothesis was used. This states that using mental imagery will significantly increase the number of words recalled from a learnt list. The results are shown in Figure 12.18.

The test statistic for the Mann–Whitney test is U and is calculated in the following way:

1. Put all the scores together and rank them as a single group, giving a rank of 1 to the lowest score and so on.

2. Now add the rank totals for participants in condition 1 (T_1) and participants in condition 2 (T_2) separately. In the example above $T_1 = 22.5$ and $T_2 = 55.5$.

3. Calculate U from the following formula:

$$U = N_1 N_2 + \frac{N_L(N_L + 1) - T_L}{2}$$

Where

	From example
N_1 = Number of participants in condition 1	$N_1 = 6$
N_2 = Number of participants in condition 2	$N_2 = 6$
N_L = Number of participants in condition with largest rank total	$N_L = 6$
T_L = Largest rank total	$T_L = 55.5$

Therefore

$$U = 6 \times 6 + \frac{6(6+1)}{2} - 55.5$$

$$= 6 \times 36 + \frac{6 \times 7}{2} - 55.5$$

$$= 36 + \frac{42}{2} - 55.5$$

$$= 36 + 21 - 55.5$$

$$= 57 - 55.5$$

$$= 1.5$$

In this example there are equal numbers of participants in each condition, and although it is always preferable to have this it is by no means essential. Many unrelated group designs have a different number of participants in each condition. In such cases you can calculate U for both rank totals and then take the *smaller* value of U.

Condition 1 (no imagery instructions)	Rank (1)	Condition 2 (instructions to use imagery)	Rank (2)
4	3	12	11
5	4	8	6
2	1.5	9	7.5
9	7.5	10	9
2	1.5	11	10
6	5	14	12
Rank totals	$T_1 = 22.5$		$T_2 = 55.5$

Figure 12.18: Imagery data

4. Now check the significance value of U using Table 3 in Appendix 3. In situations where you have different numbers of participants in each condition N1 refers to the number of participants in the smaller group and N2 refers the number of participants in the larger

condition. In our example since we have six participants in each condition we just look down the column where N1 = 6 and across the row where N2 = 6 and we will find the critical value for U, which is 7. In order for the differences to be significant our calculated value of U must be less than the critical value. Since our calculated value of U is 1.5, which is less than the critical value of 7 we can reject the null hypothesis and accept the alternative hypothesis at the 0.05 significance level. In other words, the results indicate that using imagery while learning a list of words does indeed improve people's ability to recall them.

EVALUATIVE COMMENT

One of the main weaknesses of this test is that the actual scores are converted to relative positions or ranks. This means that we are losing information about the size of the differences between the scores of the groups.

RELATED (REPEATED MEASURES) T-TEST

The related (or repeated measures) t-test is used for experimental designs where the same participants take part in both conditions. It is designed to be used with parametric data. A psychologist is carrying out research into the effects of acupuncture on cigarette smoking. A sample of 10 smokers is selected for the study. The number of cigarettes they smoke before their treatment is recorded. The participants are then given a course of acupuncture. The number of cigarettes they smoke after the course of acupuncture is also recorded. The data are shown in Figure 12.19 below. We are aware that previous research has shown acupuncture to be an effective in helping people with addictive behaviours. Therefore we decide to use a one-tailed alternative hypothesis which states, 'acupuncture will significantly reduce the number of cigarettes a person smokes per day'. The null hypothesis states, 'Acupuncture will have no significant effect on the number of cigarettes a person smokes per day'.

Participant	Number of cigarettes smoked per day before treatment A	Number of cigarettes smoked per day after treatment B	Difference (d) (A – B)	D^2
1	21	14	7	49
2	30	32	–2	4
3	20	14	6	36
4	31	25	6	36
5	18	11	7	49
6	12	2	10	100
7	15	10	5	25
8	40	42	–2	4
9	35	28	7	49
10	10	5	5	25
Total			Total = 49 (Σd)	Total = 377 (Σd^2)

Figure 12.19: Smoking data

The related measures t-test is calculated in the following way:

1. Calculate the differences between participants' scores by subtracting their scores in the second condition from their scores in the first condition (A − B).

2. Add up the differences, counting minus scores as minuses. (Note that the symbol Σ means the 'sum of'. So Σd means the sum of all the difference (d) scores and in the example above $\Sigma d = 49$)

3. Now square the sum of the differences. This is written as $(\Sigma d)^2$ which in the example above is $49 \times 49 = 4998$.

4. Square the differences. In other words multiply the number by itself, so for participant 1, the difference between their first and second scores was 7. The square of 7 is 7×7 which is 49. One of the rules of mathematics is that if you square a minus number (e.g. participant 2) then you lose the minus sign. Now add up the squared differences (Σd^2) and in the example above $\Sigma d^2 = 377$).

(Note the difference between $(\Sigma d)^2$ which means add up all the differences and square the total and Σd^2 which means square the differences and add them up.)

5. The value for *t* can be found using the following formula where N is the number of participants:

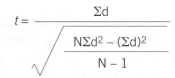

$$t = \frac{\Sigma d}{\sqrt{\dfrac{N\Sigma d^2 - (\Sigma d)^2}{N - 1}}}$$

In this formula the symbol $\sqrt{}$ means 'find the square root'. This is the opposite of squaring a number and means you have to calculate the number which when multiplied by itself will give you the number inside the square root symbol. So the square root of 4 is 2 and the square root of 9 is 3 and so on. Most calculators have a function key which will calculate the square root of a number.

When we put in the values from the example above we get

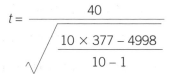

$$t = \frac{40}{\sqrt{\dfrac{10 \times 377 - 4998}{10 - 1}}}$$

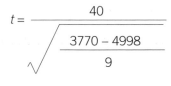

$$t = \frac{40}{\sqrt{\dfrac{3770 - 4998}{9}}}$$

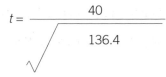

$$t = \frac{40}{\sqrt{136.4}}$$

$$= \frac{40}{11.7}$$

$$= 3.42$$

6. In order to test the significance of the calculated value of t we need to find the degrees of freedom (df) for an related measures t-test which is $N - 1 = 9$.

7. Now look up the significance level of your calculated value for t using Table 4 in Appendix 3. Look down the left-hand column until you reach the appropriate degrees of freedom (in our example it is 9). Decide whether you are using a one-tailed or a two-tailed hypothesis and look across the row for the critical value for t. If the critical value for t is smaller than your calculated value then we can reject the null hypothesis and accept the alternative hypothesis. The critical value for t using a one-tailed hypothesis and $9df$ is 1.883 which is smaller than our calculated value of 3.42. This means that we can reject the null hypothesis and accept the alternative hypothesis.

EVALUATIVE COMMENT
The results of the related t-test indicate that there is a significant difference between the two conditions. In other words, the data in our example suggest that acupuncture can significantly reduce the number of cigarettes people smoke per day.

INDEPENDENT T-TEST

The independent (or unrelated) t-test is designed to be used when there are different people in each condition. The test assumes that the data is parametric. Suppose a teacher was interested in comparing two methods of teaching children to read. She has a class of 20 children and she teaches 10 of them using the first method and the other 10 are taught using the second method. At the end of term all the children have a reading test and their performance is scored out of 20. The data are shown in Figure 12.20 below. There is no previous research that has compared the two methods of teaching and so a two-tailed alternative hypothesis is used which states, 'The teaching method will have a significant effect on children's ability to read'. The null hypothesis states, 'The teaching method will have no significant effect on children's ability to read'.

The t for independent groups can be calculated in the following way.

1. Calculate the square for each individual score in both conditions (see columns A and B).

2. Add up the all the scores from participants who were taught using teaching method 1 (Σx_1).

3 Add up all the squared scores of participants who were taught using teaching method 1 (Σx_1^2).

4. Add up the all the scores from participants who were taught using teaching method 2 (Σx_2).

5. Add up all the squared scores of participants who were taught using teaching method 1 (Σx_2^2).

6. Calculate the means for each group (M_1 and M_2).

7. Square the total scores of participants who were taught using teaching method 1 (($\Sigma x_1)^2$).

8. Square the total scores of participants who were taught using teaching method 2 (($\Sigma x_2)^2$).

Teaching method 1 Reading test scores $(\times_1)$	A Scores squared $(\times_1{}^2)$	Teaching method 2 Reading test scores $(\times_2)$	B Scores squared $(\times_2{}^2)$
20	400	4	16
10	100	3	9
12	144	15	225
6	36	8	64
17	289	9	81
16	256	7	49
15	225	10	100
11	121	9	81
9	81	5	25
8	64	3	9
Total $\Sigma \times_1 = 124$	$\Sigma \times_1{}^2 = 1716$	$\Sigma \times_2 = 73$	$\Sigma \times_2{}^2 = 659$
Mean $M_1 = 12.4$		Mean $M_2 = 7.3$	
$(\Sigma \times_1)^2 = 15376$		$(\Sigma \times_2)^2 = 5329$	

Figure 12.20: Teaching method data

9. The value for *t* can be calculated using the following formula where N_1 is the number of participants in condition 1 and N_2 is the number of participants in condition 2. This formula is by far the most complex you will have to cope with for A Level psychology, so just be careful and take your time!

$$t = \frac{M_1 - M_2}{\sqrt{\dfrac{\left(\Sigma \times_1{}^2 - \dfrac{(\Sigma \times_1)^2}{N_1}\right) + \left(\Sigma \times_2{}^2 - \dfrac{(\Sigma \times_2)^2}{N_2}\right)}{(N-1) + (N_2 - 1)}}\left(\dfrac{1}{N_1} + \dfrac{1}{N_2}\right)}$$

$$t = \frac{12.4 - 7.3}{\sqrt{\dfrac{\left(1716 - \dfrac{15376}{10}\right) + \left(659 - \dfrac{5329}{10}\right)}{(10-1) + (10-1)}}\left(\dfrac{1}{10} + \dfrac{1}{10}\right)}$$

$$t = \frac{5.1}{\sqrt{\dfrac{\left(1716 - 1537.6\right) + \left(659 - 532.9\right)}{18}} \times \dfrac{1}{5}}$$

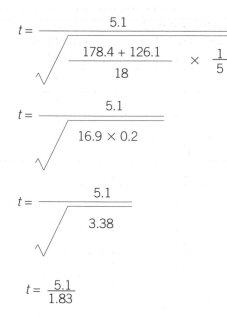

$$t = \frac{5.1}{\sqrt{\dfrac{178.4 + 126.1}{18} \times \dfrac{1}{5}}}$$

$$t = \frac{5.1}{\sqrt{16.9 \times 0.2}}$$

$$t = \frac{5.1}{\sqrt{3.38}}$$

$$t = \frac{5.1}{1.83}$$

$$t = 2.78$$

10. Calculate the degrees of freedom for an independent t-test using the following formula:

$$df = (N_1 - 1) + (N_2 - 1)$$
$$= (10 - 1) + (10 - 1)$$
$$= 9 + 9$$
$$= 18$$

11. Now look up the significance level of your calculated value for t using Table 4 in Appendix 3. Look down the left-hand column until you reach the appropriate degrees of freedom (in our example it is 18). Decide whether you are using a one-tailed or a two-tailed hypothesis and look across the row for the critical value for t. In our example we used a two-tailed hypothesis. If the critical value for t is smaller than your calculated value then we can reject the null hypothesis and accept the alternative hypothesis. The critical value for t using a two-tailed hypothesis and $18df$ is 2.101 which is smaller than our calculated value of 2.78. This means that we can reject the null hypothesis and accept the alternative hypothesis.

EVALUATIVE COMMENT

The results of the independent t-test indicate that there is a significant difference between the two sets of scores. In other words, the data in our example suggest that the method used to teach the children to read does indeed have a significant effect on their reading ability. If we inspect the mean scores then it is clear that teaching method 1 (mean score = 12.4) is better than teaching method 2 (mean score = 7.3).

Statistical tests of association

SPEARMAN'S RANK ORDER CORRELATION

Spearman's rank order test of correlation is designed to be used with non-parametric data. It should be used when the data are measured on an ordinal scale or when the data does not meet the parametric assumptions. The test statistic for this test is Spearman's rho (pronounced 'row').

As with all tests of correlation it is used when we are interested in people's performance on two different variables. In other words it is a related design. Suppose we are interested in the relationship between extraversion and going out to clubs. We know that extraverts tend to be outgoing and sociable, but does this mean that the more extraverted a person is the more likely they are to go out to nightclubs? In investigating this question we design a questionnaire which includes a measure of extraversion and a measure of how frequently the respondent goes to nightclubs. Our one-tailed alternative hypothesis states, 'There will be a significant positive correlation between levels of extraversion and the frequency with which people go to nightclubs'. The null hypothesis states, 'There will be no significant correlation between levels of extraversion and the frequency with which people go to night clubs'. We are predicting a positive relationship between extraversion and going to clubs. This means that we are expecting people who are very extravert will also go to clubs quite frequently. We select nine people to complete our questionnaire and the results are shown in Figure 12.21 below.

Participant	Level of extraversion (A) (1–10)	Frequency of going to night clubs (B) (1–5)	Rank A	Rank B	Difference (d) (Rank A – Rank B)	Difference squared (d²)
1	10	5	1	1	0	0
2	3	1	8	8.5	−5	.25
3	6	3	5.5	5	.5	.25
4	5	4	7	2.5	4.5	20.25
5	9	3	2	5	−3	9
6	8	4	3	2.5	.5	.25
7	2	1	9	8.5	.5	.25
8	7	3	4	5	−1	1
9	6	2	5.5	7	−1.5	2.25
						$\Sigma d^2 = 33.5$

Figure 12.21: Nightclub attendance and extraversion data

Spearman's rho can be calculated in the following way.

1. Rank all the scores on variable A (level of extraversion), giving 1 to the highest score and so on. Then do the same for the scores on variable B (frequency of going to nightclubs).

2. Calculate the difference (d) between each pair or ranked scores.

3. Square the difference (d²).

4. Add up the squared differences to calculate the sum of the squared differences (Σd^2).

5. Count how many participants you have (N).

6. Calculate the value of rho using this formula:

$$\text{rho} = 1 - \frac{6\Sigma d^2}{N(N^2 - 1)}$$

$$= 1 - \frac{6 \times 33.5}{9(81 - 1)}$$

$$= 1 - \frac{201}{9 \times 80}$$

$$= 1 - 0.28$$

$$= 0.72$$

7. Now look up the significance level of your calculated value for rho using Table 5 in Appendix 3. Look down the left-hand column until you come to the number of participants you had in your study. Decide whether you were using a one-tailed or two-tailed hypothesis and look across to the appropriate column to find the critical value for rho. If the calculated value is greater than the critical value then the relationship between the variables is significant. In the example above there were nine participants and as we were using a one-tailed hypothesis the critical value of rho is .600. The calculated value of rho is 0.72 which is greater than the critical value. This means that there is a significant relationship between extraversion and going to nightclubs.

EVALUATIVE COMMENT

The correlation coefficient of 0.72 is quite high indicating that there is strong positive correlation between extraversion and going to nightclubs. The results suggest that the more extraverted a person is the more likely they are to go to a nightclub.

PEARSON'S PRODUCT MOMENT CORRELATION

The Pearson product moment correlation is a parametric test which measures the extent to which people's scores correlate on two variables. Although Spearman's rank order test can be used with more or less any data, Pearson's test is designed to be used with data that has been measured on an interval scale. The test statistic for Pearson's test is r.

Suppose you were interested in the relationship between children's ability to read and their ability to spell words correctly. You recruit a sample of 10 children and give them a reading test, which is scored out of 20, and a spelling test which is scored out of 15. You predict that there will be a positive correlation between reading and spelling. In other words we expect children who do well on the reading test to also do well on the spelling test, and children who do badly on one test will also do badly on the other. Since we are predicting a direction we use a one-tailed alternative hypothesis which states, 'There will be a significant positive correlation between a person's reading ability and their spelling ability'. The null hypothesis states, 'There will be no significant relationship between a person's reading ability and their spelling ability'. The data are shown in Figure 12.22 on p 275.

Pearson's r can be calculated in the following way:

1. For each participant multiply their score on variable A by their score on variable B (column C).

2. For each participant square their scores on variable A (column D) and variable B (column E).

3. Calculate the total (sum) for each of the columns A–E.

4. Use the following formula, where N = the number of participants, to calculate the value of r.

$$r = \frac{N\Sigma A \times B - \Sigma A \times \Sigma B}{\sqrt{\left(N\Sigma A^2 - (\Sigma A)^2\right)\left(N\Sigma B^2 - (\Sigma B)^2\right)}}$$

$$r = \frac{(10 \times 1174) - (124 \times 81)}{\sqrt{(10 \times 1794 - 124^2)(10 \times 783 - 81^2)}}$$

$$r = \frac{11740 - 10044}{\sqrt{(17940 - 15376)(7830 - 6561)}}$$

$$r = \frac{1676}{\sqrt{2564 \times 1269}}$$

$$r = \frac{1676}{\sqrt{3253716}}$$

$$r = \frac{1676}{1803.8}$$

$$r = 0.93$$

5. Calculate the degrees of freedom (*df*) using the formula, the number of participants minus 2. In this case it is $10 - 2 = 8$. Therefore there are 8 *df*.

6. Now look up the significance level of your calculated value for *r* using Table 6 in Appendix 3. Look down the left-hand column until you come to the appropriate degrees of freedom you had in your study. Decide whether you were using a one-tailed or two-tailed hypothesis and look across to the appropriate column to find the critical value for *r*. If the calculated value is greater than the critical value then the relationship between the variables is significant. In the example above there were 8 degrees of freedom and as we were using a one-tailed hypothesis the critical value of *r* is 0.5494. The calculated value of *r* is 0.93 which is greater than the critical value. This means that there is a significant positive correlation between reading ability and spelling ability.

Participant	Reading test score (20) (Variable A) A	Spelling test score (15) (Variable B) B	A × B C	A² D	B² E
1	11	7	77	121	49
2	19	13	247	361	169
3	8	8	64	64	64
4	5	3	15	25	9
5	15	9	135	225	81
6	14	7	98	196	49
7	20	14	280	400	196
8	17	11	187	289	121
9	8	6	48	64	36
10	7	3	21	49	9
Total	$\Sigma A = 124$	$\Sigma B = 81$	$\Sigma A \times B = 1172$	$\Sigma A^2 = 1794$	$\Sigma B^2 = 783$

Figure 12.22: Reading and spelling data

EVALUATIVE COMMENT

The correlation coefficient of 0.93 is extremely high showing that there is a very strong positive correlation between reading ability and spelling ability. The results indicate that if a person is good at reading then they are good at spelling and if they are poor at reading then they are also poor at spelling.

CHI-SQUARED TEST OF ASSOCIATION

The chi-squared test (pronounced 'ki' squared) is designed to be used with nominal data. This means that rather than having a score, such as their performance on an intelligence test, we can only put our participants into categories. When using the chi-squared test it is important to remember that each participant can only be put into *one* category. This means that in each category we will have frequency data which indicates how many of our participants were placed in that category. In other words it can be used in situations where we have an unrelated design. Suppose we wanted to find out if the use of public transport as a way of getting to school was significantly different between a city centre school and a school that is in the suburbs. Fifty pupils at each school were asked to indicate whether or not they used public transport to get to school. The results are shown in Figure 12.23 below. Of the 50 pupils attending the city centre school 39 used public transport and 11 used some other means of getting to school. Whereas 15 pupils attending the school in the suburbs used public transport, 35 used some other method of getting to school.

The chi-squared test is concerned with the difference between the frequencies we actually observe and those that we would expect to occur by chance if there was no association between the type of school and use of public transport. In other words the test compares the actual number of children in each category with the number that we would expect to be in each category. Our data collection has given us the observed frequencies shown in Figure 12.23, but we still need to calculate the expected frequencies. In order to calculate the expected

	City centre school	School in suburbs	Total
Use public transport to get to school	39 (A)	15 (B)	54
Do not use public transport to get to school	11 (C)	35 (D)	46
Total 50	50	100	

Figure 12.23: Observed frequencies of public transport use by school children in two schools

frequencies we need to take into account the totals of each row and also the total of each column. For example we need to take into account the fact that in total 54 children used public transport to get to school. From this we can then work out how many children from each school we would expect to use public transport. If the type of school was not associated with the type of transport children used then we would expect the total of 54 to be equally divided between both types of school. In other words, we would expect the total of 54 to be made up of 27 children from each school. If the observed results are due to chance then they should be more or less the same as the expected results. On the other hand, if there is some association between the type of school and type of transport then there will be a considerable difference between the observed and expected scores. It is normal to use a two-tailed hypothesis with a chi squared test. Our alternative hypothesis could be stated as, 'There will be a significant association between the type of school children attend and the type of transport they use to get there'. The null hypothesis could be stated as, 'There will be no significant association between the type of school children attend and the type of transport they use to get there'. The chi-squared test calculates the difference between the observed and expected values. The larger the difference the more likely the result will be significant.

Chi squared can be calculated in the following way:

1. From the observed frequencies (O) calculate the total of each row and column.

2. Label each cell using a number or a letter. In the example above I have used the letters A–D.

3. Calculate the expected frequency (E) for each cell using the following formula:

$$E = \frac{R \times C}{T}$$

R = row total

C = column total

T = overall total of all cells

Expected value for cell A $= \frac{R \times C}{T} = \frac{54 \times 50}{100} = 27$

Expected value for cell B $= \frac{R \times C}{T} = \frac{54 \times 50}{100} = 27$

Expected value for cell C $= \frac{R \times C}{T} = \frac{46 \times 50}{100} = 23$

Expected value for cell $D = \dfrac{R \times C}{T} = \dfrac{46 \times 50}{100} = 23$

4. Calculate the degrees of freedom using the following formula:
$df =$ (number of rows − 1) × (number of columns − 1).
Using the data from our example, $df = (2 − 1) \times (2 − 1) = 1$.

5. The value of chi squared can be calculated using the following formula:

$$\text{Chi squared} = \Sigma \frac{(|O - E| - 0.5)^2}{E}$$

In mathematical formulae the use of straight lines (i.e. $|O - E|$) rather than curved brackets means that when the subtraction is carried out any minus signs are ignored. So if the observed score (O) was 10 and the expected score (E) was 15 then the answer would be 5. So the formula above means that for each cell we have to, (1) subtract the expected value from the observed value, (2) ignore any minus signs, (3) subtract 0.5, (4) square the result of step 3, and (5) divide the answer by the expected value. When you have done this for every cell, the final step (6) add up the results of you step 5 calculations. This sounds more complicated than it really is! The calculations for our example are shown below.

Cell	Step 1 $(O - E)$	Step 2 $\|O - E\|$	Step 3 $(\|O - E\| - 0.5)$	Step 4 $(\|O - E\| - 0.5)^2$	Step 5 $\dfrac{(\|O - E\| - 0.5)^2}{E}$
A	$39 - 27$ $= 12$	12	11.5	$11.5^2 = 132.25$	$132.25 \div 27$ $= 4.9$
B	$15 - 27$ $= -12$	12	11.5	$11.5^2 = 132.25$	$132.25 \div 27$ $= 4.9$
C	$11 - 23$ $= -12$	12	11.5	$11.5^2 = 132.25$	$132.25 \div 23$ $= 5.7$
D	$35 - 23$ $= 12$	12	11.5	$11.5^2 = 132.25$	$132.25 \div 23$ $= 5.7$

Step 6
$4.9 + 4.9 + 5.7 + 5.7 = 21.2$

Therefore the value for chi squared calculated for the data in our example is 21.2.

6 Now we can look up the significance level of chi squared using Table 7 in Appendix 3. Normally a two-tailed hypothesis should be used with a chi squared test. With one degree of freedom the critical value for chi squared is 3.84. Our calculated value for chi squared is 21.2 which is greater than the critical value. This means that our results were significant at the 5% level and we can accept the alternative hypothesis. In other words there is a significant association between the location of the school and the type of transport children use to get there.

EVALUATIVE COMMENT

Unfortunately there are two different formulae that are used to calculate the chi-squared statistic. One is used when there is one degree of freedom and the other in situations where the number of degrees of freedom is greater than 1. In situations where there are more than one degrees of freedom then the following formula is used:

$$Chi\ squared = \frac{\Sigma(O - E)^2}{E}$$

In principle there is no limit to the number of cells that can be used in a chi-squared test. For example, it is quite common to have 3 × 2 and 3 × 3 matrices.

12.2.4 The factors affecting the appropriate choice of statistical test

Choosing an appropriate statistical test depends on several factors including the type of data and the experimental design.

LEVELS OF MEASUREMENT

REFLECTIVE Activity

Consider the following statements:

(a) Sarah is an attractive woman.

(b) Sarah is more attractive than Sharon.

(c) Sarah is twice as attractive as Carol.

Which of the statements contains the most information?

Which of the statements contains the least information?

The statements in the reflective activity above are about Sarah and two of them compare Sarah to other women. Each of the statements provides a different type of information about Sarah. In the first statement we are putting Sarah into a category, the 'attractive women' category. In the second statement we are comparing Sharon and Sarah and deciding that Sarah is more attractive than Sharon. In other words we are putting Sarah and Sharon into an order in terms of how attractive we think they are. The last statement provides the most information because not only does it tell us that Sarah is more attractive than Carol it also tells us how much more attractive she is. The three statements correspond to the three main 'levels of measurement' used in psychological research, nominal, ordinal and interval.

THE NOMINAL LEVEL OF MEASUREMENT

The nominal level of measurement is used in situations where we are interested in putting people into categories. We use the nominal level of measurement quite frequently in our everyday lives. For example, we identify people as 'men' or 'women', or we can categorise them according to the country where they were born, 'English', 'French', 'Irish', 'Italian' 'German' and so on. The important point to bear in mind here is that when we are using categories like this, people can only be placed into one of the categories. In psychological research we typically use categories during studies than involve observation. For example, if we were interested in whether children aged 2 years played on their own with other children then we could set up a study which observed a group of 20 of them playing. The results could be presented in the following way:

Type of play	Alone	With others
Number of children	14	6

Figure 12.24: Type of play of 2-year-old children

In this example, only six of the 20 children played with other children, whereas 14 played alone. This would seem to indicate that 2-year-old children tend to play on their own rather than with other children. If we wanted to we could increase the number of categories. For example, we might be interested in comparing the types of play of boys and girls. We repeat our observations but this time use a sample of 15 boys and 15 girls. The results are presented below:

Type of play	Alone	With others
Number of girls	10	5
Number of boys	11	4

Figure 12.25: Type of play of 2-year-old children

The results would appear to suggest that there is no real difference between the type of play of boys and girls at this age. They both have a preference to play on their own. So the nominal level of measurement simply places participants into a category. In the case of Sarah she was placed in the category of 'attractive' rather than 'unattractive' and the children were categorised as either playing alone or with other children. This is a level of measurement that provides the least amount of information about our participants. Nominal data simply tells us that one participant is different from another. It does not tell us anything about the quantity of the difference.

THE ORDINAL LEVEL OF MEASUREMENT
Ordinal measurement means that participants can be ranked in some sort of order. In Sarah's case we said that she was, 'more attractive than Sharon', but we did not say by how much. Using ordinal level of measurement we can rank our participants from highest to lowest. For example, we could rank all our friends in terms of their attractiveness. The first person in the ranking is the most attractive and the next person is the second most attractive and so on. When you have ordinal data you are making one assumption, that is, the numbers are ordered. In other words, the person who you have ranked as number one is the best, number 2 the second best and so on. The ranking does not assume that the difference between the first and second ranked person is the same as the difference between the third and fourth ranked person.

THE INTERVAL LEVEL OF MEASUREMENT
The interval level of measurement uses a scale with equal intervals, such as seconds, percentage scored in a test or the number of items recalled in a test of memory. Intervals on the scale are of an equal size which means that the difference between 20 seconds and 30 seconds is the same as the difference between 30 seconds and 40 seconds. Interval data is data that is on a continuous numerical scale with equal intervals between points. It is always possible to reduce interval data to ordinal data. Suppose Kathryn solves a problem in 12 seconds, Joshua solves it in 15 seconds and Amelia takes 20 seconds to solve it. The time they take to solve the problem is interval data. But we can easily convert their times to ordinal data: Kathryn is first, Joshua second and Amelia third. But by doing this we are losing information about the size of the differences between Kathryn, Amelia and Joshua.

TYPE OF DESIGN
Research designs fall into two broad categories: those that are looking for a difference between two conditions or groups and those that are looking for a relationship between two variables. If we consider research designs that are looking for a difference between two conditions then we

can either have the same participants in each condition or different participants in each condition. Designs where the same participant takes part in each condition are known as related designs. On the other hand designs where you have different participants in each condition are known as unrelated designs. Whether you decide to use a related or unrelated design depends on a number of factors. Generally speaking related designs are preferable because we have the same people in each condition therefore we can assume that any differences are likely to be due to the effect of the independent variable. There are several alternative terms that are used in statistics books that mean the same as related and unrelated (see Figure 12.26). Correlational designs are always related because we are interested in the relationship between participants' performance on two variables.

Type of design	Participants
Related (repeated measures)	Same participants in each condition.
Unrelated (independent groups)	Different participants in each condition.
Correlational	Same participant has scores on two variables or score of one person similar to score to another person.

Figure 12.26: Summary of different types of research design

CONDITIONS FOR PARAMETRIC TESTS

If we intend to use parametric tests then there are certain criteria that should be met. The first of these is that the level of measurement should be interval. If the data is not interval then a non-parametric test should be used. Second the sample data that we are using should be drawn from populations that are normally distributed. In other words if we were able to collect data from the whole of the target population it would have the bell-like shape that is characteristic of a normal distribution. In practice it is very difficult to determine whether or not this would be the case. In some cases we might have information from other research that the variable we are testing is normally distributed. Third, the variances of the two samples should not be significantly different from each other. This is referred to as homogeneity of variance and essentially means that the distribution of the scores in each condition should have a similar pattern. Fortunately parametric tests are fairly robust which means that if the criteria are not met exactly then the tests can still be used. Parametric tests only become unreliable if the criteria are poorly met. A list of parametric tests and their non-parametric equivalents is presented in Figure 12.27.

	Tests looking for a difference		Tests looking for an association
	Related design	Independent design	Correlational design
Parametric	Related *t*-test	Independent *t*-test	Pearson's product moment correlation coefficient
Non-parametric	Wilcoxon	Mann–Whitney *U*	Spearman's rho Chi squared

Figure 12.27: Parametric tests and their non-parametric equivalents

EVALUATIVE COMMENT

The nominal level of measurement provides us with the least amount of information. It simply tells us that one person is different from another. In other words they can be placed in a different category. The ordinal level of measurement provides us with more information than the nominal scale. It tells us what order people can be placed in. But we do not know what the difference between the ranks really is. The interval level of measurement provides us with the most information. Not only does it tell us what order people are in, but it also tells us how different people are from each other. There is a considerable debate in psychology about the extent to which scores on psychological tests, such as intelligence quotient (IQ) tests are really interval data. If the scores are really interval data then the difference in intelligence between people who score 90 and those who score 100 should be the same as the difference in intelligence between people who score 60 and those who score 70. This view has been challenged by some psychologists and statisticians on a number of grounds. For example, we cannot assume that all the items in a test are at the same level of difficulty. So if two people have exactly the same score on an IQ test, such as 95, they are quite likely to have got a different set of answers correct. It is argued that this makes comparisons problematic. However, in most cases psychologists treat the data from IQ tests and other psychological scales as interval data. When research produces data that is based on estimates, such as how attractive a person is, then it is probably safer to assume that the ratings should be reduced to an ordinal level.

12.3 Issues in research

This section discusses four important issues associated with carrying out psychological research. The first part addresses the advantages and disadvantages of different methods of research. This is followed by a discussion of the strengths and weaknesses of quantitative and qualitative approaches to research. The third part looks at the concepts of reliability and validity. The final part of this section addresses ethical issues in psychological research.

Advantages and disadvantages of different methods of research

One of the goals of psychology is to develop a better understanding of human behaviour and conscious experience. Psychologists use a variety of different techniques to collect data which helps them develop theories and explanations of why people behave and feel as they do. Each of these methods has their own particular strengths and weaknesses. This section outlines the main advantages and disadvantages of experiments, interviews, questionnaires, observational studies and case studies as methods of research in psychology. The main advantages and disadvantages of each method are summarised in Figure 12.29 on p.284.

EXPERIMENTS

In an experiment researchers 'manipulate some aspect of a situation and examine the impact on the way participants respond' (Westen 2002). Experiments have a number of advantages and are still the most common method of research used in psychology. They are carried out in carefully controlled environments. Typically experiments take place in a laboratory but it is also quite common for researchers to carry out experiments in more natural settings such as schools and the workplace. Experiments carried out in everyday settings are referred to as 'field experiments'. Although field experiments have a higher ecological validity than laboratory experiments they have some drawbacks as well. For example, it is much more difficult to control extraneous variables in field experiments. Overall, experiments have several advantages over other research methods, largely because great care is taken to ensure that all the variables – independent variables, dependent variables and extraneous variables – are carefully controlled. This means that it is possible to change one variable at a time and look at the effect that it has on the behaviour we are interested in. Experiments follow a standardised procedure. All participants in one condition have the same instructions and perform the same tasks under the same conditions. This means that it is easy for other researchers to replicate the experiment. However, experiments are not without their disadvantages. For example, complex social phenomena such as violence and the effects of divorce on children are extremely difficult to study using an experimental method. There are just too many complex variables involved which means that isolating them and manipulating them under experimental conditions is more or less impossible. It has been argued that laboratory experiments have low ecological validity since many of the tasks that people perform and the conditions under which they perform them, bear little resemblance to everyday life. Related to this is the problem that the experience of participating in a laboratory experiment can often have little relevance for the participants. Pressing a button in response to particular stimuli or learning lists of words is not something that most people can relate to their everyday lives. When people are taking part in an experiment they are usually aware of the general aims of the research. One of the consequences of this is that some participants will behave in a way that they think will please the researcher rather than acting as they would normally. The term 'demand characteristics' is used to refer to cues and clues that participants pick up about what is expected from them in experiments.

INTERVIEWS

There are two types of interview that are frequently used in psychological research, structured interviews and semi-structured interviews. In structured interviews each participant is asked exactly the same questions in the same order. Many of the questions will have a fixed set of responses that the participant has to choose from. This means that the whole procedure is standardised and the data collected can be summarised and analysed quite quickly. It also means that it is possible to interview large numbers of people fairly efficiently. One of the main disadvantages of structured interviews is that any interesting answers or issues raised by the participants cannot be followed up. Semi-structured interviews use a combination of fixed questions, usually to collect background information about the participant, and open-ended questions where participants are given the opportunity to talk about particular topics. The fixed questions might include age, occupation, gender and any other information that is needed for the study. When participants are answering the open-ended questions the researcher is quite likely to ask further questions to get the participants to clarify points or say more about issues that seem to be interesting and relevant to the research. The term 'unstructured interview' is used to refer to interviews where there are no fixed questions at all. In practice most interviews have some fixed questions, even if it is just basic information about age and gender. Semi-structured and unstructured interviews generate huge amounts of data which enables interesting topics to be explored in some depth. They are also capable of dealing with complex social issues such as coping with bereavement, violence and parenting. The complexity of the data collected using semi-structured and unstructured interviews means that the process of analysing it can be very time consuming. However, since the interviews are not standardised it means that replicating the research can be difficult.

PRACTICAL Activity

Think about the psychological research you are familiar with. List three topics that could be investigated using an experimental approach and three topics that could be investigated using interviews. Discuss your topics with your classmates and justify your chosen research methods.

OBSERVATIONAL STUDIES

Observational studies normally take place in a natural setting, although some studies do take place in a laboratory setting where particular situations have been created for the participants. There are two main forms of observational study, participant observation and non-participant observation. In participant observation the researcher becomes part of the group they are studying and takes part in the group's activities as well as recording the behaviour of the group. In non-participant observation the researcher is separate from those being observed and records the behaviour but does not take part in any of the activities. One of the main ethical issues associated with observational studies is consent. Participants should normally be aware that they are taking part in a study and have the right to withdraw at any point. If participants are unaware that they are being studied they are unable to exercise their right to withdraw. However, there is the problem that if participants know they are being observed they may either knowingly or unknowingly change their behaviour One advantage of observational studies is that participants are behaving naturally in an everyday environment. This means that the studies have high ecological validity. Observational studies also tend to focus on 'whole behaviours' rather than breaking behaviour down into small units.

QUESTIONNAIRES

Questionnaires are often used to obtain the views of large numbers of people about specific issues or topics. For example, if we were interested in attitudes towards different types of schools or drug use we could collect information from a large number of people through the use of a questionnaire. The questions on a questionnaire can be either 'closed' or 'open'. Closed questions provide people with a fixed set of responses, whereas open questions allow people to express what they think in their own words. Examples of closed and open questions are given in Figure 12.28. The responses to closed questions are easy to summarise and quantify whereas the responses to open questions are much more difficult to summarise and analyse. This is because each response reflects the unique views of the individual completing the questionnaire. But in some ways the rich detail provided by open questions can provide useful insights into the topics being researched. One problem encountered when using questionnaires, especially when there are a fixed number of responses is 'response set'. What can happen is that people stop reading the questions and just tick the same answer all the way down the page. This is most likely to occur when the questionnaire is several pages long.

Closed questions	Open questions
I would describe myself as someone who goes to the cinema: a) Never b) Occasionally c) Frequently.	Describe how you felt last time you went to the cinema.
I really like going to the cinema: a) Strongly agree b) Agree c) Neutral d) Disagree e) Strongly disagree.	What are the things you really like about your local cinema?

Figure 12.28: Examples of closed and open questions

PRACTICAL Activity

Imagine you have been asked to carry out some research into the leisure activities of young people. You have been asked to find out what leisure activities young people take part in. You are not sure whether to collect data using a questionnaire or to carry out an observational study. Make a list of the advantages and disadvantages of each research method in relation to this particular research question.

CASE STUDY

Case studies are carried out in many different branches of psychology, including clinical psychology, educational psychology, occupational psychology and cognitive psychology. As the name suggests case studies involve an in-depth investigation of a single case. The 'case' is often a person, but in occupational psychology the 'case' could be a factory or a department within a company. One the main characteristics of case studies is that they use several different methods to collect information. For example, in clinical psychology a case study of a person with a mental health problem might use structured and semi-structured interviews, questionnaires and observation as ways of collecting data. Case studies can collect data over a relatively long period of time (a longitudinal study) which means that any changes that occur can be noted. So in clinical psychology it is possible to observe how a person responds to different treatments and different situations. One of the main advantages of using a case study approach is that an in-depth understanding can be developed of an individual case, whether that case is a person, a school or an organisation. Case studies are capable of coping with a

Research method	Advantages	Disadvantages
Experiments	• Have a standardised procedure. which makes replication easy • Can control extraneous variables. • Can establish cause and effect. • Can manipulate variables one at a time and observe the effect. • Accurate measurement of the dependent variable can be achieved.	• Have difficulty coping with complex social phenomena such as divorce and violence. • Have problems with ecological validity. • Often have little relevance for the participants. • Have problems with demand characteristics.
Structured Interviews	• Produce data that is easy to quantify and analyse. • Are standardised. • Have high reliability. • Are easy to replicate. • Produce results that are generalisable.	• Rely on self-report data which can be problematic. • Participants can only give answers to the questions asked. • Important information may be overlooked.
Semi-structured or unstructured Interviews	• Produce large amounts of detailed data. • Have high validity. • Are very flexible which enables interesting issues to be explored in depth. • Are useful when dealing with complex social phenomena such as divorce and violence.	• Are difficult to replicate. • Are difficult and time-consuming to analyse. • Produce data that is difficult to quantify. • Rely on self-report data which may be biased. • Difficult to establish cause and effect relationships.

Observational studies	• Are typically carried out in a natural environment which means that participants are behaving naturally. • Have high ecological validity. • Tend to look at behaviour as a whole rather than breaking it down into smaller units. • Can identify important issues that are worthy of further more detailed investigations.	• Participants' behaviour may change if they know they are being watched. • Demand characteristics may influence the data collected. • Cause and effect may be difficult to establish. • Observer bias can be a problem. • Observing people without their knowledge raises ethical issues.
Questionnaires	• Large amounts of data can be collected very quickly and easily. • Questionnaires using closed questions are highly replicable. • Closed questions are easy to score and quantify. • Open-ended questions can provide rich detail.	• Rely on self-report data which may be biased. • Data may be biased by response rates. • Social desirability effects may influence responses. • Response set may influence responses.
Case studies	• Case studies can be longitudinal which provides information about what happens over a period of time. • Rich qualitative data can be collected. • A single case study can provide the basis for changing existing theories or developing new theories. • Can deal with complex social phenomena.	• Replication is difficult. • In some case studies retrospective data is collected which may be biased. • The approach usually focuses on single cases which can make generalisation a problem. • The views and beliefs of the researcher are more likely to bias the interpretation of the data than in some other research methods.

Figure 12.29: Summary of the strengths and weaknesses of major psychological research methods

range of complex social issues ranging from mental health to teaching methods in a school. However, because the researcher may spend a considerable amount of time with the same individual or organisation there is the danger that their views and interpretation of the data becomes biased in some way. For example, the extent to which the researcher likes or dislikes the person they are studying may influence the way in which they make sense of the data. Clearly, since case studies are based on single unique cases replication and generalisation can be a problem.

EVALUATIVE COMMENT

All research methods have their advantages and disadvantages. As a researcher you need to be aware of these and be able to choose the method (or methods) that is appropriate for the research question you are investigating. Several research methods rely on 'self-report' as a means of collecting data where participants have to provide information about themselves. Self-report measures can be consciously or unconsciously biased in a number of ways. For example, people may answer in a particular way to make a good impression or because they think they are saying what the researcher would like to hear. People's memory for things that have happened in the past or their beliefs about how they will behave in the future can be wildly inaccurate. However, these problems do not mean that self-report measures should be

abandoned. Rather it means that with any research method we should always be aware of its limitations and drawbacks as well as its strengths.

Strengths and weaknesses of quantitative and qualitative methods

Quantitative approaches to research are concerned with measurement and converting any information collected into a numerical form. Whenever we count or sort people into different categories we are engaged in a process of quantification. Quantitative approaches to research are usually associated with the traditional scientific approach to carrying out research. A hypothesis is generated from a theory. The hypothesis is expressed in a way that indicates how the variables will be measured. In other words it is operationalised. The operational hypothesis is tested through the use of an experiment or some other form of empirical data collection. One of the key features of this approach is that it starts with a theory which then gives rise to some predictions, or hypotheses. The alternative hypothesis will be typically stated in terms of differences between conditions or associations between variables. In order to investigate the differences or associations we need to convert our data into numbers that can be used in an appropriate statistical test.

Qualitative research is concerned with the meanings that people attach to events and people's experiences. In qualitative research theories tend to come after the data collection rather than before it. Because of this it is often referred to as 'hypothesis generating' rather than 'hypothesis testing' research (Robson 1993).

PRACTICAL activity

Make a list of the differences between the following activities:

1. Imagine you are a geologist who has been given the job of finding oil in a particular region. Describe what you would do in order to try and find a large underground oilfield. Bear in mind the fact that you will have detailed geological maps available and you know what geographical features are likely to be associated with underground oil.

2. Imagine you are an explorer who has been given the task of finding out more about an area of a South American rain forest. Because it is overgrown it cannot be seen clearly from the air. There are rumours that an ancient civilisation used to inhabit the area, but there is no clear cut evidence that this is the case.

In the activity above the approach taken by the geologist would most likely be similar to that taken by a psychologist conducting quantitative research. She would know what she was looking for and have information about what kinds of features were associated with underground oil. She would form a hypothesis about where oil was likely to be and test this out by drilling. On the other hand, the approach taken by the explorer is likely to be similar to that taken by a psychologist conducting qualitative research. He would gather information about the area by walking through it in different directions, and perhaps by talking to people who lived in the area or had some experience of it. If he found any evidence of a lost civilisation he would document it carefully. This evidence could be used to develop theories about the nature of the ancient civilisation, when it existed, how it came to be there and so on.

There has been considerable debate in psychology about the relative merits of quantitative and qualitative research. It is only relatively recently that qualitative approaches have become generally accepted within mainstream psychology. Perhaps one reason for the resistance to qualitative approaches is that they challenge the traditional 'scientific' approach to doing research. Bryman (1988) suggests that the debate about the relative merits of qualitative and quantitative approaches revolves around two main issues. First there is the practical matter of deciding which approach is best suited to the research question we are faced with. Some research questions are best answered by the use of laboratory-based experiments and questionnaires. Other research questions need data collected using interviews or participant observation in order to be answered. So the issue here is to ensure that the research method chosen is appropriate to the research question being asked. The second issue identified by Bryman (1988) is more fundamental to the whole question of carrying out psychological research. Here quantitative and qualitative methods are seen as separate and distinct approaches to doing research. Quantitative methods are based on a 'scientific' approach which seeks to establish cause and effect by testing specific hypotheses. On the other hand, qualitative approaches are concerned with a search for meaning and understanding. Qualitative approaches are sensitive to the context within which behaviour occurs and also the different meanings that can be placed on thought and behaviour. Both qualitative and quantitative approaches to research have their strengths and weaknesses which are summarised in Figure 12.30.

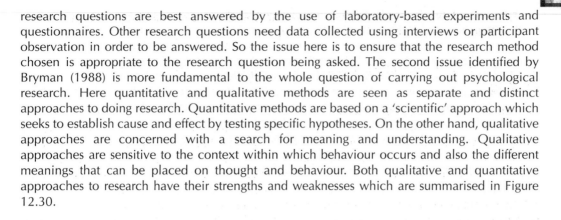

Qualitative research	
Strengths	**Weaknesses**
Can be useful in generating new theories and new perspectives on phenomena.	Is typically difficult to replicate.
Focuses on issues that are meaningful and important to the participants. Can be seen to have high face validity.	Can generate huge amounts of data which can be time consuming and difficult to analyse.
Can be used in situations where it is inappropriate to quantitative methods, for example, counselling and clinical psychology.	It can be difficult to control extraneous variables.
Enables behaviour to be studied in context rather than manipulating in an artificial setting.	It is difficult to establish cause and effect relationships.

Quantitative research	
Strengths	**Weaknesses**
Easy to replicate.	Tends to have low ecological validity.
It is possible to control for the effects of extraneous variables.	It is not very useful in generating new theories
Can identify cause and effect relationships.	Not really appropriate to carry out research in some areas of psychology, for example, counselling or clinical psychology.
Can be used to test predictions made by existing theories.	Often the research has little relevance to the participants.

Figure 12.30: The main strengths and weaknesses of qualitative and quantitative research methods

EVALUATIVE COMMENT
There are a number of contrasts between quantitative and qualitative approaches to research in psychology. Although there are still some psychologists who take an extreme position and

reject one approach completely, it is becoming more common for researchers to acknowledge the strengths and weaknesses of both approaches. For example, our understanding of how students learn has been improved through a combination of both quantitative and qualitative research (Entwistle *et al*. 1971; Entwistle and Marton, 1994). Which approach psychologists adopt depends on a combination of factors including their own personal beliefs and the nature of the topic being investigated. In many situations it is quite likely to be the case that quantitative and qualitative approaches can complement each other. It is quite common for qualitative methods to be used to investigate topics where there is little existing research. The information collected in this way can be used to suggest hypotheses which can be tested using quantitative methods. However, it is becoming increasingly common for qualitative research to follow quantitative research, especially in cases where it has become clear that existing theory is inadequate.

Reliability and validity

The terms 'reliability' and 'validity' are commonly used in psychological research. Reliability refers to the extent to which research findings can be repeated. Imagine you carried out a study on one day and repeated the same study on a different day. If you get the same, or very similar results on both occasions you can say the research is reliable. Reliability is a measure of the extent to which the instrument will give the same reading when measuring the same thing on different occasions. Imagine you bought a thermometer and decided to test its accuracy by checking the reading it gives for boiling water. On Tuesday you place it in a pan of boiling water and it gives a reading of 100°C. You are happy that you have spent your money wisely. But if you repeat the test on Wednesday and you get a reading of 92°C and again on Thursday and it gives a reading of 127°C for boiling water you would not be happy. The thermometer is clearly unreliable.

REFLECTIVE Activity

Amy's parents are a little bit concerned that her reading skills aren't as good as her abilities with numbers. After a discussion with her teacher they arrange for Amy to be seen by a psychologist. The psychologist gives Amy a psychological test that aims to assess her reading ability. After the test the psychologist tells Amy's parents that she scored 75 out of 130 which is about average for girls of her age.

How confident can Amy's parents be that the test score accurately reflects Amy's reading ability? How could we investigate whether or not the test is accurately measuring Amy's reading ability?

If the reading test Amy completed is reliable then if she did it again in a couple of days' time her score should be very close to 75. One of the ways of checking the reliability of the Amy's reading test is called test-retest reliability. This involves giving the test to a group of people on two occasions and looking at the correlation between the scores. If the test is reliable then people's scores should be similar each time they take the test and we would expect there to be a high correlation between the scores. In test-retest reliability we would normally expect the correlation coefficient to be 0.7 or higher.

Reliability is also an issue in observational research where there is more than one observer involved. Typically in observational research observers will be rating or coding different types of behaviour. It is important that all the observers are using the rating scales or codes in the same way. One of the ways in which this can be checked is to set up a situation where the observers rate the same behaviours. Their scores can then be compared using correlation. If there is a strong positive correlation between the scores of the different observers then we can say that there is good inter-rater or inter-observer reliability.

As well as being reliable we also expect research to produce results that can be trusted as being valid. It is possible to identify two forms of validity in psychological research. The first is referred to as 'internal validity'. One aspect of internal validity is concerned with the extent to which any significant effects we have found reflect a real cause–effect relationship. In other words we are concerned with the question, 'Was it really the independent variable affecting dependent variable or were our results due to some extraneous variable?' Another aspect of internal validity is related to the use of psychometric tests such as personality tests and is concerned with the question, 'Is the test measuring what it claims to be measuring?' In other words if we are using a test that claims to measure extraversion is it really measuring extraversion and not some other aspect of an individual's personality? This is often referred to as 'construct validity'. The second form of validity is referred to as 'external validity'. External validity is concerned with the extent to which we can generalise our findings to other settings or other populations. In any research the sample used is taken from a target population. For example, we might identify pupils in our school as the target population, so the question here is, 'Can our results be generalised to pupils at other schools?' Another aspect of external validity is concerned with the location or setting where the research was conducted. For example, if the research was conducted in a laboratory will the findings generalise to 'real world' settings? This aspect of external validity is often referred to as 'ecological validity'. The key questions associated with the different forms of validity are presented in Figure 12.31.

Type of validity	Key questions
Internal validity	• Is the independent variable responsible for the changes in the dependent variable? • Is the test measuring what it claims to be measuring? (Construct validity).
External validity	• Can we generalise our results to other populations? • Can we generalise our results to other settings? (Ecological validity).

Figure 12.31: Internal and external validity

EVALUATIVE COMMENT

One of the common criticisms made of laboratory-based research is that it lacks ecological validity, in other words the findings cannot be generalised to other settings. However, well controlled studies have a high internal validity, which in some ways compensates for the problems with generalisability. If the findings of carefully controlled laboratory based research support a particular theory then we can begin to explore the practical applications of the theory. On the other hand just because research is carried out in a naturalistic setting does not mean that it is ecologically valid. There are many examples of poor research that has been carried out in 'real world' settings. The key for all research is to be clear about how it will establish its reliability and validity.

12.3.4 Ethical considerations

The British Psychological Society (BPS) (2000) has issued a code of ethics for conducting psychological research with human participants. A copy of the *Ethical principles for conducting research with human participants* can be downloaded from their website (http://www.bps.org.uk). It is important that participants in psychological research have confidence in the people who are carrying out the research. If they do not then it is unlikely that the research will be reliable, valid or ethically sound. In general, when designing and carrying out psychological research it is essential that the standpoint of the potential participants is considered at all times. Any potential threats to their psychological well-being, physical health and dignity should be removed. We live in a multi-cultural and multi-ethnic society and it is therefore important to bear in mind the different values and beliefs that are held by participants in any research. The main ethical considerations for psychological research are given below.

CONSENT

A distinction can be made between what has been referred to as 'simple consent' and 'informed consent'. Simple consent refers to situations where the potential participant is given little, if any, information about the study they are being asked to take part in. For example, the researcher might just approach someone and ask if they would like to take part in an experiment. Recruiting participants in this way is considered to be unacceptable. The BPS ethical principles state, 'The investigator should inform the participants of all aspects of the research or intervention that might reasonably be expected to influence willingness to participate'. Informed consent refers to situations where participants are provided with all the information that is relevant to their participation in the research. In other words participants know in advance what they are expected to do before they agree to participate. Research with children is a little more complicated since the law regards people under the age of 16 years as juveniles and unable to make such decisions for themselves. This means that informed consent should be obtained from parents or from people *in loco parentis* such as teachers. Nevertheless, wherever possible informed consent should be obtained from children.

DECEPTION

Deception involves participants being deliberately misled or given incorrect information about the nature of the research. The BPS ethical principles state, 'The withholding of information or the misleading of participants is unacceptable if the participants are typically likely to object or show unease once debriefed'. So providing participants with information *after* they have taken part in a piece of research is not sufficient. Even in situations where the deception might appear to be quite harmless it must be considered very carefully, because the participant's consent is never fully informed. This is clearly a problem in some types of research. For example, if you were interested in how well people can recall information that that they were told specifically to remember. One of the ways in which some psychologists deal with this issue is to ask potential participants if they would mind being temporarily deceived during the experiment. This means that although they do not know the purpose of the study they are consenting to being deceived. Even in cases like this, if there is any doubt about whether participants are likely to object or feel uneasy about the experiment then advice should be sought from an ethics committee. As the BPS ethical principles states, 'Debriefing does not provide a justification for unethical aspects of an investigation.'

DEBRIEFING

Once the data have been collected the researcher should provide the participants with any additional information to make sure they fully understand the nature of the research. It is unacceptable if participants go away from the research feeling anxious or uncomfortable about their role in it. One aspect of the debriefing is that is enables the researcher to discuss with the participants what it was like to take part in the research. This means that the researcher can monitor any unexpected consequences or misunderstandings that participants have of the research. Debriefing also provides the opportunity for participants to ask any questions about the research and clarify any issues they are unsure about. As a general rule participants should be in the same frame of mind as they were at the start of the study.

WITHDRAWAL FROM THE RESEARCH

When participants are being given information about the research they must be told that they can withdraw from it at any point. They can stop at any point during the research. Even if participants have taken part fully in the research they still have the right to withdraw any consent they have previously given. This means that participants have the right to insist that any

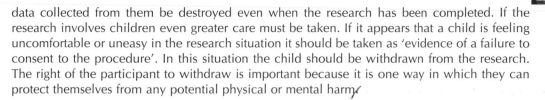

data collected from them be destroyed even when the research has been completed. If the research involves children even greater care must be taken. If it appears that a child is feeling uncomfortable or uneasy in the research situation it should be taken as 'evidence of a failure to consent to the procedure'. In this situation the child should be withdrawn from the research. The right of the participant to withdraw is important because it is one way in which they can protect themselves from any potential physical or mental harm.

CONFIDENTIALITY

Participants must be assured that the information and data they provide in a piece of research is confidential. In any reports or publications that arise from the research it should not be possible to identify any individual. In certain situations participants may agree beforehand to be identified in reports or to allow information about themselves to be given to someone else. But normally participants would expect that any information they provide will be treated confidentially and kept anonymous.

PROTECTION OF PARTICIPANTS

The BPS ethical principles states that 'Investigators have a primary responsibility to protect participants from physical and mental harm during the investigation'. This means that people carrying out research must go to considerable lengths to ensure that they are aware of any potential consequences of their investigation. Participants should feel no worse about themselves after they have taken part in the study than they did before.

ETHICS AND OBSERVATIONAL STUDIES

Normally people being observed as part of a research project will have given their informed consent. Observing people without their consent should only be carried out in situations where those being observed would expect to be observed by strangers. Just because people are in a public space does not mean that it is acceptable to observe them without their consent. Even in public spaces people have a right to privacy if they believe they are unobserved. It is also important to bear in mind that different cultures hold different views about what they find acceptable.

PRACTICAL activity

Imagine you are a psychologist who is interested in finding out the effect that being depressed has on students' ability to remember information. You are interested in this because you have read research that suggests that depression is a common problem among university students. You decide to carry out a laboratory experiment in which you induce depression in one group of students and compare their performance on a memory task with a control group. The technique you are going to use to induce depression is to get the participants to read aloud a set of statements in which they say things about themselves which are likely to make themselves depressed. For example, 'I feel so bad I want to go to sleep and never wake up'.

1. Discuss with your classmates the ethical issues this study raises.

2. How would you overcome the ethical issues you have identified?

EVALUATIVE COMMENT

Conducting research with people raises a number of ethical issues, some of which go beyond considering the welfare of participants. There is always the potential problem that the findings of psychological research can be used in ways that were never intended by the researchers. For example, research which discovered ways of reducing prejudice could be used to manipulate people. One final word of caution, if a person's rights and dignity are infringed then there is the possibility of legal action. In the United Kingdom there has been an increase in legal actions taken by members of the public against professionals, such as medical practitioners. **Research being carried out as part of a GCSE or A Level course is subject to the same ethical principles as any other psychological research.**

See Appendix 3 for information concerning questions that appear in the examination paper. The assessment of knowledge and understanding (AO1) and analysis and evaluation (AO2) assessment objectives is also given in Appendix 1.

12.4 Sample questions

SAMPLE QUESTION 1

A psychologist wanted to find out if emotionally positive words such as 'friendship' and 'relaxed' are recalled better than emotionally negative words such as 'argument' and 'unhappiness'. Previous research has shown that emotionally positive events are more likely to be remembered than emotionally negative events.

The psychologist recruited 10 participants for the experiment. The participants were told that that they would be asked to learn a list of words and then after a short delay they would be asked to recall them.

The participants were given 10 minutes to read and learn a list of 40 words. There were 20 emotionally positive words and 20 emotionally negative words on the list.

The participants then watched a short film for 20 minutes. They were then asked to write down all the words on the list that they could remember.

The psychologist recorded the number of emotionally positive and emotionally negative words that each participant recalled.

A summary of the findings is shown in Figure 12.32 below.

	Mean number of words recalled	
	Emotionally positive words	**Emotionally negative words**
Mean	9.35	5.64
Standard deviation	2.75	2.96

Figure 12.32: Mean number of emotionally negative and emotionally positive words recalled

(a)   State a suitable alternative hypothesis for the study.

   (AO1 = 2)   *(2 marks)*

(b)   The mean scores could be compared using a related t-test. Give *two* criteria that should be considered when deciding to use this test.

   (AO3 = 2)   *(2 marks)*

(c)   The psychologist found a significant difference between the two conditions at the 5 per cent (0.05) level. Explain what is meant by the phrase 'found a significant difference between the two conditions at the 5 percent (0.05) level.

   (AO2 = 2)   *(2 marks)*

(d)   The psychologist used a list of 20 emotionally positive words and 20 emotionally negative words. Identify and discuss two factors that should have been considered when the psychologist was selecting words for the list.

   (AO1 = 2, AO2 = 2)   *(4 marks)*

(e) The psychologist used a related design in this study. Identify and explain *one* advantage of using a related design.

(*AO1 = 1, AO2 = 1*)   (*2 marks*)

(f) A psychologist wanted to compare memory for emotionally negative and emotionally positive events. Identify two ethical considerations should be taken into account when designing such a study. Discuss how they could be addressed by the psychologist to ensure that the study met ethical guidelines.

(*AO1 = 2, AO3 = 4*)   (*6 marks*)

Total AO1 marks = 9 Total AO2 marks = 5 Total AO3 marks = 6 Total marks = 20

QUESTIONS, ANSWERS AND COMMENTS

SAMPLE QUESTION 2

A psychologist was interested in finding out if the mood people are in affects the size of tip they leave at a restaurant. Previous research has shown that people in a good mood are more likely to leave a tip than people in a bad mood.

The psychologist recruited 40 participants for an experiment. The participants were told that they would be asked to read a short story and then they would be asked to complete a questionnaire.

Twenty participants were put into a good mood by reading a funny short story full of jokes. The other 20 were put into a bad mood by reading a short story about a person with cancer.

After reading the short story each participant was taken to another room where they were given the questionnaire to fill in. One of the questions on the questionnaire asked them to imagine they had just had a meal at a restaurant. They were told that food was food was good and the service was excellent. The participants were asked to write down how much money they would leave as a tip for the waitress.

A summary of the findings is shown in Figure 12.33 below.

	Amount of money left as a tip (pounds sterling)	
	Participants put in a good mood	**Participants put in a bad mood**
Mean	2.34	1.17
Standard deviation	0.75	0.68

Figure 12.33: Mean (in pounds sterling) and standard deviations of the amount of money left as a tip by participants

(a) State an alternative null hypothesis for the experiment.

(*AO1 = 2*)   (*2 marks*)

(b) The psychologist wanted to see if there is a significant difference between the mean amount of money left as a tip by the two groups of participants.

(*AO1 = 1, AO2 = 3*)   (*4 marks*)

(i) Name an appropriate statistical test the psychologist could use. Justify your answer.

(*AO1 = 1, AO2 = 3*)   (*4 marks*)

(ii) Should the psychologist use a one- or two-tailed test? Justify your answer.

(*AO1 = 1, AO3 = 1*)   (*2 marks*)

(c)   The psychologist assumed that participants were put in a good or a bad mood depending on the story they had read. Explain *one* way in which the psychologist could have checked on the mood of the participants after they had read the story.

(AO1 = 1, AO2 = 1)   *(2 marks)*

(d)   Identify and outline *one* advantage and *one* disadvantage of using the experimental method in psychology.

(AO1 = 2, AO2 = 2)   *(4 marks)*

(e)   Identify and discuss *two* ethical considerations raised by this study.

(AO1 = 2, AO3 = 4)   *(6 marks)*

Total AO1 marks = 9   Total AO2 marks = 6   Total AO3 marks = 5   Total marks = 20

Answer to 2(a)

People in a good mood will not leave significantly more money as a tip in a restaurant than people in a bad mood.

Comment: The null hypothesis is accurately stated. This answer would be given the full two marks.

Answer to 2(b) (i)

An independent *t*-test could be used. The reason why I would use this test is because the data is parametric. It is measured on an interval scale and the standard deviations are similar. This means that the variance is similar which means that a parametric test can be used. The design of the experiment is an independent measures design.

Comment: This answer has identified the correct test and has given an accurate justification referring to interval data and the fact that the variance or spread of scores in the two groups is similar. It also pointed out that the study used an independent measures design. An answer which suggested that a Mann–Whitney test could be used would also be given marks provided it made an accurate case for treating the data as ordinal rather than interval. The answer above would be given the full 4 marks.

Answer to 2(b) (ii)

I would use a two-tailed test because there are two groups.

Comment: This answer is wrong! The fact that there are two groups has no bearing on whether a one-tailed or two-tailed test is used. What is important is whether or not a directional hypothesis is used. The correct answer is that a one-tailed test should be used because previous research has indicated the direction of the results, namely, people in a good mood are expected to leave more money than people in a bad mood. The answer would be awarded no marks.

Answer to 2(c)

The psychologist could have constructed a Likert scale for the participants to fill in. The scale could cover the range of their mood on a five point scale. This would show what mood the participant was in. An example is shown below:

1	2	3	4	5
Very good mood	Good mood	Neutral	Bad mood	Very bad mood

Comment: The answer has described and explained one way of checking the mood of participants. The use of a diagram is very helpful here since it makes it clear what the candidate is referring to. The answer would be awarded the full two marks

Answer to 2(d)

A disadvantage of the experimental method is that it can lack ecological validity. Ecological validity is a type of external validity and it means that the findings of the study cannot be generalised to other settings. Experiments carried out in a laboratory setting do not always reflect what would happen in a real life setting.

An advantage of experiments is that you can control the independent variables and measure the dependent variable accurately. This means that you can establish cause and effect relationships. In the restaurant experiment we can say that the mood of the participants caused the differences in the amount of money they said they would leave.

Comment: The answer has identified correctly an advantage and a disadvantage of using experiments to carry out research in psychology. The answer uses appropriate terms such as 'ecological validity' and goes on to explain the advantage and disadvantage. A good answer that would be awarded the full 4 marks.

Answer to 2(e)

The two ethical issues raised by the study are consent and the right to withdraw. Some of the participants were put into a bad mood by getting them to read a story about a person with cancer. This might have been upsetting for some of the participants. They were not told about this before they took part in the experiment. This means that they were not able to give their informed consent to participate. The BPS guidelines state that researchers should tell participants about parts of the research that might influence whether or not they take part. Reading a story about a person with cancer might be something that some people did not want to do. It does not say that participants were told that they had the right to withdraw. The BPS guidelines state that participants should be told about their right to withdraw from the study at any time. If the experimenter did not tell the participants about their right to withdraw the experiment was not being carried out in an ethical way.

Comment: This is another good answer which identifies and discusses two ethical issues. The answer also relates the ethical issues to the study. This answer would be awarded the full 6 marks.

The answer to the whole question would score 18 out of 20, making it an excellent answer overall.

Sample questions, answers and comments

Appendix 1
Coursework (A2 Module 6)

All students who have completed the AS course in Psychology, AQA Specification B will have already planned, implemented and written the report of an independently designed practical investigation for the Unit 3 assessment of the course. In the A2 AQA Specification B there is also a requirement that each student should complete a second practical investigation, but there are some key differences between these two investigations and their assessment, as shown in Figure 1.

PYB3 Practical investigation	PYB6 Practical investigation
There are 30 separate skills available for the report – each skill awarded 0/1/2 marks.	There are 60 marks available for 21 skills and the marks are in a banded marking scheme which allocates up to 4 marks for some skills.
The report will be marked by the examination board as if it were an examination script, just like PYB1 and PYB2.	The report is marked by the supervising teacher and the marking at the centre is moderated by the examination board.
Each report must be the independent work of an individual student. Group work is not permitted.	The work can be entirely independent – which allows access to all 60 marks, or students may work in small groups of up to 3 and the marks available will be reduced according to the input of each group member.
Analysis of data is only required to be at the level of descriptive statistics.	If appropriate to the study, analysis of data should be at a level of using inferential statistics tests.

Figure A1: 1 Skill marks for AS PYB3 and A2 PYB6

Clearly, you are expected to build on the coursework skills acquired at AS level, but in addition, you will have to demonstrate a greater breadth and depth of understanding of the processes involved in research in psychology.

There are some very important points to remember when you are thinking about the investigation you will design, implement and submit as a report.

A1.1 The marking scheme

You have to be sure that you understand the marking scheme and are aware of all the skill marks and what each skill criterion means, (you will find information about this in what follows). The investigation you design must address effectively each of the skill marks. It will not matter if your investigation is an original idea or an innovative method, if the report you write does not contain information related to the skills and their definitions, which are given on the marking scheme, then you will not gain many marks for all your hard work. This is exactly the same principle that applies in the examination papers. When a candidate produces an excellent essay, which is **not** a suitable answer to the question set, markers adhere to the marking scheme and will not give the answer top marks because of its lack of relevance to the question set. Similarly, teachers and moderators cannot disregard the marking scheme and give full credit if the evidence for each of the skill marks is not presented in the report. So, if you want to gain top marks you will need to understand the marking scheme and make sure that you design an investigation that will allow you to gain maximum access to all the skill marks.

Skill	Components of skill		Marks of skill
Skill A Design	A1 Relevance of background material A2 Formulation of aim(s) A3 Statement of hypotheses A4 Design decisions A5 Ethical considerations A6 Independence in design	 Total marks Skill A	4 marks 2 marks 2 marks 4 marks 4 marks 3 marks 19 marks
Skill B Implementation	B1 Implementation of design decisions B2 Dealing with participants B3 Independence in conduct of the investigation	 Total marks Skill B	3 marks 3 marks 2 marks 8 marks
Skill C Analysis and interpretation of data	C1 Choice and application of techniques for data analysis C2 Presentation of data C3 Explanation of results C4 Relationship to background material C5 Implications of result C6 Limitations of generalisation C7 Suggestions for improvements C8 Suggestions for further research	 Total marks Skill C	4 marks 4 marks 3 marks 3 marks 2 marks 2 marks 2 marks 2 marks 22 marks
Skill D Communication	D1 Written components D2 Quality of communication D3 Abstract D4 References	 Total marks Skill D	3 marks 3 marks 3 marks 2 marks 11 marks
		Total marks	60 marks

Figure A1.2: PYB6 skills components and marks available for each skill

A1.2 Independence in coursework and working in groups

The marking criteria make it clear that teachers and moderators can only give credit for the *independent work* of each candidate. However, it is possible to work as a member of a small group – up to a maximum of three group members at a time. You will have to decide which approach suits you best. When you work on your own, you will be able to access all of the 60 marks which are available on the marking scheme. When working in a group your teacher will have to adjust each member's individual marks to take into account the fact that you had help from the other members of the group in designing and implementing the investigation. Having already had an opportunity to work independently for PYB3 in your AS course, it is not really difficult to extend this to PYB6, so you will need to think carefully about whether you wish to share some of the marks with others or not.

Remember, it is clearly stated in the specification that it is the candidate who is to:

- identify and define a problem or testable hypothesis
- formulate a plan and,
- outline the procedure to be followed.

Your teacher is expected to provide you with all the information you need about things like how to choose a statistics test and so on. This will help you to make choices. You will only be allowed to proceed with the investigation when your proposal has been approved by your teacher.

A1.3 The Marking criteria for PYB6

The following information will help you to understand exactly how to gain the marks for each of the coursework skills. Remember, you must give the detail in your report since the moderator cannot see what you considered or planned or said to participants. Be as explicit as you can so that the moderator can agree to marks that your teacher awards.

A1.3.1 Skill A: Design

A1 RELEVANCE OF BACKGROUND MATERIAL

Moderators are instructed to look for a variety of sources including both theoretical information and prior research in the background material presented, normally in the Introduction section of the report. Candidates are required to provide critical comments highlighting methodological weaknesses of the theories or research of others and to evaluate the material cited. Comprehensive and focused coverage is expected. A common error here is for Introduction sections to lack focus. This happens when candidates fail to choose material which is relevant, and instead rely on writing all they know or can copy out about an area rather than the construction of a 'coherent scene' for their investigation. Therefore, be sure to write clearly and accurately about relevant theories and research.

A2 FORMULATION OF AIM(S)

This should be very clear from the background cited and specific rather than general. It is often disappointing for moderators to read that many candidates want to 'see if X was right' as the aim for their investigation. A better approach is to focus on the key variables of the study and aim, for example, to see if manipulating A in some specific way does affect B.

A3 STATEMENT OF HYPOTHESES

The null and alternative/experimental hypotheses should be presented as *testable statements* including the word 'significant' if inferential analysis is proposed. The choice of producing a one- or two-tailed alternative hypothesis (H_1 or H_A) must be apparent from the background. If it is incorrectly stated, for example, that the hypothesis under test is 'two-tailed' – moderators will restrict the award for this skill to 1 mark.

There should be coherence in the writing related to these three skills and candidates often make it difficult for moderators to follow their thinking by: criticising a theorist or researcher in their Introduction section highlighting how theory or research had 'moved on'; immediately setting up an aim to 'see if the criticised researcher *was right'*, then in the Discussion section suggesting improvements based on not doing the investigation *they chose to implement!*

A4 DESIGN DECISIONS

The *method* chosen, for example, an experiment, must be explained. Variables – independent variable *(IV)*, dependent variable *(DV)* or *key variables* must be operational and extraneous variables *(EVs)* – extraneous variables which might confound the results, should be identified with their possible effect explained *not* merely listed. Also, any controls suggested to eliminate or minimise the effects of extraneous variables should result in *control* of the extraneous variables identified. Many candidates claim that the possible tiredness or fatigue of the participants is an extraneous variable. There is often then a suggestion that conducting the investigation at the same time of day for all participants will control this. Of course, it will not because people are different and get tired at different times of the day. Other controls related to design must be identified and justified, such as the target population. Think about exactly which group of people you expect to confine your results to. The sampling method must be correct for the description provided and experimental design used, and not named only. Task *construction* should be described and justified and detail of apparatus needed to conduct the study provided. The investigation should include *all* essential controls and be *replicable* for full credit. This is an extremely demanding skill criterion and not many candidates report the detail required for full credit. You will need to be very organised and ensure that materials are in the Appendix of your report, if the moderator is to be sure he or she could replicate your investigation from the information you have provided.

A5 ETHICAL CONSIDERATIONS

This is a design skill and therefore detail is needed of the issues *considered*, their identification in the study and how they are to be controlled. This cannot be a list, or even just the BPS guidelines presented without justification. The key to gaining marks here is for the candidates to explain their considerations. These marks *cannot* be awarded for implementation, or conducting an ethical investigation – that is B2. Moderators need to know what issues were considered, why these were deemed to be important and what was designed to overcome the issues.

In total 7 marks are available for skill A5 and its partner B2 and many candidates are given full credit by their teachers even though there are serious omissions in other parts of the report. You have to remember that the moderator cannot see what you have done and how you did it so the description you provide is very important. Too often, people under the age of 16 years have been used in investigations with little evidence of proper parental consent. In some cases participants were placed in a situation which bordered on the unethical with little consideration of the effects this might have on them. Many participants are told they have the right to withdraw from the study but *only* after they have finished participating. This means participants cannot actually withdraw from taking part in the study but can only withdraw any data collected from their participation. Surprisingly, some candidates seem to think that stating participants have the 'right to counselling' removes any need to consider whether the investigation is ethically sound. If this is said, there needs to be explanation of how participants might exercise this right.

A6 INDEPENDENCE IN DESIGN OF THE INVESTIGATION

Top marks are only available for candidates who devise their own materials/tasks *or* provide a full rationale for their decision to use a published 'measuring tool' such as a psychometric test measuring some aspect of personality. You must be very careful here. There are some tests or scales, such as personality or IQ scales, which are copyright protected. Even if these are published in a textbook it does not mean you can just copy them and use them in your investigation. If tasks are taken from books/websites and merely administered by the candidate, rather than being *based on* published material then full marks are unlikely to be awarded by the moderator. Think of it in this way: if your teacher gave you a word list to use, you could not claim to have designed the task and the same is true if you take something from a book or website. The marking of your report for PYB6 is concerned with giving you credit for the work *you* have done. The word list you devise might not be perfect but you should be able to explain why it is adequate for the task you have devised.

Skill B: Implementation

Moderators are guided by the centre marks for this skill domain, but skills that have been credited in the design domain of Skill A actually have to be carried out with appropriate evidence in the report to support the centre marks so that the moderator is able to agree the marks at your centre with confidence.

B1 IMPLEMENTATION OF DESIGN DECISONS

Full marks are awarded for an appropriate experience of the participants who should be asked to perform a *competently constructed* 'task'. The Procedure description is always scrutinised carefully by moderators so make sure that you have implemented a 'competent task'.

B2 DEALING WITH PARTICIPANTS

Clear evidence of exactly what was requested of participants, for example, *verbatim/spoken* detail, is required and any debriefing presented must actually debrief the participants by explaining the purpose of the task they completed. Moderators will also check for the presence of ethical issues, information given and consent letters if these have received credit as being considered for skill A5.

B3 INDEPENDENCE IN CONDUCT OF THE INVESTIGATION

A check is made of your teachers' marks. These are expected to agree with the candidate's own description of the Procedure.

Skill C: Analysis and interpretation of data

In this section there must be *full detail* and *justification* for full marks to be awarded. Raw data and calculations must be included in the appropriate sections of the report and moderators will at the very least look at these and check probability levels and critical values used by candidates. Of course, there are many statistical packages which can be used for the computation of descriptive and inferential statistics available today and there is no requirement that you should work through the computation of a statistics test by longhand. *But*, you must remember to provide a full *justification* for your chosen techniques for data analysis. Similarly, you must think very carefully about how to present *summaries* of your data. The need is not to produce a journal article but to gain the marks available for the various skills. Results sections must have descriptive summaries – remember to choose measures of central tendency and dispersion, percentages, which are appropriate to the hypothesis(es). In general you should not present raw values in the Results section of your report.

C1 ANALYSIS CHOICES AND APPLICATION

There must be *justification* for the *choice* of descriptive statistics. Choice of inferential statistics test and the decision over whether or not to use an inferential statistical test must be accurately explained. The conditions for a test are not sufficient justification unless they are *applied* to the data obtained. The information must explain, for example, why a Mann-Whitney rather than an unrelated *t*-test was appropriate. 'The data is ordinal' is often an incomplete explanation. Candidates usually mean that their numerical data are not from a safe interval scale. Moderators expect to see parametric conditions discussed, not stated. Levels of measurement (ratio, internal, ordinal and nominal) should be explained and not merely named. Probability level (e.g. 0.05 or 0.01) should be chosen *before* calculation of the test. Many candidates use an inferential statistical test with no explanation of the reasons for their choice. Even if the choice of test seems to be correct, the marking scheme requires *justification* for full marks to be achieved. You must be sure that you understand which test to use to analyse your data and you must explain why the choice of test is appropriate.

C2 DATA PRESENTATION

Tables of results must be in summary form and labelled correctly, including headings. If graphs are necessary, as in correlations, axes and headings must be correct. Inappropriate graphs/tables restrict candidates to 2 marks. For 3 or 4 marks the choices must be *appropriate*. There should be a verbal summary, which moves the reader from descriptive to inferential analysis. Remember to comment on the descriptive statistics you have presented and then explain the reasons for the inferential test chosen. In the Results section you must also present a summary of your inferential analysis, but the calculations should be in the Appendix to your report. A common error is for candidates to arrange their data using variables which are not the key variables under test. Do not suddenly present comparisons of male and female performances or performances of younger or older participants if gender or age were not variables given in the aims or hypotheses of your investigation.

C3 EXPLANATION OF RESULTS

There should be accurate reference to rejection or not of Ho – null hypothesis, and if appropriate, acceptance of Hi – alternative/experimental hypothesis. Additionally original and final significance levels should be given. You must give a full explanation of the results you have obtained, especially if a directional (one- or two- tailed) hypothesis has not been supported. It is important to note that the descriptor for this skill refers to *explanation* in relation to the aims and hypotheses, not *description*.

C4 RELATIONSHIP TO BACKGROUND MATERIAL

The candidate must refer to all relevant material cited in the Introduction and explain the 'fit' with that material for full credit. What you must not do is ignore all the theories or research you cited in the Introduction section of your report and introduce new material (theory and/or research) evidence in the Discussion section. The skill descriptor clearly states, *previously cited background.*

C5 IMPLICATIONS OF RESULTS

This is the 'conclusions' skill and the candidate is expected to draw *conclusions based on* results and not resort to restating results or hypothesis. Many candidates fail to demonstrate that they understand the implications of what they have found from their data and often resort to reiterating past research. This will not gain marks. Make sure that you can explain what you think your results indicate about the particular aspect of human behaviour you have been researching.

C6 LIMITATIONS OF GENERALISATIONS

In this skill the candidate must explain *why* the limitation is a limitation – a list of possible limitations will not suffice. The real issue is that of *generalisation* and you cannot gain credit here for recognition of methodological flaws in your design. Therefore, you must go back to the sample and your target population and explain exactly which group you can relate these results to and what restrictions there may be about generalising to a wider population or range of groups.

C7 SUGGESTION FOR IMPROVEMENTS

The suggestion(s) must be explained showing exactly how they would improve the study and it is at this point candidates need to highlight problems with the design and implementation of their investigation which could then be improved by the suggestion(s) made. Again, information in the form of a list will not be sufficient so you should show that you have a good understanding of how to change your design to improve the reliability and/or validity of your investigation.

C8 SUGGESTION FOR FURTHER RESEARCH

The suggestion(s) must be appropriate and should not be, for example 'do the improved study', which will already be credited in the skills for C7. Information related to a change of a key variable or methodology will be acceptable and you could comment on any patterns you have noticed in your data which might bear further investigation.

SKILL D: COMMUNICATION

The emphasis for this skill domain relates to the need for accurate use of terminology and appropriate format of the report and is based on the AS experience and clarity in the presentation of materials from published sources.

D1 WRITTEN COMPONENTS

Candidates must present the report using the following format developed in the AS course: Title, Introduction, Method, Results, Discussion, References and Appendix. All sections must be clear and organised. If you have missed out a section or included material that should be in the Appendix in the main body of your report, you will not gain full credit for this skill.

D2 QUALITY OF COMMUNICATION

At the top end of the range candidates are expected to have an excellent grasp of terminology, spelling, punctuation and grammar to achieve full marks.

D3 ABSTRACT

The summary must follow the AS requirements below and include the following detail:

- the background theory and research on which the investigation is based – this should be brief

- the aim(s) and hypothesis(es) of this investigation

- detail of the research method used, e.g. experiment/observation and the design chosen, for example 'related' as in repeated measures and 'unrelated' as in independent groups

- the sampling method and sample of participants

- the results of the investigation including appropriate statistical information

- the conclusion drawn about the relationship between results obtained and hypothesis(es)

- how the findings were interpreted, (not how they were displayed).

This may seem to be a great deal of writing, but you should remember that you are merely asked to provide a succinct and accurate summary of your report. You are not doing something that involves new information, just producing a different version of your report.

D4 REFERENCES

All references are required in conventional format. This includes putting them in alphabetical order for full marks. This is a step up from the AS course where the requirement is for one complete reference. You must use the format of *name,* (surname and initial), *date of publication, title, publisher.* For full credit you need to provide a reference for every theory or piece of research you have cited in your report.

Now you should be ready to design your investigation. One extremely important point to bear in mind is that this module is worth 30% of your A2 course and will be converted to a total mark out of a possible 90 UMS marks. You should be spending a comparable amount of your time on this module, making sure that you convince your teacher and the moderator that you understand what you are doing and what you have discovered from conducting the practical work.

Finally, remember, research is what psychology is about – suggesting a theory about behaviour, formulating an appropriate hypothesis and testing the hypothesis to see if it seems to hold true and support the theory. Psychologists want to find out what people actually do and then explain the reasons for the behaviour observed and measured. Conducting an investigation will give you real insight into human behaviour and you should enjoy the opportunity to do this as part of your A level course.

Appendix 2

Questions and assessment objectives in the A2 examinations

A2.1 Question selection and question structure

The questions that appear in the A2 examination papers for Unit 4 Child Development and Options, and Unit 5 Perspectives, Debates and Methods in Psychology are all structured in a certain way. An explanation of the principles and structure of question setting is given below. Note that for Unit 4, only the topic area of Child Development is dealt with. For the option topics of Atypical Behaviour, Contemporary Topics and Health Psychology see the appropriate separate text books.

Unit 4 Child Development

Unit 4 Child Development contains four topic areas: social development, cognitive development, moral development and exceptional development. There are four questions on the examination paper, with one question on each of the aforementioned topic areas. All candidates must answer **at least one** question from these four child development topic areas, and up to a maximum of two of the four questions. Which one or two questions the candidate answers is entirely the candidate's choice. For each of the four topic areas there are two subsections in the specification as follows:

Social Development	attachment and separation
	self and others
Cognitive Development	Piaget's theory of cognitive devleopment
	alternatives to Piaget
Moral Development	Piaget and Kohlberg
	alternatives and evaluation
Exceptional Development	autism and learning difficulties
	gifted children

To ensure that a candidate is prepared for answering a question from any one or two of these four main topic areas each of the two subsections must be fully covered.

Each of the four questions in Child Development is structured in the same way. All questions carry 20 marks and 30 minutes are allocated for answering in the examination. All these four questions conform to the following three-part structure:

- three subsections per question: (a), (b) and (c).

- subsections (a) and (b) can be worth between 2 and 6 marks, making a total of 8 marks.

- subsection (c) will always be worth 12 marks.

Two assessment objectives – AO1 knowledge and understanding, and AO2 analysis and evaluation – are examined in these questions. For more details on assessment objectives see the next section of this Appendix. For each 20-mark question 10 marks are for AO1 knowledge and understanding, and the other 10 marks are for AO2 analysis and evaluation. If we take one of the sample questions from Chapter 1 Social Development, the way in which the marks for AO1 and AO2 are distributed across the three subsections can be seen.

(a   Describe one way in which caregiver–infant interactions might contribute to the formation of attachment.

(AO1 = 3, AO2 = 0).

(b)   Outline and briefly discuss one method used by psychologists to measure attachment.

(AO1= 2, AO2 = 3)

(c)   Discuss at least one function of attachment.

(AO1 = 5, AO2 = 7)

(Total AO1 marks = 10, Total AO2 marks = 10) Total = 20 marks

From this you can see that subsection (c) carrries a majority of AO2 marks. Hence to score a high mark in subsection (c) of any of the four Child Development questions requires candidates to provide a substantial amount of analysis and evaluation. See section (b) later in this Appendix for more information of what is meant by analysis and evaluation.

Unit 5 Perspectives, Debates and Methods in Psychology

Perspectives, Debates and Methods in Psychology contains three main areas of psychology, with topic areas in each as follows:

1. Behaviourist, cognitive, psychoanalytic and humanistic perspectives.

2. Debates in psychology – the scientific approach and debates in psychology

3. Methods in psychology – inferential statistics (statistical inference and statistical tests), and issues in research.

The examination paper, for which two hours is allowed, has two questions for (1) above, two questions for (2) above and a single, compulsory question for (3) above. Each question is worth 20 marks and candidates should spend up to approximately 40 minutes answering each question. Candidates must choose one question from Perspectives, one question from Debates in Psychology and all candidates do the compulsory Methods in Psychology question.

The two questions for Perspectives and the two questions from Debates in psychology are structured in the same way as the Child Development questions. This means that each question is divided into three subsections, with 3 marks for subsection (a), 5 marks for subsection (b) and 12 marks for subsection (c). To ensure that candidates are in a position to answer one of the two questions in the Perspectives part of the examination paper, all four perspectives (behaviourist, cognitive, psychoanalytic and humanistic) need to be covered. In addition, the biological perspective (from the AS part of the specification) should also be covered. Candidates must be prepared to make comparisons between two or more of these perspectives. In the Debates in Psychology part of the examination there is one question on the scientific approach and one on the Debates in Psychology topic areas. Hence, candidates must cover one of these topic areas fully in order to be in a position to answer a question on Debates in Psychology.

The compulsory Methods in Psychology question presents a short description, usually with data, of an empirical study in psychology. The description is followed by a series of short questions about the study. To answer this question candidates must cover *all* elements of the inferential statistics and issues in the research topic area of this unit.

The two questions associated with the Perspectives and Debates in Psychology topic areas of this unit examine AO1 and AO2 assessment objectives in the same way as for Child Development, i.e. 10 marks for AO1 and 10 marks for AO2. Also, as with Child Development, the 12-mark subsection (c) part of each of these four questions carries a majority of marks for AO2 Analysis and evaluation. The Compulsory Methods in psychology question examines all three assessment objectives; AO1, AO2 and AO3 Psychological investigations (see Figure A2.1).

A2.2 Assessment objectives

The term ' assessment objectives' sounds complicated. It is not, but it is very important that you understand the three assessment objectives of the AQA Specification B A2 Psychology. This is because the questions, mark schemes and actual marking of the answers that you write in the examination all directly relate to them. There are three assessment objectives, as shown in Figure A2.1.

Assessment objective	Explanation
AO1 – Knowledge and Understanding	Involves knowledge and understanding of psychological theries, terminology, concepts and methods in psychology. Communication of knowledge and understanding should be clear and effective. A2 candidates should also be able to show knowledge and understanding of psychological principles, perspectives and applications of psychology.
AO2 – Analysis and Evaluation	Involves the analysis and evaluation of psychological theories, concepts, studies and methods in psychology. Communication should be clear and effective. A2 candidates should also be able to analyse and evaluate psychological principles, perspectives and application of psychology.
AO3 – Psychological Investigation	Design, conduct and report psychological investigations choosing from a range of methods, and taking into account issues of reliability, validity and ethics, and collect and draw conclusions from data.

Figure A2.1: Explanation of the three assessment objectives used for A2 level psychology

Assessment objective 3 (AO3) relates solely to Unit 5 and the question on Methods in Psychology. You are referred to Appendix 1 where the assessment of skills related to the practical report write-up that you have to do are dealt with fully.

AO1 Knowledge and understanding: This assessment objective concerns how much you know about and understand theories, concepts, methods and studies in psychology, and how well you are able to offer written descriptions of these different aspects of psychology. Terms used in questions on the examination papers which attempt to assess AO1 knowledge and understanding include the following:

Give	Outline
Identify	State
List or name	Describe

How effectively you can communicate, in written form, your knowledge and understanding of psychology will directly affect the marks you are awarded when answering questions with the above terms in them.

AO2 Analysis and evaluation: This assessment objective concerns how well you are able to use your knowledge and understanding of psychology to provide critical evaluation and application to everyday life. Analysis and evaluation requires you to be able to discuss strengths and weaknesses, advantages and disadvantages, shortcomings and application of theory, concepts and research findings in psychology. The skills of analysis and evaluation are higher level cognitive or intellectual skills which you would have to demonstrate in written form to gain the higher grade at A2 level psychology. Terms used in questions which assess AO2 analysis and evaluation include the following:

Discuss	Distinguish
Evaluate	Explain
Apply	Compare

In each of the 12 chapters of this textbook there are numerous sections headed 'Evaluative Comment'. These evaluative comments are designed to help develop your skills of analysis and evaluation. It is very important that you not only understand the point being made in an evaluative comment, but that you are able to discuss and expand it further. One way to do this is to get together with a group of three or four of your classmates and discuss the evaluative comment further. Another way is to hold a discussion based on an evaluative comment in class. You may also be able to develop the point further by taking up some of the suggestions for further reading given at the end of each chapter.

A2.3 Assessment objectives and examination questions

In each of the specimen questions given at the end of each chapter an indication of marks for AO1 knowledge and understanding, and AO2 analysis and evaluation is provided.

If you look at each subsection of the question you will see that (c) has the most AO2 marks attached to it. As we have seen earlier, key terms like 'discuss', 'explain', 'distinguish', 'evaluate', etc. indicate a requirement for AO2 analysis and evaluation.

In order to understand better what examiners award marks for when marking what you write in examinations you are referred to past examination papers and associated schemes of marking. The schemes of marking are detailed and are what the examiners use to determine the marks to award for what you write in an examination. These are available from the AQA, or visit their website at www.aqa.org.uk.

When studying, revising and preparing for the A2 examinations for Unit 4 and Unit 5 you must ensure that you provide analysis and evaluation (critical discussion) when the terms given above are present in the wording of the question. One of the most common problems with answers to questions, especially to subsection (c), is that too much is written that is descriptive (knowledge and understanding) and not enough that represents critical discussions (analysis and evaluation). It is tempting to write down all that you know about the topic under examination. However, lots of description will not score any of the marks for AO2 in the question!

For the 12 mark sub-section (c) questions in both Unit 4 and Unit 5 the following guidelines generally apply:

- 'Describe and discuss' indicates that there are 5, 6 or 7 marks for AO1 knowledge and understanding, and 7, 6 or 5 marks for AO2 analysis and evaluation.

- 'Discuss' indicates slightly fewer marks for AO1 (4 marks) and more marks for AO2 (8 marks).

A2.4 Recommendations

The above explanation of how questions are set, structured and assessed in Unit 4 and Unit 5 at A2 level is important to understand. Read this Appendix carefully and ask your teacher if there are bits that you do not clearly understand. Remember that success at examinations is about studying hard, good examination preparation and being well-organised. Success is not, and never should be, about luck, so prepare well and you should do well in your examinations.

Appendix 3
Statistical tables for Chapter 12 - research methods

	One-tailed		Two-tailed	
N	.05	.01	.05	.01
5	0	–	–	–
6	0	0	–	–
7	0	0	0	–
8	1	0	0	0
9	1	1	0	0
10	1	1	0	0
11	2	1	1	0
12	2	2	1	1
13	3	2	1	1
14	3	2	2	1
15	3	3	2	2
16	4	3	2	2
17	4	4	3	2
18	5	4	3	3
19	5	4	4	3
20	5	5	4	3
25	7	7	6	5
30	10	9	8	7
35	12	11	10	9

Figure A3.1: Critical values in the binomial sign test

Calculated S must be equal to or less than the table (critical) value for significance at the level shown.

Source: Clegg, F. (1982) *Simple statistics*. Cambridge University Press, Cambridge.

	One-tailed		Two-tailed	
N	.05	.01	.05	.01
5	1	–	–	–
6	2	–	1	–
7	4	0	2	–
8	6	2	4	0
9	8	3	6	2
10	11	5	8	3
11	14	7	11	5
12	17	10	14	7
13	21	13	17	10
14	26	16	21	13
15	30	20	25	16
16	36	24	30	19
17	41	28	35	23
18	47	33	40	28
19	54	38	46	32
20	60	43	52	37
21	68	49	59	43
22	75	56	66	49
23	83	62	73	55
24	92	69	81	61
25	101	77	90	68
26	110	85	98	76
27	120	93	107	84
28	130	102	117	92
29	141	111	127	100
30	152	120	137	109

Figure A3.2: Critical values in the Wilcoxon Test

Calculated T must be equal to or less than the table (critical) value for significance at the level shown.

Source: Wilcoxon, F. and Wilcox, R. A. (1964). Some rapid approximate statistical procedures, American Cyanamid Company, New York

	N1																			
N2	1	2	3	4	5	6	7	8	9	10	11	12	13	14	15	16	17	18	19	20
1	–	–	–	–	–	–	–	–	–	–	–	–	–	–	–	–	–	–	–	–
2	–	–	–	–	–	–	–	–	–	–	–	–	0	0	0	0	0	0	1	1
3	–	–	–	–	–	–	0	0	1	1	1	2	2	2	3	3	4	4	4	5
4	–	–	–	–	0	1	1	2	3	3	4	5	5	6	7	7	8	9	9	10
5	–	–	–	0	1	2	3	4	5	6	7	8	9	10	11	12	13	14	15	16
6	–	–	–	1	2	3	4	6	7	8	9	11	12	13	15	16	18	19	20	22
7	–	–	0	1	3	4	6	7	9	11	12	14	16	17	19	21	23	24	26	28
8	–	–	0	2	4	6	7	9	11	13	15	17	20	22	24	26	28	30	32	34
9	–	–	1	3	5	7	9	11	14	16	18	21	23	26	28	31	33	36	38	40
10	–	–	1	3	6	8	11	13	16	19	22	24	27	30	33	36	38	41	44	47
11	–	–	1	4	7	9	12	15	18	22	25	28	31	34	37	41	44	47	50	53
12	–	–	2	5	8	11	14	17	21	24	28	31	35	38	42	46	49	53	56	60
13	–	0	2	5	9	12	16	20	23	27	31	35	39	43	47	51	55	59	63	67
14	–	0	2	6	10	13	17	22	26	30	34	38	43	47	51	56	60	65	69	73
15	–	0	3	7	11	15	19	24	28	33	37	42	47	51	56	61	66	70	75	80
16	–	0	3	7	12	16	21	26	31	36	41	46	51	56	61	66	71	76	82	87
17	–	0	4	8	13	18	23	18	33	38	44	49	55	60	66	71	77	82	88	93
18	–	0	4	9	14	19	24	30	36	41	47	53	59	65	70	76	82	88	94	100
19	–	1	4	9	15	20	26	32	38	44	50	56	63	69	75	82	88	94	101	107
20	–	1	5	10	16	22	28	34	40	47	53	60	67	73	80	87	93	100	107	114

Figure A3.3(A): Critical values of Mann-Whitney U for one-tailed test at .01

For any N1 and N2 the calculated value of U is significant if it is equal to or less than the table (critical value)

N1																				
N2	1	2	3	4	5	6	7	8	9	10	11	12	13	14	15	16	17	18	19	20
1	–	–	–	–	–	–	–	–	–	–	–	–	–	–	–	–	–	–	0	0
2	–	–	–	–	0	0	0	1	1	1	1	2	2	2	3	3	3	4	4	4
3	–	–	0	0	1	2	2	3	3	4	5	5	6	7	7	8	9	9	10	11
4	–	–	0	1	2	3	4	5	6	7	8	9	10	11	12	14	15	16	17	18
5	–	0	1	2	4	5	6	8	9	11	12	13	15	16	18	19	20	22	23	25
6	–	0	2	3	5	7	8	10	12	14	16	17	19	21	23	25	26	28	30	32
7	–	0	2	4	6	8	11	13	15	17	19	21	24	26	28	30	33	35	37	39
8	–	1	3	5	8	10	13	15	18	20	23	26	28	31	33	36	39	41	44	47
9	–	1	3	6	9	12	15	18	21	24	27	30	33	36	39	42	45	48	51	54
10	–	1	4	7	11	14	17	20	24	27	31	34	37	41	44	48	51	55	58	62
11	–	1	5	8	12	16	19	23	27	31	34	38	42	46	50	54	57	61	65	69
12	–	2	5	9	13	17	21	26	30	34	38	42	47	51	55	60	64	68	72	77
13	–	2	6	10	15	19	24	28	33	37	42	47	51	56	61	65	70	75	80	84
14	–	2	7	11	16	21	26	31	36	41	46	51	56	61	66	71	77	82	87	92
15	–	3	7	12	18	23	28	33	39	44	50	55	61	66	72	77	83	88	94	100
16	–	3	8	14	19	25	30	36	42	48	54	60	65	71	77	83	89	95	101	107
17	–	3	9	15	20	26	33	39	45	51	57	64	70	77	83	89	96	102	109	115
18	–	4	9	16	22	28	35	41	48	55	61	68	75	82	88	95	102	109	116	123
19	0	4	10	17	23	30	37	44	51	58	65	72	80	87	94	101	109	116	123	130
20	0	4	11	18	25	32	39	47	54	62	69	77	84	92	100	107	115	123	130	138

Figure A3.3(B): Critical values of Mann-Whitney U for one-tailed test at .05

For any N1 and N2 the calculated value of U is significant if it is equal to or less than the table (critical value)

	N1																			
N2	1	2	3	4	5	6	7	8	9	10	11	12	13	14	15	16	17	18	19	20
1	–	–	–	–	–	–	–	–	–	–	–	–	–	–	–	–	–	–	–	–
2	–	–	–	–	–	–	–	–	–	–	–	–	–	–	–	–	–	–	0	0
3	–	–	–	–	–	–	–	–	0	0	0	1	1	1	2	2	2	2	3	3
4	–	–	–	–	–	0	0	1	1	2	2	3	3	4	5	5	6	6	7	8
5	–	–	–	–	0	1	1	2	3	4	5	6	7	7	8	9	10	11	12	13
6	–	–	–	0	1	2	3	4	5	6	7	9	10	11	12	13	15	16	17	18
7	–	–	–	0	1	3	4	6	7	9	10	12	13	15	16	18	19	21	22	24
8	–	–	–	1	2	4	6	7	9	11	13	15	17	18	20	22	24	26	28	30
9	–	–	0	1	3	5	7	9	11	13	16	18	20	22	24	27	29	31	33	36
10	–	–	0	2	4	6	9	11	13	16	18	21	24	26	29	31	34	37	39	42
11	–	–	0	2	5	7	10	13	16	18	21	24	27	30	33	36	39	42	45	48
12	–	–	1	3	6	9	12	15	18	21	24	27	31	34	37	41	44	47	51	54
13	–	–	1	3	7	10	13	17	20	24	27	31	34	38	42	45	49	53	56	60
14	–	–	1	4	7	11	15	18	22	26	30	34	38	42	46	50	54	58	63	67
15	–	–	2	5	8	12	16	20	24	29	33	37	42	46	51	55	60	64	69	73
16	–	–	2	5	9	13	18	22	27	31	36	41	45	50	55	60	65	70	74	79
17	–	–	2	6	10	15	19	24	29	34	39	44	49	54	60	65	70	75	81	86
18	–	–	2	6	11	16	21	26	31	37	42	47	53	58	64	70	75	81	87	92
19	–	0	3	7	12	17	22	28	33	39	45	51	56	63	69	74	81	87	93	99
20	–	0	3	8	13	18	24	30	36	42	48	54	60	67	73	79	86	92	99	105

Figure A3.3(C): Critical values of Mann-Whitney U for two-tailed test at .01

For any N1 and N2 the calculated value of U is significant if it is equal to or less than the table (critical value)

N1																			
N2	1	2	3	4	5	6	7	8	9	10	11	12	13	14	15	16	17	18	19	20
1	–	–	–	–	–	–	–	–	–	–	–	–	–	–	–	–	–	–	–	–
2	–	–	–	–	–	–	–	0	0	0	0	1	1	1	1	1	2	2	2	2
3	–	–	–	–	0	1	1	2	2	3	3	4	4	5	5	6	6	7	7	8
4	–	–	–	0	1	2	3	4	4	5	6	7	8	9	10	11	11	12	13	13
5	–	–	0	1	2	3	5	6	7	8	9	11	12	13	14	15	17	18	19	20
6	–	–	1	2	3	5	6	8	10	11	13	14	16	17	19	21	22	24	25	27
7	–	–	1	3	5	6	8	10	12	14	16	18	20	22	24	26	28	30	32	34
8	–	0	2	4	6	8	10	13	15	17	19	22	24	26	29	31	34	36	38	41
9	–	0	2	4	7	10	12	15	17	20	23	26	28	31	34	37	39	42	45	48
10	–	0	3	5	8	11	14	17	20	23	26	29	33	36	39	42	45	48	52	55
11	–	0	3	6	9	13	16	19	23	26	30	33	37	40	44	47	51	55	58	62
12	–	1	4	7	11	14	18	22	26	29	33	37	41	45	49	53	57	61	65	69
13	–	1	4	8	12	16	20	24	28	33	37	41	45	50	54	59	63	67	72	76
14	–	1	5	9	13	17	22	26	31	36	40	45	50	55	59	64	67	74	78	83
15	–	1	5	10	14	19	24	29	34	39	44	49	54	59	64	70	75	80	85	90
16	–	1	6	11	15	21	26	31	37	42	47	53	59	64	70	75	81	86	92	98
17	–	2	6	11	17	22	28	34	39	45	51	57	63	67	75	81	87	93	99	105
18	–	2	7	12	18	24	30	36	42	48	55	61	67	74	80	86	93	99	106	112
19	–	2	7	13	19	25	32	38	45	52	58	65	72	78	85	92	99	106	113	119
20	–	2	8	13	20	27	34	41	48	55	62	69	76	83	90	98	105	112	119	127

Figure A3.3(D): Critical values of Mann-Whitney U for two-tailed test at .05

For any N1 and N2 the calculated value of U is significant if it is equal to or less than the table (critical value)

Source: Runyon, R. P. and Haber, A. (1976) *Fundamentals of behavioral statistics*, Addison Wesle, Reading, MA.

	One-tailed		Two-tailed	
df	.05	.01	.05	.01
1	6.314	31.821	12.706	63.657
2	2.920	6.965	4.303	9.925
3	2.353	4.541	3.182	5.841
4	2.132	30747	2.776	4.604
5	2.015	3.365	2.571	4.032
6	1.943	3.143	2.447	3.707
7	1.895	2.998	2.365	3.499
8	1.860	2.896	2.306	3.355
9	1.833	2.821	2.262	3.250
10	1.812	2.764	2.228	3.169
11	1.796	2.718	2.201	3.106
12	1.782	2.681	2.179	3.055
13	1.771	2.650	2.160	3.012
14	1.761	2.624	2.145	2.977
15	1.753	2.602	2.131	2.947
16	1.746	2.583	2.120	2.921
17	1.740	2.567	2.110	2.898
18	1.734	2.552	2.101	2.878
19	1.729	2.539	2.093	2.861
20	1.725	2.528	2.086	2.845
21	1.721	2.518	2.080	2.831
22	1.717	2.508	2.074	2.819
23	1.714	2.500	2.069	2.807
24	1.711	2.492	2.064	2.797
25	1.708	2.485	2.060	2.787
26	1.706	2.479	2.056	2.779
27	1.703	2.473	2.052	2.771
28	1.701	2.467	2.048	2.763
29	1.699	2.462	2.045	2.756
30	1.697	2.457	2.042	2.750

Figure A3.4: Critical values in the t-test

Calculated value for t is significant if it is equal to or larger than the table (critical) value

Source: Lindley, D. V., and Miller, J. C. P. (1973) *Cambridge elementary statistical tables*, Cambridge University Press, Cambridge.

	One-tailed		Two-tailed	
N	.05	.01	.05	.01
5	.900	1.000	1.000	–
6	.829	.943	.886	1.000
7	.714	.893	.786	.929
8	.643	.833	.738	.881
9	.600	.783	.683	.833
10	.564	.746	.648	.794
12	.506	.712	.591	.777
14	.456	.645	.544	.715
16	.425	.601	.506	.665
18	.399	.564	.475	.625
20	.377	.534	.450	.591
22	.359	.508	.428	.562
24	.343	.485	.409	.537
26	.329	.465	.392	.515
28	.317	.448	.377	.496
30	.306	.432	.364	.478

Figure A3.5: Critical values of Spearman's rho

The calculated value of rho is significant if it is equal to or larger than the table (critical) value

Source: Olds, E. G. (1994) The 5% significance levels for sums of squares of rank differences and a correction, *Annals of Mathematical Statistics*, 20, The Institute of Mathematical Statistics

	One tailed		Two tailed	
df = N–2	.05	.01	.05	.01
1	.9877	.9995	.9969	.9999
2	.9000	.9800	.9500	.9900
3	.8054	.9343	.8783	.9587
4	.7293	.8822	.8114	.9172
5	.6694	.8329	.7545	.8745
6	.6215	.7877	.7067	.8343
7	.5822	.7498	.6664	.7977
8	.5494	.7155	.6319	.7646
9	.5214	.6851	.6021	.7348
10	.4973	.6581	.5760	.7079
11	.4762	.6339	.5529	.6835
12	.4575	.6120	.5324	.6614
13	.4409	.5923	.5139	.6411
14	.4259	.5742	.4973	.6226
15	.4124	.5577	.4821	.6055
16	.4000	.5425	.4683	.5897
17	.3887	.5285	.4555	.5751
18	.3783	.5155	.4438	.5614
19	.3687	.5034	.4329	.5487
20	.3598	.4921	.4227	.5368
25	.3233	.4451	.3809	.4869
30	.2960	.4093	.3494	.4487
35	.2746	.3810	.3246	.4182
40	.2573	.3578	.3044	.3932
45	.2428	.3384	.2875	.3721
50	.2306	.3218	.2732	.3541
60	.2108	.2948	.2500	.3248
70	.1954	.2737	.2319	.3017
80	.1829	.2565	.2172	.2830
90	.1726	.2422	.2050	.2673
100	.1638	.2301	.1946	.2501

Figure A3.6: Critical values of Pearson's product moment correlation coefficient
The calculated value of r is significant if it is equal to or larger than the table (critical) value

Source: Fisher, R. A. & Yates, F. (1974) *Statistical tables for biological and agricultural research*, Longman Group Ltd, London.

df	.05	.01
1	3.84	6.64
2	5.99	9.21
3	7.82	11.34
4	9.49	13.28
5	11.07	15.09
6	12.59	16.81
7	14.07	18.48
8	15.51	20.09
9	16.92	21.67
10	18.31	23.21

Figure A3.7: Critical values of chi squared

The calculated value of chi squared is significant if it is equal to or larger than the table (critical) value

Source: Lindley, D. V., & Miller, J. C. P. (1973) *Cambridge elementary statistical tables,* Cambridge University Press, Cambridge.

Glossary

Adult attachment interview An interview procedure developed by Mary Main to assess the type of attachment relationship a parent had as a child. Main suggested that understanding of attachment relationships based on one's own childhood experiences would affect the type of attachment relationship a parent had with his or her own children.

Acceleration The speeding up of a child's progress through school, either by extra tuition or by moving the child up into a higher class.

Accommodation Modifying an existing schema to fit a new situation. Leads to development of additional schemas.

Actualisation See *self-actualisation*.

Adaptation The child's construction of set of schemas which accurately match his/her environment.

Affectionless psychopathy An inability to have feelings for another person.

Altruistic behaviour Prosocial behaviour carried out even when there is no obvious benefit to the actor.

Anal personality In Freudian theory results from fixation at the anal stage and consists of the traits of orderliness, miserliness, and obstinacy.

Anal stage is a psychosexual stage of development in Freudian theory. It occurs during the second year of life when the child gains control of anal muscles and is being toilet trained. Fixation at this stage may lead to the **anal personality**.

Animism The child's belief that inanimate objects have feelings and intentions.

Applied behavioural analysis (ABA) A rigorous and highly structured therapy for autism based on a behaviour modification and using a system of reinforcement.

Artificial intelligence is concerned with getting computers to perform tasks that are regarded as requiring intelligence; there is not necessarily an attempt to simulate human intelligence.

Assimilation Cognitively dealing with a new situation by applying an appropriate schema to it. An infant might assimilate a graspable object by bashing it on a table.

Attachment An affectional tie or bond between two people, usually characterised by attachment behaviours such as proximity seeking and separation distress.

Attachment figure The preferred object of attachment, for example, a parent would most usually be an attachment figure for a young child.

Autism A mental disorder resulting in wide ranging and severe deficits including problems in social interaction, language and communication and repetitive or stereotyped behaviours.

Autistic savant A person with autism who displays remarkable ability or skill in a particular area, for example, the ability to produce detailed drawings from memory.

Autonomous stage See *moral relativism*.

Aversion therapy A form of behaviour therapy which involves pairing an unpleasant stimulus with an undesired behaviour.

Behaviour shaping The use of reinforcement to get an individual to perform a complex activity. In behaviour shaping, reinforcement is given for successive approximations to the desired behaviour until a long sequence of behaviours is performed for a single reward.

Behaviourist perspective An approach to psychology that states that behaviour is learnt through association between response and consequence.

Biological determinism The view that all behaviour and thought is determined by the action of the brain and nervous system.

Categorical self The ability to place oneself and others in categories, for example, according to age and gender.

Central coherence The tendency to process information for its general meaning or gist rather than process the specific individual elements.

Centration The child's tendency to deal only with one aspect of a situation at a time. The pre-operational child finds it difficult to take into account the effect of two factors.

Chunking A memory technique that involves the combination of several small units of information into fewer larger units, thereby increasing the amount of information that can be retained in short-term memory.

Class inclusion An understanding that some classes of objects include other classes of objects. For example the class of 'flowers' includes the class of 'roses'. A class inclusion test might involve showing a child some pictures of flowers and asking, 'Are there more roses or more flowers?'

Classical conditioning is a form of learning in which a stimulus (the CS) acquires the ability to cause a behavioural response originally evoked by another stimulus (the UCS).

Cognitive maps are mental representations that an organism has of features of a physical area.

Cognitive neuropsychology is a relatively new area of psychology where the workings of the brain are linked to cognitive processes. Often people with brain damage are used to understand which cognitive processes are affected and impaired.

Cognitive perspective An approach to psychology that emphasises the role of thinking and understanding in behaviour.

Cognitive processes are mental processes, which we may or may not be aware of, that are involved with thought, perception, memory and attention.

Cold parenting hypothesis A theory of autism according to which the disorder is due to cold and unresponsive parenting. See also the *refrigerator mother*.

Communication theory A theory of attachment suggesting infants and young children attach to those with whom they are best able to communicate.

Comparative psychology The field of psychology that involves the study of non-human species and extrapolation or generalisation of the findings to human behaviour.

Compenential intelligence Identified by Sternberg (1988) as the type of intelligence measured by an IQ test.

Compensation a *mental operation* which involves understanding that a transformation of the dimension might cause a balancing transformation in another dimension. For example, if a rubber band is streached it will become thinner.

Concordance A mathematical estimation of the likelihood that a behaviour trait or characteristic is inherited. Concordance is expressed as a percentage and is based on correlation.

Concrete operations One of Piaget's stages of cognitive development, in which the child is first able to perform logical operations on real (concrete) objects and situations.

Conditioning involves learning associations between events that occur in the environment.

Connectionist network is a parallel processing model of cognitive processes which in its simplest form has input units, hidden units and output units.

Conscience Part of the *superego* which tends to inhibit wrong actions, and leads to guilt following wrongdoing.

Conscious in Freudian theory is that which you are aware of at any time.

Consciousness is the awareness a person has at any time of stimuli from the environment, body or state of mind.

Conservation The ability to understand that redistributing material does not affect its mass, number or volume.

Conservation tests Simple tasks Piaget devised to find out whether children could perform the *operation* of *conservation*. For example the 'three beakers test'.

Constructivism A view of cognitive development which suggests that the child builds up a mental model of the world and the processes which happen.

Contextual intelligence Identified by Sternberg (1988) as the type of intelligence required to integrate the processing of information with demands of the situation.

Continuous development The view that child development happens gradually and continuously and not in a series of distinct stages. See *Stage Theory*.

Critical period A period of time after birth during which a specific behaviour or ability is acquired or develops.

Cross-sex play Play with a member of the opposite sex.

De-centring The child's ability to take more than one factor into account when judging situations. Achieved in the stage of concrete operations according to Piaget.

Defence mechanisms in Freudian psychoanalysis operate at an unconscious level by the ego. Defence mechanisms such as repression, sublimation, reaction formation, help deal with inner conflicts between the id, ego and superego.

Deficiency needs in Maslow's hierarchy of needs are those of physiological needs, safety needs, belongingness and love needs, and self-esteem needs. See also *Growth needs*.

Demand characteristics where the participants in an experiment try to guess what the experiment is about and may behave to please (or displease) the psychologists. Results in bias and error in psychological research.

Deprivation Losing something one has once had: in relation to attachment, the loss of an attachment figure, either short-term or long-term.

Determinism The view that human behaviour and thought is determined by forces outside of the person, in the environment, and beyond the person's control. See also 'soft' and 'hard' determinism.

Discovery learning Learning things by discovering them for yourself as a result of active exploration. Piaget assumed that children learn through active self-discovery during play rather than by instruction.

Disequilibrium A situation in which a new experience cannot be easily assimilated using existing schemas. Leads to accommodation.

Dizygotic twins Twins from two separately fertilised eggs who have the same genetic similarity as ordinary siblings (50%). Dizygotic twins are sometimes known as fraternal or non-identical twins.

Double blind study A study where the researcher administering the test or procedure is unaware of the aim of the study. Using a double blind technique means that the results are less likely to be affected by demand characteristics and researcher expectations.

Double-standard Socially-accepted rules which are different for different social groups e.g. for men and women.

Dualistic is to do with the mind-body debate whereby a dualistic view states that the mind and body are two separate things, possessing different qualities or properties. *Note* 'mind-brain identity' is the view that the mind is the same or identical to the brain and no more than this.

Dyscalculia A learning difficulty affecting mathematical performance.

Dysgraphia A disorder of writing possibly involving a combination of cognitive and perceptual motor deficits.

Dyslexia A learning difficulty affecting reading ability.

Dyseidetic dyslexia A type of dyslexia where reading involves laboriously sounding out both familiar and unfamiliar words.

Dysphonic dyslexia A type of dyslexia where some whole words can be recognised, but component sounds of unfamililiar words cannot be analysed.

Dyspraxia A learning difficulty affecting motor co-ordination.

Echolalia Repetition of speech sounds or syllables characteristic of infants in the pre-linguistic stage, but also seen in the speech of people with autism.

Ego in Freud's structure of the personality operates according to the reality principle at both conscious and unconscious levels. The ego employs defence mechanisms to help deal with internal conflicts.

Egocentrism The inability to perceive the world or other people from the point of view of others. According to Piaget egocentrism is characteristic of children under the age of 7 years.

Ego-ideal Part of the *superego* which tends to lead to good actions.

Electra complex Experienced by girls during the *phallic stage*. A conflict between sexual desire for father and fear of punishment by mother.

Empirical approach Obtaining knowledge, information and data through observation and through our senses.

Empiricist A philosophical position which claims that all learning and human characteristics comes from experience. Represents the nurture side of the nature/nurture debate.

Enactive mode One of Bruner's modes of representation, in which an object or situation is represented by means of actions – i.e. body movements.

Endorphins Opium like substances released when the body is stressed or aroused.

Enrichment Provision of extra activities and opportunities for learning and stimulation.

Environmental determinism is the view most associated with the radical behaviourism of Watson and Skinner stating that all behaviour is under the control of environmental forces of reward and punishment.

Environment or nurture in the nature-nurture debate is the view that all learning, behaviour and personality comes from environmental experiences.

Environmentalism is the view that all behaviour of an organism results solely from experience, with heredity playing no role.

Evolutionary psychology is the study of the evolutionery origin of human behaviour patterns, for example, sexual behaviour, jelously and human emotions.

Existential philosophy asks fundamental questions about what it is to be human and what is the meaning of life. Influenced the development of humanistic psychology.

Existential self The understanding that the self exists as a separate entity, with a past and a future.

Experimenter bias This occurs when the wishes, attitudes, and beliefs of the psychologist as an experimenter interfere with the participants in an experiment to produce bias.

Experiential intelligence Identified by Sternberg (1988) as the type of intelligence necessary for automatic processing and dealing with novel situations.

Expiatory punishment The view that a person has to pay for wrongdoing, possibly by harsh and arbitrary punishment.

Extinction of a behaviour occurs when the behaviour ceases to be emitted or repeated.

Folk psychology the beliefs, values, attitudes and morals that are held by a culture or sub-culture.

Formal operations One of Piaget's stages of cognitive development, in which the child is capable of abstract thought and able to perform logical operations on hypothetical objects and situations.

Fragile-X syndrome A genetic disorder caused by a defective gene in the X chromosome which results in mental retardation.

Free will is a central principle of humanistic psychology. It is to do with seeing a person as having free choice over what to do. Also related to the idea of personal responsibility.

Fully functioning person was put forward by Carl Rogers and is to do with a person achieving goals, ambitions and life aspirations. People who are able to self-actualise.

Gender concept The ability to label one's own and others' gender correctly.

Genital stage starts at puberty and in Freudian theory represents appropriate direction of the sexual instinct to heterosexual pleasure and intercourse.

Genome scanning A technique involving the analysis of DNA from an individual to allow for identification of individual genes at specific gene locations on chromosomes.

Gestalt psychology A school of psychology holding the view that humans are best studied as organised, structured wholes and not analysed into numerous component parts. See also *holism*.

"Good boy/girl" orientation A stage in Kohlberg's theory of moral development in which good behaviour is seen as what gains approval from others.

Growth needs in Maslow's humanistic psychology are the needs for self-actualisation. Self-actualisation is to do with personal growth and realisation of potential.

Hard determinism. An extreme determinism viewpoint in which all behaviour and thought is regarded as caused by forces outside of the person's control.

Hedonism The belief that what is pleasurable is morally good.

Hedonistic behaviour Behaviour directed towards one's own pleasure.

Heredity The traits, predispositions and characteristics inherited from a person's parents and ancestors. Represents the nature side of the nature/nurture debate.

Heritability coefficient. A number between 0 and 1.0 representing the extent to which a human characteristic is genetic in origin. A value of 1.0 means entirely genetic, a value of zero that genetics play no role at all.

Heteronomous stage See *Moral realism*.

Holism. The view that the whole person has to be studied rather than component parts or smaller aspects, a view subscribed to by humanistic and Gestalt psychologists.

Horizontal decalage. A situation in which a child shows cognitive abilities characteristic of more than one stage, for example can conserve number but not volume.

Hot-housing The process of exposing a child to early enrichment and intensive encouragement with the specific aim of developing skills or abilities. Hot-housing normally involves provision of opportunity for prolonged and intensive practice of skills.

Humanism See humanistic psychology.

Humanistic psychology Known as the 'third force' in psychology; adopts the principles of free will and holism to focus on human subjective perceptions and experience. Developed by Carl Rogers and Abraham Maslow.

Iconic mode One of Bruner's modes of representation – representing an object or situation by means of mental pictures.

Id is the most primitive, unconscious part of the mind in Freudian theory of personality. It operates according to the pleasure principle. The sex (life) and aggressive (death) instincts originate in the id.

Ideal self The kind of person we would like to be.

Identification Adopting a range of attitudes, values and behaviours from a role model, especially a parent.

Idiographic approach An approach in psychology which recognises the uniqueness of the individual in terms of experiences, feelings, motivations, etc. Often employs qualitative methods.

Immanent justice The belief that unpleasant events which happen by chance after wrongdoing are actually punishments.

Imprinting Instinctive following behaviour shown in species that are mobile from birth whereby newborn animals follow the first large, moving object they see.

Inductive method The use of induction is where single observations are made, regularities noticed, and generalisations or theory inferred from the observations. Represents a common-sense view of science.

Insight Thinking or problem solving involving incubation of relevant information followed by the sudden realisation of a solution.

Instrumental hedonism orientation A stage in Kohlberg's theory of moral development in which good behaviour is seen as what brings rewards.

Interactional synchrony A process whereby the movements and utterances of an infant and adult are synchronised in time.

Internal working model A theory of attachment whereby the child's understanding of his or her earliest attachment relationship acts as a model for all future relationships.

Internalisation A process by which children develop their own set of moral (and other) beliefs, as a result of contact with parents and peers and everyday experience.

Introspection is to do with attempting to look at one's own mind and how mental processes, perception, attention, etc., operate and work. Used by Wilhelm Wundt over 100 years ago. Suffers from being subjective.

Intuitive period The later part of Piaget's *pre-operational stage*, in which children's judgements are influenced by the appearance of objects. As a result children are 'fooled' by *conservation tests*.

Jonah complex comes from Maslow's theory of humanistic psychology. It is to do with fear of success: in males fear of responsibility and in females fear of career success.

Latent stage in Freudian theory occurs between the age of 5–6 years until the onset of puberty. No psychosexual development is said to take place during this stage.

Law of acquisition as stated by the radical behaviourists B. F. Skinner says that the strength of a behaviour increases when it is followed by reinforcement.

Learning is a relatively permanent change in the behaviour, thoughts and feelings of an organism resulting from prior experience.

Libido Freud's term meaning sexual motivation.

Longitudinal study A study which takes place over a period of time, where the researcher studies the same individual or group of participants on more than one occasion.

Lovaas technique A behaviour modification technique involving the use of positive reinforcement to encourage speech in children with autism.

Magnocellular theory A theory of dyslexia according to which the disorder results from defects in large magna cells in the visual pathway.

Maternal deprivation The loss of a mother figure or primary attachment figure. The consequences of such loss were popularised as a *theory of maternal deprivation* in the 1950s by John Bowlby.

Maturation Development which is genetically-programmed, and appears to follow a biological timetable. The best example is physical growth, including the timing of the onset of puberty.

Mediational processes are the cognitive processes or mental events that take place between stimulus and response. Usually referred to as stimulus-organism-response.

Meta-analysis Research involving the collation of results from a number of separate studies to enable an overall view of findings on a particular research topic.

Meta-cognitive awareness An awareness of one's own cognitive processes and abilities.

Mind–body debate Philosophical debate of central importance to psychology in which the mental and the physical are seen as different. The dualist view is that the mental and physical must interact in some way. The monist view is that the mind is the brain. See mind-brain identity theory.

Mind–brain identity theory. The view that the mind is identical to the brain, and that all mental processes can be understood to be functions and operations of the brain.

Modelling is where an individual observes another person and imitates the observed behaviour on a future occasion. Modelling is a key concept in observational learning or social learning theory.

Monotropy A key feature of Bowlby's theory of attachment according to which a child can attach to only one attachment figure.

Monozygotic twins Twins from a single egg that divides after fertilisation. Monozygotic twins are sometimes referred to as identical twins because they have 100% of genes in common.

Moral cognition The ability to think about moral issues.

Moral comparison A technique for studying moral understanding in which the partisipant is asked to compare the naughtiness of two individuals.

Moral comparison technique Children compare two contrasting stories of wrongdoing. Used by Piaget to study moral reasoning.

Moral dilemma A situation in which a person has to chose between two alternative actions, both of which involve some degree of wrongdoing.

Moral dilemma technique Use of a moral dilemma story to get participants to make moral statements. Used by Kohlberg.

Moral realism A stage in Piaget's theory of moral development, in which children make judgments based on the authority of parents and others, and judgements based on the seriousness of the consequences of actions. Also known as the *heteronomous stage.*

Moral relativism A stage in Piaget's theory of moral development, in which children make judgements based on their own internalised moral beliefs, and take account of an actor's intentions. Also known as the *autonomous stage.*

Morality of care A tendency to think about the effects of actions on the feelings and needs of others, on relationships and on the prevention of harm.

Morality of justice A tendency to think about whether or not society's rules have been broken, and about appropriate punishment.

Motherese A simplified and exaggerated form of language used by adults and older children when addressing young children and babies.

Multiple intelligences A theory of intelligence suggesting that intelligence comprises six separate domains.

Nativist A philosophical view that states that human characteristics are innate or a result of nature.

Nature The influence of genetic factors, including *maturation* on development.

Nature/nurture debate A disagreement about what determines psychological development. Nativists believe that *nature* is the main influence, whereas *empiricists* believe that *nurture* is the main influence.

Need for cognition is a personality variable. People high in need for cognition enjoy thinking about a task or problem and have a need to understand the world.

Negative reinforcement occurs when a response (or behaviour) is strengthened due to the removal of an adverse (painful or unpleasant) stimulus. See aslo *positive reinforcement.*

Nomothetic approach An approach in psychology that looks for similarities between people and attempts to establish general laws about human behaviour. Often employs quantitative methods and laboratory experiments.

Non-conscious is used by cognitive psychologists in preference to the word unconscious. Refers to mental or cognitive processes that take place outside of conscious awareness.

Nurture The influence of environmental factors, such as learning from other people, on development.

Object concept A child's awareness that objects exist independently of us in the world, and continue to exist even if we are not observing them. See *object permanence.*

Object permanence The ability to react to the disappearance of a previously-present object, for example by searching for it. See *object concept.*

Object relations theory was developed by the psychoanalyst Melanie Klein and takes as central concern the relationship a person has with other people, most notably parents and significant others in a person's life.

Observational learning takes place when the behaviour of a person results from the observation and imitation of the behaviour of another person. Also known as social learning theory.

Oedipus complex occurs during the phallic stage and revolves around the child desiring the opposite sex parent and wishing to get rid of the same sex parent. The resolution of the Oedipal conflict results in appropriate gender identity.

Operant conditioning is a type of learning that occurs through either reinforcement or punishment of a behavioural response.

Operation A type of logical thought process. A transformation we can make to mental representations, for example in adding, subtracting, multiplying and dividing.

Oral stage is a psychosexual stage of development in Freudian theory. It occurs in the first year of life and is centred around the mouth and oral pleasure. Fixation at this stage may result in an oral personality in adulthood.

Organismic theory treats the individual in terms of physical and mental aspects as a unified whole. Developed by Kurt Goldstein and influenced the development of humanistic psychology.

Overt behaviour. That which can be objectively observed, measured and is amenable to scientific research.

Paradigm Suggested by Thomas Kuhn to characterise a mature science. A paradigm is a set of shared assumptions about the subject matter and methods of enquiry of a science. Kuhn saw psychology as in a pre-science stage.

Parallel processing or connectionist model of cognitive processes is the view that information is processed at a number of levels or different places in the brain at the same time.

Peak experiences are feelings of ecstasy, and deep, satisfying feelings of satisfaction. Some people regard peak experiences as mystical or spiritual. To do with humanistic psychology.

Personal growth in humanistic psychology is the idea that the person grows and changes throughout life. Personal growth comes about through self-actualisation, peak experiences and freedom from fear or threat.

Personal orientation inventory is a standardised questionnaire to measure the extent to which a person achieves self-actualisation.

Person-centred approach or client-centred approach is to do with humanistic psychology. Developed by Carl Rogers and focuses on the person's subjective experience of the world.

Pervasive mental disorder a severe disorder of childhood affecting many aspects of behaviour and functioning.

Phallic stage is the third stage of psychosexual development in Freudian theory. Here boys and girls gain pleasure from playing (masturbating) with their genitals. The most important aspect of the phallic stage is the **Oedipus complex**.

Phenomenology is a philosophical method developed to examine human experience and how people live their lives. To do with subjective experience and humanistic psychology.

Phenylketonuria (PKU) An inherited disorder affecting metabolism. The damaging effects of the disorder can be completely prevented if the individual follows a strictly regulated diet from birth.

Philosophy A method of rational enquiry using logic, reason and argument to find knowledge and truth. Derived from the Greek word *philosophia* which means the love of wisdom.

Phonological deficit A processing difficulty resulting in the inability to identify and distinguish speech sounds or phonemes.

Positive behaviour is a term used by behaviourists to characterise behaviour that is performed by an organism (human or other animal) that is directed at achieving a goal or objective.

Positive regard in Rogers' person-centred humanistic approach is to do with how others judge and evaluate a person. See also *unconditional positive regard*.

Positive reinforcement occurs when a response (or behaviour) is strengthened because it is followed by a reward or reinforcement. See also *negative reinforcement*.

Precocial species Animals that are mobile from birth.

Preconceptual period The early part of Piaget's *Pre-Operational Stage*, in which children's judgements show *egocentrism, animism* and *centration*.

Preconscious in Freudian theory represents thoughts and memories that a person can bring to consciousness with relative ease.

Pre-operational stage One of Piaget's stages of cognitive development, in which the child's understanding of the world is shaped by appearances (intuition) rather than logical thought.

Private experience Is unique to the individual, subjective and not easily investigated using scientific procedures.

Privation Never having had the chance to form an attachment relationship with anyone.

Projection is a psychoanalytic defence mechanism whereby an individual projects or attributes unwanted or painful thoughts and feelings onto another person.

Prosocial behaviour Socially-desirable behaviour, such as helping. In contrast with antisocial behaviour such as aggression.

Protest, despair, detachment A sequence of behaviours seen in separation situations.

Psychic determinism is best represented by Sigmund Freud's view that all thought and behaviour is determined by unconscious forces associated with the sex and death instincts.

Psychoanalytic theory A theory developed by Sigmund Freud emphasising the importance of unconscious motives.

Psychodynamic approach An approach to psychology developed by Sigmund Freud emphasising the importance of unconscious motives.

Psychosexual development The development of the self, which Freud believed was strongly influenced by sexual motivation.

Psychosexual stages are Freudian stages of development. There are three stages: the oral stage, the anal stage, and the phallic stage. The stages are linked to the sexual instinct.

Psychosocial development according to Erikson takes place over eight stages from birth to old age, five psychosocial stages take place in childhood and teenage years.

Punishment and obedience orientation A stage in Kohlberg's theory of moral development in which wrongdoing is judged on the basis of what is punished.

Punishment by reciprocity The view that a punishment should be limited, appropriate to the wrongdoing, and tend to reform the wrongdoer.

Punishment reduces the likelihood of a behaviour occurring in the future or stops it happening at all.

Purposive behaviour is a term used by behaviourists to characteise behaviour that is performed by an organism (human or other animal) that is directed at achieving a goal or objective.

Radical behaviourism is an extreme form of behaviourism which is solely concerned with observable behaviour as an object of scientific psychology.

Reaction formation is a psychoanalytic defence mechanism in which a person behaves in the opposite way to which he or she actually thinks or feels.

Reciprocal determinism A concept put forward by Albert Bandura in an attempt to bring idiographic and nomothetic approaches together.

Reductionism The view that to understand human beings, psychologists have to analyse and reduce the whole to the simplest component parts. Consciousness, for example, may be reduced to the action of neurons in the brain.

Refrigerator mother A type of mother who is cold and unaccepting of her child. See also the *cold parenting hypothesis*.

Reinforcement is a stimulus that increases the likelihood of behaviour occurring in the future. Positive reinforcement occurs when a behaviour is strengthened because it is followed by a reward. Negative reinforcement strengthens a behaviour because it is followed by removal of an aversive stimulus.

Replication Is an important aspect of experiments and empirical research more generally in scientific psychology. In principle an experiment in psychology should be capable of replication to produce the same results.

Repression is a defence mechanism in psychoanalysis which keeps disturbing, threatening, and unpleasant thoughts at an unconscious level and so stops such thoughts becoming conscious.

Resilience Hardiness or resistance to the ill effects of deprivation or privation.

Retrospective phenomenological assessment is a modern type of introspection in which a person is asked to report (usually verbally) on their experiences. See also *introspection*.

Reversibility A mental operation in which a previous operation is undone. For example the ability to know that if a pack of 52 cards is dealt out equally to four players, there will still be 52 cards when they are all collected again.

Scaffolding Support and prompting, usually provided by an adult, which helps a child achieve cognitive tasks they could not achieve alone.

Schedules of reinforcement include fixed and variable ratios, and fixed and variable interval schedules of reinforcement.

Schema A cognitive structure consisting of a set of linked mental representations of the world, which we use both to understand and to respond to situations.

Secondary drive theory A theory of attachment according to which infants attach to those who feed them.

Self-actualisation is concerned with psychological growth and realising the true and full potential of an individual. Central to Maslow's humanistic theory of human needs.

Self-concept in humanistic psychology has two components. These are self-worth and the ideal self. The ideal self is our idea of how we should be and may differ from how we are.

Self-disclosure The giving of personal or even intimate information about oneself to others.

Self-esteem The evaluative dimension of self.

Self-image Factual or descriptive information a person has about him- or herself, including information about looks and social roles.

Self-worth in Rogers' person-centred theory is to do with how we value and regard ourselves. Conceptualised on a continuum from high to low.

Sensitive responsiveness The ability of an attachment figure to determine the meaning of and respond appropriately to signals given off by an infant or young child.

Sensorimotor stage One of Piaget's stages of cognitive development, in which the child's understanding of the world is restricted to sensations and movements, and the here and now.

Separation anxiety A consequence of separation from an attachment figure, which continues long term and results in fear of future separations.

Serial processing or the serial processing model of cognitive processes is the early view of cognition whereby stimuli are processed in a bottom-up or automatic way by the person. See also *parallel processing*.

Seriation The ability to put concrete objects (or their representations) into a logical sequence e.g. by size.

Significant other A person whose opinion is valued above that of other people.

Skinner Box is a piece of equipment developed by the radical behaviourist B. F. Skinner. A hungry animal, typically a rat, is placed in a box which has transparent sides. In the Skinner Box is a lever and food tray. The rat has to learn to press the lever to get the reward of food.

Social learning see *observational learning*.

Social learning An approach to psychology that emphasises the role of observation and imitation in learn behaviour.

Sociometric status The popularity status of an individual as assessed in a *sociometric study*.

Sociometric study A technique used to assess popularity: relationships between members of a group are assessed through interviews and then represented diagrammatically to show the popularity status of each individual.

Soft determinism. A deterministic view of human behaviour but one which also allows people to exercise a degree of freewill.

Splitting is a primitive defence mechanism in object relations theory in which the young infant splits objects (people) and part objects (for example, the breast) into good and bad objects.

Spontaneous recovery occurs when a previously learnt behaviour that has been extinguished recurs in the absence of any new reinforcement.

Stage theory Stage theories assume that development occurs in a universal and invariant sequence of stages. Each stage is qualitatively different from the next. Each child goes through the stages in the same order, and no stage can be missed out. See *continuous development*.

Stimulus discrimination occurs when an organism that has learnt a response to a specific stimulus does not respond to new stimuli that are similar to the original.

Stimulus generalisation occurs when an organism that has learnt a response to a specific stimulus responds in the same way to other stimuli that are similar to the original stimulus.

Strange Situation (The) A controlled observation procedure developed by Mary Ainsworth to assess type of attachment.

Sublimation is a psychoanalytic defence mechanism in which unconscious sexual and aggressive thoughts are transformed and channelled into socially acceptable behaviour such as work, art and literature.

Subliminal perception is the perception of stimuli and processing of information that takes place outside of conscious awareness. To do with non-conscious information processing.

Substitution A *mental operation* used in algebra. For example. For example being able to work out the sum $3a + 2b$ knowing that $a = 4$ and $b = 3$.

Superego in Freud's structure of the personality is made up of the ideal self and conscience. In Freudian theory the superego develops as a result of the Oedipus complex.

Symbolic mode One of Bruner's modes of representation in which an object or situation is represented by means of something else, such as a word which (even though it does not resemble the object) stands for the object or situation.

Systematic desensitisation is a behavioural therapy used to treat people with phobias or fears.

Thematic apperception test (TAT) A type of projective personality test in which the respondent is asked to write a story about characters in a picture. The themes in the story are then analysed for information about the respondent's personality.

Theory of mind An explanation for autism according to which the disorder results from an inability to understand the minds of others.

Theory of mind mechanism (ToMM) An extension of the theory of mind explanation for autism according to which an innate, maturational mechanism underlies the development of a theory of mind.

Token economy programme A programme of reinforcement involving token rewards for instances of desired behaviour. The tokens can then be exchanged for primary rewards such as food or visits, etc.

Tourette's syndrome A disorder in which an individual shows uncontrollable motor tics/mannerisms and verbal outbursts.

Unconditional positive regard is where people accept a person for what they are – the person is shown love and respect in all aspects of their personality.

Unconscious According to Freud, the mind is largely unconscious and has the greatest influence on thoughts, feelings and behaviour. Unconscious thoughts are outside of awareness and cannot be directly brought to consciousness.

Vicarious reinforcement occurs in observational learning when the observer sees another person being reinforced for behaving in a certain way.

Visual perceptual deficit A processing difficulty involving problems in detecting elements or features of visually presented information and/or problems in the perception of such information.

Zone of proximal development The gap between what a child can achieve unaided, and what s/he can achieve with the help and support of other people.

References

ABRANAVEL, E. & DEYONG, N. (1991) Does object modelling elicit imitative-like gestures from young infants?, *Journal of Experimental Child Psychology*, 52, 22–40

ADAMS. H. E., WRIGHT, L. W. & LOHR, B. A. (1996) Is homophobia associated with homosexual arousal?, *Journal of Abnormal Psychology*, 105, 440–445

AINSWORTH, M. D. S., BLEHAR, M., WATERS, E. & WALL, E. (1978) Patterns of attachment. Erlbaum, Hillsdale, NJ

ALLPORT, G. W. (1937) Personality: a psychological interpretation, New York: Holt

ANTONUCCI, T. C. & LEVITT, M.J. (1984) Early prediction of attachment security: a multivariate approach. Infant Behaviour and Development, 7, 1–18

ARGYLE, M. (1983) The psychology of interpersonal behaviour (4th Edn). Penguin, Harmondsworth

ASCH, S. (1955) Opinions and social pressure, *Scientific American*, 193, 5, 31–35

ASPERGER, H. (1944) Die 'aunstisehen Psychopathen' im Kindesalter. *Archiv für psychiatrie und Nervenkrankheiten*, 117, 76–136

Association of Educational Psychologists (1998) Inquiry into highly able children, June 1998, AEP

AYER, A. J. (1959) Privacy, Proceedings of the British Academy, 45, 43–65

BANCROFT, D. (1995) Language impairment and dyslexia. In D. Bancroft & R. Carr (Eds) Influencing children's development, Blackwell, Oxford

BANDURA, A. (1965) The influence of models' reinforcement contingencies on the acquisition of initiative responses, *Journal of Personality and Social Psychology*, 1, 589–95

BANDURA, A. (1969) Principles of behaviour modification, New York: Holt, Rinehart and Winston

BANDURA, A. (1967) The role of modelling in personality development, In C. Lavatelli & F. Stendler (Eds), Readings in childhood and development, New York: Harcourt Brace Jovanovich.

BANDURA, A. (1986) Social foundations of thought and action, Englewood Cliffs, NJ: Prentice Hall

BANDURA, A., ROSS, D. & ROSS, S. A. (1963) Imitation of film-mediated aggressive models, *Journal of Abnormal and Social Psychology*, 66, 3–11

BARNES, P. (1995) Personal, social and emotional development of children. Open University Press, Milton Keynes

BARON, R. A. & RICHARDSON, D. R. (1994) Human Aggression, Second Edition, New York: Plenum Press

BARON-COHEN, S., LESLIE, A. M. & FRITH, U. (1985) Does the autistic child have a theory of mind? *Cognition*, 21, 37–46

BARON-COHEN, S., RING, H. A., BULLMORE, E. T., WHEELWRIGHT, S., ASHWIN, C. & WILLIAMS, S. C. (2000) The amygdala theory of autism. *Neuroscience and Biobehavioural Reviews*, 3, 355–364

BARON-COHEN, S., TAGER-FLUSBERG, H. & COHEN, D. J. (Eds) (1993) Understanding other minds: perspectives from autism, Oxford: Oxford University Press

BARTAK, L. & RUTTER, M. (1973) Special education treatment of autistic children: a comparative study, I *Journal of Child Psychology and Psychiatry*, 14, 161–179

BASS, D. M. (1994) The evolution of desire, New York: Basic Books

BAUM, W. M. (1994) John B. Watson and behaviour analysis, In J. T. Todd & E. K. Morris (Eds), Modern perspectives on John B. Watson and classical behaviourism, Westport, CT: Greenwood Press

BECK, A. (1991) Cognitive therapy: a 30-year retrospective, *American Psychologist*, 46, 368–375

BECK, A. T. & WEISHAUR, M. E. (1995) Cognitive therapy, In R. J. Corsini & D. Wedding (Eds), Current psychotherapies, 5th Edition, Itasca, IL: Peacock

BEE, H. (1989) The developing child, 5th Edn,, New York: Harper Collins

BEE, H. (1992) The developing child, 6th Edn, New York: Harper Collins

BEE, H. (2000) The developing child, 9th Edn, Boston: Allyn and Bacon

BELL, A. (2002) Debates in psychology, Hove, Sussex: Taylor & Francis

BELSKY, J. (1984) Determinants of parenting: a process model. *Child Development*, 55, 83–96

BELSKY, J. (1988) The 'effects' of infant day-care reconsidered. *Early Child Research Quarterly*, 3, 235–272

BENTLEY A. (1966) Musical ability in children and its measurement, London: George G. Harrap & Co. Ltd

BETTLEHEIM, B (1967) The empty fortress, New York: Free Press

BIGELOW, B. J. & LA GAIPA, J. J. (1975) Children's written descriptions of friendship: a multi-dimensional analysis, *Developmental Psychology*, 11, 857–858

BLASI, A. (1980) Bridging moral cognition and moral action: A critical review of the literature. *Psychological Bulletin*, 88, 1–45

BLOOM, B. S. (1985) Developing talent in young people, New York: Ballantyne Books

BODEN, J. M. & BAUMEISTER, R. F. (1997) Repressive coping: distraction using pleasant thoughts and memories, *Journal of Personality and Social Psychology*, 73, 45–62

BODER, E. (1971) Developmental dyslexia: prevailing diagnostic concepts and a new diagnostic approach. In H. R. Myklebust (Ed.) Progress in learning disabilities, Vol. 2, New York: Grune and Stratton

BOEHNKE, K., SILBEREISEN, R. K., EISENBERG, N., REYKOWSKI, J. & PALMONARI, A. (1989) Developmental pattern of prosocial motivation: A cross-national study. *Journal of Cross-Cultural Psychology*, 20, 219–243

BOWLBY, J. (1946) Forty-four juvenile thieves, London: Balliere, Tindall and Cox

BOWER, T. G. R. (1971) The object in the world of the infant, *Scientific American*, 225 (4), 30–38

BOWER, T. G. R. (1979) Human development, San Francisco: W.H. Freeman

BOWER, T. G. R. & WISHART, J. G. (1972) The effects of motor skill on object permanence, *Cognition* 1, (2), 28–35

BOWLBY, J. (1953) Child-care and the growth of love, Harmondsworth: Penguin

BOWLBY, J. (1969) Attachment, London: Hogarth Press

BOWLBY, J. (1951) Maternal care and mental health, Geneva; World Health Organisation, Breakwell, G.M., Hammond, S. & Fife-Shaw, C. (2000) Research methods in psychology, 2nd Edn, London: Sage Publications

BREMNER, J. G. (1994) Infancy, 2nd Edn, Oxford: Blackwell

BRITISH PSYCHOLOGY ENTRY HERE

BRODY, G. H. & SHAFFER, D. R. (1982) Contributions of parents and peers to children's moral socialization, *Developmental Review*, 2, 31–75

BRUNER, J. S. (1966) Towards a theory of instruction, Cambridge, MA: Harvard University Press

BRUNER, J. S. & KENNEY, H (1966) The development of the concepts of order and proportion in children, New York: Wiley

BRYANT, P. & BRADLEY, L. (1985) Children's reading problems, Oxford; Blackwell

BRYMAN, A. (1988) Quality and quantity in social research, London: Unwin Hyman

BUHRMESTER, D. (1996) Need fulfilment, interpersonal competence, and the developmental context of early adolescent friendship. In W. M. Bukowski, A. F. Newcomb & W. W. Hartup (Eds) The company they keep: friendship in childhood and adolescence. Cambridge: Cambridge University Press

BUSS, D. M. (1994) The evolution of desire, New York: Basic Books

CACIOPPO, J. T. & PETTY, R. E. (1982) The need for cognition, *Journal of Personality and Social Psychology*, 42, 116–131

CAPRA, F. (1975) The tao of physics, Berkeley, CA: Shambhale

CARLSON, N. (1994) Physiology of behaviour, 5th Edn. MA: Allyn and Bacon Needham Heights

CARSON R. C. & BUTCHER, J. N. (1992) Abnormal psychology and modern life, 9th Edn. New York: Harper Collins

CASSIDY, J. (1986) The ability to negotiate the environment: an aspect of infant competence as related to quality of attachment, *Child Development*, 57, 331–337

CATTELL, R. B. (1983) Structured personality-learning theory: a multivariate research approach, New York: Praeger

CHASE, W. G. & SIMON, H. A. (1973) Perception in chess. *Cognitive Psychology*, 4, 55–81

CHEYNE, J. A. (1971) Effects of imitation of different reinforcement combinations to a model, *Journal of Experimental Child Psychology*, 12, 258–269

CHEZ, M. G., BUCHANAN, C. P., BAGAN, B. T., HAMMER, M. S., MCCARTHY K. S., OVRUTSKAYA, I., NOWINSKKI, C. V. & COHEN Z. S. (2000) Secretin and autism: a two part clinical investigation. *Journal of Autism and Developmental Disorders*, 30(2), 87–98

CHILD, D. (1997) Psychology and the teacher, London: Cassell

CHOMSKY, N. (1959) Review of verbal behaviour by B. F. Skinner, Language, 35, 26–58

CHOMSKY, N. (1965) Aspects of a theory of syntax, Cambridge, MA: MIT Press

CHRISTIE, P. & WIMPORY, D. (1986) Recent research into the development of communicative competence and its implications for the teaching of autistic children, *Communication*, 20, 4–7

CLARKE, A. M. & CLARKE, A. D. B. (1976) Early experience; myth and evidence, London: Open Books

COIE, J. D. & DODGE, K. A. (1983) Continuities and changes in children's social status: a five-year longitudinal study. *Merrill-Palmer Quarterly* 29, 261–282

COLBY, A., KOHLBERG, L,, GIBBS, J. & LIEBERMAN, M. (1983) A longitudinal study of moral development, Monographs of the Society for Research in Child Development, 48 (1–2, Serial No. 200)

COLBY, A., KOHLBERG, L. & KAUFFMAN, K. (1987a) The measurement of moral judgment (Vol. I), Cambridge: Cambridge University Press

COLBY, A., KOHLBERG, L., SPEICHER, B., HEWER, A., CANDEE, D., GIBBS, J. & POWER, C. (1987b) The measurement of moral judgment (Vol. II), Cambridge: Cambridge University Press

COMINGS, D. E. & COMINGS, B. G. (1991) Clinical and genetic relationships between autism-pervasive developmental disorder and Tourette syndrome: A study of 19 cases. *American Journal of Medical Genetics*, 39, 180–191

CONDON, W. S. & SANDER, L. W. (1974) Neonate movement is synchronized with adult speech: interactional participation and language acquisition, *Science*, 183, 99–101

CONSTANZO, P. R., COIE, J. D., GRUMET, J. F. & FARNILL, D. (1973) Re-examination of the effects of intent and consequence on children's moral judgements. *Child Development*, 44, 154–161

COOK, R. C. (1993) The experimental analysis of cognition in animals, *Psychological Science*, 4, 174–178

COOLEY, C. H. (1902) Human nature and the social order, New York: Scribner

COOLICAN, H. (2000) Research methods and statistics in psychology, 2nd Edn, London: Hodder & Stoughton

COON, D. (2002) Psychology: a journey, United States: Wadsworth, Thomson Learning

COOPERSMITH, S. (1967) The antecedents of self-esteem, San Francisco: Freeman

COURCHESNE, E. (1991) Neuroanatomic imaging in autism, *Pediatrics*, 87, 781–790

COWEN, E. L., PEDERSON, A., BABIGIAN, H., IZZO, L. D. & TROST, M. A. (1973) Long-term follow-up of early detected vulnerable children, *Journal of Consulting and Clinical Psychology*, 41, 438–446

COX, A., RUTTER, M., NEWMAN, S. & BARTAK, L. (1975) A comparative study of infantile autism and specific developmental language disorders, I, Parental characteristics. *British Journal of Psychiatry*, 126, 146–159

CRAWFORD, M. & MARACEK, J. (1989) Psychology reconstructs the female: 1968–1988, *Psychology of Women Quarterly*, 13, 147–165

CRONBACH, L. J. (1957) The two disciplines of scientific psychology, *American Psychologist*, 12, 671–684

CSIKSZENTMIHALYI, M. (1990) Flow: the psychology of optimal experience, New York: Harper Perennial

CURTISS, S. (1977) Genie: a psycholinguistic study of a modern day 'wild child', London: Academic Press

DAMON, W. (1977) The social world of the child, San Francisco: Jossey-Bass

DANIELS, M. (1988) The myth of self-actualisation, Journal of Humanistic Psychology, 28, 7–28

DASEN, P. (1975) Concrete operational development in three cultures, Journal of Cross-Cultural Psychology, 6, 156–172

DAVIDSON, J. E. & STERNBERG, R. J. (1985) Cognitive development in the gifted and talented. In F. D. Horowitz & M. O'Brien, (Eds) The gifted and talented developmental perspectives, 37–74, Washington DC: American Psychological Association

DAWSON, M. R. (1998) Understanding cognitive science, Oxford: Blackwell Publishers

DE CARVALHO, R. J. (1991) The founders of humanistic psychology, New York: Praeger

DEARY, I. (2000) Simple information processing – an intelligence, In R. J. Sternberg (Ed.), Handbook of intelligence, New York: Cambridge University Press Diagnostic and Statistical Manual of Mental Disorders, 4th Edn. (1994) American Psychiatric Association, Washington DC

DIEN, D. S. (1982) A Chinese perspective on Kohlberg's theory of moral development. Developmental Review, 2, 331–341

DODGE, K. A., SCHLUNDT, D. C., SHOCKEN, I. & DELUGACH, J. D. (1983) Social competence and children's sociometric status: the role of peer group entry strategies, Merrill-Palmer Quarterly, 29, 309–336

DONALDSON, M (1978) Children's Minds, London: Fontana Press

DOUVAN, E. & ADELSON, J. (1966) The adolescent experience, New York: Wiley

DUCK, S. W. (1991) Friends for life, Hemel Hempstead: Harvester-Wheatsheaf

DUNN, J. (1993) Young children's close relationships beyond attachment, London: Sage

DWORETSKY, J. P. (1981) Introduction to child development, St Paul, M: West Publishing Co

EISENBERG, N. (1983) Children's differentiations among potential recipients of aid. Child Development, 54, 594–602

EISENBERG, N. & HAND, M. (1979) The relationship of pre-schoolers' reasoning about prosocial moral conflicts to prosocial behaviour, Child Development, 50, 356–363

ELLIS, A. (1989) Inside rational-emotive therapy: a critical appraisal of the theory and therapy, New York: Academic Press.

ELLIS, A. (1995) Rational-emotive therapy, In R. J. Corsini & D. Wedding (Eds), Current psychotherapies, Edn, Itasca, IL: Peacock

ELLIS, A. W. (1973) Reading, writing and dyslexia: a cognitive analysis, 2nd Edn, London: Erlbaum

ENTWISTLE, N. J, & MARTON, F. (1994) Knowledge objects: understandings constituted through intensive academic study, British Journal of Educational Psychology, 64(1), 161–178

ENTWISTLE, N. J., ENTWISTLE, J., & COWELL, M. D. (1971) The academic performance of students: I. Prediction from scales of motivation and study methods, British Journal of Educational Psychology, 41(3), 258–267

ERICSSON, K. A. & SIMON, H. A. (1980) Verbal reports as data, Psychological Review, 87, 215–251

ERIKSON, E. (1963) Childhood and society, 2nd Edn, New York: Norton

ERIKSON, E. (1968) Identity, youth and crisis, New York: Norton

ERIKSON, E. (1969) Ghandi's truth, New York: Norton

ERWIN, P. (1998) Friendships in childhood and adolescence, London: Routledge

EYSENCK, H. J. (1952) The effects of psychotherapy: an evaluation, Journal of Consulting Psychology, 16, 319–324

EYSENCK, H. J. (1990) The decline and fall of the Freudian empire, Washington DC: Scott-Townsend

EYSENCK, M. (Ed.) (1998) Psychology: an integrated approach, Harlow: Addison Wesley Longman Ltd (In particular Chapter 21)

FARTHING, G. W. (1992) The psychology of consciousness, Englewood Cliffs, NJ: Prentice Hall

FEYERABEND, P. K. (1975) Against method: outline of an anarchistic theory of knowledge, London: New Left Books

FINE, R. (1990) The history of psychoanalysis, New York: Continuum

FISHER, S. & GREENBERG, R. P. (1977) The scientific credibility of Freud's theories and therapies, New York: Basic Books

FISHER, S. E., FRANCKS, C., MARLOW, A. J., MACPHIE, I. L., NEWBURY, D. F., CARDEN, L. R., ISHIKAWA-BRUSH, Y., RICHARDSON, A. J., TALCOTT, J. B., GAYN, J., OLSEN, R. K., PENNINGTON, B. F., SMITH, S. D., DEFRIES, J. C., STEIN, J. F. & MONACO, A. P. (2002) Independent genome-wide scans identify a chromosome 18 quantitative-trait locus influencing dyslexia, *Nature Genetics*, 30, 86–91

FISHER. S. & GREENBERG, R. P. (1996) Freud scientifically reappraised: testing the theories and therapies, New York: Wiley

FLANAGAN, C. (1996) Applying psychology to early childhood development, London: Hodder & Stoughton

FLANAGAN, C. (2000) AS/A level psychology: essential word dictionary, Oxford: Philip Allan Updates

FLAVELL, J. H. (1978) The development of knowledge about visual perception. In C. B. Keasey (Ed.) Nebraska symposium on motivation, Vol. 25, Lincoln: University of Nebraska Press

FOLSTEIN, S. E. & PIVEN, J. (1991) Etiology of autism: genetic influences, *Pediatrics*, 87, 767–773

FREEMAN, J. (1979) Gifted children: their identification and development in a social context, Lancaster: MTP Press

FREEMAN, J. (1997) Gifted children growing up, London: Cassell

FREUD. S. (1900) The interpretation of dreams, London: The Hogarth Press

FREUD, S. (1905/1977) Fragment of an analysis of a case of hysteria (Dora), The Pelican Freud Library, Volume 8, Harmondsworth: Penguin

FREUD, S. (1909/1977a) Analysis of a phobia in a five year old boy (Little Hans), The Pelican Freud Library, Volume 8, Harmondsworth: Penguin

FREUD, S. (1909/1977b) Notes upon a case of obsessional neurosis (The Rat Man), The Pelican Freud Library, Volume 9, Harmondsworth: Penguin

FREUD, S. (1922) Beyond the pleasure principle, London: Hogarth Press

FREUD, S. (1933/1973) New introductory lectures on psychoanalysis, Pelican Freud Library, Volume 2, Harmondsworth: Penguin

FREUD, S. (1933/1964) New Introductory lectures on psychoanalysis, Stamford Edn, Vol. 22, London: Hogarth Press

FREUD, S. (1961) Some psychical consequences of the anatomical distinction between the sexes. In J. Strachey (Ed. and Trans.), Standard edition of the of the complete psychological works of Sigmund Freud (Vol. 19). London: Hogarth Press

FREUD, A. & DANN, S. (1951) An experiment in group upbringing, *Psychoanalytic Study of the Child*, 6, 127–168

FRITH, U. (1989) Autism: explaining the enigma, Oxford: Blackwell

FROMM, E. (1941) Escape from freedom, New York: Holt, Rinehart & Winston

GALLAGHER, J. J. (1958) Peer acceptance of highly gifted children in elementary school. *Elementary School Journal*, 58, 465–470

GARCIA, J. (1989) Food for Tolman: cognition and cathexis in concert. In T. Archer & L. G. Nilsson (Eds) Aversion avoidance and anxiety: perspectives on adversely motivated behaviour, Hillsdale, NJ: Erlbaum

GARCIA, J. & KOELLING, R. (1966) Relation of cue to consequence in avoidance learning, *Psychonomic Science*, 4, 123–124

GARDNER, H. (1983) Frames of mind, New York: Basic Books

GAZZANGIA, M. S. (1970) The bisected brain, New York: Appleton-Century-Crofts

GAZZANGIA, M. S. (1985) The social brain: discovering the networks of the mind, New York: Basic Books

GEISELMAN, R. E., FISHER, R. P., MACKINNON, D. F. & HOLLAND, H. L. (1985) Eye witness memory enhancement in police interview: cognitive retrieval mnemonics versus hypnosis, *Journal of Applied Psychology*, 70, 401–412

GEISELMAN, R. E., FISHER, R. P., MACKINNON, D. F. & HOLLAND, H. L. (1986) Enhancement of eye witness memory with the cognitive interview, *American Journal of Psychology*, 99, 385–401

GELMAN, R. (1969) Conservation acquisition: a problem of learning to attend to the relevant attributes, *Journal of Experimental Child Psychology*, 7, 167–187

GESCHWIND, N. A. & BEHAN, P. O. (1984) Laterality, hormones and immunity. In N. Geschwind & A. M. Galaburda (Eds) Cerebral dominance: the biological foundations, Cambridge, MA: Harvard University Press

GESCHWIND, N. & GALABURDA, A. M. (1985) Cerebral lateralization: biological mechanisms, associations and pathology, A hypothesis and a program for research. *Archives of Neurology*, 42, 428–458 (5)

GILLIGAN, C. (1977) In a different voice: women's conceptions of self and morality, *Harvard Educational Review*, 47, 481–517

GILLIGAN, C. (1982) In a different voice: Psychological theory and women's development, Cambridge, MA: Harvard University Press

GOLDFARB, W. (1943) The effects of early institutional care on adolescent personality. *Journal of Experimental Education*, 12, 106–129

GOLDSTEIN, K. (1939) The organism, New York: American Book Co

GOODNOW, J. J. (1969) Problems in research on culture and thought, in D. ELKIND, and ??????

J. FLAVELL (Eds) Studies in cognitive development: essays in honour of Jean Piaget, Oxford: Oxford University Press

GOTTESMAN, I. L. (1991) Schizophrenia genesis, New York: W. H. Freeman

GOULD, S. J. (1981) The mismeasure of man, New York: Norton

GREENWALD, A. G., SPANGENBERG, E. R., PRATKANIS, A. R. & ESKENAZI, J. (1991) Double-blind tests of subliminal self-help audio tapes, *Psychological Science*, 2, 119–122

GROSS, M. (1993) Exceptionally gifted children, Routledge: London

GROSS, R. (1999) Themes, issues and debates in psychology, London: Hodder & Stoughton

GROSS, R. D. (2001) Psychology, the science of mind and behaviour, 4th Edn, London: Hodder and Stoughton

GROSSMAN, K. E., GROSSMAN, K., HUBER, F. & WARTNER, U. (1981) German children's behaviour towards their mothers at 12 months and their fathers at 18 months in Ainsworth's strange situation, *International Journal of Behaviour Development*, 4, 157–181

HAPPE, F. (1999) Understanding assets and deficits in autism. Why success is more interesting than failure, *The Psychologist*, Vol 12, No. 11, 540–546

HARLOW, H. F. (1959) Love in infant monkeys, *Scientific American*, 200, 68–74

HARRIS, S., MUSSEN, P. H. & RUTHERFORD, E. (1976) Some cognitive, behavioral, and personality correlates of maturity of moral judgment, *Journal of Genetic Psychology*, 128, 123–135

HARTER, S. (1988) The determinations and mediational role of global self-worth in children. In Eisenberg, N. (Ed.) Contemporary topics in developmental psychology, New York: Wiley-Interscience

HARTSHORNE, H., & MAY, M. S. (1928–1930) Studies in the nature of character. Vol. 1: Studies in deceit. Vol. 2: Studies in self control. Vol. 3: Studies in the organization of character, New York: Macmillan

HASLAM, S. A., & MCGARTY, C. (1998) Doing psychology: an introduction to research methodology and statistics, London Sage

HATANO, G. & INAGAKI, K. (1992) Desituating cognition through the construction of conceptual knowledge. in P. LIGHT and G. BUTTERWORTH, (Eds) Context and cognition, London: Harvester

HAZAN, C. & SHAVER, P. R. (1987) Romantic love conceptualised as an attachment process, *Journal of Personality and Social Psychology*. 52(3), 511–524

HEIDEGGER, M. (1927) Being and time, New York: State University of New York Press

HEIDER, F. (1958) The psychology of interpersonal relations, New York: John Wiley & Sons

HENDERSON, N. D. (1982) Human behaviour genetics, *Annual Review of Psychology*, 33, 403–440

HERMELIN, B. & O'CONNOR, N. (1967) Remembering of words by psychotic and sub-normal children, *British Journal of Psychology*, 58, 213–218

HESS, W. R. (1957) The functional organisation of the diencephalem, New York: Grune & Stratton

HINDE, R. A., TITMUS, G., EASTON, D. & TAMPLIN, A. (1985) Incidence of 'friendship' and behaviour with strong associates versus non-associates in pre-schoolers, *Child Development*, 56, 234–245

HOBSON, R. P., OUSTON, J. & LEE, T. (1988) What's in a face? The case of autism, *British Journal of Psychology*, 79, 441–453

HODGES, J & TIZARD, B (1989) IQ and behavioural adjustment of ex-institutional adolescents, *Journal of Child Psychology and Psychiatry*, 30, 53–76

HOFFMAN, L. W. (1974) Fear of success in males and females, *Journal of Consulting and Clinical Psychology*, 24, 353–358

HOFFMAN, M. L. (1970) *Moral Development*, In P. H. Mussen (Ed.) Carmichael's manual of child psychology, Vol. 2, New York: Wiley

HOFFMAN, M. L. (1975) Altruistic behaviour and the parent-child relationship, *Journal of Personality and Social Psychology*, 31, 937–943

HOFSTEDE, G. (1980) Culture's consequences: international differences in work-related values, Beverly Hills, C: Sage

HOLLINGWORTH, L. S. (1942) Children above IQ 180, New York: World Books

HOLMES, D. R. & MCKEEVER, W. F. (1979) Material specific serial memory deficit in adolescent dyslexics, *Cortex*, 15, 51–62

HORNSBY, B. & SHEAR, F. (1976) Alpha to omega, London: Heinemann Educational Books

HOWE, J. (1999) Genius explained, Cambridge: Cambridge University Press

HYLAND. M. E. (1989) There is no motive to avoid success: the compromise explanation for success-avoiding behaviour, *Journal of Personality*, 57, 665–693

INHELDER, B. & PIAGET, J. (1958) The growth of logical thinking from childhood to adolescence, New York: Basic Books

ISABELLA, R. A., BELSKY, J., & VON EYE, A. (1989) Origins of infant-mother attachment: An examination of interactional synchrony during the infant's first year, *Developmental Psychology*, 25, 12–21

JACOBSEN, S. W. (1979) Matching behaviour in the young infant, *Child Development*, 50, 425–430

JAMES, W. (1890) The principles of psychology, New York: Henry Holt & Company

JANOS, P. M. (1983) The psychological vulnerabilities of children of very superior intellectual abilities. Unpublished doctoral dissertation, Ohio State University

JENKINS, J. M., SMITH, M. A. & GRAHAM, P. J. (1989) Coping with parental quarrels. *Journal of the American Academy of Child and Adolescent Psychiatry*, 28, 182–189

KALAT, J. W. (1992) Biological psychology, 4th Edn, Pacific Grove; CA: Brooks/Cole

KANDEL, D. B. (1978) Homophily, selection and socialization in adolescent friendships, *American Journal of Sociology*, 84, 427–436

KANNER, L. (1943) Autistic disturbance of affective contact, Nervous Child, 12, 17–50

KEMP, S. & STRANGMAN, K. T. (1994) Consciousness – a folk theoretical view, *New Zealand Journal of Psychology*

KILSTROM, J. F. (1984) Conscious, subconscious and unconscious: a cognitive view, In K. S. Bower & D. Meichenbaum (Eds), The unconscious reconsidered, New York: Wiley.

KILSTROM, J. F., BARNHARDT, M. & TATARYN, D. J. (1992) The psychological unconscious: found, lost and regained, *American Psychologist*, 47, 788–791

KING, P. M. (1985) Formal reasoning in adults: a review and critique. in R. A. MINES and

K. S. KITCHENER (Eds) Adult Cognitive Development, New York: Praeger

KLAUS, H. M. & KENNELL, J. H. (1976) Maternal infant bonding, St. Louis: Mosby

KLEIN, J. (1987) Our need for others and its roots in infancy, London: Routledge

KLEIN, M. (1932) The psychoanalysis of children, London: Hogarth Press

KLEIN, M. (1964) Contributions to psychoanalysis, 1921–1945, New York: McGraw-Hill

KLEIN, M. (1975) Envy and gratitude, and other works, New York: Delta Books

KLINE, P. (1984) Psychology and Freudian theory: an introduction, London: Methuen

KOHLBERG, L. (1963) The development of children's orientation towards a moral order: 1. Sequence in the development of moral thought, *Human Development*, 6, 11–33

KOHLBERG, L. (1975) The cognitive-developmental approach to moral education, Phi Delta Kappa, June, 670–677

KOHLBERG, L. (1976) Moral stages and moralization: the cognitive-developmental approach. In T. Lickona (Ed.) Moral development and behaviour: theory, research and social issues, New York: Holt, Rinehart & Winston

KOHLBERG, L. & KRAMER, R. (1969) Continuities and discontinuities in childhood and adult moral development, *Human Development*, 12, 93–120

KÖHLER, W. (1929) Gestalt psychology, New York: Liveright.

KREPPNER, J. M., O'CONNOR, T. G., DUNN, J., ANDERSEN-WOOD, L. & the English and Romanian Adoptees (ERA) Study Team. (1999) *British Journal of Developmental Psychology*, 17, 319–332

KROSNICK, J. A., BETZ, A. I., JUSSIM, L. J. & LYNN, A. R. (1992) Subliminal conditioning of attitudes, *Personality and Social Psychology Bulletin*, 18, 152–163

KUGELMASS, S. & BREZNITZ, S. (1967) The development of intentionality in moral judgment in city and kibbutz adolescents, *Journal of Genetic Psychology*, 111, 103–111

KUHN, T. S. (1970) The structure of scientific revolutions, 2nd Edn, Chicago: University of Chicago Press

KUJAWSKI, J. H. & BOWER, T. G. R. (1993) Same-sex preferential looking during infancy as a function of abstract representation, *British Journal of Developmental Psychology*, 11, 201–209

KULIK, J. A. & KULIK, C. C. (1984) Effects of accelerated instruction on students, *Review of Educational Research*, 54, 409–425

KUPERSCHMIDT, J. B. & COIE, J. D. (1990) Preadolescent peer status, aggression and school adjustment as predictors of externalising problems in adolescence, *Child Development*, 61, 1350–1362

LACHMANN, R., LACHMANN, J. L. & BUTTERFIELD, E. C. (1979) Cognitive psychology and information processing, Hillsdale, NJ: Lawrence Erlbaum Associates

LADD, G. W. & GOLTER, B. S. (1988) Parents' management of pre-schoolers' peer relations: is it related to children's social competence? *Developmental Psychology*, 24, 109–117

LAMB, M. E. (1977) Father-infant and mother-infant interaction in the first year of life. *Child Development*, 48, 167–181

LAUPA, M. & TURIEL, E. (1986) Children's conceptions of adult and peer authority, *Child Development*, 57, 405–412

LAZARUS, R. S. (1991) Cognition and motivation in emotion, *American Psychologist*, 46, 352–367

LEARY, M. R. (1995) Introduction to behavioral research methods, Pacific Grove, CA: Brooks/Cole

LEBOYER, M., BOUVARD, M. P., LAUDAY, J. M., TABUTEAU, F., WALLER, D., DUGAS, M., KERDELHUE, B., LENSING, P. & PANKSEPP, J. (1992) Brief report: a double blind study of naltrexone in infantile autism, *Journal of Autism and Developmental Disorders*, 22, 309–319

LESLIE, A. M. (1987) Pretence and representation: the origins of 'theory of mind', *Psychological Review*, 94, 412–426

LEVER, J. (1976) Sex differences in games children play, *Social Problems*, 23, 478–487

LEVITT, M. J., GUACCI-FRANCO, N. & LEVITT, J. L. (1993) Convoys of social support in childhood and early adolescence: structure and function, *Developmental Psychology*, 29, 811–818

LEWIS, G. (1995) Bringing up your talented child, Sydney: Harper Collins

LEWIS, M. & BROOKS-GUNN, J. (1979) Social cognition and the acquisition of self, New York: Plenum

LICKONA, T. (1976) Research on Piaget's theory of moral development. In Lickona (Ed.) Moral development and behavior: theory, research, and social issues, New York: Holt, Rinehart & Winston

LORENZ, K. Z. (1935) 'The companion in the bird's world', *Auk*, 54, 245–273

LOVAAS I. O. (1977) The autistic child: language development through behaviour modification, New York: Holsted Press

LOVAAS I. O., FREITAS, L., NELSON, K. & WHALEN, C. (1967) The establishment of imitation and its use for the development of complex behaviour in schizophrenic children. *Behaviour Research and Therapy*, 5, 171–181

MAIN, M., KAPLAN, N. & CASSIDY, J. (1985) Security in infancy, childhood, and adulthood: a move to a level of representation. In I. Bretherton & E. Waters, (Eds), Growing points of attachment theory and research. *Monographs of the Society for Research in Child Development*, 50 (1–2, Serial No. 209)

MAIN, M. & SOLOMON, J. (1990) Procedures for identifying infants as disorganised/disoriented during the Ainsworth Strange Situation. In M. T. Greenberg, D. Cicchetti & E. M. Cummings, Attachment in the pre-school years, Chicago: University of Chicago Press

MARR, D. (1982) Vision: a computational investigation into the human representation and processing of visual information, San Francisco, CA: Freeman

MASLOW, A. H. (1962) Toward a psychology of being, New York: Van Nostrand

MASLOW, A. H. (1970) Motivation and personality, 2nd Edn, New York: Harper & Row

MAUTNER, T. (Ed.) (2000) The Penguin dictionary of philosophy, Harmondsworth: Penguin Books

MCADOO, W. G. & DE MYER, M. K. (1978) Personality characteristics of parents. In M. Rutter & E. Schopler (Eds) Autism: a reappraisal of concepts and treatment, New York: Plenum

McGARRIGLE, J. & DONALDSON, M. (1974) Conservation accidents, *Cognition*, 3, 341–50

McGARRIGLE, J., GRIEVE, R. & HUGHES, M. Interpreting inclusion: a contribution to the study of the child's cognitive and linguistic development. (In Donaldson 1978)

MELZOFF, A. N. & MOORE, M. K. (1977) Imitation of facial and manual gestures by human neonates, *Science*, 198, 75–78

MERCKELBACH, H., ARNTZ, A. & DE JONG, P. (1991) Conditioned experiences in spider phobics, *Behaviour Research and Therapy*, 29, 333–335

MESSER, D. J. (1978) The integration of mother's referential speech with joint play. *Child Development*, 49, 781–787

MILGRAM, S. (1963) Behavioural study of obedience, *Journal of Abnormal and Social Psychology*, 67, 371–378

MITCHELL, P. (1997) Introduction to theory of mind: children autism and apes, London: Arnold

MUNJACK, D. J. (1984) The onset of driving phobias, *Journal of Behaviour Therapy and Experimental Psychiatry*, 15, 305–308

MURRAY, L. & TREVARTHEN, C. (1985) Emotional regulations of interactions between two-month-olds and their mothers. In T. M. Field and N. A. Fox (Eds) Social perception in infants, Norwood, NJ: Ablex

NELSON, S. A. (1980) Factors influencing young children's use of motives and outcomes as moral criteria, *Child Development*, 51, 823–829

NEWMAN, L. S., DUFF, K. J. & BAUMEISTER, R. F. (1997) A new look at defensive projection: thought suppression, accessibility and biased person perception, *Journal of Personality and Social Psychology*, 72, 980–1001

NISBETT, R. E. & WILSON, T. D. (1977) Telling more than we can know: verbal reports on mental processes, *Psychological Review*, 84, 231–295

NYITI, R. M. (1982) The validity of 'cultural differences explanations' for cross-cultural variation in the rate of Piagetian cognitive development. In D. A. Wagner and H. W. Stevenson (Eds) Cultural perspectives in child development, San Francisco: W. H. Freeman

ODEN, S. & ASHER, S. R. (1977) Coaching children in social skills for friendship making, *Child Development*, 48, 495–506

OHNISHI, T., MATSUDA, H., HASHIMOTO, T., KUNIHIRO, T., NISHIKAWA, M., UEMA, T. & SASAKI M. (2000) Abnormal regional cerebral blood flow in childhood autism, *Brain*, 123, Part 9, 1838–44

ORNE, M. T. (1962) On the social psychology of the psychological experiment: with particular reference to demand characteristics and their implications, *American Psychologist*, 17, 776–783

OST, L. (1991) Acquisition of blood and injection phobia and anxiety response patterns in clinical patients, *Behaviour Research and Therapy*, 29, 323–332

OWEN, F. W. (1978) Dyslexia – genetic aspects. In A.L. Benton & D. Pearl (Eds.) Dyslexia: in appraisal of current knowledge, New York: Oxford University Press

PARKE, R. D. & SAWIN, D. B. (1980) The family in early infancy: social interactional and attitudinal analyses. In F. A. Pedersen (Ed.) The father-infant relationship: observational studies in a family context, New York: Praeger

PENNINGTON, D. C. (Ed.) (2002) Introducing psychology: approaches, topics and methods, London: Hodder & Stoughton

PENNINGTON, D. C. (2003) Essential personality, London: Hodder & Stoughton

PERNER, J., FRITH, U., LESLIE, A. M. & LEEKHAM, S. R. (1989) Exploration of the child's theory of mind: knowledge, belief and communication, *Child Development*, 60, 689–700

PIAGET, J. (1952) The origins of intelligence in children, New York: International University Press

PIAGET, J. (1963) The origins of intelligence in children, New York: Norton

PIAGET, J. (1932) (trans. M. Gabain), The moral judgment of the child, New York: Free Press, 1965

PIAGET, J. & INHELDER, B. (1956) The child's conception of space, London: Routledge & Kegan Paul

PIAGET, J & SZEMINSKA, A. (1941) (C. Cattegno and trans. F. M. Hodgson), New York: W. W. Norton & Co

PIVEN, J., ARNDT, S., BAILEY, J., HAVERCAMP, S., ANDREASEN, N. C. & PALMER, P. (1995) An MRI study of brain size in autism. *American Journal of Psychiatry*, 152, 1145–1149

PLACE, V. T. (1956) Is consciousness a brain process? *The British Journal of Psychology*, 47, 42–51

PLOMIN, R. (1996) Nature and nurture, In M. R. Merrens & G. C. Brannigan (Eds), The developmental psychologists: research adventures across the life-span, New York: McGraw-Hill

PLOMIN, R., De FRIES, J. C., McCLEARN, G. E. & RUTTER, M. (1997) Behavioural genetics, 3rd Edn, New York: Freeman

PLOMIN, R., OWEN, M. J. & MCGUFFIN, P. (1994) The genetic basis of complex human behaviours, *Science*, 264, 1773–1739

POPPER, K. R. (1963) Conjectures and reputations; the growth of science knowledge, London: Routledge and Kegan Paul

POPPER, K. R. (1969) Conjectures and refutation, London: Routledge & Kegan Paul

POSNER, M. (1978) Chronometric explorations of mind, Hillsdale, NJ: Lawrence Erlbaum Associates

POWELL, R. A. & BOER, D. P. (1995) Did Freud misinterpret reported memories of sexual abuse as fantasies?, *Psychological Reports*, 77, 563–570

POWELL, S. D. (1999) Autism. In D. Messer and S. Millar (Eds) Explaining developmental psychology: from in infancy to adolescence. London. Arnold

PRIOR, M. & WHERRY, J. S. (1986) Autism, schizophrenia and allied disorders. In H. C. Quay and J. S. Wherry (Eds) Psychopathological disorders of childhood (3rd Edn), New York: Wiley

RENZULLI, J. S. (1986) The three ring conception of giftedness: a developmental model for creative productivity. In R. J. Sternberg and J. Davidson, (Eds.) Conceptions of giftedness, Cambridge: Cambridge University Press

REST, J. (1973) The hierarchical nature of moral judgment: the study of patterns of preference and comprehension of moral judgments made by others, Journal of Personality, 41, 86–109

RHINEHART, L. (1999) The dice man, London: Harper Collins

RICHARDSON, K. (1994) Interactions in development. in J. OATES (ed.) The foundations of child development, Oxford: Blackwell/The Open University

RICHARDSON, T. M. & BENBOW, C. P. (1990) Long term effects of acceleration on the social and emotional adjustment of mathematically precocious youths, Journal of Educational Psychology, 82, 464–470

RICHERT, E. S., ALVINO, J. J. & MACDONNELL, C. (1982) National report on identification: assessment and recommendations for comprehensive identification of gifted and talented youth, Washington DC: US Department of Education, Education Information Resource Centre

RITVO, E. R., FREEMAN, B. J., MASON-BROTHERS, A., MO, A. & RITVO, A. M. (1985) Concordance for the syndrome of autism in 40 pairs of afflicted twins, American Journal of Psychiatry, 142, 74–77

RITVO, E. R., FREEMAN, B. J., PINGREE, C., MASON-BROTHERS, A., JORDE, L., JENSON, W. R., MCMAHON, W. M., PETERSON, P. B., MO, A. & RITVO, A. (1989) The UCLA – University of Utah epidemiologic survey of autism: prevalence, American Journal of Psychiatry, 146, 194–199

ROBERTSON, J. & ROBERTSON, J. (1968) Young children in brief separation: a fresh look, Psychoanalytic Study of the Child, 26, 264–315

ROBINSON, H. B. (1981) The uncommonly bright child. In M. Lewis, & L. A. Rosenblum, (Eds) The uncommon child, New York: Plenum

ROBSON, C. (1993) Real world research, Oxford: Blackwell

ROGERS, C. R. (1951) Client-centred therapy: its current practice, implications and theory, Boston: Houghton Mifflin

ROGERS, C. R. (1959) A theory of therapy, personality and interpersonal relationships, as developed in the client-centred framework. S. Koch (Ed.) Psychology: a study of science, Vol. 3, New York: McGraw-Hill

ROGERS, C. R. (1961) On becoming a person, Boston: Houghton Mifflin

ROGERS, C. R. (1977) Carl Rogers on personal power, New York: Delacorte

ROGERS, C. R. (1980) A way of being, Boston: Houghton Mifflin

ROKEACH, M. (1960) The open and closed mind, New York: Basic Books

ROSE, S. A. & BLANK, M. (1974) The potency of context in children's cognition: an illustration through conservation, Child Development, 45, 499–502

ROSENBERG, M. (1979) Conceiving the self, Basic Books, New York

ROSENTHAL, R. & FODE, K. L. (1963) The effects of experimenter bias on the performance of the albino rat, Behavioural Science, 8, 183–189

ROSENTHAL, R. & JACOBSON, L. (1968) Pygmalion in the classroom: teacher expectations and pupil's intellectual development, New York: Holt

ROSENTHAL, R. (1966) Experimenter effects in behavioural research, New York: Appleton-Century-Crofts

RUBIN, Z. (1980) Children's friendships, Cambridge, MA: Harvard University Press

RUNCO, M. A., EBERSOLE, P. & MRAZ, W. (1991) Creativity and self-actualisation, Journal of Social Behaviour and Personality, 6, 161–167

RUTTER, M. (1981) Maternal deprivation reassessed, 2nd Edn Harmondsworth: Penguin

RUTTER, M. (1985) The treatment of autistic children. Journal of Child Psychiatry, 26 (2), 193–214

RUTTER, M., SILBERG, J., O'CONNOR, T. & SIMINOFF, E. (1999) Genetics and child psychiatry: empirical research findings, *Journal of Child Psychology and Psychiatry*, 40: 19–55

RUTTER, M. and the English and Romanian Adoptees Study Team (1998) Developmental catch-up and deficit after severe global early deprivation, *Journal of Child Psychology and Psychiatry*, 39, 465–476

RUTTER, M., TIZARD, J. & WHITMORE, K. (1970) Education, health and behaviour, London: Longman

RYLE, G. (1963) The concept of mind, Harmondsworth: Penguin

SCHAFFER, D. R. (1988) Developmental psychology: childhood and adolescence, 2nd edn, New York: Brooks/Cole Publishing Company

SCHAFFER, H. R. & EMERSON, P. E. (1964) The development of social attachments in infancy, *Monographs of the Society for Research in Child Development*, 29, No. 94

SCHAFFER, R. D. (1996) Social development Oxford: Blackwell

SCHIFFER, F., ZAIDEL, E., BOGEN, J. & CHASAN-TABER, S. (1998) Different psychological status in the two hemispheres of split-brain patients, *Neuropsychiatry, Neuropsychology and Behavioural Neurology*, 11, 151–156

SCHNEIRLA, T. C., ROSENBLATT, J. S. & TOBACH, E. (1963) Maternal behaviour in the cat. In H. L. Rheingold (Ed.) Maternal behaviour in mammals, New York: John Wiley

SCHULTZ, D. P. & SCHULTZ, G. E. (2000) A modern history of psychology, 7th Edn, Fort Worth: Harcourt College Publishers

SELIKOWITZ, M. (1998) Dyslexia and other learning difficulties: the facts, 2nd Edn, Oxford: Oxford University Press

SELMAN, R. L. (1980) The growth of interpersonal understanding, New York: Academic Press

SERAFICA, F.C. (1982) Social-cognitive development in context, London: Methuen

SERBIN, L. A., TONICK, I. J. & SETRNGLANZ, S. H. (1977) Shaping co-operative cross-sex play, *Child Development*, 48, 924–929

SEXTON, T. L. & WHISTON, S. C. (1994) The status of the counselling relationship: an empirical review, theoretical implications and research directions, *The Counselling Psychologist*, 22, 6–78

SHAH, A. & FRITH, U. (1993) Why do autistic individuals show superior performance in the block design task? *Journal of Child Psychology and Psychiatry*. 34, 1351–1364

SHEFFIELD, M., CAREY, J., PATENAUDE, W. & LAMBERT, M. J. (1995) An exploration of the relationship between interpersonal problems and psychological health, *Psychological Reports*, 76, 947–956

SHELDON, P. M. (1959) Isolation as a characteristic of highly gifted children, *Journal of Educational Sociology*, January, 215–221

SHETTLEWORTH, S. J. (1998) Cognition, evolution and behaviour, New York: Oxford University Press

SHOSTRUM. E. L. (1963) Personal orientation inventory, San Diego: EdITS/Educational and Industrial Testing Service

SHOSTRUM, E. L. (1977) Manual for the personal orientation dimensions, San Diego: EdITS/Educational and Industrial Testing Service

SIMPSON, E. L. (1974) Moral development research: a case study for scientific cultural bias, *Human Development*, 17, 81–106

SKINNER, B. F. (1953) Science and human behaviour, New York: Macmillan

SKINNER, B. F. (1957) Verbal behaviour, New York: Appleton

SKINNER, B. F. (1974) About behaviourism, New York: Vintage Books

SLOMAN, L. (1991) Use of medication in pervasive mental disorders. *Psychiat. Clin. N. Amer.* 14, 165–182

SMETANA, J. G. (1981) Pre-school children's conceptions of moral and social rules. *Child Development*, 52, 1333–1336

SMETANA, J. G. (1985) Pre-school children's conceptions of transgressions: Effects of varying moral and conventional domain-related attributes, *Developmental Psychology*, 21, 18–29

SMITH, P. B. & BOND, M. H. (1999) Social psychology across cultures, Second Edition, Hemel Hempstead: Harvester-Wheatsheaf

SMOLENSKY, P. (1995) On the proper treatment of connectionism. In C. McDonald & G. McDonald (Eds) Connectionism: debates on psychological explanation, Cambridge, M: Blackwell

SNAREY, J. R. (1985) Cross-cultural universality of social-moral development: a critical review of Kohlbergian research, *Psychological Bulletin*, 97, 202–232

SNOW, C. E. & FERGUSON, C. A. (Eds) (1977) Talking to children, Cambridge: Cambridge University Press

SNOWLING, M. J. (1985) Children's written language difficulties, Windsor: NFER Nelson

SNOWLING, M. J. (1987) Dyslexia, Oxford: Blackwell

SPIEGLER, M. D. & WEILAND, A. (1976) The effects of written vicarious consequences on observers' willingness to imitate and ability to recall modelling cues, *Journal of Personality*, 44, 260–273

STACKHOUSE, J. (2000) Barriers to literacy development in children with speech and language difficulties. In D.V.M. Bishop & L.B. Leonard (Eds) Speech and language impairments in children: causes, characteristics, intervention and outcome, Hove: Psychology Press

STANLEY, J. C. & BENBOW, C. P. (1983) Extremely young college graduates: evidence of their success, *College and University*, 58 (4), 361–371

STAPLETON, M. (2001) Psychology in practice, education, London: Hodder and Stoughton

STEIN, G. L., KIMIECSK, J. C., DANIELS, J. & JACKSON, S. A. (1995) Psychological antecedents of flow in recreational sport, *Personality and Social Psychology Bulletin*, 21, 125–135

STEIN, J. F. & TALCOTT, J. B. (1999) Impaired neuronal timing in developmental dyslexia – the magnocellular hypothesis. *Dyslexia*, 5, 59–78

STERNBERG, R. (1988) The trairchic mind: a new theory of human intelligence, New York: Viking

STERNBERG, R. J. (1996) Successful intelligence, New York: Simon & Schuster

STERNBERG, R. J. (2001) Psychology: in search of the human mind, Fort Worth: Harcourt College Publishers

STERNBERG, R. J. & GRIGORENKO, E. L. (Eds) (1997) Intelligence, heredity and environment, New York: Cambridge University Press

STERNBERG, S. (1966) High speed scanning in human memory, *Science*, 153, 652–654

STEVEN, A. (2001) Jung: a very short introduction, Oxford: Oxford University Press

STORR, A. (2002) Freud: a very short introduction, Oxford: Oxford University Press

STRAKER, A. (1983) Mathematics for gifted pupils, Longman, Harlow

STUNKARD, A. J. (1991) Review of Schwartz, H. J. (Eds), Bulimia: psychoanalytic treatment and therapy, *Psychiatric Annals*, 19, 279

SUOMI, S. J. & HARLOW, H. F. (1972) Social rehabilitation of isolate-reared monkeys. *Developmental Psychology* 6, 487–496

TAKAHASHI, K. (1990) Affective relationships and their lifelong development. In P. B. Baltes (Ed. *et al.*) Life-span development and behaviour, Vol 10, Lawrence Erlbaum Associates, Hillsdale

TERMAN M. L. & ODEN, M. (1959) Genetic studies of genius: Vol. 5. The gifted group at mid-life, Stanford, CA: Stanford University Press

TERMAN, L. M. (1925) Mental and physical traits of a thousand gifted children, Genetic studies of genius Vol. 1 Stanford CA: Stanford University Press

TERMAN, M. L. & ODEN, M. (1947) Genetic study of genius, Stanford, CA: Stanford University Press

The British Psychological Society (BPS) (2000). Ethical Principles for Conducting Research with Human Participants. http://www.bps.org.uk

THOMAS, L. & COOPER, P. (1980) Incidence and psychological correlates of intense spiritual experience, *Journal of Transpersonal Psychology*, 12, 75–85

TIETJEN, A. M. (1986) Prosocial moral reasoning among children and adults in a Papua New Guinea society. *Developmental Psychology*, 22, 861–868

TICHENER, E. B. (1990) A textbook of psychology, New York: Macmillan 1910 to 1909

TOLMAN, E. C. (1932) Purposive behaviour in animals and men, New York: Appleton

TORRANCE, E. P. (1970) Causes for concern. In Vernon, P. E. (Ed.) Creativity, Harmondsworth; Penguin

TRONICK, E. Z., MORELLI, G. A., & WINN, S. (1987) Multiple caretaking of Efe (Pygmy) infants, *American Anthropologist*, 89, 96–106

TURIEL, E. (1978) Social regulations and domains of social concepts. In W. Damon (Ed.) New directions for child development: Vol. 1 *Social cognition*, San Francisco: Jossey-Bass

TURIEL, E. (1983) The development of social knowledge: Morality and convention, Cambridge University Press

VAN TASSEL-BASKA, J. (1989) Profiles of precocity, a three-year study of talented adolescents. In Van Tassel-Baska, J. & Olszewski-Kubilius, P. (Eds) Patterns of influence on gifted learners, New York: Teachers College Press

VAN WIERINGEN, J. C. (1978) Secular growth changes. In F. Falkner & J. M. Tanner (Eds) Human Growth, Vol. 2, New York: Plenum

VERGNES, N. (1975) Déclechment de reactions d'agression interspécific après lesion amygdalienne chez le rat, *Physiology and Behaviour*, 14, 271–276

VYGOTSKY, L. S. (1978) Mind in society, Cambridge, MA: Harvard University Press

WALDROP, M. F. & HALVERSON, C. F. (1975) Intensive and extensive peer behaviour: longitudinal and cross-sectional analyses, *Child Development*, 46, 19–26

WALKER, L. J. (1984) Sex differences in the development of moral reasoning: a critical review, *Child Development*, 55, 677–691

WALKER, L. J. (1989) A longitudinal study of moral reasoning, *Child Development*, 60, 157–166

WALKER, L. J., DEVRIES, B., and TREVETHAN, S. D. (1987) Moral stages and moral orientations in real-life and hypothetical dilemmas. *Child Development*, 58, 842–858

WASSERMAN, E. A. (1993) Comparative cognition: beginning the second century of the study of animal cognition, *Psychological Bulletin*, 113, 211–228

WATSON, J. B. (1919) Psychology from the standpoint of a behaviourist, Philadelphia: Lippincott.

WATSON, J. B. (1930) Behaviourism, New York: Norton

WEINBERGER, J. L. & SILVERMAN, L. H. (1990) testability and empirical verification of psychoanalytic dynamic propositions through subliminal psychodynamic activation, *Psychoanalytic Psychology*, 7, 299–339

WEISKRANTZ, L. (1997) Consciousness lost and found, Oxford: Oxford University Press

WATSON, J. B. & RAYNOR, R. (1920) Conditioned emotional reactions, *Journal of Experimental Psychology*, 3, 1–4

WEITEN, W. (2002) Psychology: themes and variations, 5th Edn, London: Wadsworth

WESTEN, D. (1999) Psychology: mind, brain and culture, New York: John Wiley & Sons.

WESTEN, D. (2002) Psychology: brain, behavior and culture, New York: John Wiley

WHITTAKER, E. M. (1982) Dyslexia and the flat earth, *Bulletin of the British Psychological Society*, 35, 97–99

WILLIAMS, C. D. (1959) The elimination of tantrum behaviour by extinction procedures, *Journal of Abnormal and Social Psychology*, 59, 269

WINDELBAND, W. (1894) History and natural science, Strasbourg: Heitz

WINNER, E. (1998) Uncommon talents: gifted children, prodigies and talents, *Scientific American Presents*, 9 (4), 32–37

WOLF, M., RISLEY, T., & MEES, H. (1964) Application of operant conditioning procedures to the behaviour problems of an autistic child, *Behaviour Research and Therapy*, 1, 305–312

WOLPE, J. (1958) Psychotherapy by reciprocal inhibition, Stanford, CA: Stanford University Press

WOOD, D. J., BRUNER, J. S. & ROSS, G. (1976) The role of tutoring in problem solving. *Journal of Child Psychology and Psychiatry*, 17, 89–100

WOOD, D. J. & MIDDLETON, D. J. (1975) A study of assisted problem-solving. *British Journal of psychology*, 66, 181–191

YOUNG, A. & BLOCK, N. (1996) *Unsolved mysteries of the mind: Tutorial essays in cognition.* Oxford, Taylor & Francis Publishers

ZIMBARDO, P. G. (1969) The human choice: individuation, reason and order versus deindividuation, impulse and chaos In W. J. Arnold & D. Levine (Eds) Nebraska Symposium on Motivation, Lincoln: University of Nebraska Press

Index

O

P